# THE JOHNS HOPKINS UNIVERSITY STUDIES IN HISTORICAL AND POLITICAL SCIENCE

Under the Direction of the Departments of History,
Political Economy, and Political Science

SERIES LXXV
(1957)

NUMBER 1

BRITONS IN AMERICAN LABOR

# BRITONS IN AMERICAN LABOR:

## A HISTORY OF THE INFLUENCE OF THE UNITED KINGDOM IMMIGRANTS ON AMERICAN LABOR, 1820–1914

By

### CLIFTON K. YEARLEY, JR.

GREENWOOD PRESS, PUBLISHERS
WESTPORT, CONNECTICUT

208505

**Library of Congress Cataloging in Publication Data**

Yearley, Clifton K
    Britons in American labor.

    Reprint of the ed. published by Johns Hopkins Press,
Baltimore, which was issued as ser. 75, no. 1 of Johns
Hopkins University studies in historical and political
science.
    Bibliography: p.
    1. Labor and laboring classes--United States--History.
2. British in the United States--History. I. Title.
II. Series: Johns Hopkins University. Studies in
historical and political science, ser. 75, no. 1.
[HD8066.Y4 1974]      331.6'2'42073      73-13822
ISBN 0-8371-7120-2

Originally published in 1957 by The Johns Hopkins Press, Baltimore

Reprinted with the permission of The Johns Hopkins University Press

Reprinted in 1974 by Greenwood Press,
a division of Williamhouse-Regency Inc.

Library of Congress Catalog Card Number 73-13822

ISBN 0-8371-7120-2

Printed in the United States of America

TO
CARLYN,
MICHAEL AND THOMAS

# PREFACE

Although the historic movement of the American has been westward toward the Pacific, his cultural orientation has always been eastward toward Europe. In the seventeenth and eighteenth centuries his basic inheritances, law, government, manners, and mores came across the Atlantic, and they came primarily, though not exclusively, from Great Britain. Subsequently, generation after generation the American environment worked its will on these legacies, reshaping them, fitting them into new patterns. By the nineteenth and early twentieth centuries such furious energies were being invested in the creation of the new American civilization that these forces from abroad were, relative to earlier years, largely taken for granted, examined superficially, or ignored. Increasingly immigration was treated as a statistical phenomenon, as a matter of numbers; there seemed to be little awareness of its underlying implications for American society, except perhaps among the staunch nativists or the humanitarians who romanticized the melting-pot. In addition, protected from the ordinary vicissitudes of European affairs by the tranquilizing influence of the British fleet and the hostage that was Canada, the American Government assumed a posture of aloofness from events overseas, and the many excellent diplomatic histories since produced have necessarily underscored this official isolation. Time and events, however, are conspiring to modify these portraits. At present, as second generation immigrants are greatly altering America's political complexion, as a half century of total wars invokes new concepts, if not a renascence, of the Atlantic Community, historians are probing beneath the formalities of governments in order to reappraise the effects of immigration. What they are discovering, essentially, is that the stream of men and ideas across the Atlantic to the economic frontiers of the United States flowed on unchecked through the years of "isolation," and that European influences, indeed, were as subtle and as powerful a leaven as ever. How ironic that during a period when the greatest migrations in history swept to America, the American Government was dedicated to isolationism, while today, as the flood of migration has been

9

reduced to a trickle, official relations between the United States and Western European states are closer than ever.

This study is designed to open further an inquiry into the impact of men and ideas from the United Kingdom upon the early modern labor and labor reform movements in the United States. Basically it is a story of the English, Scotch, and Welsh. The Irish, it is true, have not been entirely ignored, but they have, I confess, been consciously neglected, first because Professor Carl Wittke has already placed them generally in the American context, and second, because the sources pertaining to the Irish in American labor, despite my belief in the enormous importance of these people, are most unrewarding in the period with which I am concerned here.

For the many services rendered me I am particularly grateful to the staffs of the following libraries: the Johns Hopkins University Library, the Wisconsin State Historical Society, the University of Wisconsin Library, the University of Michigan General Library, the American Federation of Labor Library and Files, the Illinois Historical Survey, the Library of the University of Illinois, the Library of the Catholic University of America, the Library of Congress, the Harvard University Library, the Boston Public Library, the New York Public Library, the Library of the Peabody Institute, the Enoch Pratt Library, the U. S. Department of Labor Library, the Library of the Manchester Co-operative Union, the Massachusetts Historical Society, and the Maryland Historical Society.

For his careful reading of the entire manuscript and his many suggestions I owe an especial debt to Professor Charles A. Barker of the Johns Hopkins University. My thanks must also go to Professor C. Vann Woodward and Professor Mark Perlman of the Johns Hopkins University, Henry Pelling of Queen's College, Oxford, William G. Carleton of the University of Florida, Mr. Denis Flanagan of Holyoake House, Manchester, Mr. John Frey and Miss Florence Thorne of the American Federation of Labor, Mark Starr, Solomin Barkin, Richard Heindel, Josephine Harper, and my wife, Carlyn P. Yearley, for their guidance, counsel, and criticism. The shortcomings of this study are, of course, my responsibility alone.

Gainesville
May, 1956

# TABLE OF CONTENTS

PAGE

INTRODUCTION . . . . . . . . . . . . 13

PART ONE: TOWARDS TRANSATLANTIC ALLIANCE

    I. Workers of the World . . . . . . . 25
    II. Agitators and Ideas, 1800-1862 . . . . . 34
    III. A Basis for Understanding . . . . . . 45

PART TWO: STRENGTHENING TIES

    I. Collaboration . . . . . . . . . . 51
    II. Alliance . . . . . . . . . . . 57
    III. Fraternity . . . . . . . . . . 80

PART THREE: COBBETTS AND HUNTS

    I. The Organizers . . . . . . . . . 84
    II. General Labor Reformers . . . . . . 94
    III. Moderate Socialists . . . . . . . 106
    IV. Miners . . . . . . . . . . . 123
    V. Metalworkers . . . . . . . . . 142
    VI. Textile Workers . . . . . . . . 147
    VII. Organizers in Other Trades . . . . . 150

PART FOUR: THE GREAT EXAMPLE

    I. England, The Model . . . . . . . 153
    II. Industrial War and Peace . . . . . 170
    III. The Amalgamateds . . . . . . . 183

PART FIVE: SELF-HELP, THE PLANTING OF AN IDEA

    I. Panacea and Propagandists . . . . . 192
    II. Co-operation and the Crispins . . . . 224

PAGE

PART SIX: SELF-HELP, THE SPREAD OF AN IDEA

    I.   Transition: Ideas and Men . . . . . . . 229
   II.   Portrait of a Prophet . . . . . . . . . 233
  III.   Sources of the Faith . . . . . . . . . 237
  IV.   Self-Help Among the Grangers . . . . . . 243
   V.   Self-Help Among the Sovereigns of Industry . . 257

PART SEVEN: TOWARD A CO-OPERATIVE COMMONWEALTH

    I.   The Co-operative Wave . . . . . . . . 266
   II.   Two Veterans and the Knights of Labor . . . 276
  III.   Self-Help Among the Knights . . . . . 283
  IV.   The Seed Sown . . . . . . . . . . 294

PART EIGHT: THE WANING OF BRITISH INFLUENCE

    I.   New Patterns . . . . . . . . . . . 303
   II.   Conclusions: British Men and Ideas . . . . 311

NOTES ON SOURCES . . . . . . . . . . . 318

INDEX . . . . . . . . . . . . . . 323

# INTRODUCTION

## 1860–1900

Largely within a single generation the old America yielded to the new. By 1900 the man who as a youth had marched with Grant or Lee could peer backward into an agrarian past and forward from the threshold of the twentieth century into the world's most highly industrialized society. As a child he might have heard the spinning wheel and worn homespun; as a man of middle years he probably donned materials woven in the great mills of Fall River or Burlington or Gastonia and pieced in the garment districts of Manhattan. Probably as a boy he had known the field and the furrow and had believed that his future lay on the land; but as a man each passing year increased the likelihood that his career would lie in the city. Long before the close of the century chances were great that the mud and sweat of the farm would have proven uncongenial to him and even less attractive to his children. Like many this man too might have retained vivid memories of the West of the buffalo trace, the emigrant trail, the cowboy and Indian, but at the turn of the century railroads lay over trace and trail; bison, cowboys, and Indians were largely stuff of the pulps; and Frederick Jackson Turner had already commented brilliantly upon a frontier that was officially closed. If there were new frontiers they were industrial, and the fact was that they had decades earlier begun to provoke fresh patterns of thought and action. Values were changing markedly in response to a changed environment. And men who recalled the rarer spirits of their youth might well have agreed with the poignant suggestion of Henry Adams that the " survivors of the forties " had become mere " bric-a-brac from the time of Louis Philippe; stylists; doctrinaires; ornaments that had been more or less suited to colonial architecture, but which never had much value in Desbrosses Street or Fifth Avenue." [1] By 1900 force lay with coal, steel, and steam, with the financial and industrial

---

[1] Henry Adams, *The Education of Henry Adams: An Autobiography* (New York: The Book League, 1928), p. 238.

genius that controlled them, and with the vast property-holding middle class.

Of the new industrial order Americans were extraordinarily proud—justly so, within limits. To prodigious resources they were applying prodigious energies, and they were producing great wealth. Amid a bumper crop of statistics they were reaping a harvest of goods. For every ton of pig iron produced in 1880, four tons were produced in 1900; each ton of steel manufactured in 1880 was matched by ten tons in 1900; every ton of coal mined in 1870 was surpassed by eight tons mined in 1900; and for every barrel of oil pumped from the ground in 1870, twelve were being pumped out in 1900. And tons and barrels, like nearly everything else, were measured in millions and tens of millions. The last ten years of the century were fairly typical of the trends that had begun thirty years before. During those tumultuous years, the number of industrial establishments increased 44 per cent, capital increased by 51 per cent, the value of manufactures by 34 per cent, the number of wage earners by 24 per cent, and the excess of exports over imports rose by almost 150 per cent.[2] Equally as remarkable were the figures on population, and the statistics of innovation and combination. The proliferation of goods was by no means the sole cause of national satisfaction. As the productive base of the new civilization was being laid Americans prided themselves on having retained their freedom and on having advanced political democracy beyond any other people. Nearly a generation before the enfranchisement of England's urban workers in 1867, universal white male suffrage was a reality in most American states, and fifteen years before the vote was extended to England's farm laborers, the Negro was entitled to vote in America. Moreover, since political democracy had sprung mainly from the economic and social democracy of the agrarian frontier, its peculiar emphasis contributed during the years of industrialization to the blurring of class lines, and, in view of the wide dissemination of property, the masses who had newly come into their inheritance could rest content upon the assumption that their government was best because it governed least.

[2] *Final Report of the Industrial Commission* (Washington: U. S. Government Printing Office, 1902), Vol. XIX, pp. 34-35 37, 39, 40-41, 217-219, 491, 506.

Change, however, did not bring accommodation for everyone, and the results of titanic transformations were in some respects catastrophic. Suffering or dislocation came to men and women in every stratum of society, but there is little doubt that their incidence fell most heavily upon those least able to bear economic shocks. Unfortunately, given the direction and velocity of these changes the best will in the world could not have prevented social trauma. Institutional and psychological tools were simply not at hand to facilitate adjustment to a new situation. In addition, such institutions could not possibly spring full blown from the soil, and even the modification of existing institutions and attitudes required time. For some people there was bound to be pain; it was an inevitable part of the industrial revolution. Yet serious difficulties that were susceptible of mitigation were often grossly aggravated by ruthlessness, social myopia, and smug complacency. American society was coming up by its bootstraps and for many citizens, infatuated by a glittering materialism, dedicated to the cult of prosperity, a rising standard of living made palatable things that minorities were finding noisome, if not oppressive. Many tacitly accepted, even if they did not openly espouse, a social Darwinism that explained away the broadening gulf between poverty and wealth while it held out alluring rewards to those who entered the competitive struggle unreservedly. Others, reasoning along traditional lines, concluded that the unlovely sores of the new order could be cured by appeals to the ballot, while the few who found freedom from restraint enormously profitable were inclined to exorcise the complaints of the critical as assaults upon the very pillars of civilization.

Just as disturbingly, American concepts of democracy, forged in an agrarian and egalitarian age, were, in several respects, proving ill-adapted to the new circumstances. Individualism in matters economic was heavily underscored in the midst of society's growing complexity and interdependence; governmental negativism, except in relation to a favored few, was encouraged in situations where, as reformers and workers were beginning to realize, government alone could be the efficient actor. Similarly the intense localism and sectionalism of politics thwarted the deft handling of national problems, and invited inefficiency and corruption that stunned the observant. In the realm of ameliorative social and industrial legislation, the United States generally lagged years and in some areas decades behind England and less democratic countries of the Continent. And property, once a means to the achievement of self-respect, was tending to become an end in itself, so much so that those who appeared to menace or sought to modify it were pronounced anathema. Where fundamental analysis of this basic institution was necessary, one heard only the whirring of wheels.

Within this framework of change and crisis there emerged a sizable laboring population and a serious labor question. Each decade after 1860 the census showed a marked increase in the number of wage earners, so that for every worker in mill, mine, and workshop in 1860, there were eighteen such workers by 1910.[3] A concomitant of this growth in the size of the labor force was a rising incidence of strikes, lockouts, and industrial violence. The twentieth century, of course, has no difficulty enumerating the blessings that undeniably (though we should remember, not automatically) accrued to workingmen as a result of the factory system, specialization, and mass production. Well-intentioned employers tried even in the nineteenth century to point out to dissatisfied toilers how the path ahead would certainly grow smoother.[4] Nevertheless, these blessings were not manifest to a large number of workers who were shaken and unsettled by the new forces. "We have gone through . . . a revolution in the last twenty years,"[5] declared one of their leaders in 1885 and not many were prepared to contest this. Nor was the magnitude of the revolution a mystery to those concerned with improving the workingman's lot. "The introduction of the system of aggregated labor in the factory and in the development of the principle of the division of labor, thus made practicable, have gradually reduced the once free artisan to a new serfdom. . . . He is no longer the master of a craft. He is a bit of a process. He does a fraction of the

[3] *Final Report of the Industrial Commission,* 1902, XIX, 491.

[4] *Ibid.,* p. 537.

[5] U. S., Congress, Senate, Committee on Education and Labor, *Report of the Committee of the Senate upon the Relations between Labor and Capital,* 48th Cong., 1885, Vol. II, p. 438.

complete job. Of the rest of the process he knows nothing. Consequently he cannot stand by himself. . . . He literally has no base for personal independence "[6]—such was the standard observation. Status, bargaining power, personal association with the employer, and a sense of identity were things that were slipping from the worker's life. New adjustments to technology, the task of learning new skills and new disciplines were in themselves trying experiences, and they were met by men already beset by strong feelings of insecurity as they discovered themselves becoming marionettes in an impersonal economic system. However one weighs the justice or injustice of these complaints against the "new feudalism," privileged legislation, and the rest, these complaints were a reality that a democracy could not ignore. Yet many of the controlling assumptions upon which society relied were largely those of a frontier farming community. Small wonder that men of the cities and the mills began opening their eyes "to see at last that a democratic country which rarely legislates for the *demos* . . . is something of a fraud."[7]

From its first moments of self-consciousness, however, American labor and its leadership agreed overwhelmingly to strive for improvement within the ambit of a democratic system. Labor organizations were often militant, vociferous, and as the nineteenth century saw it, radical, but their methods were nearly always moderate, hence liberal. Revolutionary tactics were occasionally suggested, revolutionary groups were formed, but they were rare exceptions and neither their tactics nor their ideologies gained acceptance among American workingmen. Basically the labor movement must be viewed as an effort to readjust, not as an attempt to revolt. George McNeill spoke for the mass of mechanics and laborers when he proclaimed that labor looked "to no red-handed or bloody reprisals of its wrongs. . . . The disciplined ranks of all divisions of the Grand Army of Labor march to the music of liberty and law. . . . He is an enemy . . . who seeks to hasten the liberation of the poor by the force of dynamite or of arms."[8]

[6] *Ibid.*, II, 564.
[7] U. S., Senate, *Report . . . upon the Relations between Labor and Capital*, 48th Cong., 1885, II, 564.
[8] *The Labor Movement: The Problem of To-day*, ed. George McNeill (Boston: A. M. Bridgman & Co., 1887), p. 468.

The job of welding institutions that would give power and meaning to the lives of many workingmen was by its very nature long term, piecemeal, and for the most part quite unsensational. Such an undertaking, and labor was quick to realize it, could succeed only after the property-holding middle class and workingmen as well had received instruction in the lessons of industrial democracy. Because its leadership was liberal, labor's tasks were very largely educational. In view of the powerful stress that the democratic credo placed upon individualism and upon property, workingmen were obviously embarked on a project of heroic proportions, for everywhere strange ideas and strange organizations that seemingly challenged the established faiths stirred fierce opposition. The reasons were rooted in American life fully as much as they were rooted in American capitalism. "The average middle class American who does not work for wages," an alert friend of labor declared in 1885, "is led by the nose into believing that this [effort to organize labor] is all some sort of European howl that has been gotten up; some sort of communism." And, he added with penetrating insight, "they all look back to the days when they were born in some little American village where, if a man had $50,000, he was supposed to be a magnate, and penury was not a common thing. They have seen their time and opportunity of getting on in the world, and they think that is the condition of society to-day, when it is a totally different condition." [9]

Confronting the rapidly unfolding problems of their industrial revolution, trying to create out of their own resources the institutions that would bring them status, security, and power, American labor and labor-reform leaders began drawing upon the fund of experience accumulated by the pioneers of industrialism, the men and women of Great Britain. Workingmen in the British Isles were generally recognized, as we shall see, as the first to evolve trade unions, co-operatives, and their own fraternal and political organizations. Through economic and parliamentary struggle, and most significantly through the education of the public, they had obliged "the men of wealth"

[9] U. S., Senate, *Report . . . upon the Relations between Labor and Capital,* 48th Cong., 1885, II, 438.

to do things "they perhaps would not otherwise have done."[10] Moreover because British workers, contrary to those in the United States, had achieved their democratic objectives after the industrial revolution was already upon them, their democratic philosophy was voiced in different accents. Being principally a movement of wage earners and country laborers, rather than a movement instigated by agrarians, British democracy was not merely political but was industrial as well. Thus for workingmen in the United States certain aspects of this democracy across the Atlantic were pregnant with suggestion. Distinctions between the peoples and the labor movements of the two nations, of course, rendered some of the practices and ideas of British workingmen useless in the United States and required modification of others. On the whole American labor faced stouter opposition and was less homogeneous (despite wide diversities within labor's ranks abroad) and less class conscious than British labor. Notwithstanding this, workingmen in the United States proved amazingly eclectic.

The ideas and men that American workers were to make extensive use of were for the most part conveniently at hand. For while the industrialization of the Republic was underway so, too, was the greatest folk movement of history, and the United States was its principal terminus. Not since the last centuries of the Roman Empire had there been any such spectacle as the mass movement of European peoples that began again in the sixteenth and seventeenth centuries and reached its climax in the nineteenth. Between 1850 and 1910 over twenty-four million Europeans poured into the United States. Until 1900 about one in every three of these immigrants was an inhabitant of the United Kingdom, and even after the enormous influx of southern and eastern Europeans in the first decade of the twentieth century nearly one in five immigrants came from Great Britain and Ireland.[11] In a sixty year period,

[10] U. S., Senate, *Report . . . upon the Relation between Labor and Capital*, 48th Cong., 1885, II, 434.

[11] See U. S., Congress, Senate, *Reports of the Immigration Commission, Immigrants in Industry, Statistical Review of Immigration, 1819-1910*, 61st Cong., 3rd Sess., 1910, Senate Doc. 756. U. S., Congress, Senate, *Reports of the Immigration Commission, Immigrants in Industry*, 61st Cong., 2d Sess., Vol. XVI. *Final Report of the Industrial Commission*, 1902, XIX, 957-62. I have relied

in other words, more than half as many persons entered the United States from the United Kingdom as had lived in Great Britain at the opening of the nineteenth century. To be sure, not all of these people stayed in America. Experience in mill towns and factories, in the tenements of the fast growing cities, led many who had hopefully taken passage to the conclusion that the worst evils of industrialism were less avoidable in the United States than they were at home, and they went back. Some came merely for seasonal work in mines or textile mills, or to take advantage of temporarily high wages, and they went back. But the vast majority stayed on, and in greater numbers than any other body of immigrants they took up industrial pursuits.[12]

No immigrants in the world were so competent to make positive contributions to American industry and labor as these men and women. With thousands of them came attitudes and disciplines that are the very core of industrialism, disciplines that it had taken decades to develop in Great Britain. To the raw industrial armies of the United States these men were seasoned troops, cadres around which new industrial recruits were marshalled. What the Huguenots had been to certain English trades in the late seventeenth century these immigrants were a hundred thousand times over to American industry nearly two centuries later. Every major industry and most of the lesser ones felt their impact, especially since many English, Scotch, and Welsh immigrants rose to become superintendents or foremen as the result of their experience and skill.[13] Information on these people is incomplete, yet official samplings of the occupations of over a quarter of a million British workers who entered the United States between 1873 and 1918 show that about forty per cent claimed to be skilled men, while only twenty-five per cent regarded themselves as unskilled.[14] This

heavily on the analyses of Rowland Berthoff, *British Immigrants in Industrial America* (Cambridge: Harvard University Press, 1953), pp. 1-11.

[12] U. S., Census. *Eleventh Census of the United States,* 1890, Vol. II, pp. 484-88. Berthoff, pp. 21-23. Stanley C. Johnson, *History of Emigration from the United Kingdom to the United States* (London: Routledge & Co., 1913).

[13] *Report of the Industrial Commission on Capital and Labor in Manufacturing and General Business* (Washington: U. S. Government Printing Office, 1901), Vol. VII, p. 620.

[14] U. S., Senate. *Reports of the Immigration Commission, Immigrants in*

was a substantially higher percentage of skilled workers, and a lower percentage of unskilled workers than was found in any other immigrant group examined.

Just as skill was a hallmark of these men and women, so too was that "corporate sense of labor" of which T. S. Ashton has written.[15] Workingmen's clubs, friendly societies, reformist political organizations, Chartist groups, co-operatives, and trade unions all physically were left behind them but, like pieces of the old clod, their spirit and an understanding of their purposes and methods clung to the English, Scotch, and Welsh, and to a lesser extent to some of the Irish, who transplanted their fortunes to the New World. Insofar as these people modified their new environment and shaped the actions or ideas of American workingmen in this respect, they materially altered and affected the course of American democratic thought.

Whatever impressions the British and Irish left upon the labor movement of the United States, they must be weighed in the light of certain reservations and evaluted in their proper perspective. We must remember that the labor movement in America was a minority and not a mass movement in the years between 1860 and 1910. No more than a few thousand of the nation's 970,000 wage earners were organized in 1860. Even as late as 1910, despite notable strides in the progress of unionism, only eleven per cent of nearly 19,000,000 workers were union members. White collar workers pulled this percentage down, of course, and some industries did show appreciable numbers of trade unionists. Miners, for instance, and workers in the building trades had, respectively, twenty-seven per cent and sixteen per cent of their men organized.[16] Nevertheless, mass unionization is a recent American phenomenon. The size of the nineteenth century labor movement, consequently, had the effect of magnifying rather than of diminishing British and Irish influences.

*Industry, Abstracts of Reports,* 61st Cong., 3rd Sess., 1910, Senate Doc. 747, Vol. I, pp. 172-73. Also see U. S., Bureau of Statistics on Commerce and Navigation, *Annual Reports,* 1873-1891. U. S., Commissioner-General of Immigration, *Annual Reports,* 1896-1918. Berthoff, pp. 21-28.

[15] Thomas S. Ashton, *The Industrial Revolution* (London: Home University Library, Oxford Press, 1949), p. 132.

[16] Leo Wolman, *The Growth of American Trade Unions, 1880-1923* (New York: Macmillan, 1924), pp. 85-86. See Chapter 4 for a detailed discussion of the extent of unionism.

Significant as British and Irish immigrants were we must also remember that they were not the only Europeans whose activities and ideas affected American labor. Singled out for special attention there is always the danger that they will tend to loom too large in the total picture. Yet who could write the history of many of the trades without serious consideration of the Germans, or for that matter, of the Scandinavians? Similarly, southern and eastern European immigration in the first decade of the twentieth century materially affected the structure and thought of American labor. Only when seen in conjunction with the work of other nationalities can the activities of the British and Irish be fully and accurately assessed. Despite the emphasis here on the influences that were brought to America, moreover, it should be made clear that ideas and influences moved in both directions across the Atlantic. If labor in the United States drew on the lessons of British industrial democracy, the British in their turn were touched by American progress in the fields of social and political democracy. We need allude only briefly to the role of American ideas—Henry George's in particular—in the revival of British socialism, the march towards extension of the franchise, the organization of certain craft unions and women's trade unions, and the unionization of the unskilled.

Furthermore, although our attention will be focused on a special group of immigrants, it is essential that we underscore the fact that the basic causes and forces that gave rise to the American labor movement were indigenous. If not a single immigrant had entered the United States after the Civil War, a labor movement would unquestionably have arisen anyway. John Mitchell, the famed mine unionist, was absolutely correct when he insisted that the American labor movement " grew up spontaneously on American soil from the needs of American workingmen." [17] Such also is the viewpoint expressed by the greatest of the labor historians, John R. Commons, and his distinguished associates [18] and it is not going too far to suggest

[17] Henry Pelling, " The Knights of Labor in Britain, 1880-1901," *Economic History Review,* IX (1957), 313-31. John Mitchell, *Organized Labor: Its Problems, Purposes and Ideals* (Philadelphia: American Book and Bible House, 1903), p. 239.

[18] John R. Commons, et al., *A History of Labour in the United States* (4 vols.; New York, Macmillan, 1918-1935).

that nearly every student would agree with them as to the native origins, as well as to the uniqueness in some respects, of the American movement.

Nevertheless, the distinctiveness and isolation of American labor can easily be overstressed. John Commons himself, though he did not pursue the point at length, was well aware that the rise of labor in America was a response to the same general forces that were giving stimulus to labor movements elsewhere.[19] He detected its kinship with a general Western movement. Given the international character of the industrial revolution, the new closeness of communication that came with the late nineteenth century, and tens of millions of Europeans on the move, circulating their ideas, utilizing their training, American labor could not have been immune to outside forces. It was no less subject to European influences than was American capitalism. A veritable bridge of human beings linked it to Europe, and especially to labor in Great Britain. The critical questions here, then, do not relate to the indigenous conditions that nourished labor organization. Rather, in seeking to augment the work of Commons, they are designed to determine whether the labor movement in America would have been substantially different if British and Irish men and ideas had been subtracted from it; whether it would have passed through its formative stages as rapidly or in the same direction; whether survival or success would have been easier without influence from across the Atlantic. The answers to questions of this kind must inevitably reflect too upon the venerable controversies that have raged around the problems posed by immigration. Would the United States have benefited, as nativists claim, by the absence of certain immigrant elements? Did they divert from its true objectives? Did they drag down the workingman's standard of living? Put more positively, if labor in the United States has helped preserve and extend concepts of economic and industrial democracy, and if, as we believe our evidence shows, these concepts stemmed from or received reënforcement from the working people of the United King-

[19] John R. Commons and John B. Andrews, *A Documentary History of American Industrial Society* (11 vols.; Cleveland: Arthur H. Clark, 1910-11), Vol. IX, p. 43.

dom, then these men and women have exerted an important influence on one of the major forces in American life.

Finally, labor itself has never been clear as to the extent or even as to the existence of British and Irish influences, and random comments on this matter have run the gamut of extremes. Nineteenth century labor leaders, as we will shortly see from their personal papers, writings, and public statements, gave every indication that British influences were present and were important, but there is incomplete agreement about them. Some felt British ideas had made unions too conservative and unaggressive, or that imported co-operative ideas detracted from the pursuit of what were regarded as more significant objectives. Some denied or ignored the presence of any foreign influences, especially after the turn of the century. In this connection it would be wise to remember, however, that everyone of stature in the labor movement was obliged to minimize any foreign influences, British or otherwise, if only because labor was continually under attack from enemies who denounced it as un-American.[20] Other labor leaders, like John Swinton,[21] found British experiences useful but nevertheless remained almost entirely unaware of their own eclecticism.

As to precisely when these influences were greatest, precisely how extensive they actually were, or even whether they were exerted continuously, no conclusive or perhaps even satisfactory answer is possible, either from the past or the present. Accurate measurement of influence, even if it can be satisfactorily defined, is at best hazardous. Particularly is this so when the subjects of scrutiny are not intellectuals, when they are not very often articulate, and when there are distressing gaps in the historical record. As always under such circumstances the historian must ultimately rely upon his own judgment and intuition.

[20] John Mitchell is a case in point. The United Mine Workers Union, which he led, as well as all of the earlier American mine unions were organized and structured by British and Irish miners. The British and Irish formed their main leadership. Yet Mitchell, a close student of British labor himself, played down these influences.

[21] John Swinton, *A Momentous Question* (Philadelphia: Keller Co., 1895), pp. 269-75.

# PART ONE

# TOWARD TRANSATLANTIC ALLIANCE

---

## I. Workers of the World: Craftsmen and Chartists

Early in June, 1848, the British government arrested six Chartist leaders. Charged with seditious speech and unlawful assembly they were speedily convicted and imprisoned at Tothill Fields, Millbank. One of the prisoners was Ernest Jones, a former Middle Temple barrister of thirty who had become a Chartist official. Until a collapse necessitated his removal to the prison hospital, Jones endured nineteen months of solitary confinement. Subjected to the "silent system" he was not permitted to talk to anyone or to write. Through days of silence, however, scribbling with a makeshift pen and his blood, he produced his article of faith, *The New World*. This poem, and its prose introduction, were dedicated to "the people of the United Kingdom and the United States," whose destinies he believed to be inseparable. Contrasting the "decaying monarchy" of Old World England against the rising promise of the New World Republic, he arraigned England as the "plague stricken hulk of a stately wreck" within whose "death fraught ribs" lay an impoverished population. Outstripping the world in mechanical power, she was employing her vast energies only "to displace labour and starve unwilling idlers." "Every factory" he pronounced "more corrupt than a barracks, more painful than a prison and more fatal than a battlefield." Hope lay across the ocean in the "New Atlantis" where Americans, despite much of the "Dead Sea apple" on their shores, were enjoying a life free from the "corrupt legislation" and industrial misery of his own land.

Although Jones held a high opinion of Americans, he rightly regarded them as mere apprentices in industrialization. Unless they were wise enough to ponder Britain's lessons, therefore, he implied that the blight scourging his nation would soon

span the sea. Out of the conviction that Anglo-American
fortunes were linked, that the problems of the industrial
revolution should be broached jointly, he insisted fervently
that "between the men of England and America should be
eternal union." [1]

Reformers are seldom objective; imprisoned men seldom
achieve balance; and romantic poets rarely transcend emotionalism. Ernest Jones was all three—reformer, convict, and poet.
His biases are manifest; the patent inaccuracy of his comments
on English society are apparent in the light of new histori-
ography. Nonetheless, he illustrated the vigor of a growing
international outlook that captivated a number of British workingclass leaders at mid-century. 1848, in fact, was more than
a year of general European rebellion and unrest. A new cos-
mopolitanism among the more skilled and articulate workers
transformed the revolutionary ferment of 1848 into a spirit
that breached political boundaries. "Workers of the World"
proved as meaningful a rallying cry to those who did not
marshal behind the red banner as to those who did. A decade
earlier John Francis Bray had seemed an anomaly when he
wrote, "On the broad principles of equal rights will Labour
now take its stand,—not Labour in the United Kingdom only,
but in France, and the United States, and the world at large." [2]
But in '48 he moved with the current as the mainstream of
events caught up with him. "The present," he announced, "is
not a merely local movement, it is not confined to country,
colour, or creed—the universe is the sphere in which it acts." [3]
Although Bray was writing in England, close to the sources
of the new internationalism, his fellow countrymen—for he
was American-born—were likewise moved by the upheavals
abroad. The doughty artisans of the Franklin Typographical
Society of Boston, not unmindful of the internationalism of

---

[1] *Ernest Jones, Chartist: Selections from the Writings and Speeches of Ernest Jones*, ed. John Saville (London: Lawrence, 1952), pp. 133, 145.

[2] John Francis Bray, *Labour's Wrongs and Labour's Remedy, or the Age of Might and the Age of Right* (Leeds: D. Green, 1839), p. 13.

[3] Max Beer, *A History of British Socialism* (2 vols.; New York, Harcourt Brace, 1921), Vol. 1, p. 243. *Socialism in American Life,* eds. Donald Egbert and Stow Persons (2 vols.; Princeton: Princeton University Press, 1952), Vol. I, pp. 45-46.

the great printer for whom their organization was named, assembled on the 1st of April, 1848 and dispatched a long and glowing address to the printers of Paris congratulating them on their role in the recent events in France. A month later a mass meeting of mechanics was held in Faneuil Hall, a meeting place associated with the dissents of an earlier day, and expressions of support and grateful sympathy were sent to the workers of France, to the Chartists of England, and to the Repealers of Ireland.[4] Not only was American socialism given a fillip by the tumultuous developments overseas, but the cause of labor reform generally received a powerful stimulus.

To a surprising extent British workers appear to have realized that capitalism, industrialism, and the train of problems that came in their wake were Western, not narrowly national, phenomena and certainly thinkers such as Bray hammered this intelligence home as forcefully as possible. Viewing their struggle for the good life within the framework of an international trend towards democracy, they reasoned that the survival of their cause might well be contingent upon its becoming as widespread as the forces opposing it. Full of missionary zeal that sprang from moral conviction as much as from economic oppression, they shouldered the " workingman's burden." Whenever freedom was on trial they joined with other elements in British society as its champions. Their land became a refuge for liberals and democrats, succoring Greek and Polish revolutionaries, furnishing asylum for Marx, Mazzini, Garibaldi, and Kossuth, supplying a haven for thousands of artisans and laborers uprooted from the Continent.

Inevitably the attention of British labor focused upon the United States. Labor and labor-reform leaders saw the Republic standing in the same relationship to England as England stood to the rest of Europe. Many of them evidenced a natural and unstrained affinity for America. Language, culture, and traditions were, in part, common inheritances that they shared with a majority of Americans and, if the two peoples were markedly dissimilar in many respects, they were also alike in others. Undoubtedly the most powerful bond between the two nation-

[4] McNeill, pp. 114-15.

alities, however, was the fact that the United States was as much of an economic frontier for the men and women of the United Kingdom as it was for its own citizenry. An abundance of land, relatively high wages, or the promise of the same, and the opportunity to become capitalists lured hundreds of thousands of Britain's finest mechanics and artisans to its shores. Those who had seen America first-hand might, as one Scotch immigrant did, "tell the people at home, if they are doing well, to stay where they are,"[5] but scant heed was paid to the doubters. There was an irresistible pull exerted on many Britons when they learned that American mechanics paraded in "sleek coats, glossy hats, gay watchguards, and doeskin gloves,"[6] or that clerks wore broadcloth, that factory girls carried umbrellas, and swineherds wore spectacles.[7] Unfortunately many learned too late that the promised land had special disabilities. However, emigration funds began to make their appearance early in the forties as one feature of trade union activity, and they grew increasingly important in subsequent years. Before the outbreak of the Civil War, in fact, Americans were already complaining of their overcrowded labor markets and were urging British workers to abandon this form of subsidized emigration. British labor agitators, including many Chartists, also found the United States temporarily congenial when repressive or discriminatory practices at home made their work hazardous. Thus whatever its shortcomings, America seemed to offer many people of the United Kingdom release from the more unpleasant features of existence there.

Despite the cheerful perspective in which many Britons viewed the United States, it became increasingly clear towards mid-century that Republican institutions were providing inadequate insurance against "wage slavery." "The American workingmen, like the English workingmen," declared one observer, "form a foundation for the whole social pile to rest upon: they are each crushed into the earth by the accumulated weight of an aristocracy and a trading class . . . and no mere

---

[5] James Stirling, *Letters from the Slave States* (London: 1857), p. 366.

[6] Harriet Martineau, *Society in America* (3 vols.; New York: Saunders & Co., 1837), Vol. II, p. 63.

[7] *Ibid.*, I, 12. Also see Max Berger, *The British Traveller in America, 1836-1860* (New York: Columbia University Press, 1943), Chap. 8.

change of government prevents the division of society into these various classes. . . . The vulture money-monger is the same, whether he be called a monarchist or a republican." [8] Watching the accumulation of wealth and the steady expansion of American industry, although it had not hit its stride before the sixties, British artisans concluded that their fight had been joined across the sea. In the dawn of this realization, conditions favorable to the establishment of closer relations between British and American labor commenced taking shape, and the perceptive Ernest Jones, alive to these circumstances, announced to his followers, " The same song is now singing on both sides of the Atlantic! Swell the chorus, Englishmen! till it rings from shore to shore." [9]

American labor, however, was slow to fall into step with labor overseas. Between 1820 and 1850 wage earners accounted for only a small fraction of the labor force. Whatever stirrings existed were necessarily feeble since only a handful of workingmen were organized. Labor, to be sure, had often taken the field against employers; occasionally in local skirmishes it had held the field. Associations such as Thomas Skidmore's in New York State and a number of craft unions as well had managed to develop significant local power. By the eighteen thirties some unionists were extending local organizations in hopes of creating national bodies of workingmen, and they were meeting with success. Nevertheless, in the broad context of an overwhelmingly agrarian nation, labor had barely begun to feel the incubus of sweeping industrial change. Actually on economic grounds artisans often had scant incentive to combine against their masters, particularly since shops were small and personal relationships between men and masters were still possible. As often as not their complaints were political or social; serious concern with labor economics was a much later phenomenon. Thus while unions showed a certain spontaneous vitality now and then, few of them mobilized permanent strength and nearly every recessional trend proved fatal to most of them. [10] Wage earners and craftsmen did, in some

---

[8] Bray, p. 19.

[9] Saville, p. 145.

[10] For general studies see, Commons, *History of Labour*, I; Nathan Fine, *Labor*

instances, furnish recruits for the various co-operative and experimental communities that flourished by the hundreds in the thirties and forties. These utopian and communitarian experiments were rather the symptoms of a labor movement than a cohesive, large-scale uprising of workingmen.

Nevertheless in the midst of these early organizational activities British men and ideas were at work. The traditional crafts were among the first to feel their impact. Tailors, for example, were organized in some American cities very early in the nineteenth century; by 1806, in fact, they had established several small craft unions. Not unexpectedly, considerable impetus towards the formation of these bodies came from emigrant British tailors whose own history of organization, particularly in London and Westminster, dated back to the beginning of the eighteenth century.[11] Many of these men continued their affiliation with the Journeyman Tailor's Union at home,[12] and their corporate spirit was kept alive. Another representative of the more venerable crafts, the Hatter's Guild, which had functioned in England well before the American Revolution, gave to the hatters of the United States their fundamental laws and regulations, most of which were transmitted by emigrants.[13] Likewise the glass blowers, among whom there were a number of Britishers, retained their old regulations such as the "bound boy laws" under which apprentices had to work five years for their masters, receiving only half the wages they actually earned.[14] Since these crafts were scattered throughout eastern cities and towns, it would be interesting to know what bearing, if any, they had upon the thinking or actions of unorganized American craftsmen. Craft traditions also remained vital among the Massachusetts Block Printers, the only

and Farmer Parties in the United States, 1828-1928 (New York: Rand School, 1928), pp. 1-23.

[11] Beatrice and Sidney Webb, The History of Trade Unionism (1st ed. rev.; London: Longmans, Green & Co., 1920), pp. 44, 47.

[12] McNeill, p. 71. John R. Commons, Races and Immigrants in America (New York: Macmillan, 1913), pp. 152-55. Benjamin Stolberg, Tailor's Progress (New York: Doubleday, 1944), pp. 25-85.

[13] McNeill, pp. 388-89.

[14] Report of the Industrial Commission, . . . Manufacturing and General Business, 1901, VII, 110.

union of its kind in the United States. Composed exclusively of English immigrants, this organization won notoriety throughout New England for having secured a ten hour work-day years in advance of American workingmen,[15] and we must certainly suspect that it stimulated the agitation of this subject. Similarly, efforts of a group of Boston laborers to forge a general assembly of the city's workingmen in 1834, although a response to local economic and social conditions, were a conscious imitation of England's Grand National Consolidated Trades Union formed the year before.[16]

In early agitational work Britons sometimes stood out in bold relief. Of the more colorful and important of such men was John C. Cluer, whose field of operation encompassed most of the New England textile centers. A Scotsman, Cluer like many of the immigrant organizers was a former Chartist. He probably arrived in the United States in the late thirties; in any event, he brought with him an extensive knowledge of the British short-hour movement and British methods of labor agitation. In 1845 he scored a notable success before the working people of Lowell, and over the course of the next few years he became the best known Ten Hour advocate in New England. At the Lynn Ten Hour Convention in 1846, one of the earliest gatherings of its kind, Cluer was a key personality. Since war between Britain and America seemed at the time to be the likely outcome of the Oregon controversy, he was instrumental in securing the passage of a resolve stating: " Far from regarding the laboring man on the other side of the water as our enemy, and shooting him as such, we regard him as our friend, and will do all in our power to better his condition." [17] Subsequently he recommended that the Convention's resolution be published in the " people's paper," the Chartist-sponsored *Northern Star*, so that " scores of thousands " could read of the American worker's stand. Moreover in hopes of breaking the " long hour " system then in general

---

[15] McNeill, p. 120.

[16] Charles Persons, Mabel Parton, and Mabelle Moses, *Labor Laws and Their Enforcement,* ed. Susan Kingsbury (London: Longmans, Green, & Co., 1911), p. 13.

[17] Commons, *Documentary History.* VIII, 114. McNeill, p. 105.

use throughout manufacturing centers, he called for a meeting of men and masters to discuss and solve this rankling issue, and a formal statement embodying his views was passed.[18]

However novel and enterprising his suggestion of a joint meeting between owners and operatives, the fact remains that nothing came of it and Cluer fell back again on typical Chartist tactics. He petitioned the Massachusetts legislature to redress the grievances of the textile operatives and when the appeal went unheeded he tried quixotically to instigate a " general strike." But before he could put his master plan into operation, the mill owners discovered that his respect for the institution of matrimony was less than profound and turned his indiscretions against him.[19] Cluer thereafter conducted his agitations in Boston and fully forty years later he was still a man of some stature among the workingclass leaders of New England.[20]

Other Chartists whose rebelliousness was unimpaired by the misfortunes of the movement in England shifted their energies to the United States. Many of these fiery personalities turned up in the chief coal mining regions during the fifties and early sixties. In the anthracite fields of northeastern and northcentral Pennsylvania, in the " river coal " and bituminous fields near Pittsburgh, westward for hundreds of miles into the Hocking, Mahoning, and Tuscarawas valleys of Ohio, and the Belleville tract of Illinois, they labored as the harbingers of mine unionism. Among the densely settled Welsh, Scotch, and English miners in the Pennsylvania anthracite fields, for instance, John Bates set about organizing what was probably the first mine union in America. Described as a man " imbued with the lofty ideals of Chartism," Bates, in 1849, founded and served as president of an historic, though short-lived, union that bore his name. Supposedly, although we have no details about it, the union was modelled on " Chartist principles." [21] Following the loss of what was hopefuly labelled a " general strike," a

---

[18] Commons, *Documentary History,* VIII, 115-17.

[19] McNeill, p. 105. Kingsbury, pp. 39-41.

[20] McNeill, p. 105.

[21] Andrew Roy, *History of the Coal Miners of the United States* (Columbus: J. L. Trauger Printing Co., 1907), p. 75.

term that found much favor with the early agitators, Bates disappeared from the labor scene, allegedly with union funds, and the organization dissolved.

Two other Chartists, Daniel Weaver and Thomas Lloyd, picked up the threads of mine unionism, undertaking organizational work in the coal fields of eastern Missouri and in the adjacent Belleville tract of southwestern Illinois. A self-educated man, a disciple of the Chartist gospel, Weaver was familiar with conditions in the Staffordshire mines, having labored in them as a youth. His departure from England was apparently hastened by his political convictions. When he started proselytizing American miners he was already a man "ripening in years." His contemporaries accounted him "a deep thinker, logical reasoner," and a "plain energetic speaker."[22] Weaver's co-worker, Thomas Lloyd, had much the same background. He emigrated from Wales and settled in the Belleville tract where he conducted his first American unionizing campaigns. Like Weaver, he was a skilled agitator with the impressive combination of natural vigor and old country labor experience.

Together, in the early sixties, these two "talked up the benefits to be derived from . . . general organization,"[23] aroused the miners, and alerted them to the virtues of concerted action. Late in 1860, Weaver, laying the foundations for a crusading, nationally organized union of coal miners, published "What Might Be Done?"—one of the most important addresses ever circulated among these men in the United States. In the text Weaver spelled out in dramatic terms the crying need for united action. His insistence that labor learn how to exercise its power upon legislatures was very probably a reflection of his Chartist career; it certainly blended well, however, with the prevailing political-mindedness of the American workingmen of this period. Moreover, Weaver's plea stressed the necessity for shelving whatever animosities divided miners. "Let there be no English, no Irish, Germans, Scotch, or Welsh," he declared; "rally round the standard of the Union—the union of the state and the unity of the miners."[24]

[22] McNeill, p. 247. Mitchell, p. 363.
[23] McNeill, p. 244.
[24] *Ibid.*, p. 245.

The fruits of this address and the agitation that paralleled it were harvested on January 28, 1861. Secession was already underway and the Civil War lay just a few months ahead, yet a gathering of miners in St. Louis was able to bring forth the American Miners' Association, first of the national mine unions in the United States.[25] The Association's constitution was largely the handiwork of Weaver, and, as might have been expected because of his leadership in mine unionism, he became first president of the new national, Lloyd quite logically serving with him as secretary. Considering the critical days during which it was launched, it is not surprising that the union did not prosper greatly, nor that both Weaver and Lloyd soon slipped back into less important functions. Lloyd achieved some notoriety while the conflict raged by leading the miners who supplied coal for the Union's Western armies. After the war both of the old Chartists battled on for the redress of their grievances, vigorously haranguing the miners of Missouri and Illinois to fight for their rights and castigating them for their inconsistency.[26] The Association, nevertheless, lost power in the bituminous fields and finally passed out of existence in 1868.

## II. Agitators and Ideas: 1825–1862

Labor agitation extended beyond the pitheads and the mining valleys; it found nourishment wherever British and Irish immigrants congregated in appreciable numbers. By the fifties, English and Welsh organizers were stirring the glassblowers of Philadelphia to action, and in that same city as well as in parts of New England, shoemakers and textile operatives were undergoing conversions to the cause of organized labor. In New York State Robert MacFarlane, formerly a Scottish dyer, organized one of the more successful workingmen's associations during the mid-forties, the Mechanics' Mutual Protection Association. Like so many other immigrants, MacFarlane was haunted by memories of the industrial evils he had experienced at home. "The factory system," he wrote,

[25] McNeill, p. 244. Roy, p. 62. The best account of the American Miners' Association is by Edward Wieck, *The American Miners' Association* (New York: Russell Sage Foundation, 1940).

[26] *Belleville Advocate*, May 28, 1868. Also see edition of July 20, 1866.

" has been long rooting out the Anglo-Saxon energy of England, and fear of a most serious result to the physical constitution and moral nature of the people, has compelled the Government to arrest the destroying Angel that was hovering over the pent up walls of Leeds, Manchester, and Glasgow." And he added, " In our country, the evil is but faintly discerned because we are young in manufactures, but, Oh! I have seen enough of it to convince me of its future evils, unless we stand between the living and the dead." [27]  The Protective Association, initially organized in Buffalo as a secret society, admitted both mechanics and masters. Superficially the organization's purposes appeared innocuous enough: " We do not wage war against wealth; we would not tear down the proud pinnacles that have been created above us. We are not the levelers of the French Revolution," declared the Association's leader. But he also added in a speech delivered to the membership, " Hitherto we have scarcely been known, we have marched along in silence and under a cloud, but like Gideon . . . our lights are in our pitchers and we shall yet bear down with the swoop of the falcon, and the victorious shout of a fair remuneration for American mechanical labor, and a ten hour system for American factory operatives." [28]

Catching on with working people, the MacFarlane organization spread throughout New York State; in fact, its leader claimed that in 1847 there were thirty-eight locals scattered not only through New York, but also through Ohio, Michigan, Pennsylvania, and Wisconsin.[29]  Moderates who repudiated use of the strike, the members appear to have concentrated on securing the more popular reforms, abolition of prison labor, shorter hours, and improved educational facilities for their children. Despite the promise of its early bloom, however, the Association proved about as ephemeral as most contemporary organizations, lasting only a few years. MacFarlane himself, thanks to his versatility, managed to keep his ideas in circulation after the collapse of the Association, for after moving from Buffalo to Albany in 1848 he became the editor variously

[27] Cited in Commons, *Documentary History*, VIII, 259.
[28] Commons, *Documentary History*, VIII, 254.
[29] *Ibid.*, VIII, 251.

of the *State Mechanic*, the *Mechanics' Mirror*, and the influential *Scientific American*. Seventeen years later he retired to his old trade and died in Brooklyn.

Several agitators were sensational enough to attract national attention. One such man was the Welsh immigrant, George Henry Evans, whose contributions to American labor-reformism still require analysis. Evans, who spent most of his life in New Jersey and New York, played no direct part whatsoever in the British labor movement; in fact he had come to the United States while a child. Nevertheless, through his editorship of *The Man*, *The Working Man's Advocate*, and *Young America*, the most powerful radical papers of the twenties, thirties, and forties,[30] he introduced many British ideas to workingmen in this country. By centering attention on the ideas of Robert Owen, sometimes through attacks upon them, he gave them additional currency, while the political programs of the Chartists, certified by his praise, probably impressed more workingmen than might otherwise have been the case. Evans was more than just a successful editor. Colorful and vital, he left his imprint on several labor reform groups, as well as on the Industrial Congresses of 1845 and 1847.[31] In co-operation with Thomas Ainge Devyr,[32] an Irishman with experience in English labor, he founded the National Reform Association and dedicated it to winning labor's "natural rights." Furthermore, in order to forestall the rise of industrial evils such as those afflicting the British, Evans improvised a land reform panacea whereby the government, from the inexhaustible bounty of the national domain, would parcel out homesteads to workingmen. As panaceas went, this one fitted easily into the American environment, but it was neither original nor for that matter even an American idea. Evans and Devyr both borrowed heavily from the English agrarian radical, Thomas Spence, whose writings appeared in the United States in 1829.

Evans' notoriety was rivalled by the fame of a man for

[30] *Ibid.*, VII, 30-33, 288, 291.
[31] Commons, *Documentary History*, VIII, 23, 25-26, 288, 303. McNeill, p. 109.
[32] U. S., Senate, *Report . . . upon the Relations between Labor and Capital*, 48th Cong., 1885, II, 836-38.

whom, intellectually, he seems to have had very little regard, Robert Owen. When Owen first arrived in the United States in the autumn of 1824 he had already become an inspiration to working people in his own country, and thanks to the careful and frequent reviews of his achievements by American papers, he had acquired a small following on these shores. Although he remained in the United States less than a year on his initial visit, and came only occasionally thereafter, he unquestionably catalyzed discussion of labor problems by presenting intelligible alternatives to the existing order of things; no one has seriously challenged his claim to being the father of American socialism or co-operation. Perhaps best known today for his communitarian experiment in 1825 at New Harmony, Indiana, Owen may well have done his most effective work in this country through less sensational writing and speaking that served to increase the self-consciousness of laboring people.[33]

Evans and Owen reflected only segments of the traditions and opinions that were carried into the United States by thousands of British immigrants. Lessons that these people had culled from struggles at home were not forgotten, and many of them, even after relocation in their new homes, continued to feed at the intellectual well-springs that once nourished them in the Old World. The career of William Heighton, fortunately, provides us with a classic example of this. A native of Oundle, Northhamptonshire, Heighton was the moving spirit behind the Mechanics' Union of Trade Associations of Philadelphia in 1827, an organization some students consider the first genuine evidence of a labor *movement* in America. According to a recent and careful study,[34] Heighton and his followers derived their salient economic ideas from the writings of Ricardian socialists whose works, curiously enough, seem to have been more easily obtainable in the United States during the twenties than they were in England. In particular, Heighton drew substance from the

---

[33] Commons, *Documentary History,* X, 292-293; also 213-214. On Spence see *ibid.,* VII, 29-30.

[34] Louis H. Arky, "The Mechanics' Union of Trade Associations and the Formation of the Philadelphia Workingmen's Movement," *Pennsylvania Magazine of History and Biography,* LXXI (April, 1952), pp. 142-176.

concise and inflammatory productions of John Gray, a Scottish economist, whose *Lecture on Human Happiness* (1825) argued the case for a more equitable distribution of wealth. Gray, we are told, owed much to the work of Robert Owen and it is of interest to note that Heighton, having borrowed from Gray, greatly impressed Owen himself when the great man was in Philadelphia in 1827. Subsequently, as Gray's writings were being circulated in America, particularly in Philadelphia and New Harmony, Heighton's work, based on Gray, was republished by Robert Owen in England. Here indeed is conclusive evidence of a transatlantic circuit of ideas.

Employers were quick to notice the impact of the British and Irish, especially as labor began to rouse itself and native "buckwheats" grew increasingly rambunctious. What unsettling influences, indeed, were not laid at the doorstep of these immigrants? Conspiracy trials, of course, always solicited the attention of masters. In one of the most famed cases of its day, the case of the Thompsonville (Connecticut) Weavers, an employer brought a band of imported Scotch artisans to book under the English doctrine of conspiracy which had been taken over into American law. A cause célèbre in the labor world in 1824, this particular trial focused attention on Scotsmen who had disrupted operations in their employer's ingrain carpet-weaving establishment. Disgruntled about the terms of their contract they walked out, announcing to one and all that "they had broke Factories in the old country and could break this." [35] They knew their business. When Mr. Thompson threatened to import strikebreakers from Scotland, they bluntly informed him it would do him little good since "his character was well known in Kilmarnock." Even more pointedly one of the undaunted ringleaders declared, "I had lived before I ever saw Thompsonville, and I thought I could live if I were out of it, and I thought all the Thompsons put together could not starve me, and give me fair play." [36] Eventually the courts

---

[35] *The Thompsonville Carpet Manufacturing Company vs. William Taylor, Edward Gorman, and Thomas Norton,* reprinted in Commons, *Documentary History,* IV (Supplement), 25, also 47.

[36] *Thompsonville Carpet Co. vs. Taylor, et al.,* in Commons, *Documentary History,* IV (Supplement), 97.

answered for the weavers, leaving mill owners more disturbed than ever about those immigrants who had " rights " and knew how to fight for them.

The Thompsonville affair was only one of the incidents that helped establish the reputation of British and Irish immigrants among certain groups of employers. In Philadelphia in 1834 during a labor altercation, a judge who seems to have surrendered some of his judicial restraint declared that labor combinations " are of foreign origin, not in harmony with our institutions or the character of our people." [37] During a strike for shorter hours in New York in 1836 the cry went up among the masters that because the tailors involved in the dispute were mainly British the walkout was of " foreign origin." [38] The charge of un-Americanism soon became a commonplace. Early in the sixties a strike of Pennsylvania anthracite miners was described as the result of " a habit contracted in Europe, where the mass of the miners is from," [39] a reference to the overwhelming numbers of Welsh, English, Scotch, and Irish who composed the bulk of the foreign-born mine population. Along the same lines, it was the fashion among New England textile manufacturers to complain that labor troubles were fomented by the scum of the English, Scotch, and Irish, just as the growth of unionism in Fall River and surrounding mill towns was blamed directly on " foreign agitators." [40] Employers sometimes tried rooting out trade union ideas as they were carried into American factories; but by and large such efforts were vain. To a considerable extent, a few prominent employers were responsible for their own plight. They gave every encouragement to the influx of supposedly *cheap* foreign labor, yet with this labor came principles of resistance that waxed stronger year by year. Thus of the union

[37] W. S. Aubrey, " Labor Disputes in America," *Fortnightly Review*, XLVIII (1890), 244.

[38] McNeill, p. 84.

[39] *The Miners' Journal*, May 24, 1862. Despite its title this was an anti-union paper. " Miners " meant mine operators. It is a principal source for a systematic study of labor and capital in Schuylkill County, (Pa.) anthracite coal fields from 1825-1897.

[40] Carroll Wright, " Fall River, Lowell, and Lawrence," in Massachusetts, Bureau of the Statistics of Labor, *13th Annual Report*, 1882, pp. 14, 148-49, 167-68, 177.

uprisings in Lowell, where the majority of immigrants were, until the sixties, of British stock, it was reported that "these societies are all founded on the same basis, pursue the same objects and encourage the same opposition as the Trades Unions of Great Britain."[41]

The impression that Britons were instigators of labor unrest was well established by the thirties. This belief was strengthened by the fact that during a period when American men scorned factory labor, immigrants were very apt to make up a sizable portion of the mill workers in certain industrial areas. One popular speaker after another, therefore, retailed stories of their influence on the labor problem. "Within a few years past," exclaimed James Homer in an address to the Massachusetts Mechanics' Association, "there has grown up among a portion of our journeymen a restless and turbulent spirit—a spirit induced chiefly, there is reason to believe, by foreign adventurers, who have been cast upon our shores, and who have brought with them the prejudices and habits peculiar to many of the operative mechanics of England, a country in which the great mass of society is divided into two classes— one of them very rich—the other very poor, ignorant, and vicious." And he added as his parting shot, "In New York, it is said, the trade unions are almost entirely of foreigners."[42]

When they did not feel their livelihoods threatened by immigrants, American workingmen cultivated an interest in the aspirations of British labor. And whatever sympathies the alert and articulate worker mustered paved the way for acceptance of British ideas. In 1824, for example, the Commonwealth of Pennsylvania initiated the first feeble probes into child labor conditions; the following year similar investigations were authorized by the Senate of Massachusetts and by the legislature in Rhode Island.[43] In each of these instances the

[41] Charles Cowley, *A History of Lowell* (Boston: Lee Shepard, 1868), pp. 199-207.

[42] James L. Homer, "An Address delivered before the Massachusetts Charitable Mechanics' Association at the Celebration of their Tenth Festival, October 6, 1836," (Boston: 1836) in the Library of the Peabody Institute, Baltimore, Maryland.

[43] Kingsbury, p. 9. For background also see J. L. Barnard, *Factory Legislation in Pennsylvania* (Philadelphia: University, 1905), and John K. Towles, "Factory

state's actions were motivated partly by pressures from workers who were guided by English discussions of the same problem. Stirred by humanitarian impulses abroad, the work of Oastler, Sadler, and Ashley, in particular, labor journals in the United States expressed growing indignation during the twenties and thirties over the physical and moral degradation of adults and children in English mills, raising the subject to a position of preëminent concern in labor circles. Humane impulses were still tender growths on both sides of the Atlantic at this time, to be sure, but the significance of industrial casualties in Lancashire was not entirely lost on parents who, with their children, labored in the factories of New England or the Middle Atlantic States.

Conditions in British industry and the worst evils of the factory system soon became a familiar tale to American operatives. The purpose of retelling this story in America was to prevent emergence of similar difficulties here. Men and women driven from the old country were especially eager to avoid enduring the same hardships twice, but they were not alone, for native sons were anxious that the New World should preserve its virginal uniqueness. When Seth Luther spoke to New England operatives in 1832 he displayed keen awareness of the more sordid aspects of English industrialism. Indeed, Luther knew English conditions so well that his audiences and early students of labor mistook him for an immigrant himself and this particular speech did nothing to enlighten them. Having emphasized the oppressed circumstances of English workingmen, he took English manufacturers to task for daring to advertise their country to the rest of mankind as the " Splendid Example." He solemnly warned his Yankee audience against permitting the spread of similar conditions in the Republic and divulged his own apprehension that already the United States was " following with fearful rapidity the ' Splendid Example ' of England." [44] In substance Luther's

Legislation in Rhode Island," *American Economic Association Quarterly,* XVI (October, 1908), 17. E. Stagg Whitin, *Factory Legislation in Maine* (Columbia University Studies in History, Economics, and Public Law, Vol. XXXIII, no. 1; N. Y.: Columbia University Press, 1908), pp. 30-32.

[44] Seth Luther, "An Address to the Working-Men of New England on the

warnings were reiterated by many others, like Charles Douglass, for instance, editor of the *New England Artisan*. Decisively influenced in his choice of a career by the publication of Richard Oastler's letters on working conditions in Yorkshire mills in 1830,[45] often mistaken for an immigrant as was his friend Luther, Douglass struck out against poor human facilities in industry and championed improved working conditions with especial vigor before the two industrial congresses of the mid-forties. Finally, in much the same vein, Robert Dale Owens, son of the great Utopian socialist, limned for his American audiences stark portraits of England's industrial plight. So serious was Britain's situation, in his judgment, that he predicted his own people faced immediately either the most sweeping reforms or a revolution that would shake the pillars of society, and he cautioned his listeners against allowing the same parlous dilemma to arise in their land.[46]

Bad as the British workingman's position was depicted, sympathetic Americans became increasingly aware of the fact that he was winning important concessions for himself. However ineffectual it really was, English factory legislation of 1802, 1819, 1833, 1842, and 1846, for instance, convinced many New Englanders they were entitled to benefits similar to those enjoyed by the benighted population of Great Britain. This feeling registered sharply in the advanced manufacturing state of Massachusetts. There, state-sponsored investigations of working conditions and analyses of British progress in this respect started a chain of events that over the long run proved of great importance to her laboring classes. The struggle to secure sound factory legislation in the United States as in Europe was prolonged; even Massachusetts did not enact significant laws on this complex subject until the mid-seventies. Nevertheless, in the course of tedious discussions, researches, and debates, workers, employers and legislators relied upon

State of Education and the Condition of the Producing Classes in Europe and America," (Boston: 1832) in the Library of the Peabody Institute, Baltimore, Maryland. Also see Louis Hartz, " Seth Luther, Agitator," *New England Quarterly*, XIII (September, 1940), 401-19.

[45] Commons, *Documentary History,* VIII, 330. McNeill, p. 96.

[46] Robert Dale Owen, *Labor: Its History and Its Prospects* . . . (Cincinnati: Herald of Truth Press, 1848), in Library of the Peabody Institute Baltimore.

English experiences[47] as their guide and ceaselessly educated themselves on the kind of laws civilized industrial societies must develop.

The observations of American workers were not centered exclusively on English industrial legislation; they also eagerly watched the contest for shorter hours of labor. Like his English counterpart, the Yankee worker sometimes realized that a reduction of hours could be won more easily if campaigns were conducted on both sides of the sea. On either side manufacturers were in competition with one another and any unilateral reduction in working hours was bound to raise opposition on economic grounds. Moreover, it was likely to provoke intense nationalist animosity. John Cluer was among the first to see the connections between the British and American short hour movements, to stir up controversy on the subject, and to goad Americans into action by reciting the progress of British workers toward shorter hours of labor. News of English success proved heartening to short hour men in the United States and unquestionably spurred them on to greater exertions. Word that the Ten Hour Law had been passed by Parliament in the summer of 1847 provided the occasion for outbursts of joy from Americans. Mass meetings were held in the principal industrial centers and congratulations were dispatched to the working people of England " on their triumph."[48] According to Robert Howard, Cheshire-born leader of the Bay State's textile operatives, by the time the Ten Hour Bill reached its final stages " the bulk of the textile operatives in the United States " were arguing that life under republican institutions ought to entitle them to privileges at least equal to those enjoyed by workers who lived under monarchical rule.[49]

Although Howard's claims may appear somewhat too enthusiastic, no one in America knew the textile workers better than he, and familiar as he was with labor on both sides of the Atlantic, he understood that gains in one nation encouraged fresh demands in the other. It is not surprising, in view of this inter-relationship, that in 1859 after the Amalgamated

---

[47] Mass., Bureau of the Statistics of Labor, *3rd An. Rept.*, 1872, pp. 28-31, 493, 497-98.

[48] McNeill, p. 112.  [49] *Ibid.*, p. 218.

Society of Engineers wrested a nine hour day from British employers, Ira Stewart's Boston Eight Hour League, the most prominent organization of its kind in the United States, claimed this as a victory for Americans too and " resolved that . . . greetings and plaudits go out to the nine hour engineers of England." [50]

While the British won more leisure time, Americans gained new talking points but it should be stressed that influences moved both ways. In March, 1844, for example, as Lord Shaftesbury expounded his case for the Factory Bill, he referred to American developments for the support of his cause. " I perceive by the papers of the 1st of February," he declared, " that a Bill has been proposed in the Legislature of Pennsylvania, to place all persons under the age of sixteen, within the protection of the ' ten hours ' limit. I never thought that we should have learned justice from the City of Philadelphia." [51] Men in both countries, in other words, careless in the assessment of their intelligence, grasped at straws to drive home their reforms.

Despite their interest in the British labor situation, Americans made almost no efforts whatever in the early decades of the nineteenth century to co-operate formally with labor overseas. To be sure, they admired English achievement, but they considered themselves, and correctly so in most respects, better off economically than workers abroad. Owen's heroic struggles, the formation of the Grand National, and subsequent endeavors along this line elicited cheers from America; the objectives of the Chartists, the accomplishments of men like Feargus O'Connor were praised in the labor press; and the rise of " new model " unionism during the fifties touched off considerable discussion among Americans, yet if they thought seriously of collaboration with British trade unionists or labor reformers, there is little evidence of it. Certain groups of Englishmen, hoping to overcome the indifference or frigidity of their cousins across the sea, put out feelers. Thus in June 1847 the English Fraternal Democrats, whose blend of Marxist and Chartist ideology attracted such men as Ernest Jones and

---

[50] McNeill, p. 145.
[51] Great Britain, 3 *Hansard's Parliamentary Debates*, LXXIII (1844), 1098.

George Julian Harney, dispatched a message, apparently calling for co-operation, to the second Industrial Congress. The communication was well received by George Henry Evans and the other delegates and it evoked " considerable discussion " but nothing came of it.[52]

British influences in America prior to the Civil War were, on the whole, only intimations of things to come. They did not for the most part set in motion the forces that were to sustain a labor movement; nevertheless, they did very materially color American thought and action. Labor developments across the Atlantic were faithfully reflected in the early battles for factory legislation, shorter hours of labor, and improved working conditions. British agitators and ideas helped shape the structure, principles, and organizing techniques of some of the early craft unions and labor-reform organizations, and immigrants like Cluer and Heighton played an important role in their leadership. Furthermore, they established or contributed to co-operative and associative enterprises, mainly of the Owenite variety, as well as to land reform panaceas. Immigrants from the United Kingdom were among the chief labor editors of the thirties and forties; and in conjunction with the fairly sophisticated speaking and writing of Warwick's Thomas Brothers [53] or Robert Dale Owen, a host of lesser propagandists and agitators through activities that ranged from lecturing to conducting strikes,[54] ceaselessly and surely educated the new proletarians.

### III. A BASIS FOR UNDERSTANDING: 1862–1875

The eminent American historians, Charles and Mary Beard, once described the Civil War as the " Second American Revolu-

---

[52] Saville, pp. 20-21. McNeill, p. 109. G. D. H. Cole and Raymond Postgate, *The British Common People, 1746-1938* (New York: Knopf, 1939), pp. 254-55, 292, 294.

[53] A disciple of Paine, Brothers came to the U. S. in 1824. He founded a newspaper and wrote several labor pamphlets. Disillusioned, he returned to England and wrote anti-labor and anti-American tracts.

[54] Cheshire's James Dillon led the greatest of America's pre-Civil War strikes. See, Philip Foner, *A History of the Labor Movement in the United States* (2 vols.; New York: International Publishing Co., 1947), I, 241-42.

tion." [55] Provocative as it is, the expression is more convenient than accurate. Industrial capitalism did not burst upon the Republic overnight; like industrial change everywhere it had deep roots. The progress of American capitalism and the extension of the nation's productive facilities were well advanced before the attack on Fort Sumter. The economy did not shift the direction in which it had been moving when war came; it simply moved in the same direction with greater velocity. For working people, more sensible of the present than the past, however, industrial expansion and technological change did carry an impact that was revolutionary. Manufacturing establishments sharply increased in number; the size of the labor force grew; and urgent social, political, and economic problems developed from situations that had merely been bothersome in the past. Fed first on high wages and a war boom, labor suddenly reaped the whirlwind of the armed battle, suffering from the vagaries of inflation, then deflation, of a promising market, then sudden unemployment. And virtually overnight, or so it seemed, employers, more powerful, more impersonal, and more cohesively organized than ever, launched forth in their juggernaut.

Under stress the perspectives of American workers tended to broaden and ties based on economic self-interest and genuine sympathy developed with segments of the British labor movement. Reasons for this are more fully explored in later chapters but during the war two factors were of singular importance.

Northern workers, first of all, were profoundly grateful to English workingmen for the aid and friendship they bestowed upon the Union cause. Curiously enough, British workers felt the issues at stake were more sharply delineated than the combatants themselves did; across an ocean the war appeared to be a struggle of aristocratic against democratic principles. In fact, as English people mobilized against those privileged elements who had strong Confederate biases, one observer sensed the " old revolutionary leaven . . . working steadily." [56] No wonder

[55] *The Rise of American Civilization* (2 vols.; New York: Macmillan, 1930), II, 52.
[56] *A Cycle of Adams Letters*, ed Worthington C. Ford (2 vols.; Boston: Houghton Mifflin, 1920), I, 245.

as mass meetings were held throughout Great Britain, as expressions of goodwill flowed from British workers, Northern opinion settled on the belief that the workingclasses were the main, if not the sole, force behind the withholding of British recognition or outright aid from the Confederate States.

English loyalty was valued even more highly in the North because of the impression that the " cotton famine " had made the price of sympathy dear. American newspapers recounted the sacrifices of British workers in the Midlands, for instance, and feelings within the Union became so strong in favor of helping these gallant Englishmen that large sums of money were raised and several shiploads of staples were sent abroad to alleviate their distress even as the war was in progress.[57] High and very uncritical praise was lavished upon those who shaped labor opinions in respect to the war. Bright and Cobden, for example, employers though they were, so thoroughly galvanized labor sentiment against the South and its institutions that they became Northern heroes.[58] Thomas Hughes and Goldwin Smith were among the others placed on pedestals.[59] Britain's trade unions were also congratulated for their work; not only had they backed the Union but as one prominent labor paper exclaimed they also " did more to protect their members during the cotton distress than the government did for the rest of the population." [60] Lincoln summarized Northern opinion in his reply to the working people of Lancashire thanking them for their wholehearted support of the Emancipation Proclamation. " Under the circumstances," wrote the President, " I cannot but regard your decisive utterances upon the question as an instance of sublime Christian heroism which has not been surpassed in any age or in any country."

A powerful grip was exerted on the emotion of American

---

[57] *Fincher's Trades Review*, March 18, 1865. *The Miner's Journal*, Dec. 20, 1862; Jan. 17, 1863. F. L. Owsley, *King Cotton Diplomacy* (Chicago: University of Chicago Press, 1931).

[58] George Trevelyan, *The Life of John Bright* (London: Houghton Mifflin, 1913), p. 296. Edward L. Pierce, *Memoirs and Letters of Charles Sumner* (4 vols.; Boston: Roberts Brothers, 1894), IV, 166, 193, 206.

[59] Goldwin Smith Mss, p. 3, in The Gilman Collection (The Johns Hopkins University, Baltimore, Maryland). Cited hereafter as Gilman Coll.

[60] *Fincher's*, Apr. 16, 1864.

labor leaders many years after the war by these examples of
"Christian heroism." In the eighties, at a time when twisting
the Lion's tail had become a hobby in American politics, workingmen still remembered the wartime role of British labor
and one of their spokesmen wrote eloquently:

There is one crowning instance which Americans above all people in
the world should never forget, in which the working classes may be
said to have decided the policy of England, when the voice of the
people proved truly to be the voice of God. At a time when every
evil influence under heaven seemed combined to force England into
abetting the slaveholders' secession, when the cotton famines and
blockade runners' profits, the French despot and the *Times*, the country-
party and the ship-owners, Mr. Carlyle and half the piety of England,
were urging the country on to a course which all now feel would have
been one of headlong and ruinous folly, the workingmen of Lancashire
stood firm and fast to the holy principle of human freedom.[61]

A decade later when David Holmes came to the United States
as a fraternal delegate from the British Trades Union Congress,
it was sufficient introduction for the *American Federationist* to
describe him as "a foremost part of that sturdy stock of
Lancashire weavers who withstood the brunt of many an industrial battle, and who gave the world one of the noblest
experiences of self-sacrifice for a great principle," and then to
proceed to recapitulate the old story compounded of a hatred
of slavery, the workers' wrath and heroism, the backdown
of the British Cabinet, and Lincoln's acknowledgement of
gratitude.[62]

That the British Cabinet was not disposed to war, that by
no means all of the better people favored recognition of the
Confederacy, that the cotton famine was not really a famine
at all, that wheat was as vital as idealism in keeping Britain
neutral, that American workers had a distorted picture of the
situation of the British worker, that the British worker had
an equally distorted picture of the Federal cause, are all clear
in the light of modern research.[63] But the deep, uncomplicated
emotions nourished by Northern workers in their time of

---

[61] McNeill, p. 65.

[62] *American Federationist,* Jan., 1895.

[63] In addition to F. L. Owsley see also Samuel F. Bemis, *A Diplomatic History
of the United States* (New York: Henry Holt and Co., 1950), pp. 373, 383.

trouble were also facts that gave Anglo-American labor a common bond.

Also important in the war and post-war years was the growing conviction among Americans that Britain possessed the most progressive labor movement in the world. This complex of views was assiduously cultivated by British agitators and propagandists, whom we shall introduce in later chapters, and by a large body of American labor leaders who echoed the same refrain. The upshot of this was that Britain became the great example to American workers. The strides made in England during the fifties and sixties, the alliance between middle-class radicals and moderate-tempered, skilled workers, the formation and success of the "new model" unions and co-operatives, and a host of alternatives and solutions to labor problems that had been tested in England were impressed upon laborers in the Republic. To the mechanic in Philadelphia or Boston or Cincinnati, the British worker was presented as a tough, plucky fellow who while opposed to revolution was nonetheless intelligently aggressive. More and more recitals of his successes entered into labor literature.

During the war and afterward, the British reciprocated by sustaining an interest in American labor. Despite the reports of many disillusioned immigrants who came to the Republic only to discover the environment less agreeable than it had been home, despite a swelling volume of criticism, workmen abroad still tended to regard the United States as a land of opportunity. Especially did the defeat of the slave power seem to be a gain for the horny-handed. Through the years labor's Christian socialist allies, like J. M. Ludlow and Lloyd Jones, co-operators like George Jacob Holyoake,[64] and many trade unionists had evidenced active hostility to the "peculiar institution." Consequently, when the Negro was freed, Britons rejoiced that free labor had received new impetus from the act of liberation,[65] that the end of the war meant the release

[64] J. M. Ludlow, *The Southern Minister and His Slave Convert* (London: 1863), and his *American Slavery* (London: 1864). For the anti-slavery writings of Holyoake see G. W. F. Goss, *A Descriptive Bibliography of the Writings of George Jacob Holyoake* (London: Crowther, Goodman, 1908), p.18.

[65] U. S., Senate, *Report . . . upon the Relations between Labor and Capital*, 48th Cong., 1885, I, 454.

of fresh energies into the struggle against privileged interests. Just as Wendell Phillips found the transition from anti-slavery crusading to labor reform an easy one, so too did John Francis Bray who had returned to his homeland twelve years before the opening of the conflict. Bray really spoke for men on both sides of the Atlantic in urging a renewal of the assault against the "new slavery"—industrial slavery. "If the Northern majority has the right to control a Southern majority [referring to the occupation of the South during Reconstruction] what [is] to prevent the same thing happening when force enables a group to take over the Northerner's Lowell factory?" asked Bray. "In Northern factories do not men and women toil for others—the moneyed aristocracy!"[66] With slavery exterminated men could turn to these other dangers.

Since the war, gilded by distance, assumed the appearance of a contest for democracy in the eyes of many English liberals and workingmen, it likewise stimulated discussion of this increasingly popular philosophy. American political progress, in fact, furnished English labor and its Parliamentary allies with ammunition for their battle to capture the franchise and American precedents were evoked to emphasize telling points. Moreover, as Bright commented, "We all know that they [the workers] are reading, debating, thinking, and combining and that they are well aware that in all our colonies as well as in the United States the position of their class is wholly different," and he later added that he attributed "the revival of Reform agitation to the result of the American War. Republicanism is now looking up in the world."[67] Out of this continuing British interest in the affairs of the Republic, and out of the corresponding American awareness of developments in British labor came a climate of opinion conducive to the interchange of ideas and leaders.

---

[66] John Francis Bray, "America's Destiny," (n. p., n. d.) in the John Francis Bray Papers (University of Michigan General Library, Ann Arbor, Michigan). Cited hereafter as Bray Papers.

[67] Great Britain, 3 *Hansard,* CLXXXII (1866), 66, 157-59, 223, 1403.

PART TWO

STRENGTHENING TIES

———

I. COLLABORATION

Between 1860 and 1910 several attempts, some of which were characterized by vision and imagination, were made to link British and American labor organizations. Born of the complex new problems confronting workingmen on each side of the Atlantic, motivated by practical self-interest and hopeful international altruism, these transatlantic experiments assumed varying shapes. Some were efforts to establish informal working agreements to ease joint problems; the more interesting ones represented moves towards official alliances or the federation of Anglo-American unions; others were arrangements designed to bring labor leadership into closer intercourse, to lend moral support or make possible emergency aids to organizations in grave difficulty. Potentially they held great promise and had they been entirely successful British and American labor history might have been drastically altered; as it happened they formed a framework for more significant events.

Viewed broadly, labor's ripening internationalism paralleled a trend towards greater rapport between British and American citizens generally. At the diplomatic level, despite moments of acute crisis, the last decades of the nineteenth century were marked by increasingly amicable relations between the British and American governments, as the arbitration treaties of the period indicate. Privately these were years during which prominent figures on both sides of the Atlantic spoke and wrote seriously about Anglo-American Union or about a general federation of the two nations—proposals that have been re-echoed in our own time. Joseph Chamberlain, Charles Dilke, and Lord Bryce in England, Charles Francis Adams, Thomas Bayard, John Hay, and Goldwin Smith in America were among the many who did much to publicize such suggestions. On

51

both shores of the Atlantic their articles and books were widely circulated and proved potent arguments for Anglo-American merger.[1] Each of these figures, English and American alike, was familiar to many labor leaders in the United States; frequently their names appeared in labor journals, and from time to time their opinions were directly quoted.[2] On at least one occasion an American labor figure tried personally to contact Charles Dilke on the subject of British-American relations; it was no less a person than Ira Stewart, key figure in the New England eight hour movement.[3] Underlying proposals for international alliance between the two peoples, moreover, we can detect the prevalence of the concept of Anglo-Saxon superiority, a racial theory that found as ready acceptance among workers as among their social peers, and this, too, probably strengthened feelings of kinship.

Somewhat more narrowly viewed, labor's internationalism was one of the concomitants of a shrinking nineteenth century

[1] There is a vast body of literature on this subject. See, for instance, Lionel Gelber, *The Rise of Anglo-American Friendship, 1898-1906* (London: Oxford University Press, 1938). Gelber like other students stresses the roles of Cecil Spring-Rice, Julian Pauncefote, and Theodore Roosevelt. Also see Charles C. Tansill, *The Foreign Policy of Thomas A. Bayard* (New York: Fordham Press, 1940), Chap. 16; W. R. W. Stephens, *Life and Letters of E. A. Freeman* (2 vols.; London: Macmillan & Co., 1895), Vol. II, pp. 278, 306, 379, 383; George W. Smalley, *Anglo-American Memories* (New York: G. P. Putnam, 1912), Chap. 14; Richard Heindel, *The American Impact on Great Britain, 1898-1914* (Philadelphia: University of Pennsylvania Press, 1940); O. D. Skelton, *The Life and Letters of Sir Wilfred Laurier* (2 vols.; New York: The Century Co., 1922), Vol. I, pp. 128, 168, 177; Vol. II, pp. 89, 229; *Letters and Recollections of John Murray Forbes,* ed. Sarah Forbes Hughes (2 vols.; New York: Houghton Mifflin, 1899), Vol. II, pp. 40, 108, 110-12, 118, 132, 151-52; Charles Francis Adams, *Transatlantic Historical Solidarity* (Oxford: Clarendon Press, 1913). For samples of the periodical literature see W. P. Trent, " Mr. Goldwin Smith on the U. S.," *Sewanee Review,* II (November, 1893), 1-3; Lord Bryce, " The Essential Unity of Britain and America," *Atlantic Monthly,* LXXXII (July, 1898), 22-29; R. L. Schuyler, " The Climax of Anti-Imperialism in England," *Political Science Quarterly,* XXXVI (December, 1921), 537-60. Also valuable are the extensive writings and collections of Goldwin Smith, e. g., " England and America," *Atlantic Monthly,* XIV (December, 1864), 749; "Anglo-Saxon Union," *North American Review,* CLVII (July-Dec., 1893), 170-85.

[2] John Samuel, " Tract for the Times," (n. p., n. d.) in John Samuel Papers (Wisconsin State Historical Society, University of Wisconsin, Madison, Wis.) Cited hereafter as Samuel Papers. *The Workingman's Advocate,* Feb. 22, 1868; Mar. 7, 1874.

[3] *Cigarmakers' Journal,* November, 1883. Cited hereafter as *CMOJ.*

world. Travel and communications, greatly improved, brought men closer together, increased their mobility, and facilitated the exchange of ideas. In addition, capitalism more than ever became a world-wide phenomenon—and workers soon realized it. In the mines of Pennsylvania or Colorado, for instance, English, Welsh, Scotch, and Irish immigrants used the same techniques underground as were used in the mines at home, worked for bosses dispatched by absentee Scotch or English capitalists who controlled the mines, or perhaps served English stockholders who held securities in American railroads that in turn operated the mines. This same situation also prevailed in numerous other American industries. As late as 1899 British capital held two and a half billion dollars in American railroad securities alone,[4] while hundreds of millions more were owned by capitalists on the Continent. Labor, in other words, had every incentive to augment its power by whatever alliances or agreements it could strike.

Just as capital had been internationalized, so also was the labor market and this circumstance raised problems for labor organizations that only negotiations could remedy. Inevitably difficulties arose because of the masses of British and Irish immigrants that came to the United States, and to a lesser degree as the result of sporadic return emigration to England. On the surface many issues associated with immigration appear trivial, yet to the individual workingman who hazarded thousands of miles of ocean, ill-informed of what lay ahead, they were of the utmost importance. The way in which a Scottish iron molder or a Cornish tin miner or a London engineer was received by his fellow tradesmen in the United States could make a tremendous difference to him. For those who came without union affiliations the situation could be even more trying than it was for unionists because as the nineteenth century wore on, native-born and immigrant residents of the United States alike grew increasingly restive in the face of Europeans pouring into labor markets they were trying or hoping to monopolize.

[4] Roy, Chap. 1. Berthoff, p. 59. *Final Report of the Industrial Commission,* 1902, XIX, 404. Pennsylvania, Bureau of Industrial Statistics, *Annual Report, 1880-81,* IX, 1-8, 426-29, 526-27.

All sorts of bedeviling questions arose. What, for instance, was to be done with a man who had unwittingly enlisted abroad as a strikebreaker or "scab" for an American employer? How could a Lancashire textile operative assess job possibilities, wages, the cost of living, and working conditions in, let us say, Fall River? How was the native Philadelphia molder or shoemaker to protect himself and prevent immigrant British and Irish molders and shoemakers from glutting the local labor market in slack times? What could the New York cigarmakers do to establish union facilities for incoming British cigarmakers? By what means could English unions in the United States avoid antagonizing American organizations when problems of "dual unionism" were raised? Depending upon how these questions were approached, British or Irish newcomers might work in St. Louis rather than in Boston, on a west Pennsylvania farm rather than in a Luzerne County mine; they might work at their old callings or at new ones, at high wages or low wages—or they might not work at all for many long months.

Even before the war, efforts were made to cope with such problems. Initiative came from both sides of the Atlantic, of course, and for brief periods satisfactory relations were fostered. The famed American Typographical Union, for example, was forced early in its history to deal with one of the commonest difficulties that confronted unions: immigrants glutting the labor market. Scotch and English printers were "induced to leave the comforts of the Old Country to seek precarious existence" on the American side of the ocean as the result of newspaper advertisements inserted by some of their less scrupulous comrades who hoped through a shortage of labor to depress the business of British employers paying low wages. Apprised of these affairs American printers addressed a circular to "printers of the United Kingdom of Great Britain and Ireland," to dissuade them from coming to East Coast cities and towns, and, after "extensive circulation" the message "tended in a great measure to counteract the evil contemplated by the original advertisement." [5]

[5] George Tracy, *History of the Typographical Union* (Indianapolis: Hollenbeck Press, 1913), pp. 65-70.

By and large, however, such co-operative actions were features of the post-war years when the seriousness of labor's problems was greater, and the first such moves came from men in the heavy industries. Iron molders had long expressed growing concern over the flood of British molders who were literally dumped by their unions on the American market. William Sylvis, the first statesmanlike figure among American unionists, protested to British leaders and even arranged for an exchange of union cards to ease the tension, but to no avail: [6] the dumping continued through the war years. A convinced internationalist with many British and Irish immigrants in his own union, Sylvis nevertheless continued seeking an amicable adjustment and thanks to a change in the British attitude a *modus vivendi* was worked out. Thus early in 1868, for instance, some Scottish molders were promised jobs in American industry but by the time they had arrived the employers, ignoring their offers, had hired other men. Soon in straitened circumstances, the Scotsmen placed William Sylvis in contact with Daniel Guile, colorful leader of the English ironfounders, and between them they arranged for the care of the unfortunate immigrants.[7] In order to forestall future difficulties Guile tried, insofar as he was able, to curtail the flow of molders to America while jobs were scarce.

Stimulated by such incidents Sylvis and the British considered even closer co-operation. "Need I tell you," declared Sylvis in a speech to his fellow unionists:

that the interests of labor are identical throughout the world? We suffer from the degradation of labor, let it occur where it will . . . when the news of their [European workingmen's] triumph shall be heard across the Atlantic, the workingmen of America will ring out in shouts of triumph from Maine to California.[8]

It was in this internationalist vein that British and American molders arranged for exchanges of information on job openings,

[6] *Fincher's,* Sept. 2, 1865. *Daily Evening Voice* (Boston), Mar. 31, 1865. Jonathan Grossman, *William Sylvis: Pioneer of American Labor* (Columbia University Studies in History, Economics, and Public Law, Vol. 516; New York: Columbia University Press, 1945), pp. 143-49.

[7] *The Workingman's Advocate,* Mar. 21, 1868.

[8] James C. Sylvis, *The Life, Speeches, Labors and Essays of William H. Sylvis* (Philadelphia: Claxton, Haffelfinger, 1872), p. 226. Grossman, p. 257.

the cost of living, and the general state of the trade. In fact, Sylvis' imagination leaped to the possibilities of an international agency designed to work for the world-wide alliance of labor.[9] Unfortunately in the midst of his new agreements with Guile, before he could implement his international dreams, Sylvis died, and for a while the web of relationships he had helped elaborate began to dissolve.

Then in 1872, the new president of the Iron Molders' International Union, William Saffin, announced in his inaugural address that he wanted to bring the Friendly Societies of Iron Founders in England into closer intercourse. Anxious to mitigate troubles that had developed again after Sylvis' death, he suggested that English molders refuse to contract for work prior to their arrival in the United States. This, he believed, would alleviate some of the crowding of the American molders' market in dull times and cut the hiring of scabs by employers' agents in Great Britain. Guile promised his co-operation and Saffin thereafter designated union representatives in the major ports whom new arrivals from abroad could contact for information on the state of the trade.[10] Moreover, to facilitate the flow of news between the members of the two unions, the American molders' executive department maintained a monthly correspondence with the Englishmen and published it in their trade journal. Finally, unionists who voluntarily deposited their cards with the Iron Molders within a month after their arrival in the United States were immediately accepted as members.[11]

Procedures elaborated by Sylvis, Saffin, and the British spread to or were developed spontaneously by other unions. In the early seventies, the Machinists' and Blacksmiths' Union, among whose members were the eight hour leader, Ira Stewart, and the man who later led the Knights of Labor, Terence Powderly, extended an invitation to the Amalgamated Society of Engineers to make full use of its journal to publicize ideas of benefit to workingmen on both sides of the Atlantic. The Engineers by that time had several branches in America, and they colla-

[9] Grossman, p. 257.
[10] *The Workingman's Advocate,* July 29, 1872; Aug. 16, 1873.
[11] *Ibid.,* July 29, 1872.

borated with the Americans by enacting union rules that made
for an easier exchange of members.[12] Similarly, American cigarmakers over a period of decades conducted heavy and extremely
important correspondence with their brethren in England. Full
advantage was taken of these channels of communication to
interdict immigation of "unfair men" and to assist skilled
men bound for American markets to make their transition
with greater ease.[13] Miners, tailors, carpenters, typographers,
as well as men in several other crafts, worked out equivalent
arrangements, while two of the great British amalgamated
unions opened branches in the United States primarily to serve
transient members from the Old Country.

Much was done in the post-war years to allay antipathies
that had sprung up between British and American unionists.
Easing the problems of adjustment which immigrants were
forced to make, honoring union cards, and circulating intelligence of joint interest were steps in this direction. They can
be exaggerated, for all was not sweetness and light. The
influx of British workers—not because they were British but because they were workers—raised issues that continually rankled
American labor, including former British laborers in America.
Patience and tact alone prevented more serious quarrels. Nevertheless in labor diplomacy as in international diplomacy, the
willingness to show good faith on little issues paved the way
to broader understanding about significant problems. These
seemingly petty achievements, in fact, were paralleled by and
in some cases led to more ambitious collaborative projects.

## II. ALLIANCE

The success of Sylvis' practical negotiations led him and his
followers to probe into more far-reaching schemes of co-operation after they launched the National Labor Union in August,
1866. During 1867 they entered exploratory talks with the
Marxist International Workingmens' Association in London,
after their attention had been solicited by the secretary of the
organization, J. George Eccarius.[14] National Labor Unionists,

---

[12] *Ibid.*, Aug. 24, 1872.
[13] *CMOJ*, March, 1876; McNeill, p. 369.
[14] Commons, *Documentary History*, IX, 333-350.

although they were not Marxists by any stretch of the imagination, then proclaimed common cause with this foreign organization. Preparations were made to send Richard Trevellick to Europe on behalf of the N.L.U. for the purposes of inquiring into the systems of co-operation adopted there, to negotiate, if possible, a reciprocity system between workers of the Old World and the New, and to put an end to the " unhallowed existence of the so-called Emigrant Aid Society." [15] A shortage of funds, unhappily, put the quietus on these plans for another two years. But they were not forgotten and in 1869 the Scotch-born editor of the *Workingman's Advocate*, Andrew Carr Cameron, journeyed to Basle for the International's meeting. The upshot of this was that Cameron found Continental representatives, much to his chagrin, too heavily involved in theory and too deficient in common sense to excite the interest of American workers. The British, on the other hand, had already impressed him with their practicality and their experience and Cameron returned to the United States a more powerful advocate than ever of the lessons taught by Britons.[16] Aside from reënforcing the sentiments of this influential labor editor, however, plans for co-operation proved abortive. Yet if the effort led up a blind alley, there were still other avenues to be tried.

In the year following events at Basle unrelated but fresh steps were taken towards British-American intimacy. The official journal of the Amalgamated Iron Workers of Great Britain carried a statement by the union's leader, John Kane, stating that:

I have reason to believe that the Iron Workers of the United States will be most willing to give a personal welcome to such persons as may be sent to represent the Iron Workers of Great Britain at the forthcoming American Trades Conference.[17]

Kane's counterpart in America was the Irish-born Hugh Mc-Laughlin, a man familiar with British unionism, and he replied

---

[15] *The Workingman's Advocate,* Sept. 7, 1867.

[16] Commons, *Documentary History*, X, 182 for references to Cameron; also *Western British-American*, March 19, 1888.

[17] Reprinted from the *Amalgamated Iron and Steel Workers' Journal* in *The Vulcan Record*, I (1870), p. 32.

at once to this English overture by announcing, " It only wants someone to get the ball in motion to have our respective unions united." [18] Long distance negotiations continued along this line throughout the following year and in 1873, McLaughlin's official organ, the *Vulcan Record*, released details of the discussions and explained some of the obstacles that had cropped up. The American leader personally reported, for example, that, " So deeply are we impressed with the many advantages of unionism and so essential has it become to success in all our movements of reform, that I was constrained some time since to enter into semi-official correspondence with the executive of the Amalgamated Iron Workers of Great Britain having in view the formation of a closer union among our members and fellow craftsmen on both sides of the Atlantic." [19]

Semi-official correspondence was not sufficient to satisfy the English who wanted more definite commitments, but since none was forthcoming Kane's group, from " some cause," refused to consider the American answer even though it came direct from the union chieftain. Moreover, the General Council of the Amalgamated Iron Workers was reluctant to take up the merger proposition as a special question. This did not imply that the project was defunct; on the contrary, Kane then wrote:

Now that we have a strong and powerful union and seeing that we can count more thousands than we could at that time count hundreds we believe . . . that a federal union would do much good . . . we shall most willingly give a deputation from the Sons of Vulcan a hearty welcome to our next conference, if they are appointed to represent the iron trade of the United States. We do not believe that there is one member of the Amalgamated . . . that would think of raising objections to the establishment of a federal union which will strengthen the hands of workers in both countries. We hope . . . an official document will be sent to the General Office so that no time may be wasted in effecting a complete federal union which will bring both parties nearer each other.[20]

Nonetheless time had been wasted. In the summer of 1873, the American economy was engulfed in a panic of major proportions and the Vulcans, like other nascent labor organiza-

---

[18] *Ibid.*
[19] *Ibid.*, I (1873), p. 21.
[20] *The Vulcan Record*, I (1873), p. 21.

tions, were among the foremost casualties. They hung on just
long enough to receive a desperate appeal from Kane which
indicated that disaster was not confined to one side of the
Atlantic. The English leader begged McLaughlin to spare
him whatever assistance he could in view of an impending
lockout of 9000 of the Amalgamated's men—and he renewed
the call for a federal union.[21] McLaughlin could do little more
than commiserate with his colleague across the sea so plans for
the international died, a victim of circumstance.

However, the spirit was catching. American cigarmakers
turned to the task of establishing closer ties with their fellow
craftsmen abroad, and they did so somewhat more naturally
than many other unionists could. Long before the Civil War,
as we have seen, these sociable men kept in contact for fraternal
as well as more practical reasons. Early in the seventies they
sought still closer relations and, as in the case of the iron
molders, most of the initiative came from the British. During
1871 John Walker, leader of the English cigarmakers, com-
municated with the president of the Cigarmakers' Union in
the United States, urging that arrangements be made for an
exchange of invitations to one another's conventions and that
steps be taken towards "unity between ourselves and the
Americans."[22] Hard times in the trade soon struck down these
tender proposals just as they had the attempted union of the
iron molders and it was not until 1876 that further overtures
were thought feasible. In the meantime, Walker helped
keep the concept alive by keeping his American friends informed of the latest developments in the trade in England
and by supplying them with details of his schemes of distributive co-operation.[23] Then in 1876, one of the dominant figures
among the New York cigarmakers, Adolph Strasser, called
upon his fellow unionists to join hands with the English in
their struggle for daily bread. When they had won their subsistence, Strasser declared, "We will strive to unite all the
trade and labor unions in both hemispheres into one International Brotherhood."[24] Nothing came of these heady visions,

[21] *Ibid. The Workingman's Advocate,* Aug. 16, 1873.
[22] *CMOJ,* March, 1876; *The Workingman's Advocate,* Oct. 5, 1872.
[23] *CMOJ,* June, July, Sept., Dec., 1876 for Walker's communications.
[24] *Ibid.,* Oct., 1876.

however, for it once again became essential to channel the cigarmakers' power into narrower domestic problems. But the international spirit that misfired so badly had one important, if unforeseen, result. It implanted the concept of the international solidarity of labor in the mind of a bullet-headed young English Jew then working in the Manhattan cigarmaking trade, Samuel Gompers. Throughout the rest of his life, the future leader of the American Federation of Labor remained an advocate of closer co-operation with his many acquaintances in the British labor movement.

Working quietly, a group of workers less numerous than the cigarmakers achieved international unity. These were the English and American boilermakers and iron-shipbuilders. The United Society of Boilermakers and Iron-shipbuilders, the English organization that took the initiative in forming the alliance, traced its roots back to 1832. During the sixties and seventies it became a leader among those new unions that featured benefit programs for their members; it was likewise one of the earliest to hire a professional administrative staff. Consequently, it was both energetic and prosperous. In 1881 a band of American metal workers founded the Brotherhood of Boilermakers and Iron Ship Builders and during their convention of 1884, when three British delegates appeared on the scene, they lost no time linking their own organization with England's. The American Brotherhood announced after the deal was consummated that it had "joined hands with the Boilermakers of England," and had become "part and parcel of that [the British] union." Members claimed subsequently that theirs was the only union that extended over both the Old World and the New. On the whole, British policy seems to have dominated in the American division; there was tight control over strike policy and strike funds, a considerable degree of class-consciousness, and many constitutional provisions that were British-inspired.[25] We have no evidence of how long the alliance lasted, though it was certainly ephemeral, but it

[25] *Report of the Industrial Commission, Labor Organizations, Labor Disputes, and Arbitration. Railway Labor,* 1901, Vol. XVII, p. 228. McNeill, p. 369. Webb, p. 320.

proved the practicality of union and pointed the way to more significant attempts.

The activities of the N.L.U., the iron molders, cigarmakers, and even of the more successful boilermakers, seemed uninspired compared with the plans laid by the Knights of Labor. Given the character of the order, indeed, it was almost inevitable that its members would want to sally into the international arena. Founded in 1869 by Uriah S. Stephens, a Philadelphia tailor once destined for the Baptist ministry, the Knights represented " one big union " in the most comprehensive sense. Only bartenders, bankers, and lawyers were excluded from membership. Equipped with a veritable grab bag of programs designed for all comers, they showed hospitality to most of the panaceas of the day: government ownership of transportation, land reforms, the eight hour day, distributive and productive co-operation, and a variety of social legislation and uplift programs. Originally a secret society, the Knights attracted more attention than many that operated publicly, and their ritual and chalked announcements on streets and walls of assembly meetings scared the better elements. Allan Pinkerton, whose mercenary army of detectives was always available for capitalist hire, spoke for many citizens when he described the Knights as " an amalgamation of the Molly Maguires and the Commune." [26] Actually this great gangling organization was almost entirely uninfected by revolutionary sentiments.

In 1879 Terence Powderly, a Pennsylvania machinist of Irish descent, assumed direction of the order and, at the insistence of the Catholic Church, brought it into the open and expanded its membership. Early in the eighties, as he won several victories on the American scene, he began preparation for organizing branches in England, Ireland, and Wales, as well as on the Continent, and tried in the process to forge an alliance of British and American workingmen.

The Pennsylvanian started correspondence with the leader of

---

[26] Commons, *Documentary History,* X, 33. The best general study of the Knights is Norman J. Ware, *The Labor Movement in the United States, 1860-95* (New York: Appelton, 1929) ; but also see William C. Birdsall, " The Problem of Structure in the Knights of Labor," *Industrial and Labor Relations Review,* V (1953), 532-46.

the Miners' National Association of Great Britain, Alexander Macdonald, in 1880. Macdonald, about whom we will say more in the next chapter, was a loyal friend of the American miner and a familiar figure in the coal fields of the United States. Years earlier he had labored mightily to bring miners of the two lands closer together. Upon receipt of Powderly's letters, Macdonald replied that the idea of international co-operation was agreeable to him. Powderly, of course, was exuberant for he was already satisfied that minor exchanges of information about working conditions in the two countries had produced " an incalculable amount of good." [27]

Once launched on the first steps towards his goal, Powderly felt the need for a vote of confidence from the membership in convention assembled. " Only doubt as to how far I could go in this direction [towards international union] prevented further action," he reported as he asked for their votes, and presented his plan in somewhat greater detail.

I believe the time [1880] is ripe for planting the Order in Europe and if the proper measures be taken at this session the workingmen of the world can be brought into harmonious concert of action. Correspon-dence has been had with membership across the ocean in the interests of one of our branches giving very encouraging news of the possibilities for organization in England especially. A request was made that the necessary material be sent over to the brothers so that they could com-mence work. The Grand Secretary was at once brought face to face with the question of how to convey private word to these brothers and avoid government scrutiny which would surely be directed against any effort we could make.[28]

Reaching the heart of the matter, Powderly then enquired of the members: " Can we not at this session do something whereby the benefits of union between workingmen in America and Europe may become so plain that a connecting link may be forged binding them closely together? I think we can . . . recommend it to your favorable consideration."

The Knights followed their chieftain. Armed with the assur-ance that the order supported him, Powderly then drafted a new and lengthy appeal to Macdonald.

[27] Knights of Labor, *Record of the Proceedings of the 4th Regular Session of the Knights of Labor, 1880,* pp. 175-78. Cited hereafter as KL, *Proceedings.*
[28] *Ibid.*

In several American journals lately I noticed accounts of your efforts in behalf of suffering humanity and as President of the Miners' National Union I now address you.

He began his request for affiliation by raising a practical problem of concern to each of them. "During the past year," he wrote, " a great number of miners left England and Wales for this country, a number of them came to Hyde Park in this city [Scranton, Pennsylvania]; the wages were not what they expected, labor not a plenty [sic] and a number of them went westward after a fruitless endeavor to obtain employment." Deplorable as this situation was, Powderly suggested that there was a remedy for it:

If the Miners' National Union and a National Organization of this country were to strike hands and establish a means of communicating intelligence it would be an excellent thing, *but they could go further,* they could [join] in our Grand Order through which the toiling millions of the earth could control their own destinies. You are the President of the Miners' National Union of Great Britain. I am the chief officer of the 'Knights of Labor.' Both organizations aim at one thing, the latter has a large membership of miners [and] it takes in all men who toil. We aim at Arbitration, Co-operation and everything (honorable) for the bettering of the conditions of the working man. We have a membership of three hundred thousand and [are] daily growing larger.

He finished his letter with high hopes that Macdonald might favor his idea for:

uniting the two organizations . . . or getting some means of understanding . . . so that men will not go on a wild goose chase every time a venal press starts the rumor work is plenty and wages high. . . . You are an Englishman [a Scot actually], I am an American yet with the true feeling of our kind we should feel as much interest in the one as in the other.[29]

Powderly's projected alliance was the legitimate offspring of idealism and of pressure created by immigration; he was anxious in 1880 to strengthen his organization and to alleviate some of its problems. But for reasons that are not clear, he and Macdonald suspended negotiations for several more years—critical years.

[29] KL, *Proceedings,* pp. 179-80; also pp. 73-75.

In January 1885, as the Knights grew with incredible swiftness to become the largest labor organization in the world, Powderly resumed his bid for alliance. This time he contacted Macdonald's successor, Thomas Burt, in Newcastle-on-Tyne, explaining again the value of a union with the Americans. Communications with Burt were carried on both through letters and the good offices of the Knights' English organizer, Albert Denny. In content the messages paralleled those that had been sent earlier to Macdonald—" Cannot your organization and ours," Powderly wrote, " become allied? " [30] On the scene in England with all the advantages that entailed, Denny suggested to his leader that the desired union faced serious obstacles, but Powderly urged him to push on, insisting the British ought to co-operate formally with his booming order. Meanwhile, working on the assumption that all would turn out for the best, he ordered the Knights' General Secretary to forward " such printed matter as you think will be of service to us in forming a connecting link between the Miners' organization of Great Britain and the Knights of Labor to Thomas Burt, M.P." [31]

Although the Knights enjoyed success in England and Ireland and were to derive important benefits from British co-operative and trade union experience, nothing substantial came of this final attempt at union. As in previous cases cited correspondence ceases abruptly and we are left to speculate about the reasons. Obviously unions on both sides of the Atlantic, boundlessly enthusiastic, overestimated their strength and resources. In the case of the Knights, there were special difficulties; the order expanded so swiftly between 1885 and 1887 that all of its energies were dedicated to the task of assimilating and consolidating domestic gains, and little attention could be spared proposals for international action. After 1888 the order burst like an oversized balloon and a rapid decline in membership made it increasingly unlikely that it could save itself, let alone the workers of the world.

What the Knights attempted proved untimely, yet failure

[30] Letter of Terence Powderly to Thomas Burt, January 13, 1885, in Terence Powderly Papers (Catholic University Library, Washington, D. C.). Cited hereafter as Powderly Papers.
[31] Powderly to Frederick Turner, January 13, 1885, Powderly Papers.

was not a true measure of its significance. Other workers ripe for international projects caught the possibilities inherent in transatlantic union and ignored the failures of the recent past. Foremost in the new efforts were men who turned more instinctively than most to international co-operation—dockers, or longshoremen as they are called in the United States, and seamen.

One of the first prominent figures to revive hopes of an Anglo-American labor alliance in the late eighties and early nineties was the Irish Republican hero and former Lancashire mill operative, Michael Davitt. In 1890 he began to take soundings. That year the influential *North American Review* published an article that he had written in which he explained to Americans that: "The economic relations between the two great English-speaking parts of the industrial world render it necessary that thinking men and politicians on both sides of the Atlantic should comprehend the full meaning of the [labor] movements peculiar to each country." [32]

Only thinly veiled, Davitt's thoughts of alliance represented lessons culled from his own experiences rather than wishful thinking. An Irishman, and a Fenian, he naturally recognized the efficacy of closer relations with America. During 1878, in fact, he lived in the Republic and became a follower of the great Henry George. Just as important, he was also associated with the Knights of Labor and apparently never lost interest in the trans-atlantic experiments in labor co-operation that Powderly proposed during the eighties. Davitt and Powderly, indeed, knew each other personally. Writing of events that had transpired in 1886 or 1887, Powderly described their contact: "One day when Michael Davitt was in Scranton, I, by the power invested in me as Grand Master Workman . . . initiated him into the Knights of Labor. I gave him a letter 'to the Order wherever found,' to recognize him as a member. I do not know what local assembly Davitt affiliated with, but that he did great service in organizing throughout Great Britain, I have ample evidence." [33] Thereafter the Pennsylvania

---

[32] Michael Davitt, "Labor Tendencies in Great Britain," *North American Review,* CLI (July-Dec., 1890), 453.
[33] Terence Powderly, *The Path I Trod: Autobiography of Terence Powderly,*

Irishman kept tabs on the activities of the Mayo-born Davitt. "On Tuesday evening May 8, 1888 District Assembly No. 208 of the Knights of Labor of England held their first public meeting in Smethwick . . . the past District Master Workman and orator of the occasion was Michael Davitt."[34] Continuing his reminiscences Powderly then told of the speech Davitt delivered that spring evening. "The Knights of Labor," said Davitt,

is not an American society, or an Irish society or an English society. It is a society of all these and more. It tells us that an injury to one man is the concern of all men. By its aid here in England we are enabled to meet on common ground for the first time and to each of us is given the great privilege of taking a member by the hand and calling him brother regardless of his country, creed, or condition of life.[35]

There is no doubt of Davitt's closeness to Powderly's cause; even in the late eighties both the American leader and the English press detected in this speech "the dawn of a new era among the industrial people of the British Isles."[36]

Events soon appeared to lend substance to Davitt's reading of the trends. Just before he penned an article for the *North American Review*, he watched Tom Mann's National Union of Dock Labourers[37] emerge victorious from the great London dock strike and spread, along with rival unions, to a position of importance in the major British ports. Like the union leaders, Davitt too was sensible of the additional strength labor could wield if it could paralyze ports on both sides of the Atlantic. When British shipmasters threatened to import American workers to serve as blacklegs, in fact, dockside leaders retaliated by hinting that they might ask New York longshoremen to boycott vessels of the transatlantic lines. Could it actually be done?

Davitt confessed to some reservations: "How far international co-operational of this kind may be resorted to or be made possible by the growing feeling of international brother-

---

eds. Harry J. Carman and Henry David (New York: Columbia University Press, 1940), p. 182.

[34] *Ibid.*, p. 183.

[35] *Ibid.*

[36] Carman and David, p. 183.

[37] Davitt, *North American Review*, CLI, 464.

hood among the workers of the world, is perhaps too much for mere speculation." But the reservations were not really serious according to his interpretation of the trends:

If we are to judge the growth of responsive friendly feelings among American workingmen towards the working classes of England by the establishment in Great Britain and Ireland of branches of a great American labor organization, the possibility I speak of may be, and probably is, near. Assemblies of the Knights of Labor are increasing day by day in these islands which means presumably that the working-men enrolled in such branches can be more or less influenced in their strike policies by the orders of the General Master Workman Powderly. We can only picture, on the other hand, the National Union of Dock Labourers of Great Britain forming its branches in New York and other ports on the Atlantic seaboard to recognize the conditions which would enable the leaders of the dockers on this side of the Atlantic to give effect to their policy even in the United States.[38]

During the subsequent decade Davitt's prescient speculations came to life along the waterfronts of England and America. After 1894 strenuous and imaginative efforts were made to ally British and American seafarers and the many men engaged in related maritime jobs in one cohesive international organization. Initiative stemmed largely from British dockside leaders, foremost among them Tom Mann and J. Havelock Wilson.

As much as any single individual Mann was responsible for centering attention on the unorganized potential of America's 70,000 dock workers. Already a noted figure in British labor circles by 1890, Mann was nearing the pinnacle of his career at the time he sought to enlist the co-operation of American workingmen. Just a year earlier he had thrown his weight behind the beleaguered dockers and their leader, the former street Arab and tea cooper, Ben Tillett.[39] After victory, Mann helped shape up the National Union of Dock Labourers, embarked on a course that won him the first secretaryship of the Independent Labour Party, flirted with revolutionary agitation in England and Australia, and left behind the quiet years of his association with the conservative Amalgamated Society

[38] Davitt, *North American Review,* CLI, 464.
[39] Tom Mann, *Tom Mann's Memoirs* (London: Labour Publishing Co., 1923) for a view of the Dock Strike.

of Engineers. He was not entirely unfamiliar with America; during 1883 he had worked here, and, like Davitt, had become a follower of Henry George. Upon his return to England he remained abreast of developments across the Atlantic; in the nineties he struck up correspondence with Sam Gompers, leader of the American Federation of Labor, and occasionally contributed to the *American Federationist*.[40]

J. Havelock Wilson, M.P., " the seamens' advocate in Parliament," and a man about whom we shall say more later, was an accomplished and respected leader in the nineties. He was somewhat more widely known among American workers than Mann, and his knowledge of American conditions was certainly more extensive.

Neither Mann nor Wilson created the forces that encouraged unionization among dockers and seamen in the United States. Such forces sprang from the gross malpractices of masters and shipowners, malpractices that made American waterfront life among the foulest in the world. But both men availed themselves of their opportunities. Fortunately too, they received positive assistance from officers of the International Seamen's Union, the Coast Seamen, and the American Federation of Labor. The fact that none of the American waterfront unions was very old likewise proved helpful. After 1891 only the International Seamen's Union, an amalgamation of three smaller unions (the most important of which was the Atlantic Coast Seamen's Union), could boast of effective organization,[41] and this union was eager to expand.

Anglo-American co-operation started on a limited scale during the summer of 1894. John R. Bell, a member of the Seamen's Union, travelled to England in July to look over the operations of the Labour Electoral Association and the new Independent Labour Party,[42] both of which excited interest in America. Bell soon commenced working with J. Havelock Wilson and the two went on an organizing tour among British

[40] Letters of Samuel Gompers to Tom Mann, Sept. 2, 1891; Apr. 30, 1894 in the Samuel Gompers Collection (American Federation of Labor Headquarters, Washington, D. C.). Cited hereafter as Gompers Coll.

[41] *Report of the Industrial Commission, Labor Organizations, . . . Railway Labor*, 1901. XVII, 255-57.

[42] *American Federationist*, Sept., 1894.

seafarers.[43] By September Bell was able to inform the members of his own union and the leadership of the American Federation of Labor "that my tour in company with J. H. Wilson, M.P., for the purpose of reorganizing the National Association of Sailors' and Firemens' Union has been a thorough success." What had been a "wretched picture until just before dawn" had been transformed into bright daylight, except that he and Wilson were "war weary" from their exertions.[44] Was Bell instructing or being instructed in organizing techniques? We can only guess; at any rate, he must have rendered an exciting report when he returned home that winter.

Satisfied that collaborative efforts were full of potential, the British, about a year and a half after Bell's trip, made the first bid for an alliance between English and American seamen and dockers. The first requests reached officials of the International Seamen's Union late in the summer of 1896.[45] They had been dispatched by the Dockers' Union. For several weeks the propositions, about which little is known in detail thanks to the secrecy of I.S.U. leaders, were examined and debated. Then, early in October, the I.S.U. Executive Board formally voted on the question of whether or not to enter an "international federation of maritime workers."[46] The Board reported its members heartily in favor of "world wide federation" and the creation of a "brotherhood of the sea"—in principle. In practice, it expressed reservations about the proposals. Reluctantly the I.S.U.'s Secretary, T. J. Elderkin, speaking on behalf of the Executive Board, confessed that international co-operation was not at that moment entirely feasible, mainly because, as he put it, the "first need [of American maritime workers] is federation among ourselves."[47] Nevertheless the Board, through Elderkin, remained in touch with J. H. Wilson and nothing further was done to discourage British hopes or to stop British organizers from taking up their work among American maritime laborers. The proposals,

[43] *Ibid.*, Nov., 1894.
[44] *American Federationist*, Nov., 1894.
[45] *The Coast Seamen's Journal*, Oct. 14, 1896. Hereafter cited as *CSJ*.
[46] *Ibid.*, Oct. 7, 1896.
[47] *Ibid.*

therefore, were still much alive because several trade union missionaries immediately set out for America.

Perhaps the most effective organizer who came to proselytize waterfront workers in order to create an international alliance was Edward McHugh. McHugh represented the International Federation of Ship, Dock, and Riverside Workers. Aided by a $1500 fund subscribed by the Union, he started his work in America at least as early as September 28, 1896. Even before officials of the Seamen's Union announced their decision, this indefatigable man was holding mass meetings along the New York waterfront.[48] With his associates, Bolton Hall and James R. Brown, both prominent disciples of Henry George, and with Havelock Wilson as well, he soon established and directed the American Longshoremen's Union.[49] McHugh was fitted for his tasks. Tough, intelligent, capable of fending for himself, he instantly became a success among the waterfront workers. He knew his men and once he commanded their attention his flair for the dramatic, coupled with his thoroughgoing integrity —a virtue sadly lacking in many American waterfront leaders, past and present—held them to his cause. During the autumn of 1896, he made considerable progress among longshoremen, mainly in the Greater New York area.[50] Elderkin of the I.S.U., far from manifesting any hostility towards the Englishman— although cries of dual unionism might have been raised— inserted weekly reports of his activities in the *Coast Seamen's Journal*, publicly wished him well, and expressed the hope that Britons and Americans might continue to work in harness together.[51]

Americans were quick to respond to these British organizing efforts. Emboldened by the new rumblings along the waterfronts, the fresh stirrings of unionization, the Seamen's Union served notice on shippers that if a world-wide dock strike materialized, as it threatened to do in December 1896, employers might well discover them standing shoulder to shoulder

[48] *CSJ,* Oct. 21, 1896.
[49] Charles Barnes, *The Longshoremen* (New York: Sage Foundation, 1912), p. 112.
[50] *CSJ,* Oct. 28, and Nov. 11, 1896.
[51] *CSJ,* Oct. 28, and Nov. 11, 1896; also Dec. 9, 1896.

with European and English seafarers. "The suggestion that American workingmen have nothing in common with those of other countries," declared a union spokesman, "coming from the representatives of world-wide capitalism is an insult to the former's intelligence which they will be prompt to resent whenever the occasion arises." And, the spokesman added, American workers knew perfectly well that class interests were not restricted by geographical boundaries.[52]

In this hospitable climate of opinion, McHugh was able over the course of the next few years to build the Longshoremen's Union into a formidable power. In port after port on the Atlantic seaboard he battled for better working conditions, struck at the evils of the hiring system, and denounced such practices as paying men their wages in saloons where they were more easily victimized by vicious elements. Soon he forged a chain of organizations in the major eastern ports and at the peak of his union's strength he boasted of a membership of between 13,000 and 15,000 men,[53] the bulk of them being concentrated in the New York-Brooklyn area.

Unfortunately, though early success augured well for the McHugh organization, it began falling apart in July 1898, after just over two years of operation. Failure appears to have been primarily the result of financial blunders that wiped out the union's cash reserve. Membership declined and when an attempt to reorganize under a new name also collapsed, McHugh, disillusioned, returned to England. His achievements, however, were long remembered on the waterfronts and many old-timers who were enlisted in the American Longshoremen's Union continued over the years to hope for its revival.

But we have briefly outrun our story. For, as the McHugh union was expanding, the American seamen who had given so much encouragement to the attempts to unionize the longshoremen, turned to more ambitious activities themselves. Their efforts were spearheaded by one of McHugh's associates, J. Havelock Wilson, whose purpose it was to incorporate the seafarers in a great international federation.

[52] *Ibid.,* Dec. 16, 1896.
[53] Barnes, p. 111.

Wilson was eminently well qualified for his mission. When he came to the United States in 1897 as the representative of the British Seamen's Union, he was in his mid-thirties, full of fight and vigor, and well armed with a long record of labor experience. When he was three his father died, leaving the mother and twelve children completely on their own in Sunderland. As soon as he was able he sold newspapers, served briefly as a lithographer's apprentice, and at the ripe age of twelve ran off to sea. A husky lad, he rose rapidly to become an able-bodied seaman, endured shipwreck in the South Seas, and finally after a decade of roaming the world, landed in San Francisco.[54] Turning from seafaring for a while, he moved to the Atlantic coast, and settled there for several years. Ashore he generously sampled a variety of occupations. American friends later described him as having been a Baltimore " dock-walloper," a Boston " cattle puncher," a New York skyscraper scaffold-rigger, and a high girder man on the Brooklyn bridge.[55] Moreover, we are told that he was a bulldog by nature, a giant in build and a Hercules in strength.

In any event, Wilson so fattened his purse in America that he returned to England, purchased a Temperance Hotel, married and became a man of affairs. In addition, he paid up his back dues in the Sunderland Seamen's Union and embarked in earnest upon an audacious union career. His agitational work cost him heavily; he lost property and earned a jail sentence. Yet his contributions to the National Seamen's Union won him the title of " Jack's friend" and in maritime circles a reputation that stretched around the English-speaking world.[56] Eventually labor's rise to power in Britain carried him, after two unsuccessful tries, into Parliament in 1906, where he continued to serve as the " seamen's advocate." [57] Years later when he retired from national politics he regained a position of influence in the National Union of Sailors and Firemen, and his decisions brought him under heavy fire from other labor

---

[54] International Seamen's Union of America, 11th Annual Convention, Boston, December 3-12, 1906, *Proceedings,* p. 47. Cited hereafter as ISU, *Proceedings.*
[55] ISU, *Proceedings, 1906,* p. 90.
[56] *Ibid.,* p. 47.
[57] *Ibid.,* pp. 47, 90.

leaders.[58] Nevertheless, until the end of the First World War he was a personality to be reckoned with.

Wilson's first mass meetings were held in Philadelphia shortly after Christmas 1897.[59] Before the year was out he travelled to Boston where he recruited the talents of the Scandinavian-born champion of American sailors, Andrew Furuseth, a man whose persistence had much to do with the passage of the LaFollette's Seamen's Act in Woodrow Wilson's first administration. Havelock Wilson and Furuseth addressed seven well packed gatherings of seafarers; together they functioned splendidly as an organizing team. In mid-January the pair temporarily split so that Wilson could move among the mass of unorganized men in the Port of New York,[60] where McHugh had already performed so handsomely. Though there are no detailed records of Wilson's plans, his salient objectives were clear. He sought to establish several agencies in New York and branches in the chief American ports to minister to the problems of British seamen, who often outnumbered Americans in these East coast ports.[61] Identical agencies were planned for the main British ports so that American seamen might protect their rights while abroad. All of these agencies were supposed to operate on an internationally subscribed fund solicited, not only from the British Seamen's Union who sponsored Wilson, but also from English, American and Australasian seafarers as well.[62]

Once involved in his task, Wilson was rejoined by Furuseth and additional assistance came from the Coast Seamen's Union in the shape of a large sum of money raised among its members and placed at the disposal of these two organizers.[63] Throughout January and February 1898, during the crisis in America's relations with Spain, they worked feverishly in New York, directing meetings, speaking to reform groups, belaboring such nefarious practices as "crimping," and lashing out at the maltreatment accorded British and American sailors aboard the ships of their respective and each other's nations.[64] Timely

[58] Webb, pp. 665-66, 669-70.
[59] *CSJ*, Jan. 5, 1898.
[60] *CSJ*, Jan. 12, 1898.
[61] *Ibid.*; also see Dec. 9, 1897.
[62] *Ibid.*, Dec. 15, 1897.
[63] *Ibid.*, Jan. 12, 1898.
[64] *Ibid.*, Feb. 2, 1898.

moral support was lent them by Tom Mann who was then in Australia keeping up a drumfire for unionism. Mann not only hammered away at the Australians but also exhorted the American Pacific Coast Seamen's, Firemen's and Longshoremen's Unions to enter into the burgeoning international federation.[65]

Auspiciously begun, the experiment in transatlantic co-operation and alliance soon hit serious snags. The work shouldered by McHugh, Wilson, Furuseth, Mann, and others, succumbed to the same general malaise that afflicted some of the earlier efforts at alliance. Traditional quarrels among American seamen's various trades certainly did not help matters; [66] lack of sustained financial power, petty jealousies, opposition by capital, and changes in the overall economic situation, each contributed to the erection of barriers that were, for the time, insuperable. Nonetheless, British and American seamen and waterfront workers did enter loose working agreements with one another, and the hope of closer unity in the future was not dead. Havelock Wilson, last of the British organizers to leave the waterfronts, remained in the United States long enough to attend the Nashville Convention of the American Federation of Labor as an honored representative of the British Trades Union Congress, but his return to England in March 1898 signalled the close of the planned federation.

Throughout these activities among the maritime workers, the position of Samuel Gompers, leader of the American Federation of Labor, is worth noting. Over the waterfront loomed the shadow of the redoubtable cigarmaker who helped found and then spent a lifetime leading the most powerful and enduring American labor organization. Gompers has often been charged with narrow and unduly conservative leadership. Whatever the merit of these criticisms they do not bear up well insofar as the Gompers of the nineties is concerned. His actions and words in the case of the British on the American waterfront indicate a rather broad and tolerant outlook.

It is well to remember that Gompers was thoroughly familiar

[65] *CSJ*, Jan. 19, 1898. Tom Mann's comments were reported in *CSJ*, Apr. 21, 1897.
[66] *Ibid.*, Nov. 25, 1896.

with the British labor world; his knowledge of the personalities and forces at work there was probably not surpassed by any other American union leader. To be sure, he did not always concur on the wisdom of British policies, nor did he subscribe to the ideas of some British leaders. Nevertheless, he had high regard for the methods, dedication, and élan manifested across the sea. He was not frightened by socialism in Britain; that socialism there was a gradualist variety he understood perfectly well. Hence his relationships with many of the prominent figures in British labor, socialist and non-socialist alike, remained friendly and he was able to conduct correspondence over a period of years with Tom Mann, Ben Tillett, John Burns, Henry Broadhurst, Thomas Burt, and J. Keir Hardie.

Because of Gompers' importance in American labor, the British began exploring his position on their organizing plans in America in July 1894. Ben Tillett outlined to him what the British were seeking to do and Gompers, in a reply that began "Dear Comrade," told Tillett that his plans had been placed before the seamen and longshoremen concerned. "Of course, I cannot say whether tangible results will come from this correspondence," Gompers added, "but a better spirit should be established between kindred trade unions on both sides." [67] For over a year no further progress was made and during part of that time Gompers himself was out of office, the only year during his career in the A.F.L. that he did not hold the Presidency. But when he regained power in 1896, he renewed his letters to Tillett, filling him in on the content of earlier missives that had passed between himself and Tom Mann "relative to the contemplated movement of the Seamen and Waterside Workers of Great Britain." [68] The American unions, Tillett was informed, were in the process of determining "how far they can co-operate with your movement." Gompers was candid enough to suggest, however, that at that moment events did not augur well for the British proposals; lax conditions of organization among seamen and longshoremen in the United

---

[67] Gompers to Ben Tillett, July 20, 1894; May 25, 1894, Gompers Coll. Incoming British letters were unfortunately destroyed years ago by A. F. of L. clerks who felt they cluttered up the filing cabinets.

[68] Gompers to Tillett, August 20, 1896, Gompers Coll.

States, the hue and cry of the Bryan free silver campaign, among other things, were making the future of transatlantic operations uncertain. Though the picture was bleak, Gompers still gave what encouragement he could. " I do wish . . . your movement may be crowned with success and I shall be pleased to have you give me any further information . . . that it may be made use of here to your advantage." [69]

Then, late in August 1896, Tillett wrote Gompers that operations were about to start and the American's rejoinder left no doubt of his anxious pleasure. " The conditions of the Waterside men, the Longshoremen, and Seamen is almost beyond endurance and they are justified in taking any reasonable action . . . calculated to bring them . . . better consideration for their labor. There is a greater interest manifested now in this international movement," Gompers hastened to add, " than when you first wrote me." To expedite matters Tillett was told to communicate directly with American waterfront leaders, while Gompers announced that he stood ready to aid the British in any way he could if requested to do so: " I beg to assure you, it will give me pleasure, yes afford me delight to perform it." [70] Moreover, he personally kept in touch with the seamen and longshoremen and announced that they had gone to work with a will.

As explained earlier, organization began on the Atlantic coast late in the summer of 1896; McHugh was busy in September and by November Gompers was telling Tillett of the Englishman's progress. Gompers seems to have expected McHugh to contact him personally but as he remarked to Tillett, " More than likely his work is of such a nature that privacy or secrecy may be necessary." [71] Although Gompers felt obliged to express his regrets for not having been of more use to the English up to this point, he made it clear that he had not been entirely idle. At a council meeting of the A.F.L., he told Tillett, he had broached the subject of an international alliance to the assembled leaders of the Federation and " a resolution was adopted authorizing us to co-operate with the

[69] Gompers to Tillett, August 20, 1896, Gompers Coll.
[70] Gompers to Tillett, August 29, 1896, Gompers Coll.
[71] Gompers to Tillett, November 4, 1896, Gompers Coll.

Seamen's organization in attaining the desired ends of both national organizations."[72] Moreover, a month later Gompers reported to Tom Mann that McHugh was "doing some effective work" unionizing men in the New York area.[73]

But the tide soon turned in the fortunes of the British and the ambitious plans of '96 were left high and dry. Gompers' relations with his transatlantic correspondents remained cordial; no evidence of strain or mistrust appears in the record. The proposals for international federation simply disappear from prominence. The last whisper of them came in 1900 when the A.F.L. leader wrote Tillett, "I should gladly render whatever assistance I could within my power but it is out of the question for the moment."[74]

All the evidence would suggest, though the point cannot be entirely proved, that Gompers did what he could to aid the international movement. He was a professed advocate of international co-operation throughout his life. Even if this is disallowed, however, it is clear that he was not hostile towards the British project; indeed, he praised and encouraged it. By leaving McHugh, Wilson, and the leaders of the American unions a free hand to determine their own course of action he was following the traditional role of the leader of an organization of autonomous unions, for while it is true that Gompers wielded more power than any figure in the British Trades Union Congress, for instance, and while it is true the A.F.L. was more highly centralized than the B.T.U.C., he was still not an autocrat. Local matters fell within the ambit of local unions; craft matters were the business of craft unions; even had Gompers wished to interfere in many decisions he lacked the power to do so. Moreover, although Gompers was extremely sensitive to problems of dual unionism which might have grown out of the organizational efforts on the waterfront, he made no mention of such fears in this connection.[75] Finally,

---

[72] Gompers to Tillett, November 4, 1896, Gompers Coll.

[73] Gompers to Mann, December 4, 1896, Gompers Coll.

[74] Gompers to Tillett, June 28, 1900, Gompers Coll.

[75] Later Gompers did clash with George Barnes of the Amalgamated Society of Engineers over this issue. See, e. g., Samuel Gompers, *Seventy Years of Life and Labor* (2 vols.; New York: E. P. Dutton, 1925), Vol. II, pp. 49-55.

if Gompers lent what aid he could to the drive for an international federation, it should be emphasized that such aid was, through no fault of his own, limited. If the bickerings and internecine warfare of seamen, longshoremen, and other maritime workers weakened their cohesiveness, there was not much he could do to remedy the situation immediately, and if national and international conditions militated against alliance there was still less that he could do.

Despite the abortive alliance, nevertheless, an important longshoremen's union was formed and operated for more than two years, thanks to Anglo-American co-operation; new precedents were set, and considerable headway was made in arousing maritime labor to the virtues of unionism. By the thousands waterfront workers were left more self-conscious not only about their problems but also about possible methods for resolving them. Finally, waterfront abuses were exposed by these joint teams of agitators whose general educational campaign made their alleviation a matter of more pressing concern.

Breakdown of the waterfront experiments marked the end of the more sweeping plans for alliance between British and American trade unions. There were, to be sure, occasional reverberations of the federation theme, but their character was quite different and they were lacking in force. When, for example, Daniel O'Keefe founded his Transport Workers' Union and boasted of its alliance in 1905 with the International Transport Workers' Federation, composed of "nearly all the dock workers of Great Britain, Continental Europe, and Australia was well as those in America," it was patently clear that his tenuous association with the British hinged not on any genuine international outlook but on his desire to stave off the attacks of other American unions opposed to him.[76] Similarly, Havelock Wilson, embarrassed by financial and legal difficulties in 1906, formally asked the International Seamen's Union of America to aid him and his National Sailors' and Firemen's Union. Claiming that the internationalization of capital called for the internationalization of labor action, he also asked two other American unions for money.[77] Each American

---

[76] ISU, *Proceedings, 1905*, pp. 20-21. Commons, *History of Labour*, IV, 357.
[77] ISU, *Proceedings, 1906*, pp. 44-46.

organization, recalling the Englishman's reputation, honored his requests but this form of co-operation did nothing to resurrect proposals for international alliance. All they did was remind men on both sides of the sea that closer ties had once been more than a vain hope.

### III. FRATERNITY

Fraternal relationships less boldly conceived than the international experiments still continued between British and American working people. One important American union, indeed, owed its existence to the timely aid it received from a body of internationally-minded English unionists. In 1899 the American Boot and Shoe Workers' Union was being bled white by the financial drain of strikes and administrative costs; fortunately, however, it was able to enlist the support of Tom Tracy who was about to leave for England as the American representative to the British Trades Union Congress of 1899.[78] Once abroad, Tracy laid the shoe workers' pleas before the leadership of the National Union of Boot and Shoe Operatives of Great Britain, whose prompt response in the shape of a thousand dollar loan unquestionably saved the American organization from total failure. The generous Britons were thanked formally and warmly " for the assistance they rendered this union. Such a fraternal act," declared the Americans, " should live in the memory of every member of this union, and should serve as a constant reminder that their generosity was made possible by their substantial treasury, built up under the ' High Dues and Benefits System ' and should spur us on to build our own union on similar lines." [79] Identical situations occurred in other crafts from time to time. The London compositors, for example, offered to lend their beleaguered counterparts in the New York Typographical Union (No. 6) the equivalent of $10,000 to see them through their contest with the owners of the New York *Sun*.[80] Especially in times of crisis did workers on either side of the Atlantic revive the spirit of international brotherhood.

[78] *The Shoemakers' Journal*, Dec., 1916, p. 10.
[79] *The Union Boot and Shoe Workers' Journal*, Jan., 1900.
[80] *Ibid*., June, 1900.

The American Federation of Labor established the most important and enduring fraternal ties with British labor. That it should do so was altogether natural, for its leaders greatly admired the British trade union movement and its accomplishments, and the A.F.L. and its earlier prototype, the Federation of Trades and Labor Unions, were consciously modelled after the British Trades Union Congress. It would be tedious to recite the fraternal relations between the A.F.L. and the B.T.U.C. in detail. Very briefly, however, we might recall that as early as 1881 proposals were made for the exchange of delegates at the annual conventions, and that by 1894, after a delay everyone concerned regretted, the exchange took place.[81] It would be easy to exaggerate the significance of these delegates and their visits, but as Florence Thorne, former research director of the A.F.L. observed,[82] the reverse has generally been the case and their significance has been too grossly underestimated. The journeys made by Samuel Gompers, Adolph Strasser, and top officers of the Federation's unions to Great Britain, and the return visits of many of Britain's more prominent labor leaders to the United States encouraged stimulating and continuing interchanges of opinions and ideas. Leaders from either side were placed in more amiable intercourse with one another and the processes of reciprocal observation and education were unquestionably facilitated. Moreover, this association was not without practical benefit from the American viewpoint for it enabled Gompers to import the organizing, lecturing, or writing talents of John Burns, Tom Mann, David Holmes, Ben Tillett, and J. Keir Hardie.[83] Indeed, during the nineties, as Gompers fought American socialists tooth and nail, he managed to co-operate successfully with many British socialists. To the American reformer, Henry Demarest Lloyd, for instance, Gompers wrote that he realized Burns, Mann, Tillett, and Hardie differed from Shipton, Burt, Broadhurst, and other conservative leaders, but ideological distinctions were

---

[81] American Federation of Labor, International Trade Union Congress, Turner Hall, Pittsburgh, November 15, 1881, *Proceedings,* p. 15.

[82] Interview with Miss Florence Thorne, Research Director of the A. F. of L., March, 1951.

[83] Mr. Gompers' letters to these men are located in volumes 15 through 50 of his letterbooks in the Gompers Coll.

unimportant for these men were all " serious workers." [84] And both socialists and non-socialists, as the A.F.L. leader freely admitted, gave real help to the American labor movement.

Vestiges of internationalist sentiment lingered long after British influences in American labor dwindled to insignificance. Especially among conservative unionists the desire for well-knit official relations continued for a generation after the turn of the century. The unpublished correspondence of John Frey, one of Gompers' chief lieutenants, a leader of the molders and a labor scholar, illuminates this point. From 1908 until the thirties Frey remained in close personal correspondence with William Appleton of the General Federation of Trades Unions in England. Their letters indicate that despite growing differences between segments of the two labor movements, many basic motivations for alliance or federation existed during the first thirty years of this century. Both men realized that increasing economic interdependence made closer co-operation desirable.[85] After the emergence of Bolshevism and an international communist movement both came to feel that " the united trade union movement . . . could erect the most powerful barrier against radicalism"; likewise, both believed that " a forward Trade Union policy and the American Federation of Labor " offered the means of uniting, " as nothing else can unite, all the Anglo-speaking peoples." [86]

In 1844 the remarkable Robert Owen speculated that " the Empires of Great Britain and America are, compared with other nations, in an advanced position, to commence gradually, and without any disorder to the interests of society, the greatest change that has yet occurred for the permanent benefit of the human race. . . . It is uncertain whether the United States or Great Britain will first commence this change, or whether the population of both Empires will agree to begin and progress

[84] Gompers to Henry Demarest Lloyd, July 2, 1894, Gompers Coll.

[85] Letter of William Appleton to John Frey, December 3, 1918, in Frey-Appleton Correspondence (Mr. Frey's personal files in the A. F. of L. Headquarters, Washington, D. C.). Also see Appleton to Frey, June 23, July 24, Dec. 6, 1918; June 4, Dec. 3, 1919; Frey to Appleton, June 30, 1918; Jan. 26, Sept. 13, 1920, Frey-Appleton Correspondence.

[86] Frey to Appleton, Jan. 26, 1920; Appleton to Frey, July 23, 1918, Frey-Appleton Correspondence.

together." [87] Unfortunately whatever alliance Owen might have envisaged springing up to bridge the Atlantic failed to materialize; those that were tried all aborted. Efforts by miners, seamen, dockers, boilermakers, iron founders, cigarmakers, the National Labor Union, the Knights of Labor, and the American Federation of Labor proved ill-timed, ill-considered, and ill-starred. Yet in the broadest of historical perspectives their failure was somewhat superficial; behind them lay real if unseen achievement—the evolution of a new awareness among American workers, awareness that labor problems stemming from the industrial revolution were in some respects international labor problems, awareness of the enormous value of the exchange of ideas, opinions, statistical and technical information, leaders, and propaganda, awareness of the variety of assistance workers an ocean apart could render one another, and awareness of the fund of experience accumulated abroad upon which American labor could draw in the attacks against its great problems. Beyond this, as we suggested earlier, these experiments provided a general framework within which British and Irish organizers who had taken up their tasks in the Republic helped pave the way for the rise of the modern labor movement.

[87] Commons, *Documentary History*, VII, 152.

# PART THREE

# COBBETTS AND HUNTS

---

## I. THE ORGANIZERS

In the past the labor agitator has proven an unsettling influence in the United States. Arousing the conservative instincts of the community, his tactics, objectives, and personal characteristics have earned him an abundant measure of opprobrium. By the eighteen thirties in America just as in the old country, epithets such as " spy," " Hunt," " Cobbett," and " apostle of sedition," [1] were accurate reflections of his unpopularity. Anti-labor journalists developed a stock set of labels for him: " The worst element was out last night to hear a kid-gloved, oily tongued, sleek faced demagogue hold forth in an incendiary, blood-curdling speech on the rights of horny-handed workingmen." And employers, too, knew him for what he was:

Communist, socialist, molly maguire, incendiary, blood and thunder spouter, hungry looking loafer, a sinister faced wretch whose company could be dispensed with in this community, a fellow whose appearance suggested a recent visit to the penitentiary; a fellow who violently gesticulated and frothed at the mouth for half an hour without saying anything; and a blatherskite, who had the audacity to stand before a body of workingmen to tell them of his wrongs, while he himself was dressed in a suit of broadcloth. Such creatures should be treated as they deserve by the honest toilers, and sent out of town in a suit of tar and feathers.[2]

Despite the low repute they enjoyed, these men were vital agents of industrial democracy. If they were pariahs, they were also organizers, administrators, and negotiators. They sometimes worked underground, but more often they lived in

---

[1] Seth Luther, *An Address to the Working-Men of New England* (Boston: Published by the author, 1832), Introduction.

[2] Terence Powderly, *Thirty Years of Labor* (Columbus: Excelsior Press, 1890), pp. 72-73.

full public view. They reminded workers of deep, unresolved problems, called attention to the possibilities of modifying adolescent capitalism, and despite their general inadequacies of intellect or background, they rendered the sacrifices essential to the progress of organized labor. To the general public,[3] in fact, they were Labor.

Many of the most capable organizers came to the United States from the British Isles. "There were many Englishmen who took a prominent part in the American labor movement,"[4] wrote Samuel Gompers in the nineteen twenties, and he might justly have added that there were many Scotsmen, Welshmen, and Irishmen as well. "Certain it is," declared another student of labor in 1888, "that the main impulse towards the formation of labor organizations among us has been of foreign derivation, and that alien elements have contributed by far the greater part of their membership."[5] The reference specifically applied to men from the United Kingdom and to a less extent to the Germans. A number of vigorous immigrants, to be sure, had left their mark on labor before the Civil War, as we have seen. After the conflict, however, there were more of them, they were better trained, and they possessed ampler opportunities to express their corporate spirit, and organizational genius. They no longer merely colored labor activity; they wielded upon it an influence all out of proportion to their numbers.[6]

Between 1860 and 1914 they occupied positions within the labor movement from which they directed or largely determined the conditions and policies, if not the destinies, of hundreds of thousands of men and women in trade unions, trades assemblies, and labor-reform organizations. Their greatest impact, as we shall see, was upon the more ephemeral orders of the nineteenth century rather than on the more permanent

[3] *Final Report of the Industrial Commission,* 1902, XIX, 87-73.
[4] Gompers, II, 49.
[5] Francis Walker, "The Knights of Labor," *Princeton Review,* VI (1888), 200.
[6] This chapter is based on the writer's study of the careers and activities of nearly 300 immigrant labor organizers and labor leaders who came to this country from the United Kingdom. On some of these figures there are only scattered bits of information; in other cases there are hundreds or, as in several instances, thousands of pages of material on which to base generalizations.

organizations of the twentieth century. Founders, organizers, and executives of unions, they figured prominently in the origins and growth of twenty-four great national and international unions and in more than forty additional state and local trade unions, trades assemblies, or labor-reform bodies. A more adequate record would probably disclose that their importance was even greater.[7] The great mine unions, whose 226,000 members in 1901 composed the largest and most vital contingent in the American Federation of Labor,[8] each sprang from organizations established or directed by British and Irish immigrants. Likewise among the ten more important figures associated with the National Labor Union from 1866 to 1872, half were British. Of the twenty-five foremost leaders and organizers in the Knights of Labor at the peak of its power in 1886, eleven were English, Irish, Scotch, or Welsh. Much the same was true of the American Federation of Labor, whose chief founder and President, Samuel Gompers, as well as numerous vice-presidents, like James Duncan, intellectuals, and organizers were British and Irish. No wonder the post-war unions were denounced as the "creation and creature" of the British immigrant, or that a French observer was led to declare after a survey of American labor in 1900, that "English immigrants have . . . brought with them the spirit of organization."[9]

Because some agitators and organizers came to the United States before attaining their majority, it is pertinent to inquire if their labor experience at home was sufficient to assure the transmission of British influences. Sometimes it obviously was not. Peter Arthur of Paisley, Scotland, the founder of the great Independent Brotherhood of Locomotive Engineers, was only about nine when he emigrated with his family to New York State. The British labor world seems to have left no impression on him. John Hunter Walker of Binnie Hill,

[7] The role of the Irish organizer was unquestionably very significant, but adequate records of his activities do not exist, except in a few notable cases. For the most part all these men have left us is the legacy of their Irish names.

[8] *Report of the Industrial Commission, Labor Organizations, . . . Railway Labor,* 1901, XVII, 29.

[9] Emile Levasseur, *The American Workman,* trans, T. S. Adams (Baltimore: The Johns Hopkins University Press, 1900), p. 180.

Stirlingshire, leader of the Illinois State Federation of Labor, likewise arrived in Illinois mine fields when he was only nine, and while he joined the Knights of Labor before he was eleven, there is scant indication that previous experience in Scotland counted for much. But men such as this were exceptions.

Many immigrants who had not reached manhood when they entered the United States already possessed a wealth of experience in British mines and mills and in British labor organizations. Workingclass lads like John Jarrett or Tom Phillips who could stay out of factories until twelve or so were fortunate indeed, doubly fortunate if they managed much schooling in these years. Nevertheless, even though Jarrett stayed out of the mills until the ripe age of twelve, he acquired six years of mill and union experience before he emigrated at the age of eighteen. Similarly, an Irish Manchesterian, John O'Keefe, began his mill work so early that by the time he was thirteen he claimed to have led a band known as "the staff," an adolescents' labor organization in the Whitworth Gun Factory. When he emigrated at twenty he counted nearly ten years of toil and training behind him. Nor was his case unusual. The Scotsman, Martin Irons, who won fame as a strike leader in the Knights of Labor, arrived in America when he was only fourteen with five years of industrial labor logged away, and John F. Welsh, an Irishman who came to the United States at sixteen, had gone down in the Durham mines and had been associated with the Free Colliers of Scotland. Just twenty-one when he left Derbyshire for Pennsylvania, Robert Watchorn had previously served for seven years as a member of the Derbyshire and Nottinghamshire Miners' Union, and William Scaife had worked before reaching his majority as an agitator and a leader in the Durham union of mine laborers. Many of these men, besides belonging to unions, themselves were raised, as was Josiah Dyer of the granite cutters, in families in which trade unionism was a tradition. Thus, while numerous immigrants came to America with the faces of striplings they brought with them the experience of men.[10]

[10] On Dyer see unidentified clipping in Knights of Labor Scrapbook, compiled by the late Agnes Inglis in the Joseph Labadie Collection (University of Michigan General Library, Ann Arbor, Michigan). Cited hereafter as Labadie Coll. Also see Carman and David, p. 118. Roy, pp. 281, 294-95. McNeill, p. 607.

But not all of those who emigrated and later made their mark in the American labor movement were striplings. As a group it is true they were young men, usually between twenty-one and thirty-five at the time of emigration. And the later they left the British Isles the more impressive, as a rule, was their background of labor activity. William R. Fairley, who emigrated in 1880 at the age of thirty-eight, had sixteen years of experience in the Durham Miners' Association, seven years on its executive board, as well as three years of service with the Miners' National Association of Great Britain.[11] In this and similar cases American labor reaped a full harvest of vigor and experience.

Moreover, being uprooted people, these immigrants, regardless of age, retained an unquenchable interest in developments at home. Since they feared snapping all ties, some of them remained affiliated with their old unions after emigrating. Out of this desire to retain a sheet anchor, engineers, carpenters, and miners established branches of their British unions and fraternal societies in America. Veteran unionists, as well as those less familiar with British labor, maintained correspondence with the men who stayed behind them in the old country, and consequently they were able to keep abreast of the latest hearsay on labor matters. John Samuel, Jr., a glassblower, thus kept up a heavy correspondence with British labor and co-operative leaders for nearly thirty years.[12] In New York, agitator Edward King made continual use of his contacts with Scottish iron founders, and Robert Blissert, of the Workingmen's Union of New York, prided himself on the labor ideas passed on to him by his friends, John Stuart Mill and Thomas Carlyle. The close relationship between Robert Howard, a leader of New England's textile operatives, and Lancashire spinners led the Englishmen to send him a testimonial of thanks for his services—almost as if he had never left the Midlands.[13]

---

[11] Roy, pp. 331-32.

[12] John Samuel Papers (Wisconsin State Historical Society, University of Wisconsin, Madison, Wisconsin) for this correspondence. Cited hereafter as Samuel Papers.

[13] U. S., Senate, *Report . . . upon the Relations between Labor and Capital*, 48th Cong., 1885, I, 557, 841. McNeill, p. 609.

Relations were cemented too by labor publications from Great Britain—newspapers, tracts, pamphlets—which followed their emigrating subscribers across the sea. Some immigrants, of course, kept in more direct touch with their homeland. Andrew Cameron, Richard Hinton, John Siney, and Samuel Gompers supplemented what they heard and read and remembered of Britain by making return trips. Each of these men, like all agitators, was fiercely proud of his new citizenship, each wholeheartedly gave allegiance to the United States, yet none of them ever lost awareness of his British training and background. The effect of this intercourse was to make it possible for the organizer in the United States to gain valuable perspectives on both the British and the American labor movements.

Despite the stigma borne by immigrant labor leaders and organizers, they were in an overwhelming number of cases moderate and constructive men. Most were ambitious and driving, to be sure; a few were shortsighted and selfish; a very few were firebrands; and occasionally men such as Thomas J. Morgan were identified with socialists. But the portrait of frenzied and unbalanced demagogues often presented to the nineteenth century public was a caricature. Because it was their task to incite labor to action and to impinge on the sanctity of private property, it did appear they were a menace; yet almost without exception in the cases studied, they deplored strikes, worked constantly for arbitration and conciliation, and without fatally compromising labor's objectives, urged harmony between capital and labor.

That so many vigorous men and women should have cut loose from their homeland and sailed off in moods of disgust and rebellion only to become one of the most moderate elements in American labor is remarkable. Witness by contrast the volatile character of the German immigrant agitators, who as much as any other people laid the foundation of American left wing socialism and anarchism. That John Jarrett, a leader of the iron, steel, and tin workers, should be regarded by his employers, and by other capitalists, as being far more conservative than the men he led, was very typical.[14] Nor was

---

[14] U. S., Senate, *Report . . . upon the Relations between Labor and Capital,* 48th Cong., 1885, I, 1122; III, 573.

it any more unusual that Robert Howard should be described by workers and by a United States Senator as "a man of intelligence," who had "devoted much time and study to [the] labor question," and one who "thoroughly understands the relation of capital to labor and the responsibilities and failures of each." [15] The American environment certainly encouraged this conservatism but it did not breed it in these men; their conservatism or moderation was extracted from lessons learned at home. The collapse of Chartism, the failure of revolutionary tactics on the Continent, and the rise of "common sense" or "new model" unionism in England conditioned their outlook in many cases before they emigrated.

The ocean passage did not fundamentally alter what environment had firmly set. Britons in American labor exhibited the same sense of propriety, the same self-discipline, diligence, and stability often associated with the terms "Victorian" and "bourgeois." From the fifties until the opening of the twentieth century, workingmen trained in the British movement tended to reflect middle class values. Since those who achieved prominence as organizers and labor leaders in the United States were semi-skilled and quite often skilled men, they steered their courses in the wake of the Protestant bourgeoisie that they admired so much; indeed, it was the hope of further emulating this class that caused many of them to cross the ocean in search of better fortunes. Once in America these immigrant organizers, like natives themselves, found nothing incompatible in their becoming petty capitalists as well as labor leaders. Richard Griffiths, a leading figure in the Knights of Labor and a Welshman by birth, operated a Chicago cigar and stationery store. The Scotch-born leader of the International Typographical Union, John Farquhar was, variously, an editor, a publisher, and a manufacturer of lubricants, while the Illinois miners' chieftain, John James, operated an agency for the Anchor White Star Line. John Hinchcliffe, an authority in the National Labor Union as well as an important leader of miners and tailors, served both as a lawyer and an editor while active in the labor movement, and Joseph Hockaday

---

[15] U. S., Senate, *Report . . . upon the Relations between Labor and Capital,* 48th Cong., 1885, III, 412-14.

of the International Ship Carpenters' and Caulkers' Union was a Detroit contractor. Other leaders moved in and out of the law and politics; such occupations outside of mill and mine often helped make up for the vagaries of low pay and the disability of working for impoverished unions. They did not seem to alter the dedicated service these men rendered labor.[16]

Admiration of the middle class meant, too, that the agitators tended to pattern their moral and religious conduct after the behavior of their social peers. They struggled manfully to become respectable, hence like many spokesmen for minorities they were abnormally self-conscious about their behavior. Judged by the standards of their own age, the more prominent organizers were unquestionably religious, upright men. A few like John Rae, first president of the United Mine Workers of America, had a professional interest in morality for they were preachers. Nearly all of the ranking leaders claimed to be teetotalers, and men like Robert Watchorn and Richard Trevellick vigorously battled the saloon's influence and attacked evils of "the drink" among workingmen. To set his men a sterling example in clean living, John James, a mine chieftain, went to the heroic extreme of giving up the use of tobacco, and most leaders did their utmost to keep organized labor away from females whose organizations predated the industrial revolution. Though none of the immigrants went so far as their British brethren who took to top hats and cutaway coats, they did seek to reform the American workingman's leisure hour and formal dress. Almost without notable exception, too, they were exponents of hard work, education, and the cult of self-improvement. Long after he had reached manhood John Siney learned to read and write, while Robert Watchorn spent fourteen years studying in various night schools. Those who mastered the rudiments of an education as lads often read extensively in labor literature, especially in newspapers, pamphlets, and to a lesser extent in popular and classical works of political economy.

[16] John C. Simonds, *The Story of Manual Labor in All Lands and All Ages* (Chicago: J. T. McEnnis & Co., 1887), p. 647. McNeill, p. 607. *The Workingman's Advocate,* Feb. 29, Mar. 14, 1874. Clipping from *Sunday News* (Detroit), July 28, 1889 in Knights of Labor Scrapbook, Labadie Coll.

Although little is known of the religious beliefs of many organizers, especially in the lower echelons of labor, the most important ones, men from Great Britain rather than Ireland, were Dissenters. Many were Methodists or at one time or another had received Methodist training. Of the Irish Catholics, except in the cases of a few like John Siney, we know almost nothing. Here the historian should be careful for the Irish suffered rather special handicaps. They were, for one thing, largely unskilled labor; in Protestant America such organizers as the Irish threw up, and they were numerous particularly in local unions, were unlikely to rise as high in industrial or in union circles as skilled Protestants. Thus their obscurity makes generalizations about them hazardous. Possibly the mainsprings of their behavior were not, popular opinion to the contrary, very different from those of the English, Scotch, and Welsh. In any event, among the Protestants of whom we have sufficient knowledge, middle class ideology with its overtones of stout moral conviction and religiosity endowed the organizer with a formidable sense of self-righteousness, lent him the zeal of a crusader, and contributed to making him an effective, if sometimes boorish, trade unionist and reformer.

Although there was ample room for enmity among them, it is not surprising that Scotch, Welsh, and English organizers in America generally co-operated and worked closely with one another; it is far more remarkable that these men in turn won the co-operation of Irish leaders. There is no need to dilate upon the animosity between the English and Irish, nor upon the fact that Irishmen continued in deep hostility to things English even after coming to the United States. The Fenian Irish Republican movement—though we marvel at the small number of recruits it won in the light of the enormous Irish immigration—is a case in point. Similarly, the "Irish vote" in crowded urban centers assumed generous proportions in the considerations of the politicos, and twisting the Lion's tail became, for some, an intriguing sport. Malice was bred also by British immigrants, who were placed in charge of Irishmen whom they regarded as "unfit for bossing." Conversely, Irishmen who vented their humors in mob scenes and drunken riots did little to endear themselves to anyone; and Irish terrorists such as those who operated in the anthracite fields of Pennsylvania were not above killing an Englishman or two if the opportunity arose—indeed on one occasion they beseiged an entire mine garrisoned by Englishmen. Yet of the millions of Irish and other British immigrants who mixed amicably in America one hears too little. We must wonder if the sensational eruptions that sometimes won attention have not obscured happier and more profitable relationships between Britons and Irishmen in the American labor movement as they faced common difficulties and common enemies.[17].

There is indeed excellent evidence of many such relationships. Martin Burke, for instance, an Irishman, was one of the finest organizers in the American Miners' Association, an organization whose top leaders were English and Welsh. Another Irishman, John Pollock, served as this union's secretary for a number of years, while Lancashireman Thomas Morgan worked so closely with Irishmen in the Chicago socialist and trade union movement that he wrote a special tribute to four of them before he died. Thousands of British miners in the Illinois Miners' Federation had high respect for their secretary, Irish James F. Morris. In Pennsylvania the Welshman John M. Davis labored in harness for the Knights of Labor side by side with the Irish miner, James Broderick, while the staff of John Siney's mine union was interlarded with immigrants from all parts of the United Kingdom. Perhaps it might be added that Siney who was Irish, worked intimately with Richard Trevellick, who was Cornish, to organize the Scotch, English, Welsh, Irish, and German mining population of Pennsylvania. By the opening of the twentieth century and thereafter, intimate relationships became even more apparent; among the steelworkers' union leadership Payne of South Wales, Mooney of Lancashire, Menzies and two prominent Murrays from Scotland were partners of Murphy and Molony of Ireland.[18] The upshot of

---

[17] W. T. Stead, "Incidents of the Labour War in America," *Contemporary Review*, LXVI (1894), 65-66. *The Miners' Journal*, May 27, 1865.

[18] "The Irish in the Socialist Movement," Ms. in Thomas J. Morgan Papers, Folder 36 (Illinois Historical Survey, University of Illinois, Urbana, Illinois). Cited hereafter as Morgan Papers. Eugene Staley, *History of the Illinois State*

all this was the establishment of a network of friendships that enhanced the pervasiveness of their ideas and at the same time kept these men in touch with the latest labor developments abroad. Moreover, once in power or in positions of authority these leaders easily formed cliques, managed to perpetuate themselves in office and took on the appearance of an oligarchy. Thus, as we shall see, though unions came and went the same leaders appeared over and over again in the newest organizational ventures.

## II. GENERAL LABOR REFORMERS

As the American economy underwent startling metamorphosis between 1861 and 1914, British and Irish organizers pressed their cause even in the recesses of the labor movement. Their backgrounds, activities, and influences cannot be treated exhaustively here; yet their careers in a few selected cases can be examined profitably insofar as they represent the four general kinds of labor agitation and leadership in which these immigrants were most active. Specifically, this would include general labor agitation, in which the organizer's pursuits carried him beyond the confines of craft into industrial or reform unionism, labor politics, and propaganda; and the fields of mining, iron and steel, and textile unionism.

Of the immigrant organizers engaged in general labor activities, few surpassed Richard Trevellick.[19] Because of the heavy onus he bore and the great sacrifices he made for labor his more sensitive colleagues regarded him as one of " the crucified ones." [20] Above average height, dark, powerfully built, a man of commanding presence and well elaborated ideas, Trevellick took up permanent residence in Detroit in 1862. Behind him lay a career compounded of high adventure and international

*Federation of Labor* (Chicago: University of Chicago Press, 1930), p. 189. U. S., Congress, House, *Labor Troubles in the Anthracite Regions of Pennsylvania, 1887-88,* 50 Cong., 2d Sess., 1889, H. Rept. 4127, Vol. IV.

[19] C. K. Yearley, Jr., " Richard Trevellick: Labor Agitator," *Michigan History,* XXXIX (December, 1955), 423-44, for details of Trevellick's career.

[20] Remarks by Robert Schilling in an unidentified clipping in US Mss 12A. Labor Collection: Biographies and Papers, Trevellick Memoranda, Box 2 (Wisconsin State Historical Society, University of Wisconsin, Madison, Wisconsin). Cited hereafter as Labor Coll., Trevellick Memoranda.

labor activity. Within a decade of his arrival in Michigan his stature rivalled that of the nationally famed leader of the Iron Molders' International Union, the great labor pioneer, William Sylvis, and he won himself a place among the most significant working class leaders. In the inflated estimate of his friends he was regarded as " a born orator, a natural genius, a thorough logician, a philosopher, a man of deep research, a student of human nature and society." [21] After Trevellick's death, Samuel Gompers, who was not usually prodigal with his praise, wrote that " the work he has performed in his time in the interests of labor, laid the basis for the superstructure of our labor movement today. Too much praise cannot be given him." [22]

Trevellick was born near St Mary's in the Scilly Isles, May 2, 1830. As a youth, like many Cornishmen, he must have felt the call of industrial towns and cities; indeed, at fourteen he joined the migration away from the land and became a joiner's apprentice. His master died, however, before his training was complete and he moved into the shipyards of southern England where he learned the ship carpenter's craft. There, in the Southampton ways, he labored until manhood.

As the "hungry forties" passed and prosperity swept back into urban areas, the young artisan started his agitations in the shipyards. We are told he entered a debating society of clerks, businessmen, and laborers and that he commended to this group a program calling for the reduction of the work day to eight hours. The idea was hardly original; an identical battle cry had issued from the ranks of the "Ancient Virgins" during the Owenite movement of the thirties; several textile manu-facturers had initiated a similar plan in their mills at about the same time, and John Fielden, the noted Tory reformer, laid proposals for an eight hour day before Parliament in 1847. Nevertheless in the early fifties the eight hour idea was contro-versial and Trevellick's resolution, we are informed, won him notoriety among his fellow workers. Local newspapers sup-

---

[21] Remarks made in the 39th General Assembly of Illinois quoted in " Richard Trevellick," Labor Coll., Trevellick Memoranda.

[22] *Ibid.* Also see Obadiah Hicks, *The Life of Richard Trevellick* (Joliet: J. E. Williams & Co., 1896), Memorial comments. Hicks was a labor journalist and a close friend of Trevellick.

posedly seized upon the proposal and not long afterward it was presented to Parliament where, not unexpectedly, it perished.[23]

Trevellick met setbacks of this kind in stride for he was already wedded to the labor movement. Moreover, he brought to his tasks a selfless, evangelical fervor which stemmed from his Methodism. When he was still a young man, in fact, he received Methodist instruction, and in time he also became a fierce temperance advocate. Before he departed from England, he served as an officer in several aggressive church temperance societies, fighting the immorality drink induced and attempting to curtail the dissipation of working class resources. Like many labor leaders he later credited these organizations with having provided him with invaluable training in leadership and administration.[24]

Following the demise of the hours bill, his career became an odyssey. In 1852 he abandoned England forever, shipping out as a joiner. At his destination in Australasia he claimed later in his life to have played a leading role in the formation of the first Eight-Hour League in New Zealand and to have duplicated the feat in Australia shortly afterwards. Students of labor in these lands make no mention of his name and without question he exaggerated his importance in the eight hour movement " down under " but the origins of the movement there are obscure, the history of eight hour organizations is unclear, and agitation appears to have burst forth in several places almost simultaneously. If we cannot know the extent to which he figured in these movements, we do know that they helped him mature his agitation techniques and become a very proficient " eight hour man." [25]

Just as labor ideas moved along the shipping lanes from the British Isles to Australasia and then across the Pacific to the West Coast of the United States, so also did Trevellick.

---

[23] Cole and Postgate, p. 239. John Rae, *Eight Hours for Work* (London: Macmillan, 1894), Chaps. 7 and 8. " Richard Trevellick," Labor Coll., Trevellick Memoranda. Hicks, Chap. 6.

[24] " Richard Trevellick," Labor Coll., Trevellick Memoranda. Hicks, Chap. 6.

[25] " Richard Trevellick," Labor Coll., Trevellick Memoranda. John Rae, " The Eight Hours Day in Victoria," *Economic Journal,* I (1891), 15-42. H. H. Champion, " Origins of the Eight Hours Movement at the Antipodes," *Economic Journal,* II (1892), 100-108.

He left Melbourne in 1855, sailing for London by way of San Francisco, but on the second leg of his journey his ship foundered off the coast of Peru and the next two years were full of travel and adventure. Then, late in 1856 or early 1857, a practiced agitator, he entered New Orleans and opened his American career. His personality, experience, and ideas had an immediate impact on the New Orleans labor world; he won election to the presidency of the local ship carpenters' and caulkers' union only a few months after his appearance in the Gulf port, and, exploiting his bargaining techniques, he acted swiftly to secure the coveted nine hour day for union members. On the heels of this victory he travelled to Brooklyn to join a brother then working in the shipyards; however, he soon returned to New Orleans, married and prepared to settle down.[26]

All of his plans apparently were upset by the Civil War, for he gave up his job as carpenter on a Mississippi steamer, refused a commission in the Confederate Navy, and after securing the permission of the British consul was allowed to pass through the lines to the North. Through part of 1862 he worked for the Marine Railway Company in Brooklyn, and may have held jobs in the New York shipyards. Labor's problems continued to occupy him and he undertook writing several articles on labor conditions in the shipyards for the famed Philadelphia labor newspaper, *Fincher's Trades' Review.* He did not remain in New York, however, but moved on to the rising Great Lakes port, Detroit.

Detroit was already the focal point of the Michigan labor movement and was due to become increasingly important after the war. Even before Michigan gained statehood there had been mechanics' societies and workingmens' associations scattered throughout the territory and, in Detroit, the iron molders, machinists and blacksmiths were unionized and other crafts were fast becoming unionized prior to Trevellick's arrival.[27]

[26] " Richard Trevellick," Labor Coll., Trevellick Memoranda. Hicks, Chaps. 2 and 3.

[27] " Richard Trevellick," Labor Coll., Trevellick Memoranda. Sidney Glazer, " The Michigan Labor Movement," *Michigan History,* XXIX (Jan.-Mar., 1945), 73-82.

The Cornishman fitted easily into this environment; indeed, no sooner had he secured employment with a local dry dock company and joined a branch of the International Union of Ship Carpenters and Caulkers, than he was elected president of the union.

War stimulated the expansion of the labor organizations, particularly local ones, and trades assemblies burgeoned in every major manufacturing area of the North. Such wartime restrictions as the Federal government placed on the use of the strike in vital industries appear to have been unimportant. On the whole, the new trades assemblies functioned as advisory bodies, seeking through co-operation among local unions to influence issues affecting workers. Lacking strike and benefit funds they relied heavily on propaganda and persuasion to attain their objectives. Inevitably the assemblies attracted the services of organizers ambitious to convert them into vehicles for their own advancement. Trevellick, as might have been expected, assumed a principal role in the organization and rise of the Detroit Trades Assembly;[28] he was largely responsible for the coalition of three major unions on which the Assembly's strength rested and by 1864 he had become its chief architect. Just two years after moving to Detroit, in other words, he was the city's most important labor leader, and he consolidated this position by winning the presidency of the Assembly.

In hopes of checking the menace posed by the organization of national employers' associations, Trevellick broadened the compass of his activities. Mainly through his efforts representatives from many trades assemblies gathered in Louisville, Kentucky in 1864 to form the famous but ill-starred Industrial Assembly of North America.[29] Although well conceived, insofar as it recognized problems raised by the creation of a national labor market and national alliances of capitalists, the Industrial Assembly collapsed amid the parochialism and inexperience of its membership. Thrown on his own resources after this experiment, Trevellick, always moderate and gradualist in his methods, sought to dissuade the Michigan Em-

---

[28] *Ibid.* Also see "Richard Trevellick," Labor Coll., Trevellick Memoranda. Commons, *History of Labour*, II, 22.
[29] *Fincher's*, Oct. 15, 1864. Commons, *Documentary History*, IX, 273.

ployers' Association from operating " in the wrong spirit,"
while at the same time he wisely revealed the fighting potential
of his five thousand man assembly and called for peaceful
relations between capital and labor.[30]

Trevellick's national reputation continued to grow. By the
time of Lincoln's assassination he led the Detroit Trades Assembly and the International Union of Ship Carpenters and
Caulkers as well; he had been blacklisted and had emerged
victorious from several conflicts with employers; he had won
notoriety for speaking often and vigorously in behalf of trade
unionism and the increasingly popular Rochdale Plan of distributive co-operation in Michigan and Illinois.[31] At the close
of 1865 he was one of the country's most outspoken champions
of the eight hour day, so much so that attempts were made
to lure him into the service of the Chicago Trades Assembly
as its chief lecturer. By this time, too, he numbered among
his associates William Sylvis, leader of the Iron Molders'
International Union, Jonathan Fincher, editor of America's most
influential labor paper, and Andrew C. Cameron, the labor
editor and prominent Illinois eight hour man.[32] On these firm
foundations the immigrant leader began still more significant
work.

During the summer of 1866 a workers' congress convened
in Baltimore to lay preliminary plans for the formation of
the pioneering National Labor Union. Seeking to smooth the
way for this new union's rapid expansion, Trevellick accompanied his friend William Sylvis on a tour of the South.[33]
Sylvis was the driving force behind the organization and it
was largely as a result of his efforts that the August convention in Baltimore had been arranged. Southern newspapers
followed the progress of the two organizers and recorded
some of their speeches and lectures. In New Orleans, his
old home, Trevellick excoriated the machinations of the prin-

[30] *Fincher's*, Aug. 13; Nov. 22, 1864.
[31] " Richard Trevellick," Labor Coll., Trevellick Memoranda. *The Workingman's Advocate*, Apr. 21; June 9, 1866. *Fincher's*, Aug. 19, 1865. *Chicago
Post*, Dec. 21, 1865.
[32] " Richard Trevellick," Labor Coll., Trevellick Memoranda. Hicks, Chap. 5.
[33] Hicks, pp. 46-55. " Richard Trevellick," Labor Coll., Trevellick Memoranda.
Commons, *Documentary History*, IX, 127-69. Powderly, p. 62.

cipal political parties as being at "the root of the evil cursing every Mechanic's Union in the land."[34] Workingmen, he urged, should accumulate a fund for the agitation of their cause just as Englishmen had done in order to fight effectively for the repeal of the Corn Laws. The organizational tour was strenuous. The South lay stricken in defeat, her manpower wasted, her future obscured. Sensible of this, Trevellick and Sylvis nevertheless gambled on the realization that labor's opportunity lay in effecting nation-wide alliance among workers. Yet their work was premature, its result unsatisfactory.

Trevellick played an important part in the growth of the National Labor Union. There is substantial evidence, though it is not conclusive, that he was the drafter of the organization's first platform. In any event, the platform adopted by the union at its Chicago convention in August 1867 was unquestionably his; it was, in fact, a replica of a document he had drawn up for the Michigan State Labor Convention in December 1866. The principles embodied in these platforms enjoyed great popularity in subsequent years and were, in substance, incorporated in the official policies of the Labor Reform Party, the Knights of Labor, the Farmers' Alliance, the Greenback and the Populist parties.[35]

After these initial efforts, Trevellick became a formidable personality in the National Labor Union. Like other Britishers in the order he discovered that experience gained abroad paid big dividends. He was selected to attend the meeting of the Internationale in Lausanne, though, as we have seen, a shortage of funds prevented his going. By 1869 he represented not only his own Ship Carpenters and Caulkers Union but also four other strong organizations in the National Labor Union. Still more important, his friendship with Sylvis made him a natural successor to power, so that when the great labor leader died

[34] *The Workingman's Advocate,* June 30, 1866. Trevellick had a crowded itinerary. Early in June he was in Chicago; later in the month he travelled through the South. In August he went North for a series of engagements in Indiana, Illinois, and Michigan.

[35] "Richard Trevellick," Labor Coll., Trevellick Memoranda. Clipping, n. d., from the *Journal* (Detroit) in Knights of Labor Scrapbook, Labadie Coll. See, *Labor Leaf* (Detroit), Feb. 17, 1895; *Journal* (Detroit), Feb. 15, 1895; *Evening News* (Detroit), Feb. 15, 1895. Hicks, p. 46. Powderly, p. 69.

almost in Trevellick's arms in 1869, the Cornishman soon gained control of the N.L.U. and held the presidency until the organization withered away in 1873.[36]

Prominence revealed his feats as an organizer. Through 1867 and part of 1868, before Sylvis' death, he delivered 270 speeches and created more than 47 unions. In his presidential address to the Cincinnati convention of the N.L.U. he reported that he had spent 169 days of the previous year travelling, during which time he issued 127 charters to new organizations. Many of his organizing junkets took him far afield; eighteen days, for example, were devoted to a journey through Massachusetts and to the task of "reviving New England."[37] One newspaper listing of his itinerary indicates that within the space of a few months he was in various towns and cities in North and South Carolina, Georgia, New Jersey, Pennsylvania, as well as in Ohio, Indiana, Illinois, and his adopted state. Moreover, 1870 found him launched upon strenuous efforts to help unionize men in the eastern anthracite coal fields, accompanied by another expatriate British organizer, John Siney. Together, speaking from old schoolhouses, balconies, and pitheads they breached the Schuylkill anthracite districts and broadened the base of organization already laid by Siney. Before that year had passed Trevellick had toured sixteen states and had dedicated "sleepless nights and weary days" to the formation of nearly 200 local and 3 state unions.[38]

Other significant works also claimed his energies. When the short-hour committee of the N.L.U. sought someone to present its case to the national legislators, Trevellick was selected. He at once placed himself in correspondence with President Andrew Johnson, journeyed to Washington and lobbied for nearly four months for the passage of the first

[36] "Richard Trevellick," Labor Coll., Trevellick Memoranda. *The Workingman's Advocate,* Sept. 7, 1867; Oct. 17, 1868. Commons. *Documentary History,* IX, 194, 262.

[37] "Richard Trevellick," Labor Coll., Trevellick Memoranda. *The Workingman's Advocate,* Oct. 17, 1868. Commons, *Documentary History,* IX, 262. Clipping " 1869: Labor," in Samuel Papers, Box 9.

[38] *The Workingman's Advocate,* Dec. 17, 1870; also Mar. 20; May 15, 29; June 5; July 10; Aug. 19; Dec. 11, 1869. Powderly, pp. 94-95. Commons, *Documentary History,* IX, 270-71.

national eight hour law. Although he was not alone in his work, Trevellick, in the opinion of several competent observers, was primarily responsible for the adoption of the law. It was Australasia over again, with complications, insofar as he was concerned. The statute was completely ineffective, of course, but even though bankrupted by the expense of lobbying, he returned to the Capitol in 1870 and labored to have Congress put teeth into the measure. This time he failed outright; yet with characteristic persistence he soon made a third appearance in Washington, demanding that department heads pay Navy yard workmen wages allegedly kept from them as a result of their having secured a shorter work day. Secretary of the Navy Robert W. Thompson came under fire from the former ship carpenter who urged him to " do justice to . . . men in yards and arsenals," and, though the fight was far from over, the Cornishman did win two minor victories. The Administration granted ten hours' pay for men performing eight hours of labor and the Congress passed a law, for which Trevellick had lobbied, putting letter carriers on an eight hour day, thereby keeping alive the example of shorter hours. The struggle to achieve an eight hour work day remained a major task for twentieth century workingmen. Nonetheless, Trevellick never quit the fight, and as late as 1880, while serving as an organizer for the Knights of Labor, he led a committee and published circulars demanding a bona fide eight hour day for all working people.[39]

The months just preceding and just following Trevellick's assumption of the N.L.U. presidency were full of success, but he soon discovered the organization was rife with factionalism. Early in the seventies membership declined disastrously and in 1872 the union split. Always popular, Trevellick was wooed by each faction and he made appearances before both; all the same he rode the national tide and leaned to the side of the politically-minded National Labor Reform Party—in fact, he even wrote its platform. The grateful reformers thereupon insisted that he accept their nomination for the presidency of

[39] Hicks, p. 48.  " Richard Trevellick," Labor Coll., Trevellick Memoranda. Powderly, pp. 475-76. *The Workingman's Advocate,* Jan. 22, 1870.  " Circular to the President," April 19, 1880, signed by Trevellick, Samuel Papers, Box 9.

the United States, a proposal the Cornishman's friends in Chicago, unmindful of his British origins, had made some years earlier. Of course, he had to decline. Meantime, the rump of the N.L.U. retained his services and in the face of decimated membership lists he travelled widely, issued 24 new charters and delivered 74 major addresses. But all the king's horses could not pull the National Labor Union back together again, and Trevellick was left to carve himself a new career.[40]

With the United States in the throes of a panic in 1873, this was not difficult for an agitator. Moreover, Trevellick sought to take advantage not only of working class unrest but of agrarian dissent as well. In an age still feeling its way towards industrialism it was not clear that the interests of urban labor and the interests of the farmer were radically different in many respects. Having been raised on a farm himself, the Cornishman was outspoken in his insistence that men of the soil be brought into closer alignment with organizations of urban workers. As early as 1868 the New York *Sun* described him as a man who " has done more than any others to organize the workingmen of the West, especially the agricultural laborers who have been forgotten or ignored by others." [41] He gave ample proof of this again in 1874 and 1875 when the prairies were alive with discontent, for he helped engineer the formation of the Greenback Party. This was a great catch-all party supported mainly by inflationists— easy money men—from all walks of life. Because of his numerous rural contacts, Trevellick was able to work closely with leaders of the National Grange and Farmers' Alliance as well as with workingmen, hence during the late summer of 1874 he made great headway in establishing Greenback clubs through the Mid-west. In March 1875 he was one of the principals in the Greenback Convention that met in Halle's Hall, Cleveland, nominating the chairman, serving as the convention vice-president, and as a leader of the platform and executive committees. When the money question assumed

[40] " Richard Trevellick," Labor Coll., Trevellick Memoranda. Commons, *Documentary History,* IX, 265.
[41] *New York Sun,* Sept. 26, 1868.

even more formidable proportions, he became the president of the Michigan Greenback Convention and plunged more eagerly than ever into political activity. In 1875 he supported the slate headed by the venerable manufacturer, philanthropist, and reformer, Peter Cooper, and two years later, at the Greenback meeting in Toledo, he acted as chairman during the formation of the National Greenback Party. When this national group met again for the presidential contest in 1880, Trevellick's maneuvers were responsible for placing Iowa's James B. Weaver in nomination as a candidate for the Presidency of the United States.[42]

Late in the seventies enthusiasm for Greenbackism waned, though a manipulated currency remained the ideal of many organizations, and Trevellick joined the Knights of Labor as a lecturer and organizer. Powderly, leader of the Knights, a man markedly the inferior of Trevellick, used his services widely. In 1883 he thought seriously of sending Trevellick abroad to observe English and Continental developments in trade unionism and co-operation and to help consummate the Knights' proposed alliance with Tom Burt's miners. Just as in 1867, however, the Cornishman was unable to go. Thereafter his fortunes as a labor leader fell with the fortunes of the Knights of Labor. Until 1893 he campaigned arduously for the order throughout the Mid-west but paralysis put an end to his activities in that year and he lived but two more.[43]

By and large Trevellick's career supports generalizations already applied to British and Irish organizers. Like most of them, he was able, aggressive, and idealistic, with special qualities of intelligence and integrity. He brought to the labor movement a dedicated spirit born of long experience in it and strengthened by his Methodism. His sacrifices were real; of his promised salaries he received but little. "His scanty recompense," an associate once declared, "would have disgusted even an itinerant Methodist preacher"[44]—which is very

[42] "Richard Trevellick," Labor Coll., Trevellick Memoranda. Hicks, Chap. 6. *The Workingman's Advocate*, Aug. 30, 1873; May 29, 1875; Mar. 4, 1876. Powderly to Trevellick, Oct. 23, 1883, Powderly Papers. *Journal of United Labor*, Jan., 1882.

[43] *Journal of United Labor*, Jan., 1882.

[44] Remarks made in the 39th General Assembly of Illinois quoted in "Richard Trevellick," Labor Coll., Trevellick Memoranda.

nearly what Trevellick was. Essentially a tactician rather than a strategist, his forte was speaking ability, well elaborated arguments, clarity, stamina, and forceful personality. He knew that American workers, like their British counterparts, would never rally around abstractions, and he argued pragmatically for " less gas at the convention and more work in the field." [45] Finally, despite his diverse activities he clung, as the British did, to his original trade and to a hard core of beliefs that might be called craft-mindedness.

Trevellick worked closely with other Britons in American labor; we have already cited his association with Andrew Cameron and John Siney. Similarly at the request of Andrew Roy, canny Scotch-born historian of the American miners, he moved into the coal districts of eastern Ohio, diligently trying to unionize the men there. John James secured his assistance in the Braidwood section of Illinois, while John Pollock won help from him among the men of the Tuscarawas Valley. In virtually every craft or union of importance, he could count acquaintances who like himself had emigrated from the United Kingdom.

Like almost all the agitators studied here, Trevellick was a proponent of the moderate approach. His ideas, to be sure, were liberal, and he was not above resorting to vitriolic attacks upon his opponents; yet he lived in a vigorous age, one that dispensed epithets more readily than is now the fashion, and his methods, as opposed to his oratory, were what the nineteenth century labeled sensible. He deprecated strikes and bore employers no malice, despite his conviction that labor's economic role was vastly more important than capital's. He publicly " entertained the heartiest feelings " [46] for employers and often invited them to his talks so that they might get labor's perspective on important issues.[47] In the Greenback movement, of course, he had to work side by side with many businessmen as well as reformers and laborers.

His English background and his labor experiences in Australasia, to which he alluded often, unquestionably contributed

---

[45] Trevellick quoted in *The Workingman's Advocate,* May 29, 1875.
[46] *Detroit Tribune,* Nov. 22, 1864. *Fincher's,* Dec. 3, 1864.
[47] *Fincher's,* Apr. 2; July 23, 1864.

to his success as a labor leader in America; Chartism, fear of
"English landlordism," the writings of Thomas Spence, and
a belief in the Rochdale Plan were all part of his inheritance.
Moreover, while he did not introduce the short hour concept
to Americans he did bring with him a knowledge of what
had been done in England and in Australia and New Zealand.
Without the benefit of nearly a decade of agitational work
in this field behind him we might doubt whether he would
have risen so rapidly to become "the most effective eight-hour
and labor reform stump speaker in the country," [48] or, as
another leader described him, "unmistakably the most effective
man we have in the movement today." [49]

To imply that Trevellick borrowed entirely from the capital
of his youthful experiences would, however, be a distortion
of the truth. He adapted easily to American conditions and he
learned from them; his career represents a fusion of Anglo-
American ideas and techniques. It is worth noting, for instance,
that his financial panaceas derived almost exclusively from his
observations of American problems and from his adherence
to the financial doctrines of Alexander Campbell. It was out
of his American environment, too, that he wove his opinions
on land reclamation, the place of women and Negroes in labor
organizations, and the immigrant question. [50]

### III. MODERATE SOCIALISTS

Besides Trevellick there were many other British-trained
agitators who won renown as general labor reformers. After
seventeen years at his craft in Berwick on Tweed, Andrew
Cameron, son of a Scotch printer, emigrated to North Chicago
where he rose rapidly in the Typographical Union. Remaining

[48] "Richard Trevellick," Labor Coll., Trevellick Memoranda.
[49] *The American Workman*, Sept. 10, 1870.
[50] *The Workingman's Advocate*, May 22, 1869; Feb. 17, 1872. *Baltimore Sun*,
Dec. 15, 1868. "Richard Trevellick," Labor Coll., Trevellick Memoranda.
R. Trevellick, *Money and Panics: Decisions of the U. S. Supreme Court and
the High Court of Great Britain on the Financial Question* (Detroit:By the
Author, 1893). John Maguire, *The Money Question* (The Johns Hopkins University Political Economy Collection, Vol. 158. no. 3), pp. 24-25, which quotes
a letter from Maguire to Trevellick. Commons, *Documentary History*, IX, 185-
86, 210-13. *Fincher's*, May 27, 1865.

active in his trade, he earned fame in the sixties as "the greatest labor editor of the time," and for years he was a key figure in the operations of the Illinois Grand Eight Hour League, the State Labor Assembly, and the Chicago Trades Assembly. We have already met him in the National Labor Union but he went on from there to advocacy of the Greenback panacea and a half dozen other reform movements.[51] Other careers evidenced the same breadth of interest; like Cameron there were many men who were eager recruits for reform movements. Richard Hinchcliffe, whose brother left his mark on Midwestern mine unionism, played a vigorous part in New England textile unionism and in labor journalism.[52] John O'Keefe helped mobilize the textile operatives of Rhode Island, fought for the Greenback cause, and became one of the ranking organizers for the Knights of Labor in the Northeast. Similarly, during the eighties and nineties George Gunton of Cheshire, by then already famous for his work on behalf of the Boston Eight Hour League and the Fall River textile workers, wrote important propaganda for the American Federation of Labor.[53] Others in the reform tradition were the labor writer Fred Woodrow,[54] the American-born, British-trained socialist John Francis Bray,[55] and the Chicago socialist and labor leader, Thomas J. Morgan.

Thomas J. Morgan deserves special attention as an agitator for several reasons. First, he was one of the few British craftsmen to achieve fame in the American socialist movement, and, as a consequence, his career supplies a useful check on generalizations made about his apparently more moderate colleagues in American trade and labor unions.

[51] *Western British American*, Mar. 19, 1888. Commons, *History of Labour*, II, 93, 113, 155, 162, 169. Commons, *Documentary History*, X, 182.

[52] *The Workingman's Advocate*, June 6, 1875; also see July 20, 1870.

[53] See his *The Economic and Social Importance of the Eight Hour Movement* (Washington: American Federation of Labor, 1889). Gunton wrote many such works, edited the *Social Economist*, and in later years tried to bridge the gulf between Capital and Labor by alternately praising and criticizing both.

[54] William E. Barns, *The Labor Problem* (New York: Harper & Brothers, 1886), pp. 256-59.

[55] "Notes on the Life of John Francis Bray," compiled by Agnes Inglis in Bray Papers. H. J. Carr, "John Francis Bray," *Economica*, VII (November, 1940).

Second, he drew heavily upon Britain for his ideas and he made effective use of them in the United States. And third, in applying his principles to the American scene he nearly altered the course of the American Federation of Labor, and hence the course of American unionism.

Morgan's background was substantially the same as that of other organizers, except that poverty scarred him more deeply than most. He was born October 27, 1847 in Birmingham amid an environment so harsh that he nurtured bitter memories of it throughout his life. In his own words, he entered the world " as near Hell as one can conveniently get on this Earth," [56] " so low in the social scale " that he could only " look around and upward." [57] Before he was nine he joined his parents in the Birmingham metal trades, " hammering out nails from iron bars " at the same fire with them, laboring from early morning until nightfall for subsistence.[58] Long before he turned to socialism he was heaping up the materials of rebellion, and it is no surprise to notice that as a boy he became a member of the Brass Workers' Independent Union.[59]

Morgan could describe himself accurately as a " type of the wage class." [60] Thirty-five years of his parents' productive lives were spent in the same outbuildings of a Birmingham mill. When his father died, the family was so impoverished that their employer purchased the coffin, but the young Morgan saw no generosity in this act for he blamed the employer for his father's death. The debilitating effects of factory life left him otherwise aggrieved; they worsened a squint he had developed at five,[61] about which he  was extremely sensitive, and left him with an uninspiring physique. Just over five feet tall, he smarted over his size until he learned to turn an inferiority complex to advantage by claiming he had been

[56] Clipping, " The Rights of Labor," Apr. 4, 1891, Morgan Papers, Folder 9.
[57] " Why I Am A Socialist," Ms, Morgan Papers, Folder 29.
[58] *Ibid.*
[59] "Autobiography," p. 1, Morgan Papers, Folder 1.
[60] Excerpt from *Open Court*, Morgan Papers, Scrapbook 3.
[61] Letter of Thomas J. Morgan to Henry Demarest Lloyd, July 6, 1896, in Henry Demarest Lloyd Papers (Wisconsin State Historical Society, University of Wisconsin, Madison, Wisconsin). Cited hereafter as Lloyd Papers. *Chicago Evening Post*, Feb. 24, 1894.

"cheated out of his rightful growth by the rapacity of capital."[62] More humorously, he ascribed his "unusual phrenological development" to the consistent whackings administered by factory overseers.[63] Most of his schooling took place in Unitarian Sunday schools, in that common recourse of working people, evening school, and in athenaeum courses. Aside from this formal instruction, however, he owed most of his training to the cult of self-improvement. When he quit the factory for a printing establishment, for example, he pored over most of the materials at hand, read through Cassell's Popular Library, and developed a distinct taste for "republican" literature.[64]

A "genuine product of the English factory," he "struggled somehow to manhood" and "recklessly married" an impoverished Birmingham girl from a family of twelve who had herself put six years into the mills. The grim realities of this youthful alliance encouraged them to emigrate to the United States. Thomas Morgan arrived first in May 1869, taking up work at the Illinois Manufacturing Company in Chicago; seven months later he paid for his wife's passage. Until 1873 he remained with the same firm, following it to Adrian, Michigan where he joined the Machinists' and Blacksmiths' Union that he was later to lead.[65]

The panic of 1873 prepared Morgan and his wife for socialism. He lost his job in the first onslaught of the depression and returned to Chicago only to discover that there was no work. Fifteen weeks of unemployment almost brought his family to the verge of starvation; only a fortuitous call to jury duty provided him with income sufficient to keep going. Realizing that the evils he had hoped to escape in England had caught up with him in America, he sought solutions to his problems by searching the writings of Ricardo, John Stuart Mill, Herbert Spencer, and Professor William Thornton. Meantime, he began attending Chicago socialist meetings then almost exclusively under the direction of vigorous German, Bohemian, and Scandinavian Lassalleans who had converted The Hub

---

[62] Excerpt from *Open Court*, Morgan Papers, Scrapbook 3.
[63] *Chicago Evening Post*, Feb. 24, 1894.
[64] "Autobiography," p. 1, Morgan Papers, Folder 1.
[65] "Why I Am A Socialist," Ms, Morgan Papers, Folder 29.

into the second strongest socialist center in America, and he scanned socialist literature in a small library located in the Chicago Rookery. Becoming more successful in trade union work, he soon took over the presidency of the Chicago Machinists' and Blacksmiths' Union, and not long afterward, in the fall of 1874, he made his first socialist speech—which earned him a stoning and ushered him into the cause with a strengthened martyr complex.[66]

A lifelong socialist thereafter, Morgan yet remained a moderate in that belief who, except for oratorical outbursts, acted in much the same way as other British organizers. In socialist conclaves he kept to the right of center and consistently fought revolutionaries and anarchists within the Socialistic Labor Party; in fact, early in the eighties he broke entirely with this element. Throughout his career he clung to his craft with British tenacity and this certainly tempered his socialism. For eighteen years, despite his tub-thumping performances during his leisure hours, he was well regarded by his employers at the Illinois Central Railway Car Works, and the very afternoon of the infamous Haymarket bombing, he settled a strike of his machinists in the Car Works peacefully.[67]

, Many of his actions must have puzzled socialists whose backgrounds were neither British nor American. For instance, twice during the early nineties he exhorted crowds of unemployed Chicagoans to take direct action to remedy their situation. Though no action resulted from his harangues, he was sternly rebuked by the City's Mayor. Morgan then led a delegation of workers to City Hall, thanked the Mayor for his leniency, and insisted that the delegates shake hands with His Honor. When they refused, Morgan grasped the Mayor's hand and then resigned as their leader. Similarly, while Morgan constantly attacked socialists like Morris Hillquit, John Spargo, Robert Hunter, and even the members of the British Labour Party for their compromises with capitalism, he

---

[66] " Why I Am A Socialist," Ms, Morgan Papers. Folder 29. "Autobiography," p. 1, Morgan Papers, Folder 1. *Chicago Daily Tribune*, Dec. 11, 1912. *Chicago Evening Journal,* Jan. 13, 1894. *Chicago Post*, Feb. 24, 1895.

[67] "Autobiography," p. 3, Morgan Papers, Folder 1. "Why I Am A Socialist," Ms, Morgan Papers, Folder 29. Henry David, *The History of the Haymarket Affair* (New York: Farrar and Rinehart, 1936).

did considerable compromising himself. By dint of bourgeois thrift and capitalist speculation he purchased, on the eve of the opening of the great Columbian Exposition in Chicago, a hotel which for several years afterwards afforded him a comfortable income. Still professing socialism, he gave up his trade in 1893, put himself through law school, and won some prominence locally as a lawyer. He labored mightily alongside capitalists like Lyman Gage to bring the Columbian Fair to Chicago and to swing workers in other cities behind the proposal. Often he lectured before university, church, and professional groups, and he once suggested that American workingmen should follow the example of English unionists by studying the conditions within their particular industries before they asked for wage increases from their employers. Early in the nineties when rumor had it that the Federal government would step in to care for the Chicago unemployed, Morgan announced that, " Governments were not organized to afford relief and it is foolish to look to them for aid. . . . Private charity is what must be looked to this winter." [68]  In 1893 after hearing of a colonization scheme some fellow socialists planned to launch in the West he denounced the idea as too radical, adding, " I speak with conservatism as becomes an honest man and a man of property." [69]

In spite of his bitter youth Morgan never lost his affection for his homeland. When war threatened between the United States and Great Britain over the Venezuelan question in 1895 he wrote to Henry Demarest Lloyd, by that time a close friend:

I am an Englishman, and altho' I left home in bitterness and have with much determination rid myself of all national egotism, still I cannot say with safety that I can view or discuss matters which threaten the evolution which it seems to me is being wrought out through the peculiar character of the English people. . . . I view the extension of the British Empire as an advance of civilization (frankly admitting all that is evil in it) embod[y]ing the principles of physical and mental

[68] The Provoker, Oct. 21, 1909; July 28, Feb. 24, Mar. 3, 1910. Chicago Tribune, Aug. 21, 1893. Chicago Evening Journal, Jan. 13, 1894. "Autobiography," pp. 4-5, Morgan Papers, Folder 1. See, too, the rough draft of a speech by Morgan, dated Apr. 14, 1895, Morgan Papers, Folder 46. " Relations between Employers and Employees," Morgan Papers, Folder 9.
[69] Chicago Tribune, Aug. 21, 1893.

freedom and democratic self-government with its essentials of free speech, meeting and press. In all these essentials there is in the U. S. no greater trend and in the absorption of the lesser by the greater the extension of the British Empire should be less, far less objectionable than if it were any other nation or people.[70]

Finally, at the pinnacle of his socialist career, although regarded by his contemporaries as a loyal and dedicated socialist, Morgan was written up in the first edition of WHO'S WHO in 1899 and in each subsequent edition until his death in 1912. But ideological pitfalls never worried a common sense Britisher of his ilk and he marched onward with abandon.

Restrained though he was, Morgan's skill, ability, and inde-fatigable energy made him a foremost figure among Illinois socialists. Until 1911 he moved steadily upward in the Work-ingmen's Party, the Socialistic Labor Party, and the Social Democratic Party, holding positions on executive boards, directing political activity, running once for the mayoralty in Chicago, competing many times for lesser local offices, and even for the United States Senate. By the nineties one exuberant Kansas City newspaper reported that " few if any men in the United States are better known to the workingman than T. J. Morgan." [71] His reputation did not rival Eugene Debs' or Daniel DeLeon's but he could not be dismissed casually as a lesser light.

Morgan was more than a talker; as much as anyone he was responsible for the establishment of the Chicago Trades and Labor Council, a forerunner of the extremely important Chicago Federation of Labor. His contributions to the drive for the creation of a state bureau of industrial statistics were great. Furthermore, he conducted several of his own investigations of industrial conditions in Chicago, published his findings with the help of the Trades Council, and testified with telling effect before a congressional committee that eventually came into the area to seek out the facts for itself. In 1879 he revised a comprehensive set of English Factory Acts, hammered them into ordinances, presented them to the Chicago City Council,

---

[70] Morgan to Henry Demarest Lloyd, Jan. 10, 1896, Lloyd Papers.
[71] "Autobiography," pp. 1-5, Morgan Papers, Folder 1. *Kansas City Star,* May 26, 1895.

and secured their enactment as a part of the Municipal Code. These direct importations and a set of emendations which Morgan drafted in 1883 served the people of Chicago for nearly a generation.[72]

An astute resolution writer, Morgan figured in the organization of several craft, labor, and general reform bodies in Illinois. In the mid-eighties he helped found and write the program for the Central Labor Union of Chicago. In an effort to bore from within he joined the Greenback Party and the Knights of Labor, and he played a leading role in launching the United Labor Party of Illinois, the first "independent" labor party in the United States, and a short-lived one. During the nineties he was one of the three main contenders for a position of dominance within the Illinois State Federation of Labor, perhaps the most important of such state bodies in the country.[73]

Morgan never lost sight of or touch with developments in England. Industrial legislation, trade union activity, co-operative ideas, the achievements of the chief British labor and socialist leaders, the discussions of the British Trades Union Congress and the Labour Party all continuously arrested his attention. New books, tracts, articles, or personalities coming from Great Britain he snapped up at once. He did not like everything he saw or read, but he was an interested spectator.[74]

Morgan was focused sharply in the national limelight early in the nineties when he attempted to swing the American Federation to a socialist and political actionist program. Broadly viewed, the tactics used by him and his comrades were but part of a general effort to capture major American

[72] "Autobiography," pp. 1-3, Morgan Papers, Folder 1. "Notes on the Factory Acts," Ms, Morgan Papers, Folder 15. Undated, unidentified clipping on Morgan and his relation with the Greenbackers and Knights of Labor in Morgan Papers, Folder 44. *Chicago Tribune*, Dec. 11, 1912. *Chicago Post*, Feb. 24, 1894. *The Provoker*, May 12, 1910. Staley, p. 18.

[73] "Autobiography," pp. 1-4, Morgan Papers, Folder 1. Clipping dated Mar. 12, 1887 on the "borers" and the Illinois Federation, Morgan Papers, Folder 44. *Chicago Post*, Feb. 24, 1894. Egbert and Persons, I, 239. Staley, pp. 84-100.

[74] Morgan to Henry Demarest Lloyd, Dec. 19, 1893; Sept. 8, Oct. 20, Nov. 27, 1894; July 18, Sept. 6, 1895; Jan. 10, Feb. 3, June 15, 1896; Dec. 28, 1898; June 30, 1903, Lloyd Papers. The Morgan Papers contain hundreds of clippings on British labor and co-operative developments.

labor organizations. Sapping and mining indeed had previously taken place to no avail in the Greenback Party and the Knights of Labor.[75]

Assaults on the Federation began at Detroit in 1890 when the socialists challenged Gompers' leadership by trying to seat Lucien Sanial, a representative of the Central Labor Federation of New York and a socialist, as a convention delegate. Accepting the challenge, Gompers waded into his opponents with considerable élan and it became obvious at the outset that he would best them. Morgan was present at the convention as the leader of Chicago's machinists and blacksmiths. He had been a member of the A.F.L. for several years and at the time, though a socialist, he was still a trade unionist and had not reconciled conflicts between political action and pure and simple unionism in his own mind. He viewed socialist actions in the convention as a mistake. Nevertheless, he ably defended Sanial as a matter of duty, impressing Gompers as being " small of stature . . . but prolific of words," and as an exceptionally competent parliamentary foe.[76]

The socialists were beaten but since defeat rested lightly upon them they returned to the cockpit at the Federation's Philadelphia convention in 1892. This time Morgan was the socialists' champion. At the first opportunity he laid before the delegates a proposal that foreshadowed his famed and controversial " Plank 10 " of the subsequent year. In essence it called for government ownership of the means of production and distribution.[77] Lacking in vote-appeal, the proposition was speedily interred but it served to put Gompers on notice that another showdown could not long be avoided.

Nor was it. In the summer of 1893 prior to the A.F.L.'s

[75] "Autobiography," pp. 3-4, Morgan Papers, Folder 1. Clippings dated Mar. 12, 1887 on Knights and Greenbackers, Morgan Papers, Folder 44.

[76] Gompers, I, 387. *Report of Thomas J. Morgan, Delegate of the Trade and Labor Assembly of Chicago, 10th Annual Convention of the American Federation of Labor, Detroit, Dec. 8-14, 1890.* Morgan kept numerous clippings about the Convention of Dec. 8-14 in Scrapbook 12. See also Egbert and Persons, I, 251. *Chicago Tribune,* Dec. 11, 1890. Howard Quint, *The Forging of American Socialism* (Columbia: University of South Carolina Press, 1953), Chap. 2.

[77] "Autobiography," p. 5, Morgan Papers, Folder 1. *Report of the Proceedings of the 12th Annual Convention of the AFL, Philadelphia, Dec. 12-17, 1892,* p. 39. Cited hereafter as AFL, *Proceedings.*

Chicago convention, panic descended upon the American econ-omy, and the delegates who gathered in the city in December were acutely aware of the seething discontent behind and all about them. Under such circumstances the socialists held a more promising hand than ever before and they selected Morgan to play it.

Sentiment within the Federation had grown in favor of some sort of labor party and Morgan sought to capitalize on this outlook by presenting the Convention with an eleven point political program. Mortised into the document were traditional demands for an eight hour day, the abolition of sweatshops, and government inspection of mines and workshops, but the core of the program was " Plank 10 " which called for " collec-tive ownership by the people of all means of production and distribution." Insofar as Morgan was concerned all else was subordinate to this plank, which he would have put into effect by political action. Moreover, when proposed it seemed to have a reasonable chance of acceptance. " More than passive support " appeared to come from Samuel Gompers and from Peter McGuire, one of his trusted lieutenants. The presump-tion—a false one as matters turned out—was that Gompers and McGuire, both of whom were once socialists, had returned to the fold. The convention delegates likewise ratified the program to the extent of recommending it by overwhelming vote to the attention of the Federation's constituent unions for their individual consideration during the forthcoming year. When decided, the locals were to instruct their delegates on how to vote for the program at the Denver Convention of 1894.[78]

Inspiration for Morgan's program had not sprung forth from a vacuum; events unraveling on the British labor scene were exerting their influence in the United States. There was, in fact, considerable parallelism between the courses of the two labor movements, or more properly of segments of the two movements from 1887 to 1900. On both sides of the Atlantic

---

[78] "Autobiography," p. 5, Morgan Papers, Folder 1. For general background on these events see Quint, pp. 62-67; Fine, pp. 140-42; Egbert and Persons, I, 252; Morris Hillquit, *History of Socialism in the United States* (New York: Thomas Y. Crowell, 1903), p. 299.

socialists were trying to commandeer the great trade unions, those that composed the British Trades Union Congress in Britain and those that formed the American Federation of Labor in the United States. Since the A.F.L. was consciously modelled after the Trades Union Congress, Gompers especially scanned the British labor horizon with an eagle eye—and so did Morgan. Ever since his emigration Morgan had kept abreast of British socialist and trade union progress; he was alive to the fact that British experiments contained many lessons for American labor. By 1890 his attention had centered on J. Keir Hardie, veteran leader of the Ayrshire miners. Hardie had broken with Liberalism in 1887 and had acted thereafter as a principal in the formation of the Scottish Labour Party; his twin objectives for British labor were independent political action and a moderate socialist program. In the British Trades Union Congress he sought unsuccessfully, but persistently, to win the important elements to his cause.[79]

Morgan's objectives largely coincided with Hardie's. He frankly imitated the course of action undertaken by the Scotsman when he drafted the preface and the political program submitted to the American Federation in 1893.[80] "Whereas," read the preamble to his resolve, "the Trade Unionists of Great Britain have by the light of experience and the logic of progress, adopted the principle of independent labor politics as an auxiliary to their economic action and whereas such action has resulted in the most gratifying success, and whereas such independent labor politics are based upon the following program, [here Morgan listed the eleven point program]. . . . Resolved that the Convention hereby endorses the political action of our British comrades and resolved that it be submitted to American labor and the American Federation of Labor."[81]

[79] Morgan to Henry Demarest Lloyd, Aug. 3, 1893, Lloyd Papers. In this letter Morgan refers to the writings of Keir Hardie, John Burns, and other British leaders relative to the "new political movement." "Autobiography," p. 5, Morgan Papers, Folder 1. For background see Webb, pp. 681-84; Cole and Postgate, pp. 386-89. For a new interpretation see Henry Pelling, *Origins of the Labour Party* (London: Macmillan, 1953).

[80] Morgan to Henry Demarest Lloyd, Aug. 3, 1893, Lloyd Papers. "Why I Am A Socialist," Ms, Morgan Papers, Folder 29.

[81] Morgan to Henry Demarest Lloyd, Night Message, Sept. 8, 1894, Lloyd Papers.

Whether Morgan wrote the preamble in a spirit of dis-
ingenuousness, in ignorance, or in a fit of wishful thinking
it was nonetheless inaccurate. The facts were somewhat different. At the British Trades Union Congress in 1892 Keir
Hardie had indeed proposed that the Congress' Parliamentary
Committee make preparations for financing independent political action by workingmen, but to little effect. The trade
unionists, those at any rate who voted simply agreed to study
the idea during the ensuing year. Meantime, while the unionists
were pondering their decision, Hardie, J. Havelock Wilson, and
John Burns were elected to Parliament, avowedly as members
of an independent labor party, and not long afterwards in
January 1893, the Independent Labour Party was officially
formed. Neither the new M.P.'s nor the Independent Labour
Party, however—and this is the point Morgan missed—represented the trade unions as a body. In fact, when the B.T.U.C.
met in 1893 it flatly rejected the scheme for independent
political action. Thus while Morgan was suggesting to the
A.F.L. that British trade unions had gone political, the British
trade unions were, in truth, torpedoing the idea and were
adamantly refusing to entertain Hardie's socialist program.[82]
Morgan's misconstruction of the facts soon cost him dearly.

During the spring and summer of 1894, prior to the Denver
meeting, there were several preliminary skirmishes over the
Morgan program. In Illinois, his home bailiwick, despite aid
from his friend, the highly respected Henry Demarest Lloyd,
Morgan failed to sell workingmen Plank 10 and independent
political action. Elsewhere, however, his ideas met with greater
hospitality; so many trade unionists seemed inclined towards
the program that there was every reason to hope for success
at Denver. Morgan hammered home his ideas in the *American
Federationist* in March and won support from some of the big
names in labor. In April, for example, Terence Powderly,
also writing in the *American Federationist*, backed the plan
for political action and argued that workers could make effective use of Morgan's British-style program. "We find the
workingman of Great Britain," he wrote, "setting forth a

[52] Morgan to Henry Demarest Lloyd, Dec. 19, 1893; Aug. 3; Oct. 20, 1894
Lloyd Papers.

political program which will dovetail into the reform platforms of New York and Pennsylvania as nicely as it fits into the advanced minds of Great Britain." Similarly, Tom Mann, who was then on good terms with Gompers, added his affimative appraisal of political action in the June issue of the official journal. But as the summer wore on it became clear that Gompers and his closest aides would refuse to countenance Plank 10 and would fight to destroy it at the forthcoming convention. Did Gompers have a closed mind on the subject during the month it was debated, did he change his mind during the summer, and if so what motivated his decision? To these questions we have no answer.[83]

In any event Morgan remained so confident of success that he took his wife with him to Denver as the only female delegate to the convention so that she might witness the anticipated victory. As the convention opened in the bracing Rocky Mountain air, Gompers immediately announced his opposition to political action. Reviewing the workingman's sorties into politics during the preceding year he discovered a record of unblemished disaster. It was the old story—many were called but few were chosen; the time was not ripe for a labor party. Then he threw down the gauntlet to the Morganites. Aware, as few others were, of the inaccuracies of the preamble, he wisely launched his attack upon it and bluntly refuted the notion that the British trade unions had sanctioned independent political action. Either unconscious of his error or simply unwilling to admit it, Morgan nonetheless stuck to his guns; he never really gave them up, in fact, for a year after the convention he still insisted that the British trade unions as a body had gone in for political action by "almost unanimous vote." But the A.F.L. delegates were not so intransigent; they struck out the offending preamble.[84]

Not until the afternoon of the fourth day did the combat over the "vital test," Plank 10, take place. Commonplaces,

[83] *American Federationist*, April, 1894. Also see editions of March and June 1894. *The Provoker*, July 7, 1900. Gompers to Mann, Apr. 30; May 10, 1894, Gompers Coll. Staley, pp. 113-30.

[84] AFL, 14th An. Conv., *Proceedings*, p. 10. "Why I Am A Socialist," Ms, Morgan Papers, Folder 29.

including a speech by the visiting John Burns, filled the inter-
vening days and heightened the suspense. Then the issue was
fully joined. Morgan still expected a sizable number of votes
and he counted heavily upon the moral support of Burns.
Before the sarcasm and parliamentary skill of Gompers, however, these imagined advantages proved of no avail. As if by
sheer legerdemain Morgan's proposals were amended to death
and the socialist tide was turned. Stunned, Morgan regarded
his defeat as the result of a colossal act of treason. "A careful
canvas of the voting strength of the delegates to the A. F. of L.
convention last December," he wrote a year later, " showed
a majority of 200 votes for Plank 10, but the leaders would
not permit such a result to be officially shown." Continuing,
he charged that " a part of the delegates of the great unions,
the Miners, Cigarmakers, and Carpenters, violated their instructions and as the vote of these three unions was almost half
of the entire vote, this violation of duty saved the A. F. of L.
from being placed in harmony with the labor movement of
the world which is distinctly socialistic." [85]

Morgan reserved special scorn for John Burns, whom he had
admired until the Denver Convention. Fifteen years after the
debacle he explained why his opinion of Burns, whom he was
then describing as a " $25,000 a year hireling of the Liberal
Party," [86] was drastically altered. Obviously he had expected
Burns to help him jam his program through the convention,
though precisely what form he expected Burns' aid to take is
not clear. Burns, who earlier than 1894 had conducted friendly
correspondence with Samuel Gompers, was a mild socialist,
having shifted from affiliation with the English Social Democratic Federation and the Marxist persuasion towards Fabianism.
In all probability the man was anxious to avoid giving serious
offense to anyone in America, and he did not spend all of his
time at this dramatic convention. But Morgan claimed that just
when he needed Burns most, the Englishman " went off seventy-
five miles to see a fire department exercise." [87] Morgan felt the

[85] " Why I Am A Socialist," Ms, Morgan Papers, Folder 29. AFL, 14th An.
Conv., *Proceedings*, pp. 36 ff.
[86] *The Provoker*, July 28, 1910.
[87] *Ibid.* Gompers to John Burns, Feb. 26; June 17, 1890; Feb. 9; Oct. 16,

real pyrotechnics were in Denver. After Plank 10 was rejected, Burns, with a guilty conscience, according to Morgan, paid Morgan a visit. Burns explained that his absence could not have made any difference in the outcome because the cards were stacked against the socialist plan from the start. " Tammany money," he allegedly told Morgan, " controlled the A. F. of L. and killed the program." Burns was not assaulted on the spot but Morgan ever afterwards registered only " unspeakable contempt " for his fellow countryman.[88]

Thus ended a socialist challenge that promised to alter the course of American trade unionism—not with a bang but a whimper. An epilogue to the affair was written in 1895 when J. Keir Hardie, whose work had largely inspired Morgan's campaign, was forced out of the British Trades Union Congress on almost the same grounds that had kept Lucien Sanial out of the American Federation of Labor in 1890.

Morgan's interest in Hardie outlasted the defeat of Plank 10. During the summer of 1895 Morgan and Henry Demarest Lloyd, at the request of socialist colleagues and a few trade unionists like Thomas Kidd of the A.F.L., prevailed upon Hardie to tour the United States. The purpose of the trip was to win over trade unionists to political action. Most of the expenses incurred by the Scotsman were borne at first by Morgan although Lloyd stepped in and remunerated him later on. Hardie was sensible of what his sponsors wanted him to do, hence he stayed clear of " radical elements " within the Socialist Labor Party who met him at the New York docks and tried immediately to " capture him." Morgan and Lloyd got from Hardie what they expected: an impressive display of middle-class socialism, the kind best calculated to influence American trade unionists. Hardie, of course, impressed nearly everyone who came in contact with him. Lloyd's estimate of the Scot was exuberant. " Perfectly candid, conscientious, and consistent," were his first descriptions. Hardie was a man of " unswerving integrity," and Lloyd added, " I believe *he* [as opposed to John Burns whom Morgan and Lloyd had sponsored

1894, Gompers Coll. For an interesting post-mortem of Burns see, Morgan to Henry Demarest Lloyd, Nov. 27, 1894; May 24, 1895, Lloyd Papers.

[88] *The Provoker*, July 28, 1910, for Morgan's story.

the previous fateful year] was worth doing it for. He has *character* or I will never trust my judgment of men again." [89] To Morgan, Hardie continued an inspiration: "We of the English speaking race must be up and doing," he declared, "when Keir Hardie's are beaten back by the consolidated forces of ignorance, and stupid greed; we must draw our waist belts tighter, spit upon our hand and take another and firmer hold." [90]

At the behest of Morgan and Lloyd, Hardie carried his missionary work from Atlantic to Pacific, spreading the word to unionists, socialists, and Populists, yet the most interesting of his contacts was with Eugene Debs. It was probably Morgan who informed Hardie and his companion Frank Smith of the sensational career of Debs, of his American Railway Union, of the court injunction that smashed the union's fight against the Pullman Car Company and sent Debs to jail. Not yet converted to socialism, Debs was a prize worth winning and as he sat in the Woodstock, Illinois jail, socialists planned his conversion. Victor Berger began the campaign of enlightenment but Morgan, who continued to purvey British influences, drove Hardie and Smith out to Woodstock to visit with Debs. Arrangements at the jail were anything but confining and the trio of Britons found Debs "minus his suit coat wearing a colored summer shirt and comfortably lounging in the yard of the jail." [91] "After a brief talk," wrote Morgan, "we left . . . driving with Debs through the surrounding country." Following dinner, the entire day having been spent in discussion of socialism, Morgan continued, "We returned to the jail and organized the International Bureau of Correspondence and Agitation." [92] This curious organization or, more properly, proposed organization, represented a step towards Morgan's dream of an international agency to push the work of political

[89] Henry Demarest Lloyd to Morgan, Sept. 13, 1895; Aug. 28, 1895, Lloyd Papers. Thomas I. Kidd to Morgan, June 27, 1895, Lloyd Papers.

[90] Morgan to Henry Demarest Lloyd, July 18, 1895, Lloyd Papers.

[91] Ray Ginger, *The Bending Cross: A Biography of Eugene Victor Debs* (New Brunswick: Rutgers University Press, 1949), p. 173.

[92] *The Provoker,* July 7, 1910. Morgan to Henry Demarest Lloyd, Sept. 6, 1895, Lloyd Papers. Also see, Morgan to Lloyd, Dec. 19, 1893; Oct. 20, 1894, Lloyd Papers.

agitation; something of this kind is what Henry Demarest Lloyd had had in mind when he wrote in relation to Hardie's visit of the " very, very great importance of establishing not only *relations* between different branches of our movement." [93] As usual Morgan drafted the group's statement:

We the undersigned, hereby agree to organize the International Bureau of Correspondence and Agitation: Object: To bring into active and harmonious relation all organizations and persons favorable to the establishment of the Industrial Commonwealth founded upon collective ownership of the means of production and distribution.

Debs became President; J. Keir Hardie, Vice-President; Morgan and Smith respectively became Secretary and Assistant Secretary. For a day anyway the socialists had seduced Debs and could claim momentarily to have converted him. But Debs soon refused to allow Morgan to publish the document drawn at Woodstock and he did not formally become a socialist for some time. Nevertheless, there is little doubt that his three British visitors brought his ultimate decision closer.

The incidents at Denver and Hardie's missionary tour are examples of the way international ideas and personalities colored American labor reform. Morgan's career is too intricate to trace in greater detail here but it is worth noting that he continued to keep his hand in on British labor developments and to see in things British examples by which Americans might profit. Thus when Henry Demarest Lloyd sent him a copy of one of William Cobbett's works Morgan heartily concurred with the thoughts in one passage Lloyd had singled out: " There is no principle, no precedent, no regulation favorable to freedom (except as to mere matters of detail) which is not to be found in the laws of England or the examples of our ancestors." [94]

As for the spirit of Morgan's activities, it was best summarized by one of his fellow Englishmen who observed him

[93] Henry Demarest Lloyd to Morgan, Aug. 28, 1895, Lloyd Papers. The original is in Morgan Papers, Folder 46.
[94] Henry Demarest Lloyd to Morgan, July 11, 1895, Lloyd Papers. Also see, J. Keir Hardie to Morgan, Dec. 25, 1896, Morgan Papers. Morgan kept many clippings from British papers on Hardie, including copies of *Justice*, in Folders 15 and 46.

at work in Chicago: "American Chartism," wrote the Englishman, "has a very close resemblance to the English article of the same name, so close indeed, that listening to Mr. Thomas J. Morgan . . . I thought myself once more a boy cheering . . . the labor gospel at the Chartist Hall in John Street. Mr. Morgan looked like a Chartist, spoke like a Chartist, and the spirit of Chartism was the magnetic spring by which he tied the audience together. . . . [An] effective orator . . . [he possessed] the sincerity and the zeal of a fanatic." [95]

## IV. MINERS

Most organizers from the British Isles, unlike Trevellick, Cameron, and Morgan, made their trades the main sphere of their activity. Nowhere among these trades was the network of British and Irish leaders more cohesive or significant than among coal miners.

The Welsh, Scotch, and English, in particular, were well prepared for leadership in this industry for as Britons they were especially intimate with coal. With them to the United States they brought a wealth of skill and experience. Until the widespread introduction of coal cutting machinery in the 1890's, in fact, the methods of cutting and mining were derived from practices in British mines, and the British immigrant miner moved easily from the pits of his homeland to those of the United States. Moreover, the deeply rooted in-group feelings among the miners themselves contributed to making them effective unionists and union organizers. This was the more emphatically so because they had a tradition of mine unionism that had grown in Great Britain with the production of coal. Thus as the tonnage mined between 1832 and 1875 increased nearly sixfold, county unions in Northumberland, Durham, Yorkshire, and Lancashire, as well as district unions in South Wales and Scotland were thrown up. Soon they were augmented by or merged with Martin Jude's Miners' Association (1841) or Alex Macdonald's National Miners' Association or Miners' Federation. A hard core of unionism at home, these seasoned men were scarcely less important in America. To

[95] Excerpt from *Open Court*, pp. 1104-1107, Morgan Papers, Scrapbook 3.

quote one American owner, they were in "constant turmoil" and "showed more of a tendency to organize into trade unions than native labor."[96]

Coal is found in five great provinces underlying portions of twenty-three states in the United States but in the nineteenth century the most productive areas lay in the eastern half of the nation. Anthracite seams were conveniently concentrated under five counties of eastern Pennsylvania; bituminous seams first brought into production lay in Western Pennsylvania and Maryland, in West Virginia, in the Mahoning, Hocking, and Tuscarawas Valleys of Ohio, and in the Braidwood and Belleville districts of Illinois. To each of these areas Britons and Irishmen came in large numbers, so much so that until the late nineteenth century they composed the bulk of the foreign-born mine population.[97]

During the Civil War only the American Miners' Association, established as we have seen by the ex-Chartists Daniel Weaver and Thomas Lloyd, commanded any considerable following in the booming coal districts. The locus of its power at that time was the Belleville section of southwestern Illinois and the central figure in the organization there was one of the most intelligent and versatile labor leaders of the sixties, John Hinchcliffe. Hinchcliffe was born in 1822 at Bradford in the West Riding of Yorkshire. Sent young into the factory, he was able to escape and become a tailor's apprentice, rising rapidly to become a journeyman, a master workman, and then an

[96] U. S., Senate, *Report . . . upon the Relations between Labor and Capital,* 48th Cong., 1885, II, 21-23. For general background see Cole and Postgate, pp. 273, 296; Edward Welbourne, *The Miners' Unions of Northumberland and Durham* (Cambridge, England: 1923); Richard Fynes, *The Miners of Northumberland and Durham* (Blyth, England: 1873); Webb, p. 776.

[97] U. S., Senate, *Reports of the Immigration Commission, Immigrants in Industry,* 61st Cong., 2d Sess., 1910, Senate Doc. 633, Vol. 16, Pt. 19, p. 660. *Report of the Industrial Commission, Transportation,* 1901, IX, p. 167. *Report of the Industrial Commission, Capital and Labor in the Mining Industry,* 1901, XII, pp. 16, 29, 80, 147, 149, 149, 166. *Report of the Industrial Commission, Immigration and Education,* 1901, XV, pp. 33, 80, 90-414. U. S., Senate, *Report . . . upon the Relations Between Labor and Capital,* 1885, II, 23. G. O. Virtue, "The Anthracite Mine Laborer," *Bulletin of the Department of Labor* (November, 1897), p. 751. U. S., Congress, House, *Labor Troubles in the Anthracite Regions of Pennsylvania, 1887-88,* 50 Cong., 2d Sess., 1889, H. Rept. 4127, Vol. IV, p. 165.

employer. Although he was later to lead American miners he had no mining experience himself, nor did he come from a family of miners. Nevertheless, his home was located in one of the largest mining districts in England and he absorbed a great deal of information about the industry. Moreover, he familiarized himself with the factory system, the demands of working people, and the operations of their trade societies. While a youth he enthusiastically participated in labor-reform demonstrations precipitated by Michael Sadler and Richard Oastler in their drive for a ten hour day. Chartism and Rochdale co-operative ideas also influenced him. In 1847 he emigrated, married a Pennsylvania girl, and lived for several years in the East. From 1852 until 1856 he worked as a tradesman in St Louis, moving finally to St Clair County in the heart of the southwestern Illinois coal fields in 1857.[98]

Ambitious, stout, and handsome enough to wear a look of authority, Hinchcliffe joined the Illinois Bar and assumed the editorship of the Belleville *Democrat and Daily Despatch* in 1860. Immediately afterwards he joined the American Miners' Association and soon became one of its principals. In a short while, through the columns of the *Weekly Miner* which he founded and edited, Hinchcliffe wielded considerable power, perhaps too much power. We are told that miners behind in their subscription could not secure work clearance cards until they displayed their loyalty by renewing their purchase of the official organ.[99] Accusations by the opposition press that Hinchcliffe was a "copperhead" did not arrest the rise of his popularity; in fact, among the British and German miners of his region he developed a sizable following. Before the end of the war he was able to take over leadership of the A.M.A. and hold it until the union collapsed late in the sixties. Meantime, on the strength of his reputation he served as chairman of the National Labor Union Convention in Baltimore, and as its treasurer. He was an important part of the N.L.U. Washington

[98] *The Workingman's Advocate,* Mar. 14, 1874. *Fincher's,* Sept. 3, 1864; Apr. 30, 1864 also. Powderly, pp. 64, 68-69. McNeill, p. 247. Roy, p. 67. Commons, *Documentary History,* IX, 129, 135, 137, 188-90, 334-35.
[99] McNeill, p. 247. *Fincher's,* June 4, 1864. *Belleville Democrat,* May 9, 1863; Jan. 16, 1864. *Belleville Weekly Advocate,* Sept. 25, 1863.

lobby in 1867-1868, and after the N.L.U. and the A.M.A. failed he entered labor politics. In 1871 he was elected to the Illinois House by his mining constituency in St Clair County, then to the Illinois Senate where he presented and fought for mine reform bills.[100]

Hinchcliffe, in other words, was one of those who kept mine unionism alive, if not flourishing, in Illinois, the Tuscarawas Valley of Ohio and Western Pennsylvania, but in the post-war years there was also a renascence of organization in the vital fields of the Mid-west and eastern Pennsylvania. And here again the initiative came from Britons.

Conditions were ripe for them. On the heels of wartime prosperity came hard times, long hours, truck payment, fraudulent checkweighing, and high casualties in the pits. With this tinder already heaped up, Alexander Macdonald, one of the most colorful and stimulating agitators ever to proselytize American miners, helped set it ablaze. As a child of eight, he followed his father into the Lanarkshire mines near Airdrie; mine life neither squelched his hopes nor killed his ambition. In young manhood he prepared for the University of Glasgow and, thanks to his summers in the mines, was able to pay his way. For a few years thereafter he taught school and worked briefly as a mine manager. But he was of the men and not of the masters. He threw his energies into organizational work and rose swiftly to become the acknowledged leader of the Scottish miners. Between 1855 and 1863 he emerged as " the chief single agent in the revival of mining trade unionism," [101] and as the foremost mine leader in Great Britain.

September 1867 found Macdonald dropping down the Clyde aboard a vessel heading for the United States. He was already in contact with American labor leaders and had explicitly announced the purpose of his journey:

As president of a very extended union, the national association of the operatives of Great Britain, I take the opportunity to announce that . . . [I am leaving] for a visit to the United States. . . . I shall, of

---

[100] *The Workingman's Advocate,* Mar. 14, 1874. Powderly, pp., 64, 68-69. Commons, *Documentary History,* IX, 188-90, 333-34. For general background see Wieck.

[101] Cole and Postgate, p. 335. Webb, pp. 301-307.

course, be in Illinois . . . I shall feel extremely happy to meet with the members of any or all unions of that state . . . [I hope] to bind understanding on both sides of the Atlantic in hopes it will lead to increased activity on both sides.[102]

Excitement among the miners ran high and the receptions tendered the Scotsman amid the gaunt shanty architecture of grubby mining towns were enthusiastic. The greeting arranged at Braidwood, a northern Illinois mining town named for a British immigrant, was fairly typical. Ceremonies there were placed in the hands of three hundred Scotch miners, one of whom was James Braidwood himself. Many of these men were personal acquaintances of Macdonald. It was a gala welcome. Leading a round of speeches John James, formerly of Nitshill, dwelt upon the bonds between miners of Britain and the United States. Then, turning to Macdonald, who had once been his chieftain in the Miners' National Association of Great Britain, James declared, " Yea . . . in the household of every British miner and many an American one too is heard and felt the voice of Macdonald in the words, ' Compensation to the widow and orphan,' ' fair weighing of all materials,' ' good ventilation,' and ' eight hours a day sufficient labor.' " [103]

At the end of the eulogies, Macdonald rose impressively before an audience that knew his " florid style and somewhat flashy personality " well. In his talk he recalled the great exodus of miners from Britain ten years earlier; some of them were standing before him. At that time, he announced, he had resolved " that no Atlantic shall divide us, that we shall be one in feelings, one in sentiment, one in sympathy, struggling for each other's weal, working for the advancement of a common cause." [104] He recited some of the new British techniques being used against employers in lieu of strikes, underlined the necessity of trade unions, pointed to the values of benefit funds, stressed the need of miners for educational facilities, and outlined briefly proposals for new mine legislation. Then he sounded the tocsin. American capital, he suggested, was less grasping than capital in England and

---

[102] *The Workingman's Advocate,* Sept. 14, 1867.
[103] *The Workingman's Advocate,* Nov. 2, 1867.
[104] *Ibid.* Webb, p. 301.

Scotland, yet if American miners were abused by their employers he urged them to fight capital with its own weapons—more capital wielded by well endowed unions. American mining, in his estimate, was still in its infancy, and sensing the discontent about him and the pitfalls that lay ahead, he cautioned his audience to avoid disaster by forming " a brotherhood among [themselves] in Illinois, Indiana, Ohio, Pennsylvania, and Western Maryland." Finally, underlining the spiritual values of trade unionism and co-operation rather than their " wealth getting " aspects, he praised union organization and co-operation as being designed to bring the greatest good to the greatest number.[105]

A few days later Macdonald started on an agitational tour that carried him into many small mining communities and to major urban centers like Pittsburgh, Washington, Philadelphia, and New York. Wherever there were miners, pains were taken to smooth his journey physically and financially. Everywhere miners left the pits to see or hear him. At Middlepen, Pennsylvania, after being introduced by a fellow Scotsman, James Spiers, Macdonald glanced about the crowd that had gathered to listen to him, noting the faces of old comrades from " Holytown, Glasgow, Hamilton, Wishaw, Lark Hall, Fife, Mid-Lothian, East Lothian, Galston, Hurlsford, and Kilmarnock." [106] During his trip he was re-united with four of his brothers who also worked in the American mines. Prior to his return to Scotland, he praised the advantages of life in America, but he warned her miners that they should " forthwith set about founding a Union . . . the object of which (in part) would be to resist by every constitutional means " the spread of child labor, the truck system, and other evils he had had to combat in Britain.[107]

From Lanarkshire Macdonald maintained correspondence with Andrew C. Cameron, hoping to keep Americans abreast of developments in Britain's coal fields. Insofar as he was able he sought to link his own men with those in the United

---

[105] *The Workingman's Advocate,* Nov. 2, 1867.

[106] *Ibid.,* Nov. 9, 1867. The Illinois miners gave Macdonald $178 to help him finance his tour.

[107] *The Workingman's Advocate,* Nov. 16, 1867; Dec. 14, 1867.

States; and in the meantime, reports in the American labor press of his testimony before the Royal Commission on Trade Unions kept his name and ideas in focus. The Scotsman's desire for closer transatlantic ties evoked favorable response in America, and Cameron even suggested editorially in *The Workingman's Advocate* that he felt Macdonald " could be persuaded to make the United States his permanent home and devote his services to the formation of a National Miners' Union." On both sides of the sea, miners congratulated themselves that while " statesmen and lying diplomats deal," workingmen were coming closer together of their own volition.[108]

Macdonald did return to America, though not to stay; in October 1869, he went back into the coal fields with his sponsor Andrew Cameron. Following his previous pattern he passed through the Braidwood district, then swung eastward into the Lonaconing area of Western Maryland and northeastward along the upper reaches of the Susquehanna River into Pennsylvania's Wyoming Valley. The journey was so freighted with success that he returned several more times to America, the last trip being in the summer of 1873. Throughout these years of his coming and going, he remained in contact with Cameron, Pollock, Hinchcliffe and other mine leaders, and they in turn, having been inspired by his example, riveted their attention on his achievements.[109]

Out of the ferment in the mine fields which Macdonald helped catalyze came John Siney, a disciple of British trade unionism and a man of signal importance in the history of American mine organizations. When Macdonald was touring the coal districts in 1867, Siney was at work in the anthracite fields of eastern Pennsylvania. Here the miners had rather special problems. Only a few hours by rail from the great urban coal markets, in an area of 1700 square miles, about 490 square miles of which are underlain by workable beds, lay the richest anthracite deposits in the world. If consolidated the scattered mine holdings in this region would have

---

[108] *Ibid.*, Jan. 11, Feb. 8, 15, Apr. 4, July 11, Aug. 15, Oct. 31, 1868; Jan. 2, Apr. 10, May 1, 1869.
[109] *Ibid.*, Oct. 30, Nov. 29, Dec. 2, 25, 1869; May 10, 1873. *The Miners' Journal*, Feb. 11, 1873.

covered only 22 square miles; in short, here were the makings of a natural monopoly. At first, however, the beds had been gobbled up piecemeal. Then, during the sixties, seven great railroad companies began absorbing earlier holdings, racing one another for ultimate power over the region. Competition was cutthroat and was complicated by railroads that did not hesitate to use their power as carriers to force the sale of as many properties as possible and to bring recalcitrant competitors to heel. Caught in this savage struggle, the victim of discrimination, chicanery, and the very complexity of the problems faced by the railroads in the operation of the coal mines themselves, labor suffered from the resultant unevenness of production, fluctuations of wages, and market warfare.[110]

Moreover, anthracite mining differed from bituminous mining. Anthracite seams were generally thicker, sometimes up to 70 feet; they lay farther below the surface and entailed driving shafts as much as 1500-2200 feet into the earth. And these shafts were frequently well below the level of ground water. To be sure, bituminous mining was dangerous, but the task of securing the smokeless natural coke that was anthracite was particularly hazardous. These perils, heightened by ignorance and neglect, combined with general economic circumstances to afford the mine worker a substantial basis for his grievances.[111]

John Siney was prepared to bear the burden of the anthracite miner's complaints. He was born of a peasant tenant family at Burnes, Queens County, Ireland in 1830. When he was five, a crop failure forced his family, like many others in Ireland, to emigrate to the Lancashire textile and manufacturing town of Wigan. When he was seven he was put to work in Ackerley's Cotton Mill, and while he had to fight to erase the stigma of being Irish, he liked to boast in later years that he had become the most useful boy in the mill. Better off in the

---

[110] *Final Report of the Industrial Commission,* 1902, XIX, 444-66. William J. Walsh, "United Mine Workers of America as An Economic and Social Force in the Anthracite Territory" (unpublished Ph.D. dissertation, Dept. of History, The Catholic University, 1931) for helpful information on the background events.

[111] *Final Report of the Industrial Commission,* 1902, XIX, 227, 250-52, 905-908.

mill than on the land, he nonetheless rebelled against low pay and an eleven hour day, and while still young he became a militant trade unionist. Quitting the mill as soon as he was able, he went to work in a Wigan brickyard where he organized the Brickmakers' Association of Wigan and served as its president for seven years.

Siney was an accomplished unionist when he emigrated to the United States at the age of thirty-two. The immediate cause of his departure was the death of his first wife, but he was undoubtedly lured by high wages and the promise of a fresh start. He arrived at St Clair, a mining town of about 5000 people located in the Schuylkill (Pennsylvania) anthracite fields in 1863. Unlike the thousands of Welshmen and other Britons with whom he worked, he started in the pits as an unskilled man, yet despite his lack of skill, and his Irish Catholic background, he adapted to his duties in his chamber, familiarized himself with the problems of the men, and began to exercise his flair for manipulating people.[112]

Meantime, with a Victorian will to improvement, the illiterate Siney was taught by his landlady to read and write. We are told—though the story is undoubtedly apocryphal—that his first written sentence read, " In Union there is strength." [113]

Siney began agitational work in Schuylkill's Eagle Colliery in 1868, not long after Macdonald's visit to the region. Twice during that year the miners had submitted to wage reductions; moreover, they had been forced to watch railroad interests in the State legislature emasculate an eight hour law from which they had expected much. In frustration they finally allowed Siney to lead them in a strike. In order to bargain with some hope of success, Siney formed the Workingmen's Benevolent Association of Schuylkill County, modeling it after a small union that British immigrants had set up in 1864 in nearby Carbon County. Localized at first, the Siney organization soon spread through the anthracite counties, and mine disasters like the tragedy at Avondale drove in the recruits. Likewise, because the collapse of the American Miners' Association had left a

---

[112] *The United Mine Workers' Journal,* May 11, 1916. Part of a series of articles on John Siney written by Terence Powderly.
[113] *The United Mine Workers' Journal,* May 11, 18, 25, 1916.

power vacuum, as it were, in the bituminous region of Western Pennsylvania and Maryland, eastern Ohio and Indiana, the W.B.A. won support there too. Since Siney welcomed men of any occupation in or around the mines he was encouraged in 1870 to change the union's name to Miners' and Laborers' Benevolent Association.[114]

Though he and his men challenged some of the most powerful corporate interests in America, Siney amazingly enough won concessions from them. Railroad moguls like Tom Scott and Franklin Gowen, the real owners of the mines, were forced to sit down with their men and elaborate a sliding scale and joint agreements about the price of coal and miners' wages.[115] And despite their cries of " Communists and Internationalists," employers bargained with the unionists for over five years. Nevertheless, the M.L.B.A. was under incessant attack, so much so that Siney several times asked his followers to take wage cuts rather than imperil the existence of the union. Similarly, although not all employers stooped to the trick, some charged that the M.L.B.A. and its leaders were associated with the Irish terrorists whose organization, the Molly Maguires, allegedly settled issues by murder. There can be little doubt that in communities outside of the mining districts, among people who were unaware that the frontier atmosphere still lingered in mine towns, unionists were often equated with this violent riff-raff. Moreover, while their union was weakened by the panic of 1873 and by its own decentralized structure, Siney and one of his organizers were hailed into a Clearfield County court on a charge of conspiracy and criminal revolt under a Pennsylvania law borrowed from the English Conspiracy Acts of an earlier day. The trial was a cause célèbre; Siney, thanks to his connections with the Democratic Party in Pennsylvania, was acquitted and his associate Xingo Parks, while

[114] *Ibid*. *The Workingman's Advocate*, Nov. 22, 1873. Roy, p. 77. McNeill, p. 249. Charles E. Kildeen, " John Siney: The Pioneer in American Industrial Unionism and Industrial Government " (unpublished Ph.D. dissertation, Dept. of History, University of Wisconsin, 1942). A copy of this dissertation was loaned the author by Father Robert Cornell of St. Norbert's College. See also, *American Federationist*, Jan. 1901.

[115] *American Manufacturer and Iron World*, Aug. 19, 1875. *Miners' Journal*, Aug. 13, 20, 1875 for an idea of the kind of opposition Siney faced.

convicted, had his sentence commuted. But they won the battle only to lose the war. Their trial, and the fact that employers, taking a leaf from the unionists' own book, restricted coal output (thereby lowering wages) resulted in the collapse of the union in 1876.[116]

But in the sixties and seventies leaders outlived their unions. Siney did not slip into obscurity; on the contrary, thanks to his vision of what the British miners had accomplished by organization, he went on to even more significant activities. Even as the M.L.B.A. was fighting its last battles, the call went out through Cameron's *Workingman's Advocate* for a national miners' convention. It represented an idea born in Great Britain, transmitted to America by Weaver and Lloyd, strengthened by Richard Trevellick and Alex Macdonald, and matured by John Siney. Response was encouraging and the gathering was held in October 1873 at Youngstown, Ohio. The principal organizers and agitators present were British and Irish; it is no surprise therefore that the Miners' National Union that they created was almost a complete replica of Macdonald's Miners' National Association of Great Britain. At some financial sacrifice Siney accepted the presidency and within a year he had recruited more than 21,000 men. When Sam Gompers, still on the threshold of his own career, met John Siney in New York not long after the Youngstown meeting, he accurately described the mine leader as " the most important figure in the trade," [117] for Siney had moved within the ambit of the country's chief labor leadership. There he stayed until his premature death in 1880.

Siney's methods and ideas, like his moderate temperament, came straight from Britain. The failure of revolutionary unionism and Chartism had deeply impressed him as a youth, hence

[116] Commonwealth of Pennsylvania, *Annual Report of the Secretary of Internal Affairs, Part III, Industrial Statistics* (Harrisburg: 1882), Vol. IX (1880-81), Legislative Doc. no. 8, " Labor Troubles in Pennsylvania, 1835-1881," pp. 322-26. *American Manufacturer and Iron World*, Aug. 12, Oct. 14, 1875. *Miners' Journal*, Aug. 13, 20, Sept. 3, 10, Oct. 8, 15, 22, 29, 1875. Chris Evans, *A History of the United Mine Workers of America* (2 vols.; Indianapolis: 1918), Vol. I, pp. 13-135. Roy, pp. 177-83.

[117] Gompers. I, 343. *The Workingman's Advocate*, June 21, July 16, 1873. Roy, p. 77. Evans; I, 29-30. *United Mine Workers' Journal*, May 18, 1916. McNeill, pp. 250-51.

in America, as in Wigan, he relied on Fabian tactics, arbitration, conciliation, joint agreements, and persuasion to settle disputes. Quiet, self-possessed, tactful, he suffered greatly because of his willingness to consider both sides of an issue. In trying to hold rebellious men to their contracts he was accused of "selling out" to employers—a charge for which there is no evidence. His moderation once brought a delegation of three Molly Maguires to his home to demand that he violate the law. He refused. "Siney," they told him, "when we make our report of this we will be sent back to see you, do you know what will happen?" "Yes," Siney replied, "three funerals."[118]

Although Siney flirted with the Knights of Labor, Anti-Monopolists, and the Industrial Brotherhood, his strength lay in economic rather than political action. Ordinarily he would suffer his men to take several wage cuts before striking, but when he did strike he waited until coal stocks were low. He believed in an eight hour day and thought it should be followed by a wage cut; above all he clung to his fundamental British belief in the compulsory maintenance of the standard wage through collective bargaining.[119]

Co-operation appealed to him as it did to many miners. In the summer of 1874 while visiting his sick mother in England, his imagination was fired by British miners' experiments with productive co-operation. The Miners' National Association at that time was planning a co-operative mining project to be located in America. With Macdonald's support about $250,000 was subscribed and surveys of a plot along the Cumberland River were begun in eastern Kentucky. Andrew Roy and John Siney, in fact, were placed in charge of the

[118] *United Mine Workers' Journal,* May 18, 1916. *The Workingman's Advocate,* Mar. 6, Apr. 3, 1869; June 11, 1870; Feb. 24, 1872; Oct. 25, 1873; Nov. 22, July 19, 1873; Jan. 31, Feb. 21, 29, 1874; July 17, 1875; June 6, Aug. 5-12, 1874. On the Mollies the best source is the *Miners' Journal* for the creation of the Mollies myth and for running accounts of Schuylkill County atrocities. Also see J. Walter Coleman, *The Molly Maguire Riots* (Richmond: Garrett and Massie, 1936).

[119] *United Mine Workers' Journal,* May 11, 18, 25, 1916. *Miners' Journal,* Dec. 2, 1868. Kildeen, p. 143.

survey. Unfortunately nothing came of the plan, except Siney's continued espousal of co-operation.[120]

As the leader of thousands of mine workers, Siney exercised great personal influence over the up and coming young labor lieutenants. His most important disciple was Terence Vincent Powderly, after 1879 the most publicized labor leader in America until the rise of Sam Gompers. Sensitive and impressionable, Powderly first met Siney under emotion-charged circumstances on a September morning in 1869 at the site of the Avondale mine disaster in Luzerne County, Pennsylvania. Not many hours earlier, a load of hay intended for the mine horses had ignited while being lowered down a hot air ventilating shaft. Catching onto the shaft's wooden sheathing, the fire rapidly consumed all the fresh air in the pit, and since there was no escape for the men underground except through the blazing shaft itself, one hundred and nine miners, most of them British, suffocated or burned alive. Siney and young Powderly watched rescue efforts and then, after their failure, the removal of the bodies. "Siney," wrote Powderly many years later,

... was the first man I ever heard make a speech on the labor question. I was just a boy then, but as I looked at Siney standing on the desolate hillside at Avondale, with his back toward a moss grown rock, the grim silent witness to that awful tragedy of ignorance, indifference, thoughtlessness, and greed and listened to his low earnest voice, I saw the travail of ages struggling for expression on his stern, pale face. I caught inspiration from his words and realized that there was something more to win through labor than dollars and cents for self. I realized that death, awful death such as lay around me at Avondale, was a call to the living to neglect no duty to fellow man. John Siney gave expression to a great thought at Avondale when he said, ' You can do nothing to win these dead back to life, but you can help me win fair treatment and justice for the living men who risk health and life in daily toil.' The thought expressed in that far away time became my thought.

And Powderly concluded later:

when I listened to John Siney I could see Christ in his face and hear a new Sermon on the Mount. I resolved there to do my part . . . to improve the condition of those working for a living.[121]

---

[120] *The Miners' National Record,* June 12, 1875. *The Workingman's Advocate,* Aug. 8-15, 1874.

[121] Carman and David, pp. 23-24, 35.

Influential as Siney was, there were many other mine leaders who, like himself, were disciples of Alexander Macdonald and British unionism. One of Siney's friends, for instance, was a sturdy, fierce-eyed little man with a full pointed beard, John James. James was born of a mining family at Nitshill, Renfrewshire, Scotland in 1839. Between his sixth and tenth years he received a rudimentary education. At ten he went into the pits in a region where only a few generations earlier the miners had worn iron collars to denote their bondage to their masters. During his adolescence hard times drove the family to Johnstone in search of better wages in the nearby mines. There James became a member of the Miners' Association of Great Britain, came under the influence of Macdonald, and formed a friendship with him that later had significant repercussions thousands of miles away.

James was steeped in agitational work long before he emigrated. While battling for passage of a Mine Inspection Bill in Johnstone he seized upon the miners' interest and organized a colliers' association. Retribution for this act came swiftly; dismissed, blacklisted, he tramped to Elderslie. Welcomed no more warmly there, he moved on through several other mining and industrial towns in the vicinity of Glasgow but when his father was gassed in a mine accident he was forced home to care for his family. His difficult circumstances, however, did not end his running fight with employers. Having found work at the Inkerman mines near Glasgow he was accused of fathering the publication of a letter in the Glasgow Sentinel "unfairly criticizing" the Inkerman management, and his discharge followed. He thereupon returned to Elderslie and secured a job at the Balaclava Colliery under an assumed name but somehow his reputation was revealed and he was once again fired. Now desperate, James trekked southwestward into Ayrshire where, beyond the reach of his former employers, he labored in the Denny Works. This breathing space gave him the time he needed to earn his passage money.

Promised a job in the United States, he arrived in New York in 1865 and entrained to Baltimore to meet an agent purportedly hiring men for assignment to a West Virginia mine. Upon moving into the mine field, however, it became apparent that he, of all people, had secretly been imported as a strike breaker. Fortunately, he was sufficiently self-reliant to acquit himself well: "We are Scotchmen," he told a delegation of the striking miners, ". . . and [we] are not going to take the bread out of your mouths."[122] James spurned the job, moved on to find employment at Newburgh, Pennsylvania, where he joined Hinchcliffe's American Miners' Association. For a time he worked in a succession of collieries stretching from Pennsylvania to Braidwood but when his journeyman spirit flagged he settled in Rock Valley, Illinois. In this postwar period the Illinois bituminous fields were a veritable bonanza for the union organizer and it was not long before James organized a flock of dissident miners into the Miners' Protective and Benevolent Association of the Northwest. Increasingly thereafter he figured as a principal spokesman for the unionized mine workers of Illinois, regularly contributing information to *The Workingman's Advocate*, and working closely with Hinchcliffe and Trevellick.[123]

It was out of the correspondence between James and John Siney that plans for the Youngstown Convention of 1873 and the formation of the Miners' National Association grew. According to Andrew Roy, Scotch-born historian of the American miners and an acquaintance of both men, James prepared the M.N.A.'s constitution and modeled it after the constitution of Macdonald's Miners' National Association of Great Britain.[124] Once the American union got on its feet James served as its secretary and, since his policies and outlook were essentially one with Siney's, he was the natural heir to the presidency when Siney died in 1880.

Another immigrant prominent in the Youngstown Convention and in the unfolding pattern of mine unionism was Daniel (Old Dan) McLaughlin, friend of James and Siney and Alexander Macdonald. Before McLaughlin, a Scotsman, reached the age of ten he was a veteran in the Scottish mines; his earliest memories were of the sufferings of the miner. Characteristically, his union activities began early in life and

---

[122] *The Workingman's Advocate*, Feb. 29, 1874.
[123] *Ibid.*, Feb. 3, 1872; Apr. 13, 1873; May 13, 1875.
[124] *Ibid.*, Feb. 29, 1874; Oct. 3-10, 1874. Roy, pp. 159-60. McNeill, p. 250.

by the time he was seventeen he was an able and experienced labor agitator. When he was twenty-one he assisted in the election of Macdonald to the secretaryship of the Scottish Miners' Union. For this he won the respect and thanks of the great leader, with whom he had struck up an acquaintance four years before, and McLaughlin rose rapidly to become his chief lieutenant. Secure in the union hierarchy, he nevertheless relinquished his foothold and emigrated to America in 1868.

In the Braidwood district where he settled he teamed up with John James and joined the Workers' Industrial Society, a small organization founded by Richard Trevellick. McLaughlin's efforts thereafter to unionize American miners were unsparing. And although his work was conducted in a region where armed Italians, Swedes, Belgians, and Negroes were imported as strikebreakers, where violence between militiamen and workers sometimes resulted in bloodshed, he made considerable gains. When he went to the Youngstown Convention to represent the Western Miners' Association, he was elected to the Executive Board of the Miners' National Association and shortly afterward took over the reins of the Illinois State Miners' Union as well.

As conditions in the coal industry changed swiftly in the eighties, thanks to the railroads' enlargement of the national market, McLaughlin joined in the call for a meeting of mine chieftains in Indianapolis, Indiana, late in the summer of 1885. From this gathering's deliberations sprang the National Federation of Miners and Mine Laborers, another of the great national mine unions that presaged the establishment of the more permanent United Mine Workers of America, and McLaughlin was successively chosen to serve as its president, treasurer, and chief of its Executive Board. Just a few years later, because of his following among miners, he was made a vice-president of the American Federation of Labor.

McLaughlin applied to American conditions ideas and practices he had learned in Scotland. He was unquestionably more politically-minded as a trade unionist than either James or Siney, however, and he never hesitated to stress the value of the ballot as an effective weapon for labor. He likewise played an active part in the confabulations of the Greenbackers and the Knights of Labor. Nevertheless, he was just as moderate in his tactics as his fellow immigrants, and the long years of work in a region where violence was common made him, if anything, still more moderate. As much as any other man he was responsible for elaborating the joint-convention system during the mid-eighties, a method by which unionists and employers sat down and worked out an annual wage adjustment based on a sliding scale. Basically, he always abhorred strikes except as a last resort and relied upon compromises or arbitration as a way out of immediate difficulty.[125]

Also present at Youngstown was McLaughlin's successor as the leader of the National Federation of Miners and Mine Laborers, Christopher Evans, as well as the future leader of the United Mine Workers of America, John Rae. Twenty-eight when he arrived in America from England in 1869, Evans resumed the same kind of agitational work among miners that he had conducted in the old country. He worked first among the men of Pennsylvania's Shenango Valley; then in the mid-eighties he shifted his operations to the strife-torn Hocking Valley of Ohio. During a period when "armed thugs and imported labor were transported into the Valley . . . [when] men who preached and taught temperance had barrels of beer and whiskey rolled among their hirelings to make them fighting mad . . . [and when] in their hurry they sometimes shot each other down,"[126] Evans, a modest and moderate man, emerged as a promoter of the joint conference and peaceful agreements. After his service in the Ohio Miners' Amalgamated Union and a stint as president of the Hocking Valley Mine Union he moved on to top positions in the National Miners' Federation and the American Federation of Labor. When the United Mine Workers of America was formed in 1890 he enlisted under its banner and returned to the coal fields as one of its key organizers.[127]

John Rae, who rose to become the first president of the

---

[125] *Journal of United Labor,* June, 1883. Roy, pp. 259-61. Powderly, p. 631. Gompers, I, 343. Barns, pp. 113-14. McNeill, p. 254.

[126] McNeill, p. 261.

[127] Roy, pp. 245-46. Evans, Chaps. 1-5.

United Mine Workers of America, fitted the same general pattern. He received his initial training in Scotland, having been in the mining trade from early boyhood. A great bearded man with a piercing glance, he was an evangelical preacher at the time he commenced arousing the West Virginia pitmen for the Knights of Labor. From the leadership of the Knights' constituent mine union, he climbed step by step to the job of Master Workman, and then in 1890 threw in his lot with compatriots like Robert Watchorn, formerly of the Derby and Nottingham Miners' Union, and William Scaife, formerly of the Durham Union, to create the most enduring of the miners' unions. Once ensconced in the presidency, Rae must have felt very much at home for his countrymen were all about him; Edward McKay of the United Mine Workers' Executive Board was a Scotsman, Benjamin James of the Executive Board was Welsh, while W. C. Pearce, Secretary-Treasurer, was English.[128]

Although most mine leaders eschewed active roles in general labor reform, they did in some cases display a penchant for politics. In the realm of political activity British training and experience also stood them in good stead, bringing into American legislation, for instance, policies and statutes already enacted in Britain to increase mine safety regulations and cut mine casualties. Dan McLaughlin, for example, served two years as mayor of Braidwood and two years in the Illinois legislature where he helped pass the state's first mine law in 1872. On three subsequent occasions he amended the basic law, and took a prominent part in the miners' lobby which sought passage of an anti-truck bill and a bill authorizing the establishment of a state bureau of labor statistics. Like McLaughlin, Walter Rutledge and William Scaife both performed pioneer legislative work in behalf of their fellow miners. Rutledge, a former English miner, earned the title of "father of mining laws in Illinois," where he was one of the first mine inspectors. Also an Englishman, Scaife gave up the presidency of the United Mine Workers of Illinois to enter

---

[128] Roy, pp. 281-83, 294-95. *Report of the Industrial Commission. Capital and Labor in the Mining Industry,* 1901, XII, pp. 71, 100, 138. *Journal of United Labor,* June, 1883.

the state legislature, where he fought for and secured the passage of mining legislation. Subsequently, he served on the state mining board and in the state bureau of labor statistics. Other miners, or more properly, former miners, like John Elthringham in Pennsylvania's Schuylkill County, or Andrew Roy in Ohio made the same effective use of their elective or appointative offices to secure better and safer working conditions for their old comrades.[129]

The influence of British and Irish mine organizers was greatest, of course, in the eastern half of the nation but it is worth noting that they did play a role too in the development of mine unions in the Far West. Many English, Irish, Scotch, and Welsh labored in the pits in Kansas, Oklahoma, Utah, and Colorado. Furthermore, they appeared in equally large numbers in the silver, lead, tin, and gold mining areas of the West. Mark Twain commented on their bumptious behavior in Virginia City, Nevada when the Comstock Lode was tapped, and wherever there were labor disturbances they filled their quota of men thrown into the "bull pens" at Coeur d'Alene, Bunker Hill, and the scenes of union combat in Colorado.[130]

Thus over vast stretches of the American coal fields, and to a lesser extent in other mining regions, in mountain towns, valleys, and in counties with names as unfamiliar to them as Belleville, Shenango, Tuscarawas, St. Clair, Pottsville, Jefferson, Allegheny, Lonaconing, and Luzerne, organizers from Lanarkshire, Mid Lothian, Durham, Derby, Northumberland, Lancashire, Ayrshire, and Wales literally built and then shaped and directed the first of the American miners' unions. To subtract their influences—positive and negative alike—is largely to wipe out the story of mining unionism prior to the opening of the twentieth century.

[129] *Journal of United Labor,* June, 1883. *The Workingman's Advocate,* Jan. 17, 1874. Roy, pp. 144-46, 281-83. Kildeen, p. 174.

[130] *Report of the Industrial Commission, Capital and Labor in the Mining Industry,* 1901, XII, pp. 322-38, 575, 588, 595, 611, 626. U. S., Senate, *Report of the Immigration Commission, Immigrants in Industry,* 61st Cong., 2d Sess., Senate Doc. 633, pp. 9-10. Mark Twain, *Roughing It* (New York: Rinehart Editions, 1953), p. 218. Berthoff, Chap. 4.

## V. METALWORKERS

Men from the United Kingdom played an important part also in the unionization of iron and steel workers; in the heavy industries, as in mining, the nationality of many workingmen opened a fissure that organizers could exploit. It was something of an exaggeration to claim " that nine tenths of the iron workers in the United States are natives of the British Isles or their immediate descendants," [131] but there were thousands of them, including a very large number of skilled men. The key industrial state of Pennsylvania counted 22,422 iron workers in 1880, of whom 7,947 had emigrated from the British Isles; similarly in New York State 4,523 of the state's 9,513 iron workers were natives of the British Isles.[132] As one careful student of British immigration has shown, American iron and steel mills drained off some of the best labor from British mills and " Welsh furnacemen could speak as familiarly about ' Pottsville, and Catasauqua, Hanging Rock, or Johnstown as if these places were . . . Ebbw Vale, Ynscedwyn, Pontypool, and Rhymney.' " [133] In addition to the many Britons who worked in the iron and steel trade, the industry borrowed very heavily from British technology and relied to some extent upon British capital for its operations, thus it was fitting that immigrant unionists should leave their mark on what was in some aspects so largely an American industry in name only.

While the Bessemer and Siemens-Martin processes were causing profound changes in the industry, British-trained agitators battled for the creation of unions. They launched a fight that raged furiously until the mid-nineteen thirties. If their struggle was more prolonged than the ones faced by organizers in other industries, they did not differ substantially from them in belief or behavior. Perhaps they were a bit more cautious and less politically-minded, but in general

[131] *The National Trades Review*, Mar. 31, 1866. *The Iron Molders' Journal*, Dec. 10, 1875. Cited hereafter as *IMJ*.

[132] U. S., Census, *Status of Population in the U. S. at the Tenth Census* (Washington: U. S. Government Printing Office, 1883), Vol. I, p. 731. U. S., Senate, *Report of the Immigration Commission, Immigrants in the Iron and Steel Industries*, 61st Cong., 2d Sess., 1910, Senate Doc. 633, Vols. 8 and 9.

[133] Berthoff, p. 64.

they relied upon "new model" tactics, economic pressure, arbitration, and conciliation to gain their objectives. These similarities make it necessary to treat only a few such men here.

One of the more notable "Vulcans of Albion" was John Jarrett, a wide-eyed, boyish looking figure in spite of his mustache and full beard. Jarrett was described to a Senate Committee in the mid-eighties as being " as largely and prominently engaged in the [labor] movement in the way of leadership as any man in this country." [134] Born in 1843 at Ebbw Vale, of native Welsh stock, Jarrett went into the iron mills shortly after he was orphaned at the age of twelve. When he was eighteen, he emigrated to Duncansville, Pennsylvania and then moved on to the Lochiel Mills near Harrisburg, where he labored as an iron puddler.

Insofar as he first came to the United States with no trade union experience in the mother country, he was something of an exception among the organizers under study. This deficiency, however, was soon remedied. In 1867 the settlement of property belonging to a relative called him back to England and he remained there for four years. During this time, while working at the puddler's trade, he made his labor contacts, becoming " acquainted with Mr. John Kane " who, when he met Jarrett, was the foremost unionist in the English iron industry. Kane, an excellent source of instruction, quickly " versed [Jarrett] in the principles of trade unionism." [135] Indeed, since his fifteenth year when he had entered the Gateshead Works at Newcastle-on-Tyne, Kane had been an ironworker. Identified with Chartism and other labor reforms, he subsequently fought for the creation of an iron workers' union, a goal he did not fully realize until 1863. After the formation of the Amalgamated Ironworkers' Association in that year he linked his provincial union's policies with those of the famed London Junta, a body that typified " business unionism." [136]

[134] U. S., Senate, *Report . . . upon the Relations between Labor and Capital,* 48th Cong., 1885, I, 1153.
[135] U. S., Senate, *Report . . . upon the Relations between Labor and Capital,* 48th Cong., 1885, I, 1159.
[136] Webb, p. 240.

Converted to unionism by Kane, Jarrett organized an iron-workers' union and led it to victory in a fight against wage reductions even before he returned to the United States. The American iron industry in which he once again took his place in 1872 was not one in which the progress of unionism had been encouraging. One of the first organizations of iron-workers, the Sons of Vulcan, was formed in the spring of 1858 by a band of Irishmen as a secret society. Early in the sixties it was brought into the open and a constitution was drafted; its growth nonetheless was exceedingly slow. A reorganization of the Vulcans occurred in 1868 after its finances had gone awry, and John O. Edwards, who had had trade union experience in England and Scotland, breathed new life into the order. Edwards, in turn, was succeeded by a vigorous Irishman out of Donegal, Hugh McLaughlin, who had previously helped organize a puddlers' union in Duncannon, Pennsylvania in 1863 and a similar union in Chicago three years later.[137]

Under McLaughlin, Jarrett rose to prominence and soon became vice-president of the Vulcans. Then in 1876, as a number of separate ironworkers' unions merged their strength to create the Amalgamated Association of Iron and Steel Workers, Jarrett, banking on his reputation and a series of skillful political maneuvers, rapidly worked up to the presidency. Early in the eighties he had become a national labor personality. President Arthur put him in nomination for the post of the first United States Commissioner of Labor, although the job was eventually given to the extremely competent Carroll Wright of Massachusetts.[138] Nevertheless, Jarrett stepped from this setback to prominence in the National Federation of Trades and Labor Unions, forerunner of the American Federation of Labor.[139]

[137] *The Workingman's Advocate*, Dec. 13, 1873; Feb. 14, 1874. *Report of the Industrial Commission, Labor Organizations, . . . Railway Labor*, 1901, XVII, 212. McNeill, pp. 268. 274-76, 277.

[138] Powderly, pp. 315-16.

[139] *Report of the 1st Annual Session of the Federation of Trades and Labor Unions of the U. S. and Canada, Pittsburgh, Sept. 15-18, 1881*, p. 8. U. S., Senate, *Report . . . upon the Relations between Labor and Capital*, 48th Cong., 1885, I, pp. 1118-1169. McNeill, pp. 283, 285, 294-95, 609.

In most respects Jarrett fitted the pattern of British leadership in America, insofar, that is, as so many diverse elements can be reduced to a "pattern." Through the cult of self-improvement he had transformed the rudimentary tools of his early education into a broad knowledge of labor. His approach to controversial issues was cautious and moderate. "I have based all my arguments in discussing the labor problem," he wrote, "upon the teachings of Christ. I know of nothing more beautiful than the words 'Love thy neighbor as thyself' and 'Do unto others as you would have others do unto you.' These simple truths include in themselves every essential principle necessary to the solution of the labor problem." [140] To prove his point he backed the manufacturers in his industry to the hilt by advocating a high protective tariff to safeguard their interests.[141] Moreover, he was a moral reformer. Workmen, he insisted, had to improve themselves to win respect and this meant abstention from drink. "Workmen," he declared, "must stand up against the evil of intemperance; it is a monster destroyer, not only robbing them of manhood and honor but also of the very means of earning an honest living. . . . Remove the curse of drink, and the workmen . . . are raised to a higher plane, in which all the people become thinkers and workers. The sequel is clear." [142]

Closely associated with Edwards, McLaughin, and Jarrett was another agitator out of the mills of Monmouthshire, Thomas P. Jones. Leaving home in Glenmorganshire, South Wales, as a youngster, Jones and four of his brothers entered the Harford Mills where he very nearly ended his career in a serious accident. Nevertheless he recovered and remained on the job for nine years, eventually assuming charge of a large bank of furnaces as a skilled operative. During 1846, in company with John Edwards, the future leader of the Sons of Vulcan, Jones tramped to Monkland near Glasgow, taking work in the Murray-Butteray Mill. There he began his agitation.

---

[140] Barns, p. 135.
[141] U. S., Senate, *Report . . . upon the Relations between Labor and Capital*, 48th Cong., 1885, I, pp. 1122, 1125, 1129, 1135, 1137.
[142] Barnes, p. 136.

Eager to form a union, he banded seven men together, making them swear to accept no wage reductions. Soon, the union having gained strength around this cadre, he instigated several spirited strikes, organized workingmen's clubs, and acquired the odious reputation of an organizer. Encouraged to leave the Murray-Butteray Mill, he moved to the Govan Bar Iron Works in Glasgow where he continued to press efforts to organize the men and to establish co-operative shops to aid their families. Slack times and increasing difficulties with his employers caused him to leave for America in 1862.

His agitations began at once. Learning of a prospective job at the North Chicago Rolling Mills, he visited the plant and succeeded before he was hired in getting a few of the hands to form a small union. Not long afterwards, having helped another Britisher, David Reese, organize the heaters of Bridgeport in South Chicago, Jones took over the secretaryship of their union. His talents, so vigorously exercised, were soon earmarked however for destruction by his employers. He was fired and so effectively blacklisted that for two years he earned a living by farming. But his organizing experience stood him in good stead and his connections among his native countrymen in America proved sound in the long run. Hugh McLaughlin brought him quietly into the North Chicago Mills and there in 1869, Jones, as unpretentiously as possible, established a union of iron and steel rail heaters, the Friendship Union Lodge of Chicago, earliest organization of its kind in the United States. With this group as a nucleus, Jones and his fellow lodge members called for a convention of heaters that met in Chicago late in the summer of 1872, and founded the National Association of Iron and Steel Heaters. Jones was the union's first president, and after he yielded office he was prime mover in effecting a merger of the heaters, the Sons of Vulcan, and the Iron Rollers to form the famed Amalgamated Association of Iron and Steel Workers in 1875.[143]

The Amalgamated fused the capacities of a number of Britons and Irishmen, John Jarrett, William Martin, David

[143] *The Workingman's Advocate*, Feb. 14, 1874. *Report of the Industrial Commission, Labor Organizations . . . Railway Labor*, 1901, XVII, pp. 277-82.

Reese, Daniel Harris, and Tom Jones among them. In an industry where unionism was weak during the first thirty years of the twentieth century because of employer opposition and divisions among workingmen themselves, it held nearly 32,000 men together at the peak of its power, fought at Homestead one of the most memorable strikes of the era, and until 1909 kept the spirit of unionism alive. If the strength of the early Iron Molders' International Union, an organization influenced by British ideas, were added to that of the Amalgamated a substantial case could be made for British contributions to iron and steel workers' unions, before the opening of this century. Unfortunately, by 1909 such unions were virtually wiped out. By the mid-nineteen thirties, however, emergence of the United Steelworkers' Union with its numerous British and Irish leaders and organizers served as a reminder of the earlier impact of men from the United Kingdom.[144]

## VI. TEXTILE WORKERS

The transit of organizers from Glasgow or Glenmorganshire to Chicago or the iron centers of Pennsylvania was paralleled by their movement from Lancashire to Fall River, Lawrence, and other New England textile manufacturing towns. Not that British operatives emigrated to that area exclusively; they did not. Many went into New York State and the silk mills there, some went to Chicago, others into the textile mills of New Jersey and eastern Pennsylvania. But since New England was the textile center of the nation in the nineteenth and early twentieth century, it was there that the bulk of the men and women from British mills settled. Some New England towns in the eighties were almost British colonies. "When they emigrate," stated an American consular official about the British, "they go to Providence . . . Fall River . . . Wanshuck

---

[144] U. S., Senate, *Report . . . upon the Relations between Labor and Capital,* 48th Cong., 1885, I, pp. 1169-1176. Carroll Wright, "The Amalgamated Association of Iron and Steel Workers," *Quarterly Journal of Economics,* VII (1893), 418. *Report of the Industrial Commission, Labor Organizations . . . Railway Labor,* 1901, XVII, 213. McNeill, pp. 283, 285, 299. Commons, *History of Labour,* IV, 101-109, 139-43. Leo Wolman, *The Growth of American Trade Unions, 1880-1923* (New York: Macmillan, 1924), p. 112.

. . . and Woonsocket; " [145] in Massachusetts and Rhode Island especially Britons and Irishmen were found in numbers. With them, as always, came the spirit of unionism and their union organizers. Agitation in this region was largely a British and Irish affair, and the several spinners' unions and carders' associations, not to mention other groups thrown up before the twentieth century, were primarily their handiwork. Indeed, the first national union of textile operatives in America was established by them.

Robert Howard's career is sufficiently typical to indicate immigrant influences in the textile trades. A stout man with a great mustache and a full head of wavy hair, mild-mannered but impressive, Howard was a veritable compendium of vital statistics and general data relevant to the textile industry in England and America. It may be doubted if any other unionist in America knew so much of the industry as he did. Born in Norwich, Cheshire, in 1844 or 1845, he was eight when he started earning his keep as a piecer in a Macclesfield silk mill. A little over a year later his family moved to Bollington where he took up the same tasks in another mill, and in his tenth year he moved again, this time into a Stockport mill as a bobbin boy. At fifteen he was a spinner; he had achieved some skill in his line and had become familiar with the trade in which he was to spend his life. In 1870 he was offered the job of overseer but he declined, claiming he could not perform the domineering work required. His decision was probably based on other considerations as well, however, for that same year he became president of the Spinners' Union. In this position, as in all he subsequently held, he went about his tasks vigorously; nevertheless, he discouraged striking and remained persuasive and conciliatory throughout his life. In 1873, for reasons unknown to us, he joined that enormous flood of operatives from all segments of the English textile trade who were literally pouring into the cotton, silk, hosiery,

[145] U. S., Congress, House, *United States Consular Reports, Labor in Europe,* 48th Cong., 2d Sess., 1884-85, House Executive Doc. 54, Part I, Vols. 24-25, pp. 587-1021. For citation above see, p. 623. Also see, U. S., Senate, *Reports of the Immigration Commissions, Immigrants in Industry, Woolen and Worsted Industry,* 61st Cong., 2d Sess., 1910, Senate Doc. 633, Vol. 10.

carpet weaving, and woolen industries in the United States, a flood that included not only workers but manufacturers and their machinery as well. After five years as a spinner in the Flint Mills at Fall River, Howard became a leading organizer, winning the secretaryship of the local spinners' union, the Fall River Spinners' Association. Wtihin the next nine years he served either as a leader or as a principal officer in the National Mule Spinners' Union, the Cotton Spinners' Association of Fall River, and the National Cotton Spinners' Association. Likewise, he was the associate editor of a textile newspaper, *Wade's Fiber and Fabric,* and the treasurer of the Federation of Trades and Labor Unions of the United States and Canada.[146]

Howard's behavior conformed more to that of the mine unionists than to that of the iron and steel unionists. This was particularly true of his political activity, for he played an assertive role in regular party politics in order to push workers' reform programs. Selected by both regular parties in Massachusetts, he served briefly in the State legislature in the early eighties, then declined re-nomination. Until 1885 he stayed clear of political entanglements, then suddenly decided to run for office again and went into the State Senate as a Democrat. Meantime, in and out of office he conducted extremely effective pressure campaigns. Starting in Rhode Island in 1883, he prevailed upon Governor Bourne to recommend a ten tour day for women and children, and the legislature enacted this proposal into law in 1885. The same year he secured the introduction of an identical bill in Maine. Before either of these lobbying enterprises was completed, he appeared to give testimony to the Massachusetts legislature on conditions in the textile industry; and in 1883 and 1885 he testified extensively before the Blair Committee of the United States Senate during its investigations of the relations between capital and labor.[147]

Throughout New England's textile mills were many Britons

---

[146] U. S., Senate, *Report . . . upon the Relations between Labor and Capital,* 48th Cong., 1885, I, 630-58; III, 491-501. *CMOJ,* May, 1876. McNeill, p. 609.

[147] U. S., Senate, *Report . . . upon the Relations between Labor and Capital,* 48th Cong., 1885, I, 630-58; III, 491-501. McNeill, p. 609.

and Irishmen laboring to extend unionism and to institute economic reforms. John O'Keefe in Rhode Island, Richard Hinchcliffe in Massachusetts, Robert Bower, and for a while, George Gunton in the Fall River area, and James Tansey and John Golden contributed to the formation of many local and state unions. In addition, Tansey and Golden were primarily responsible for founding the United Textile Workers of America, a great national organization that is still in operation.

## VII. ORGANIZERS IN OTHER TRADES

Actually British organizational genius manifested itself in a variety of industries. Again and again the British and Irish banded together to found American unions, and, in the early stages of their development, to dominate them and set their policies. Immigrant influence came primarily in the great labor-reform organizations, and in the coal, iron and steel, and textile unions; yet it was not confined to them.

Leaders such as James Duncan of Kincardine, and Joseph Dyer of Cornwall, both experienced in the granite or stone cutters' societies of their native regions were long prominent in the American granite cutters' union.[148] John Samuel and his son left the Welsh bottle blowers' trade to lead skilled glass bottle blowers in the United States. Tom Phillips and Richard Griffiths both became important figures among the shoe-makers.[149] Even the cigarmaking trade, a stronghold of the Germans, felt the impact of men from the British Isles. Thomas M. Dolan " never forgot the lessons . . . learned in unionism " [150] as a Liverpool cigarmaker. The organization of cigarmakers in Cincinnati was largely his handiwork and he contributed substantially to the formation of the Detroit Trades Assembly in company with Richard Trevellick. Born on the Isle of Man, William Cannon likewise rose to leadership in the Cigarmakers' International Union, and Michael

[148] *IMJ*, Oct., 1928. *Granite Cutters' Journal*, Oct., 1928. Cited hereafter as *GCJ*. McNeill, pp. 380, 607.

[149] "Autobiography," in the Thomas Phillips Papers (Wisconsin State Historical Society, University of Wisconsin, Madison, Wisconsin). Cited hereafter as Phillips Papers. Simonds, p. 647.

[150] *Detroit News*, July 28, 1889. Knights of Labor Scrapbook, Labadie Coll.

Raphael, an Englishman, led the New Haven cigarmakers.[151] John Heenan of Queens County, Ireland and Daniel Olive, a Londoner, were important in the same trade.[152] In still other crafts, William H. Foster, " the original boycotter," unionized the printers of Cincinnati and Philadelphia and then led one of the biggest American typographical unions, while a Scottish type-founder, Edward King, organized his trade in New York City.[153] Joseph Hockaday, out of Devonshire, the shipyards of southern England and the Woolwich docks, became a personality of local significance among the Detroit carpenters and caulkers and the district assembly of the Knights of Labor.[154] Robert Blissert, a student of unionism in his native England, established the Workingmen's Union of New York and the Central Labor Union of New York City, while Joseph Wilkinson helped direct the Journeyman Tailors' National Union and played an active part in the formation of the Amalgamated Trades and Labor Union of New York.[155]

Occasionally women who had emigrated from the British Isles became successful organizers. They were exceptions, of course, in a man's world and they were usually unable to rise to national prominence, nevertheless they fought hard and effectively for unionization and labor-reform. English-born Melinda Scott, for instance, won a position of leadership among the female hat trimmers of New York;[156] Maggie Macnamara founded the Brooklyn Female Burnishers' Association while two of her Irish countrywomen, Kate Mullaney and Leonora Barry, led the Troy laundresses and the women of the Knights of Labor respectively.[157] Drawing upon her British experience Mrs. Thomas J. Morgan became one of the more important women in the American labor movement.

[151] *The Workingman's Advocate,* Nov. 15, 1873. Gompers, I, 126.

[152] *The Workingman's Advocate,* Sept. 14, 1872.

[153] U. S., Senate, *Report . . . upon the Relations between Labor and Capital,* 48th Cong., 1885, I, 402-13, 557-605, 687-713; II, 70-86, 868-91. McNeill, p. 608.

[154] *Detroit Sunday News,* Sept. 6, 1891.

[155] U. S., Senate, *Report . . . upon the Relations between Labor and Capital,* 48th Cong., 1885, I, 840-61. McNeill, pp. 614-15.

[156] Alice Henry, *The Trade Union Woman* (New York: 1915), p. 75.

[157] *Ibid.,* p. 126. Commons, *Documentary History,* IX, 227.

Once a poverty stricken Birmingham girl, she conducted pioneering studies of sweated female labor in Chicago, founded three independent women's unions, and for several years led the women's division of the Knights of Labor. Probably no woman of her generation did more to relieve the plight of Chicago's unfortunate working girls.[158] Finally, Irene Ashby-Macfayden, an Englishwoman, educated at Westerfield College in London, and originally hired at the turn of the century by Samuel Gompers as an organizer, became one of the most sensational critics of child labor in the southern states. Having started her labor career by organizing girls who worked for Sir Thomas Lipton, she soon developed into an effective lobbyist for the American Federation of Labor.[159]

Thus in almost every segment of American labor, immigrants from the United Kingdom left the indelible stamp of their agitational activity; and just as significantly they left the impress of their British ideas.

---

[158] *Chicago Herald,* Aug. 21, 1891. *Chicago Daily News,* Apr. 4, 5, 1892. *Chicago Sunday Tribune,* Feb. 12, 1893. "Rights of Labor," Ms, Morgan Papers, Folder 15. Unidentified clipping "In the Dens of Sweaters," Morgan Papers, Folder 15. Gompers to Mrs. Thomas J. Morgan, Nov. 28, Mar. 11, 1892, Morgan Papers. Also see, "Autobiography," p. 4, Morgan Papers.

[159] Elizabeth H. Davidson, *Child Labor Legislation in Southern Textile States* (Chapel Hill: University of North Carolina Press, 1939), pp. 25-28.

# PART FOUR

# THE GREAT EXAMPLE

---

## I. ENGLAND THE MODEL

" England has been the model," wrote the Frenchman Emile Levasseur of American labor organizations in 1900; ". . . the ideas which circulate among the working classes cross the ocean with the tide of immigration." [1] There is little doubt that the example posed by British trade unions and British labor reform movements proved as significant in some ways as the activities of the British and Irish organizers in the United States. Unsure of themselves, not historically-minded, American leaders often allowed their thinking to assume an English orientation. Out of ignorance or scorn they paid scant attention to the fund of achievement and experience rooted in their own history upon which they might have drawn. Instead, labor spokesmen of the Civil War and post-war period either worked pragmatically, day to day, hit or miss, or else utilized England as their labor laboratory. Indeed, the number of responsible leaders who eulogized or criticized the practices and policies of British labor was so large that Britain not only became *an* example to many American workingmen, but *the* example.

At a glance this appears paradoxical. The post-war era was marked by rising nationalism, and by the emergence of several varieties of Anglophobia. " England," " Great Britain," and " The Empire " were terms that often evoked images of gold, cunning, and oppression. Yet attitudes easily entertained about governments did not always extend to peoples. There were at least two Britains in the American workingman's mind; one was aristocratic, capitalistic, and imperialistic, and the other was workingclass and increasingly democratic. In spite of this ambivalent outlook, Americans drew freely upon British capital and British commercial and industrial techniques to

---

[1] Levasseur. p. 180.

help sustain their industries, upon British economists to equip them with a rationale, and upon British and Irish laborers to lead them.

There were, of course, more specific reasons why American labor leaders and reformers were often content to watch and to follow in the footsteps of British labor. Britain, for one thing, wielded enormous prestige as the birthplace of modern trade unionism. There the movement first grew dramatically into a formidable instrument in the hands of reformers, the socially and economically underprivileged, and the skilled workers. Samuel Gompers, at the time the most impressive figure in American labor, referred to Great Britain in 1887 "as the cradle of our now universal movement,"[2] while the editor of an influential labor journal praised England in 1876 as the root and "the hotbed of unionism."[3] In the same year Richard Hinton, a highly respected labor journalist and in later years a socialist of renown, declared that "the idea of individual self-help, as well as protective organization seems to have come from British agitators;" British trade unions "afforded the groundwork" upon which workers elsewhere were building, and in his judgment through "their experience alone could the initiative creating the labor movements of the West have been formed. British unions were the elders, the forerunners of other such movements."[4]

Other opinions were strikingly similar. Spokesmen for the iron molders regarded England as "the father and the mother of trades unionism."[5] To cigarmakers it ranked as "the classic land of labor organization," where "the oldest and most powerful trades were to be found."[6] One prominent observer in 1877 depicted "the English and their descendants" as foremost among civilized peoples, as "the mother of workmen," and the "first in all matters concerned with industry." In England, he declared with unusual frankness, "there grew up

[2] AFL, *Proceedings, President's Report*, 1887, p. 10.
[3] *IMJ*, Mar. 10, 1876.
[4] Richard Hinton, "The Organization of Labor," *Atlantic Monthly*, XXVII (May, 1871), 545-48. U. S., Senate, *Report . . . upon the Relations between Labor and Capital*, 48th Cong., 1885, II, 41.
[5] *IMJ*, Jan. 10, 1878.
[6] *CMOJ*, Jan. 15, 1882.

and flourished that epidemic of justice and unreason, charity and selfishness known as trades unionism." [7] Journalists, organizers, and co-operators alike accorded the British the esteem they believed was due labor pioneers.

Some American leaders argued that Britain warranted imitation because her labor movement was " the one from which [America's] sprang." [8] It was generally acknowledged that unions established in the United States between the eighteen fifties and the eighties were British models: [9] " We in America are copyists of [England's] past efforts in this phase of human growth and development." [10] As to trade unionism generally, " England has been the teacher of the world," wrote one keen observer at the turn of the century, " and America has been her aptest pupil." [11] " Welcome to Columbia's shores, teachers of our cause," echoed the American Federation of Labor as it greeted two British fraternal delegates in the nineties.[12] American workmen were not blind to the fact that some labor problems in the United States required original treatment; nevertheless there existed a deep conviction that because American unionism derived to some extent from Britain's, events transpiring abroad had relevance in the Republic.

Linked with this belief was the feeling that American workers lagged behind the advances made across the Atlantic— a notion strong among British immigrant leaders but by no means confined to them. This sentiment was partially inspired by certain fuzzy impressions prevalent on both sides of the Atlantic relative to wages and the cost of living, and this in turn gave rise to rule of thumb comparisons between the circumstances of the British and the American workman.[13] Thus, to many persons, American workingmen appeared far less

[7] Charles Barnard, "A Scottish Loaf Factory," *Scribner's Magazine,* XIII (1876-77), 60-62.

[8] U. S., Senate, *Report . . . upon the Relations between Labor and Capital,* 48th Cong., 1885, II, 42.

[9] *Ibid.,* I, 558.

[10] *Fincher's,* Dec. 30, 1866.

[11] Nicholas Gilman, *Methods of Industrial Peace* (Boston: Houghton Mifflin, 1904), p. 19.

[12] *American Federationist,* Dec., 1894.

[13] U. S., Senate, *Report . . . upon the Relations between Labor and Capital,* 48th Cong., 1885, I, 164-67, 557-58, 631-35, 640, 1136-1137, 1163; II, 723-24.

effectual and their unions far less perfect agencies than was the case with labor and labor unions in Britain. England's workingmen, claimed an American newsman in the mid-sixties, " had more steam than we," and would therefore " reach the true goal of civilization before us." [14] In the same vein, Moncure Daniel Conway, an expatriate Virginia divine who spent many years in England, recorded that "America has some distance to journey before she will catch up with the English artisan's dream." [15] Robert Howard testified in 1881 that in terms of philosophy, organization, and achievement British unionism was substantially ahead of American unionism, and from his hardscrabble farm in Michigan, John Francis Bray added that American labor, relative to England's, was still in its infancy.[16] Even Samuel Gompers, who was fiercely proud of American labor, indicated in his correspondence with British trade unionists and socialists in the nineties that their " well drilled " and " disciplined " leaders could teach Americans a great deal.[17] His invitations to socialists, unionists, and, in one curious case, to a British anarchist,[18] to come to the United States and aid in the organizational campaigns of the A.F.L. are adequate proof of this. No one in American labor thought British laborers had reached Nirvana, but the steady accomplishment which Americans were convinced they could detect across the sea contrasted sharply with what were regarded as " fluctuations of American [organizations]." [19]

Since the industrial revolution, hence the rise of a labor movement, came later in the United States than in Britain, assertions that Americans were " behind " England hardly made sense. It is now clear that most American workers, even without the benefits of unions, materially at least, were better off than most types of British labor. But this is the wisdom of

[14] *Boston Evening Voice*, Oct. 17, 1866.

[15] Moncure Daniel Conway, " Sheffield, A Battlefield of English Labor," *Harper's Magazine*, XXXVI (Mar.-Apr.), 600.

[16] U. S., Senate, *Report . . . upon the Relations between Labor and Capital*, 48th Cong., 1885, I, 630; III, 439. For Bray's comments see an unidentified note in Bray Papers. *The Workingman's Advocate*, Mar. 3, 1873; Mar. 14, 1874.

[17] Gompers to John Burns, Feb. 26, 1890, Gompers Coll.

[18] Morgan to Henry Demarest Lloyd, July 6, 1896, Lloyd Papers.

[19] *CMOJ*, July, 1885.

hindsight; inadequate information led many organizers in the United States to claim that their movement was undergoing the same "stages" of development Britain's had years earlier. One American labor journalist in 1881 inquired what difference it made if American labor lagged " forty years behind Britain," was it not " travelling the same road?" [20] Commenting on the forces that shaped the National Labor Union, from the perspective of 1871, Richard Hinton declared that " since the germs [of unionism] were the same as in England, the end will be the same also." [21] A spokesman for the organized iron molders reënforced this thesis in 1878, stating that " the same causes, the same necessities that combines [sic] the molders of England, Ireland, Wales, and Scotland existed in free America, and produced similar results." [22] And as late as 1904 a well-informed student of labor problems wrote of British unionism and its relevance to America: " The history of this development supplies a more substantial foundation for judgement on the present and on the probable future of unionism than the much shorter record it has yet made in the United States. The permanent and essential nature of the movement can be more safely deduced from the conditions and the character of the English trade unions than from those of the American unions." Looking ahead, he added, "In all probability, American trade-unionism will repeat—either fully or with some ' short cuts '—the accomplished phases of English unionism." [23] Out of such a climate of opinion it was almost inevitable that labor leadership in the United States would give credence to the belief that English organizations were " leading the fight " for the liberation of the working classes and that the " workingmen of the United States were bound to follow."

English progress greatly encouraged the American unionist. Even in the labor world nothing succeeded like success. " We Americans," declared the doughty printer and labor journalist,

[20] U. S., Senate, *Report . . . upon the Relations between Labor and Capital*, 48th Cong., 1885, I, 323.
[21] Hinton, *Atlantic Monthly*, XXVII, 557. *IMJ*, May 9, 1879.
[22] *CMOJ*, Sept., 1887. *Fincher's*, Feb. 25, 1865.
[23] Gilman, p. 18.
[24] *CMOJ*, Sept., 1887. *Fincher's*, Feb. 25, 1865.

John Swinton, " have much to learn from the great trade and labor unions of England . . . [they] have worked wonders." " Would to God that such a spirit," he added, " such a purpose and such concord as exists in the British unions were prevalent among the wage earners of our own country." [25] Because British victories gave Americans effective talking points, the gains and losses of British artisans were carefully recorded in the labor press. Pleas for the toleration of unionism, for higher wages, shorter hours, and improved working conditions were buttressed by claims that the more progressive British working-men had secured these things. " The spirit of progress is animating the workingmen of all trades in England more than on this side of the water," proclaimed the Boston *Evening Voice* in 1866; " the struggle for wages continues under efficient and successful organizations." [26] The attenuated struggle for the eight hour day brought out typical comments. Chicago workmen were told at several big rallies in 1866 how a reduction of hours in England had been achieved without a cut in wages. In what it called " The Test for Eight Hours," the New York *Sun* cited how the Staffordshire iron strike of 1865 had resulted in shorter hours,[27] and on the same issue Gompers told an A.F.L. convention in 1889: " In England where there was an apparent adverse vote on the eight hour movement recently immense numbers of working people have made gigantic strides in improving their condition by increasing their wages and reducing the hours of labor within the past few months." Continuing, Gompers declared that the battle cry for eight hours was taken up and " reverberated throughout Great Britain with such earnestness and enthusiasm that [it] will no doubt ensure success and command the admiration of the world." [28] The observations of *The Workingman's Advocate* in 1866 were a sound example of American attitudes towards the gains of British workingmen: " We wish to point

[25] *The American Federationist,* Feb., 1895.
[26] *The Workingman's Advocate,* May 5, 1866.
[27] *Ibid.,* Apr. 21, 1866. *Chicago Post,* Dec. 21, 1865. *Chicago Tribune,* July 22, 1867. *The Workingman's Advocate,* May 11, 1866.
[28] AFL, *Proceedings, President's Report,* 1889, pp. 9-10. British Trades Union Congress. *Parliamentary Committee's Reports and Circulars* (Manchester, England: Manchester Co-operative Printing Society, 1897).

out the singular success with which the working classes [of Britain] have adapted these combinations to their own particular politics and the extraordinary power they have acquired . . . we may add . . . that workingmen all through the country are thus bettering their incomes by 10 or 20 per cent, their positions as householders must have been bettered too, and their trade unions will introduce them to the electoral franchise by an insensible operation of events." [29]

Equally impressive to Americans were labor's legislative advances in Britain, some of which resulted from unionism, some from unionists collaborating with reformers, humanitarians, and intellectuals. "I would be proud to say that the United States was ahead of England in all these [legislative] matters," wrote John Swinton, "but it would be folly so to speak in view of the experiences of both countries during the past few years." [30] English gains in this direction were, in his judgment, "of higher importance than all the labor legislation of our own Congress for the past hundred years." Moreover England was far ahead in its labor laws, in its recognition of the power of organized labor, and in its national attitude towards shorter hours and union rates of wages.[31] In a lecture delivered in the famed Boston Monday Morning Lecture Series, Joseph Cook echoed the same refrain. His views carried some weight in both England and America for reputedly he reached "more than a million readers per week" in the two countries. In any event, while praising Britain he told his listeners:

British factory laws are certainly superior to ours. I need only to invoke the visible presence before this assembly of the lofty spirits of Sir Robert Peel and Lord Shaftesbury to suggest sufficiently the historic perils of congregated labor under the factory system in large towns. Would that in the air above every manufacturing center of New England, Robert Peel and Lord Shaftesbury, colossal and admonitory in archangelic stature, might stand to teach, with one hand pointing toward Old England, and the other stretched as a shield over New England the methods of avoiding here the perils that have arisen there! [32]

---

[29] *The Workingman's Advocate*, May 5, 1866.
[30] Swinton, p. 271.
[31] *Ibid.*
[32] Joseph Cook, *Labor: with Preludes on Current Events* (Boston Monday Morning Lecture Series; Boston: Houghton Mifflin, 1881), pp. 3, 69.

The impassioned Cook continued: "What do I want? The legislation of England, which I hold in my hand provides an efficient board of factory-inspectors," and, he admonished, "you have nothing of this sort in this Commonwealth." [33] Waving an official copy of the Factory Acts he pronounced them "in advance of the best laws passed in America for the prevention of industrial and moral perils," and he thought they ought "to arrest American attention." [34]

The factory acts passed in England after 1833, notably those of 1850, 1867, and 1878, despite serious defects not readily apparent to Americans, became models which most American manufacturing states copied at the insistence of labor and reform elements. American labor leaders like Gompers, Jarrett, Howard, Morgan, and many others,[35] were familiar with the principles embodied in these acts and they fought hard to secure enactment of similar laws in the several states. Massachusetts and New York, both leaders in factory legislation, copied England closely,[36] though as late as the twentieth century they continued to "lag behind" in some respects. So many states or localities followed the lead of Massachusetts and New York, however, that the United States Industrial Commission recommended that the English Acts be adopted uniformly.[37]

Considering the lack of social and industrial legislation in the United States, it is small wonder that other pieces of British labor legislation produced a similar impact. John James and John Hinchcliffe, for instance, borrowed freely from mine legislation in Great Britain to aid them in composing identical types of legislation in Illinois.[38] Miners' leaders did the same thing in Ohio and Pennsylvania. Passage of the Coal Mines Act of 1872 by Parliament solicited widespread attention in

[33] *Ibid.*, p. 112.
[34] *Ibid.*, p. 106.
[35] See the testimony of these men before the Blair Committee in 1885 and the Morgan and Gompers papers.
[36] *Report of the Industrial Commission, Capital and Labor in Manufactures and General Business,* 1901, VII, 222-23, 815, 828. Mass., Bureau of the Statistics of Labor, *6th Annual Report* (1875), pp. 115-42; also see, *14th Annual Report* (1883), pp. 377-401. New Jersey, Bureau of Statistics of Labor and Industry, *12th Annual Report* (1889), pp. 233-303.
[37] *Final Report of the Industrial Commission,* 1902, XIX, 950.
[38] *The Workingman's Advocate,* Feb. 3, 1872; Jan. 17, 1874.

America, especially in Illinois, and Andrew Cameron prevailed upon Alexander Macdonald to mail off a long article on the subject from Glasgow to *The Workingman's Advocate*.[39]

Miners were not alone in looking to England. When Henry White, secretary of the United Garment Workers' Union, sought to bring sweating evils before the public and public officials, he drew heavily upon reports issued by the Select Committee of the House of Lords (1890) on English sweatshops.[40] In general what was true of the factory acts and mining acts was also true of legislation in the realm of social insurance, of the Employers' Liability Acts of 1880 and 1896. American labor copied both of these laws. For example, when the British abrogated the legal doctrine of common employment which had been on the statute books since 1837 (Priestly v. Fowler, 3 Meeson and Welsby, I, 6 England) and which had been followed as a precedent in American courts for many years, labor and reform groups pressured the states into making parallel changes. Thus "Alabama followed England in 1885 and Massachusetts in 1887," [41] and New York, learning from the experiences of the Royal Commission in enforcing liability laws, sought to put into operation a law based on " the character of the English Act of 1897." [42] Such a British-model law was actually passed in 1910. American courts, of course, kept abreast of developments and interpretations in British labor law; when the English held that workingmen could refuse to labor with those to whom they objected (Allen v. Flood), several American state courts followed suit.[43] It is reasonable to say that almost every major legislative or legal advance made by British working people was widely discussed and often duplicated or imitated in the chief industrial states of America.

British economic thought also filtered into the ranks of labor, and labor leaders occasionally read directly in the latest British

---

[39] *Ibid.*, Aug. 24, 1872.

[40] *Report of the Industrial Commission. Capital and Labor in Manufactures and General Business*, 1901, VII, 182-201.

[41] *Ibid.*, p. 816. John R. Commons and John Andrews, *Principles of Labor Legislation* (New York: Harpers & Brothers, 1920), Chap. 8.

[42] *Report of the Industrial Commission, Capital and Labor in Manufactures and General Business*, 1901, VII, 816.

[43] *Final Report of the Industrial Commission*, 1902, XIX, 814.

treatises. For some men, such readings were a continuation of early training or study in classical economics. Thomas J. Morgan, for instance, began his readings with Smith, Malthus, Ricardo, and snatches from classical economists, shifting later to John Stuart Mill, Thornton, Cairnes, and other of the so-called " transitional " economists.[44] Though we can never be sure of just what he actually did read, Gompers claimed to have rummaged widely in the general economic literature coming out of England.[45] The opinions of Henry Fawcett and Thorold Rogers, in addition to the men listed above, were cited frequently in the labor press, often to support the arguments of American workingmen in specific controversies. Of all the English political economists John Stuart Mill was undoubtedly the most widely respected among thoughtful American laborers; his views were frequently quoted. Ira Stewart, Richard Trevellick, Andrew Cameron, and others used his name so freely in labor speeches or writings that it appears it had wide currency among workers.[46] The precise effect of these thinkers and their ideas is impossible to tell, but workingmen were hardly interested in them for purely meditative reasons.

Faced with a critical shortage of data and statistics, American labor imported this vital ammunition from the accumulated reserves of the British working class. The value of this material can scarcely be overestimated; often trade union programs or negotiations suffered from a dearth of information. Especially was this the case until the establishment in the late seventies and in the eighties of state bureaus of industrial and labor statistics. Prior to those years, Americans gleaned what they could from abroad. During the Civil War, for instance, Jonathan Fincher seized upon the annual statement of an English amalgamated union, declaring, " This report should

[44] "Autobiography," pp. 1-5, Morgan Papers, Folder 1. Also see the rough draft of an address by Morgan dated Apr. 14, 1895 on " Wages," in Folder 9. and a group of pamphlets written by Henry Demarest Lloyd also in Folder 9.

[45] Interview with Miss Florence Thorne, A. F. of L. Research Director, March, 1951.

[46] See the Ms on " Social Reform," Samuel Papers, Box 3. *The Workingman's Advocate*, May 29, 1866; Oct. 31, 1868, and Aug. 25, Sept. 8, 1866; Nov. 7, 1868; Apr. 15, 1871; July 29, 1871. *IMJ*, Apr. 30, 1874. *CMOJ*, Feb. 1872; Nov., 1876; Jan., 1885. Commons, *Documentary History*, IX, 289-90, 294, 324. Barns, pp. 201-203, 231.

find its way to every trade union in America, that the statistical and practical information furnished therein may be employed in perfecting our preliminary steps in the work of organization." Fincher believed this intelligence to be vital to the progress of union welfare programs: " One thing is assured," he wrote; " we must have more reliable statistical information upon the various causes for benefits throughout the country, than at the moment are possessed by any organization in America, before we would dare venture upon so broad a plan of benefits." [47]

Through the sixties and seventies labor newspapers and journals constantly carried the latest figures published by British trade unions, or by Royal Commissions dealing with labor problems,[48] and labor leaders borrowed what they could from friends overseas. Powderly, for example, called upon Albert Denny, his representative in England during the eighties, " to favor me with such literature as you may come across " [49] on a variety of matters ranging from studies of co-operatives to postal savings programs for workingmen, while at the solicitation of the A.F.L., England's Henry Broadhurst agreed to render " any assistance he could . . . in the interchange of documents of mutual interest." [50] The Gompers Collection, indeed, indicates that Broadhurst and other British leaders sent over considerable amounts of valuable information. Gompers often called for special articles, studies, strike statistics, information about the Trades Union Congresses, even for reports " on whether there had been an increase of drinking among English dockers." [51] Likewise, Thomas J. Morgan made frequent use of British statistics and, as the critical Denver Convention of 1894 approached, he wired his friend Henry Demarest Lloyd to send him the latest information compiled by the Trades Union Congress.[52] Testimony given by labor

---

[47] *Fincher's,* Dec. 12, 1863. New York, Department of Labor, *16th Annual Report* (1900), p. 62.

[48] *The Workingman's Advocate,* May 5, 19; July 28, 1866; Aug. 10, 17, Sept. 21, 28; Nov. 2, 9; Dec. 7, 1867; Sept. 5, 1868; Jan. 1, 1870; May 13; June 10, 1871. *IMJ,* Feb. 28, 1873; Aug. 1875. *CMOJ,* July, 1885.

[49] Powderly to Albert Denny, Nov. 18, 1884; Jan. 12, 1885, Powderly Papers.

[50] AFL, *Proceedings, President's Report,* 1887, p. 10.

[51] Gompers to Mann, Apr. 30, 1894; Gompers to Burns, June 17, 1890; Gompers to Tillett, Aug. 20, 1895, Gompers Coll.

[52] Morgan to Henry Demarest Lloyd, Sept. 8, 1894, Night Message, Lloyd Papers.

leaders to the Senate Committee on education and labor in 1885 clearly indicates that a heavy reliance was placed upon British data to substantiate important points. Even as late as 1900, despite the advances Americans had made themselves, British sources were still important. " We are not yet in the possession of American trade union statistics covering a sufficiently long period to fully show the evil effects of the neglect to establish high dues and proper benefits, but we have at our disposal perfectly reliable figures furnished by our British trade union brothers which fully sustain our contention," [53] wrote one American at the time. Labor did not doubt the righteousness of its cause, but as the desire to be scientific grew, it used British statistics to help prove the soundness of its views.

Americans often invoked examples of British progress to prod their own men into creating organizations and passing legislation favorable to labor's cause. This was done by implying that the British were " less under the thumb of capital " than Americans. With bitter sarcasm the *Iron Molders' Journal* commented on how keenly some Americans felt themselves discriminated against: " Let British statesmen," it suggested, " question some of the Fall River mill operatives who returned to England last spring about the blessings enjoyed by mill operatives in republican America . . . then perhaps they will change their former opinions about the success and stability of republican institutions." [54] A year later the editor's views were unchanged and he issued another blast designed not so much for British as for American consumption: " The factory system of England in its worst days never equalled in atrocity the system in full force in New England today." [55] Good times or bad, American organizers tirelessly recounted stories of British strides towards influence and self-respect, and while their tales were largely hortatory, there is no reason to doubt that they believed in what they said. Writing about the Knights

[53] *American Federationist*, Jan. 1900. U. S., Senate, *Report . . . upon the Relations between Labor and Capital*, 48th Cong., 1885, I, 53-54, 164-67, 557-58, 631, 635, 673-76, 1137, 1163; II, 540, 723-24. *Final Report of the Industrial Commission*, 1902, XIX, 792, 865, 870, for examples.

[54] *IMJ*, July 10, 1875.

[55] *Ibid*., May, 1876.

of Labor in 1888, a careful American observer fairly summarized the attitudes of American labor leaders:

It is now . . . sixty years since combinations of workingmen to influence
the hours and conditions of labor or rates and terms of remuneration
were first made lawful in England. Beginning their operations amid
the distrust of the community, under the ban of the economists and
against the stern opposition of the employing class, trade unions have
made their way to general acceptance. . . . Trade unions have borne
an important part in the industrial, social, and political elevation of
the English people. Nothing less than . . . the fierce revolts which
followed the repeal of the Combination Acts of 1824-5 could have
lifted the operative class out of the horrible pits and miry clay . . .
by no shocks less rude and violent could the degraded masses have been
roused from . . . lethargy . . . [and] apathy which hopeless poverty
. . . had engendered. No succession of individual efforts would have
sufficed to create in the factory population . . . that calm, steadfast,
self-assertion which are transforming the English squirearchy into a
true democracy. Even to the present moment I for one believe . . .
that the . . . conscious efforts of the working classes of that country
through organizations by themselves created, sustained, and administered . . . have continued to be the *greatest educational force in English
life,* have done more to raise the general level of character, conduct, and
political capability throughout the Kingdom than any other agency.[56]

Imbued with such sentiments labor leaders excoriated their
fellow workingmen for their lack of courage and their failure
to fight for the substance of freedom. They tended to ignore
the fact that a gradual improvement in the worker's lot, coupled
with a host of individualistic beliefs which were vestiges of an
agrarian society, robbed the examples of British success of some
of their potency. Nevertheless, if unorganized men gave the
impression of knowing their own interests best, ranking labor
leaders discovered in Britain the epitome of progress. Across
the sea unions had raised wages and cut hours; they were stable
and well financed, compact and efficient. Through political
action they had secured mine, factory, and social legislation,
and after the seventies they were electing their own representatives to Parliament. Oversimplified and distorted, this, nonetheless, was the picture that was guilelessly presented to
American workers; and there was more.

Revelation of the moderate, middle class character of English

[56] Walker, *Princeton Review,* VI, 199.

trade unionism was certainly instrumental in modifying American conceptions that unions existed primarily to conduct strikes or to engage in anti-social activities. And this was extremely important, for American workingmen feared strikes and violence. Moreover, these fears had a basis in fact, for American labor was caught up in a tragic paradox; hating strikes and violence, it suffered greatly from both. Americans engaged in more strikes than workers anywhere else in the world; between 1881 and 1900, 33.6 persons per thousand in industries subject to strike were actually on strike each year. In Britain the corresponding proportion was 27.6 persons per thousand. Americans, furthermore, emerged unvictorious more frequently than workers elsewhere. To be sure, about 35 per cent of their strikes—which compared favorably with the British figure of 37 per cent—were completely successful. But only 16 per cent of American strikes were partially successful, compared to about 33 per cent for Britain. More ominously still, about 48 per cent of the strikes in America were entirely unsuccessful, against only 29 per cent in Great Britain.[57] American workers were taking a drubbing and they knew it. Consequently, until it was clear that unions could achieve their goals without resorting to what were considered reprehensible methods, many workingmen preferred to take their chances with capital alone. Examples of British unionism, therefore, paved the way for a general re-education of sceptical Americans; this educational process was a long term affair, as is all social change, but its importance was very great.

Few factors were of greater value in establishing confidence in trade unions, their methods, and their goals—either in England or the United States—than the work of the Royal Commission on Trade Unions instituted in February 1867. Growing out of investigations into a gunpowder explosion, rattening, and other alleged "outrages" in Sheffield, the Commission began its work largely at the insistence of Robert

---

[57] *Final Report of the Industrial Commission*, 1902, XIX, 865, 870. *IMJ*, Feb. 28, 1874; Apr. 10; Mar. 10, 1875. *CMOJ*, Apr. 15, 1882. *The Workingman's Advocate*, Feb. 3, 1871; Mar. 9, 1872; Sept. 28, 1872; July 25, 1874. U. S., Senate, *Report . . . upon the Relations between Labor and Capital*, 48th Cong., 1885, II, 538-40, 563-64. Swinton, pp. 269-75. Mitchell, pp. 44-46, 49-50, 106-107, 109, 161, 219, 272.

Applegarth, secretary of the Amalgamated Society of Carpenters and Joiners, and fellow unionists who were anxious to clear their unions of any implication in these crimes. Once under way the Commission's investigation provided both labor and capital with a public battleground. In several instances labor found itself very much on the spot. Nevertheless, the brilliant counter-attacks of its intellectual allies, notably the positivist Frederic Harrison and the M.P. Thomas Hughes, and the bungled tactics of the employers' representatives resulted in a vindication of conservative unionism. British unions won a vote of confidence from the nation at large and from many in the governing class. The *Times* declared, after the release of the Commission's findings, that " true statesmanship will neither seek to augment nor reduce [trade union] influence, but accepting it as a fact will give it free scope for legitimate development." [58] Some capitalists at least were similarly impressed, especially by the picture of union leaders serving as restraints upon rambunctious workers. Thomas Brassey, for instance, son of a contractor, placed himself squarely behind the unions in this respect, asserting that they exercised a benign influence on workingmen,[59] and there were many others who clearly agreed with him.

The Commission's Minutes of Evidence were celebrated news in the American labor press. Cameron's highly respected *Workingman's Advocate* featured lengthy excerpts from the minutes, as well as from the Majority and Minority Reports, in nearly every edition for two years. For months the testimony was front page news, getting half and sometimes full page coverage. The anatomy of unionism, its leadership, resources, structure, methods, achievements and deficiencies were all bared to public scrutiny.[60] The testimony of Alexander Macdonald, George Odger, Daniel Guile, the comments and articles drawn from men such as Frederic Harrison and Professor Beesly, proved to be of special interest to the labor journals and workingmen.[61] All told, the Commission's reports and the

[58] *Times* (London), July 8, 1869.          [59] *IMJ*, Nov. 10, 1877.
[60] *The Workingman's Advocate*, Aug. 10, 17; Sept. 21 28; Oct. 5, 9; Nov. 9, 16, 23, 1867.
[61] *CMOJ*, Nov., 1883; Jan., 1885; and July, 1879. Thomas Hughes,

debates they evoked pro and con about unionism can only be regarded as a first-rate liberal education for those numerous persons who followed them. Cameron accurately assessed their impact: " Messers Allen [leader of the Amalgamated Society of Engineers] and Applegarth . . . have rendered a valuable service to the trade unionists both of England and America by giving the most succinct exposition of their aims and objects —a service which we feel will yield its fruit despite all legislation to the contrary." [62]

In the years succeeding the Commission's investigations, American laborers received further reassurances about the acts and purposes of trade unions. In New England the granite cutters were told by their leaders that after all the hue and cry about the pernicious effects of unions in Britain, it was shown that only 6 per cent of the British trades unions' expenditures went into the support of strikes.[63] In much the same vein, E. L. Godkin's liberal paper *The Nation*, which on several previous occasions had suggested that Americans model their labor movement after Britain's, cited statistics published by Frederic Harrison indicating that the most powerful unions channeled 99 per cent of their funds into benefit programs rather than into industrial warfare.[64] Likewise the U. S. Industrial Commission of 1902 reported that " during recent years . . . 95 per cent of all changes in wages in Great Britain have taken place as the result of negotiations between employers and employes or as the result of arbitration and without strikes or lockouts." [65] Certainly the moderation of the Trades Union Congresses did nothing to discourage these views and those who wondered whether labor was abusing its new-found strength could find solace in a report by the *Nation*:

---

" Trade Unionism in England," *Century Magazine*, VI (January, 1884), 127-34. Thomas Hughes, " Trade Unionism in England." *Scribner's Magazine*, XXVIII (January, 1884), 127. Thomas Hughes, " Working Classes in Europe," *Atlas Essays: Labor and The Republic* (New York: A. S. Barnes & Co., 1878). Justin McCarthy, " Some English Workingmen," *Atlantic Monthly*, XXVI (Oct., 1870), 458-63.

[62] *The Workingman's Advocate*, Feb. 22, 1868.

[63] *GCJ*, Nov., 1882.

[64] *The Nation*, Oct. 4, 1883.

[65] *Final Report of the Industrial Commission*, 1902, XIX, 863-64.

To such fears the Congress which has just brought its sittings to a close supplies the best antidote. Not that the alarmist will not find a program . . . distasteful to him, but that if he be fair-minded, he will recognize that it is put forward by men who so far from constituting a class apart, form an integral part of the community, share its feelings and common interests and have the same differences of opinion among themselves as any other class. If he has heard much of the Socialists of the Continent or of the doctrines of the ' Internationale ' and expects to find furious denunciations of religion, marriage, and private property he will be greatly surprised. The program contains nothing so exciting. The Congress is . . . a business meeting where the special trade interests of the workmen are treated in a practical commonsense manner. . . . Throughout its proceedings there reigned a spirit . . . absolutely the reverse of anything that can be called revolutionary.[66]

This theme was reiterated in various ways. Care was taken to underscore the emergence of respectable leaders among workingmen and the fact that disreputable elements had been placed under a ban. One view in 1887 was that British unions were " led by men of the highest character and judgement," [67] while another source reported at about the same time that the training and discipline exercised in British unions made them " much more successful, reasonable, and intelligent than similar unions in the United States." [68] Americans were informed by the pro-labor New York *Tribune* that when they resorted to strikes and violence they were " blindly adopting the abandoned weapons of their English brethren," [69] and even after the uprisings of the unskilled and the re-emergence of socialism in Britain, John Swinton explained that while there were " plenty of labor strikes in England . . . only about the same number of men were concerned in the whole of them as were concerned in our own great strikes in the first half of the year 1894." [70]

Slowly but surely the main point got across: the more successfully unions were organized and able to carry on their work, " the more harmonious their relations " with employers,

---

[66] *The Nation*, Oct. 6, 1881.

[67] *Public Opinion*, III (1887), 13. Richard Hinton, " Trade Unions and Co-operation," *Old and New*, III (Jan., 1875), 69-75. U. S., Senate, *Report . . . upon the Relations between Labor and Capital*, 48th Cong., 1885, III, 439.

[68] *Public Opinion*, III (1887), 13.

[69] *New York Tribune*, Oct. 25, 1870.

[70] Swinton, p. 272. U. S., Senate, *Report . . . upon the Relations between Labor and Capital*, 48th Cong., 1885, II, 456-57.

the less likely it became anyone would start hasty, violent, or unlawful action. Stable unionism, in other words, was capable of making real contributions to workingmen and to the community.

## II. INDUSTRIAL WAR AND PEACE

George Howells of the London Junta once said of industrial warfare: "The whole question lies in a nutshell. Is brute force better than reason? If it be then a costermonger may be a greater personage than a philosopher, and Tom Sayers might have been considered superior to John Stuart Mill." [71] Increasingly this logic won favor with American laborers and their leadership. There was, to be sure, opposition to newfangled proposals for the settlement of industrial disputes. Jonathan Fincher denounced "arbitration between capital and labor" as "a humbug, a delusion, a snare;" if it had failed in England, as he thought it had, it was even "less possible" in the United States.[72] Fincher was partly right for the early industrial boards established in England between 1856 and 1860 had proven unsatisfactory. However, as the frequency of strikes and violence in the United States grew, so also did the numbers of those searching for industrial peace. Too many strikers found themselves on the losing side; too many employers suffered from the disruption of production; too many innocents like Isaiah Sanderson, a Scotsman working in a Massachusetts mill, were caught between two fires:

What I know about the strike is this: In the first place they took ten cents out of the dollar and the spinners didn't want to stand it. . . . I said I had no objections to work if the thing was settled. . . . The second night I worked in the mill there was a great crowd. . . . The superintendent wanted us not to go in the crowd. . . . I told him we might just as well get what we had to take. . . . Going through the crowd the stones began to come; the rocks just as hard as they could. Finally a few steps further I got kicked, and knocked down and beat; my eyes bunged up, my body kicked and my head and every bit of me. . . .[73]

---

[71] Nebraska, Bureau of Labor and Industrial Statistics, *1st Biennial Report* (1887-88), p. 132.

[72] *Fincher's,* Apr. 22; May 21; June 10; July 15, 1865.

[73] Mass., Bureau of Statistics of Labor, *1st Annual Report* (1870-71), p. 57.

Fortunately as individual Americans, like Sanderson, began to feel the costliness of strikes in the post-war years, arbitration boards were already functioning in Britain and were readily available for study. Revamped and fully operative, these boards were popularly identified with the work of "two great preachers of arbitration, A. J. Mundella and Rupert Kettle,"[74] yet they had an earlier history in England and in France.[75] In fact, only by drawing on French precedents like the Conseil des Prudhommes, on an English statute enacted in 1824, and on the ideas of William Falkin, a student of arbitration, did A. J. Mundella devise his own method of settling controversies. Mundella, a Nottingham capitalist but a lifelong friend of labor, established the first permanent boards of arbitration and conciliation in the English glove and hosiery trade in 1860. Having brought some peace to the industry, they served as prototypes for boards in different trades, and, as Mundella anticipated, they curtailed a rising tide of unrest, at least for a time.[76] There were two especially striking features about the English boards that were to have their appeal in America: first, arbitration remained, until the First World War, a voluntary affair into which contending parties entered of their own volition; and second, the boards enlisted the aid of umpires of considerable prestige and detachment, men like Thomas Brassey, Joseph Chamberlain, Thomas Hughes, and Sir Rupert Kettle.[77]

The British boards, as we have seen, immediately stirred discussion in America, and while they were initially given a chill

[74] Wisconsin, Bureau of Labor and Industrial Statistics, *2nd Biennial Report* (1885-86), p. 391. *Report of the Industrial Commission, Labor Organizations . . . Railway Labor*, 1901, XVII, 470. "Arbitration" was construed broadly and could mean conciliation, mediation, or even collective bargaining to late nineteenth century American labor leaders. *The Workingman's Advocate*, May 12, 1866; Aug. 31, 1867; Nov. 7, 1868.

[75] Richard Ely, "Arbitration," *North American Review*, CXLIII (Jan.-July, 1886), 321-22.

[76] W. H. G. Armytage, *A. J. Mundella* (London: Benn, 1951), pp. 32-34, 102-104.

[77] S. N. D. North, "Industrial Arbitration," *Quarterly Journal of Economics*, X (July, 1895), 407, 429-30. Barns, p. 243. Pennsylvania, Legislative Document, *Report on the Practical Operation of Arbitration and Conciliation . . . in England*, II (1878-79), no. 8.

reception by men like Fincher, they soon found a warmer welcome amid post-war readjustment. By 1866 even the *Workingman's Advocate* was taking a more judicious view of them. After the spring of 1866, in fact, favorable comments appeared often and it became apparent that the Mundella Plan as it operated in Nottingham was finding friends. Developments in Sheffield, "the battlefield of labor," warranted the scrutiny of every American, declared one influential labor paper, and it and other journals as well went on in frequent reports to describe the working methods of the British boards, including those of Judge Kettle in Wolverhampton and Coventry. From every important angle the strengths and weaknesses of the English system were explored and commented on.[78]

Direct impetus was given to the advertisement of arbitration when, early in September 1870, Thomas Hughes and A. J. Mundella travelled to the United States. Long recognized as friends of unionism, they required little introduction to organized workingmen. Basically both men came to America for the same reason; as Mundella put it, they hoped to acquaint themselves "with features of the American social and political scene bearing upon questions in agitation in Great Britain with a view to proximate legislation." [79] However, if they came to borrow, they returned home leaving American workers well compensated for the information they took with them. .

Actually, the Englishmen met with some of the most distinguished persons in the land—Emerson, Lowell, Sumner, Wendell Phillips, Goldwin Smith, David Wells,[80] and many high officials—and they spent little time hobnobbing with mechanics. Therefore the speeches of greatest interest to workers came in October and November 1870, as the two

[78] *The Workingman's Advocate,* Apr. 21; May 5; Sept. 1, 1866; Dec. 28 1867; Jan. 25; June 6; Aug. 15, 1868; Aug. 7; Sept. 25; Nov. 27; Sept. 10-17, 1869. *IMJ,* Apr. 20; Sept. 30, 1873; Apr. 10, 1875; Mar. 10, 1876. *CMOJ,* May, 1876. U. S., Senate, *Report . . . upon the Relations between Labor and Capital,* 48th Cong., 1885, I, 346, 1124, 1150; II, 460, 639; III, 513, 573.

[79] Armytage, p. 85. Chapter 5 deals with Mundella's American trip.

[80] Wells was economic advisor in several administrations and probably influenced Cleveland's views on arbitration. James Richardson, *A Compilation of the Messages and Papers of the Presidents* (Washington: U. S. Government Printing Office, 1896), Vol. VIII, pp. 394, 526.

travellers prepared to sail home. At that time, Hughes, who was reportedly feted in Boston as no other Englishman except John Bright would have been, journeyed from Boston to New York where at Cooper Union Hall he lectured before a packed gathering, mainly of workingmen, on " Work and Wealth." Much of the lecture was a recapitulation of British labor history, of how the amalgamated unions had helped diminish the incidence of strikes, and of the ways unionism had been led into peaceful channels. To his audience he suggested that moderation, peaceful progress, and co-operation offered labor its best hope for the future and he closed by inquiring: " Have you nothing to learn from the Old Country in this matter? " The talk was well received and, because it described Hughes' personal experience with arbitration, among other things, and paid tribute to Mundella (who was supposedly in the hall) it paved the way for the latter's subsequent farewell.[81]

Mundella's reception at Cooper Union Hall came two days before he left for home in mid-November. It was fully as enthusiastic as Hughes'. Presiding over the gathering of notables and laboring men was Abram S. Hewitt, the iron master, a man of broad interests and experience. The Englishman spoke as an expert on " Strikes, Arbitration, and the Civil Service of Great Britain." He explained how industrial peace had been cultivated in England, dealt with the impact of the reforms of 1867, touched briefly on co-operation, and then launched into an explanation of arbitration. That this was a great step forward he had no doubt; scarcely a trade union in England, he informed his listeners, had failed to champion the creation of boards of arbitration like those he had founded and experimented with at Nottingham. The Amalgamated Society of Engineers favored the idea and the Carpenters and Joiners, according to his estimate, maintained between twenty and thirty boards. Fairly into his subject, he devoted the balance of the lecture to further descriptions and appraisals of industrial peace, and the Civil Service.

The speech received wider circulation than it perhaps deserved because it irritated some of the labor leaders present

---

[81] *New York Tribune,* Oct. 25, 1870.

and provoked a great deal of discussion. In the liberal tradition, Mundella had announced that while he was much in
favor of unions, he believed "every man has a right to decide
for himself whether he will or will not be a member of a trade
organization." [82] Merely in passing he had touched upon a
very delicate matter indeed. Samuel Gompers, then a youngster,
attended the speech to keep abreast of the latest British labor
developments, but on this score he wholeheartedly disapproved
of Mundella's views. Nevertheless, he frankly confessed that
the Englishman's remark had inspired him to re-examine trade
union functions.[83] Taking note of these outcries, the London
*Times* reported that Mundella's talk had been universally
condemned; several critics simply pointed out that the speaker's
stand had made it hard to tell whether he was for or against
labor. Some of the criticisms, coming from people who had
done little to aid labor, carried no weight; others were ridicu-
lous distortions of the speaker's ideas.[84] Nonetheless, the
publicity attendant upon the lecture did the cause of arbitration no harm.

Within a short time, in fact, the lecture was accepted as a
step toward industrial peace, though this interpretation was
certainly over-sanguine. The most widely circulated of the
labor newspapers declared frankly that the Hughes-Mundella
talks "attracted a deal of attention among a large class of our
citizens who are anxious that Co-operation and Arbitration
should have as fair a test in America as they have had in Great
Britain, believing that equally beneficial results will follow
from their adoption in the New World as has already crowned
their efforts in the Old." The New York *Tribune*, perhaps
the most influential liberal paper in the United States, praised
both Hughes and Mundella for their work and their words.
An editorial penned shortly after Mundella's appearance at
Cooper Union left no doubt about the construction placed upon
the remarks of either man:

Two of the most memorable lectures ever addressed to the workingmen

---

[82] *New York Tribune*, Nov. 18, 1870.
[83] Gompers, I, 49-50.
[84] *Times* (London), Dec. 8, 15, 1870. *The Workingman's Advocate*, Dec. 17, 1870.

in this country have lately been delivered to great audiences in this city composed of our largest employing manufacturers and the best representatives of the laboring class, by members of the British Parliament. These two gentlemen . . . unite in making the same declaration of the superiority to our own of the English system of Trades Unions and in tendering the same advice regarding Co-operation and Arbitration to the manufacturers and artisans of this country. Advice from these distinctive, disinterested, and high authorities ought not to fall unheard on the ears of American workmen. We commend now to all workingmen this admonition [against strikes and violence] from one of their trusted friends abroad.[85]

In succeeding years Mundella's suggestions merited wide acclaim. Indirectly the amicable settlement of the Alabama Claims issue, which some laboring men feared would lead to war, lent additional force to his ideas.[86] Only a few years after the Cooper Union address labor leaders were urging arbitration upon employers as well as on the rank and file of the unions. John Siney, who was familiar with Mundella's boards of arbitration before the Englishman's New York lectures, told his anthracite miners in September 1870, " We earnestly wish that the troubles which have formerly prevailed here would cease." Encouraged by Britain's example, he felt that the miners had little to lose and much to gain by giving the principles of arbitration a chance.[87] " In England," he declared, " I can say with assurance this plan has been successful and I see no grounds for doubting the same results from an earnest and sincere application of it here." [88]

The principles of peaceful settlement were soon tested in Siney's own bailiwick when a group of miners struck under his direction in the anthracite fields of Eastern Pennsylvania. While they were idle, plans for settlement were advanced by private mine operator Eckley B. Coxe, of Drifton, Pennsylvania. Coxe read a paper before the Social Science Association's Philadelphia branch in the winter of 1870-71 dealing with arbitration abroad. He followed this up with a series of

---

[85] *New York Tribune,* Nov. 18, 1870. *The Vulcan Record,* I (1870), no. 6.
[86] McNeill, p. 229. *The Workingman's Advocate,* Jan. 14, 1871. *IMJ,* Sept. 30, 1873.
[87] *The Workingman's Advocate,* Sept. 10-17, 1870.
[88] *The Miners' National Record,* Nov. 14, 1875.

letters to Siney's official news organ, the *Anthracite Monitor*, in hopes that they would encourage the contesting parties to imitate the British and arbitrate. Coxe's general views, in fact, were broadly summarized in another paper which he wrote on the labor problem in 1871:

. . . the same ideas are floating far and wide; the same seeds are scattered by every wind over sea and shore, and if blood is shed one day in Paris, it is shed another at Scranton; if English women and children starve while their husbands and fathers strike, so do Americans; if the working classes are all in angry motion throughout Europe, they are not contented or pacific in the United States.

Co-operation, trade unionism, arbitration, and industrial partnership were his proposed solutions.[89] Coxe's persuasiveness, four months of a struggle of attrition, and the good offices of Judge William Elwell led to the selection of five arbitrators to represent the miners and an equal number to represent the employers; early in 1871 these men met at Mauch Chunk, Pennsylvania. The miners initially refused to permit Elwell to render any decisions about wages, though they were willing to let him determine conditions of employment. Somewhat later in the negotiations, however, they submitted to adjustment of the sliding scale upon which wages in the industry were then based.[90] More informal than the Mundella boards, the Mauch Chunk conference was an historic occasion; it kept a turbulent industry relatively peaceful for the next four years, left the Siney unionists a real power in the coal fields, and most significantly of all, represented what was certainly one of the earliest collective bargaining sessions in American industry.

[89] Eckley B. Coxe, " Relief of Labor," *Journal of Social Sciences: Transactions* (1871), no. 4, p. 133. The Coxe Family was one of the most important of the " independents " in the anthracite mining industry. It was not always as liberal as this in later years. Also see Roy, p. 92. Pa., Bureau of Industrial Statistics, *9th Annual Report* (1880-81), IX, 295-97. *Report of the Industrial Commission, Labor Organizations . . . Railway Labor,* 1901, XVII, 325-26. Kildeen, p. 167. Evans, I, 34-35.

[90] Pa., Bureau of Industrial Statistics, *9th Annual Report* (1880-81), IX, 295-97. Arthur E. Suffern, *The Coal Miner's Struggle for Industrial Status* (New York: Macmillan Co., 1926), pp. 18-31. Clarence E. Bonnett, *History of Employers' Associations in the United States* (New York: Vantage Press, 1956), pp. 96-97, 118. .Kildeen, p. 167. Evans, I, 34-35.

Mundella's ideas also took root among workmen and employers in New England. Testimony of British immigrants before a Massachusetts labor commission, for instance, clearly indicates how deeply arbitration had impressed them while they were laboring in Britain, and how its general concepts had been brought with them to the United States.[91]

Elsewhere, nearly every major trade union leader showed some understanding of the practices used abroad to effect settlements. Samuel Gompers, Robert Howard, John Siney, John James, James Pollock, Hugh McLaughlin, William Sylvis, Richard Griffiths, Terence Powderly and many others spoke favorably of Mundella's work or of other systems of peaceful settlement that had been experimented with in Britain.[92] John Jarrett spoke for many men when he testified that " arbitration and conciliation are bringing employers and working men closer together all the time in England and we need to adopt methods here whereby employers and men will be brought closer together." [93] The cigarmakers felt that " the trade unions of Great Britain teach many lessons, one of which is that strikes may be averted by arbitration." *The Workingman's Advocate*, especially after 1868, began giving details of how the Mundella and Kettle plans actually worked, and the iron molders learned that arbitration had become " an established principle " on the other side of the Atlantic, one they ought to consider using.[94]

Labor's sympathizers and allies were especially exuberant about arbitration. R. Heber Newton, the Episcopal divine of New York, thought it was " proving to be the missing coupling between Capital and Labor in England and France," and he

[91] Mass., Bureau of the Statistics of Labor, *2nd Annual Report* (1871), pp. 136, 143, 148.

[92] S. M. Jelley, *The Voice of Labor* (Philadelphia: H. J. Smith & Co., 1891), p. 244. U. S., Senate, *Report . . . upon the Relations between Labor and Capital*, 48th Cong., 1885, I, 5, 10, 16, 22, 85-88, 139, 209, 245, 377, 404. *Report of the Industrial Commission, Labor Organizations . . . Railway Labor*, 1901, XVII, 695-96. Hicks, Chap. 6.

[93] U. S., Senate, *Report . . . upon the Relations between Labor and Capital*, 48th Cong., 1885, I, 1124.

[94] *CMOJ*, May, 1876. *The Workingman's Advocate*, Jan. 25; June 6; Aug. 15, 1868. *IMJ*, Apr., 1873; Apr. 10, 1875; May 10, 1876; Aug., 1879.

exhorted Americans to turn to it.[95] Professor Edwin R. A. Seligman announced that there " can be no doubt that the system of arbitration and conciliation, as initiated by Mundella and Kettle, is susceptible of immense development in the future." [96] Another friendly observer enthusiastically declared that arbitration " is already becoming a substitute for strikes in England where the trade unions are adopting this new weapon," [97] and Justice T. M. Cooley, writing amid the uprisings of 1886, summarized what many people were thinking about English arbitration. " Especially," wrote the Justice, " should the experience of England be valuable, the government and habits of thought, of action among the people of that country resembling our own. Statutory tribunals may be established with such compulsory powers as would be admissible in free government. Such tribunals have been provided for in England . . . [although] they are not resorted to. . . . The tribunal most likely to be of value would be one established by the parties themselves. . . . Tribunals of this sort are found exceedingly valuable in England and their use has steadily increased with best results." [98] Implicit in all these remarks was the tacit assumption that capital and labor were primarily moderate in outlook, that there was no irreconcilable difference between them.

Yet while many unionists favored peaceful procedures they also recognized the stubborn problems of applying them or getting them to work under uniquely American conditions. English methods flourished under circumstances that had little validity in the United States, namely, the existence of powerful cohesive unions capable of exercising a degree of countervailing power, a strong sense of responsibility among the conflicting parties, impartial umpires, and sound governmental legislation. Thus while supporting arbitration in principle, Andrew Cameron demurred on these very points and, in fact,

[95] Barns, p. 147.
[96] *Ibid.*, p. 54.
[97] U. S., Senate, *Report . . . upon the Relations between Labor and Capital,* 48th Cong., 1885, II, 539.
[98] T. M. Cooley, "Arbitration in Labor Disputes," *Forum,* I (June, 1886). pp. 310-11.

he soon became an advocate of compulsory arbitration.[99] Similarly, Hugh McLaughlin, leader of the Sons of Vulcan, publicly announced that his organization was "ready and willing" to accept arbitration but he charged that employers consistently rejected the idea.[100] Obviously, successful negotiations were largely contingent on both parties wielding considerable power which in turn commanded respect. Richard Ely, a keen student of labor who was fully sensible of this, argued that the opportunities for industrial peace would increase markedly as trade unions gained in strength.[101] Union leaders, unfortunately, were often unable to discipline their men long enough to confront capital with sufficient power to command respect. In the anthracite fields, for instance, Siney's agreements about a sliding scale and the peaceful resolution of differences were wrecked in part by the rank and file unionists in 1874-5. Siney proved unable to persuade them that the course of wisdom lay in caution or that the bread lines were not the fault of their employers but were due rather to more general economic circumstances, hence the men tossed over their agreement, struck, and left Siney discredited and martyred.[102] Ironically, too, workingmen believed that they had taken most of the initiative in seeking arbitration, therefore, when they were rebuffed on account of their weakness they were more bitter than ever. Yet weakness, by and large, was something they alone could effectively remedy. It was altogether too much to expect that employers who saw the realities of the situation would forfeit bargaining advantages for the sake of sentiment.

Where arbitration was put into effect along British lines, unions were, as Richard Ely suggested, fairly stable. John Jarrett, chief of the Amalgamated Association of Iron and Steel Workers and an admirer of Mundella and Kettle, was among the first to press for adoption of their ideas in the United States.

---

[99] Staley, pp. 163-64. *The Workingman's Advocate,* Apr. 19, 1873.
[100] *Ibid.,* Aug. 19, 1873.
[101] Ely, *North American Review,* CXLIII, 327-28.
[102] Evans, I, 35. Siney was remembered years later by mine leaders such as John Mitchell as a martyr to the cause of labor. *United Mine Worker's Journal,* May 11, 18, 25, 1916.

Jarrett, as the capitalists with whom he bargained admitted, was a great force for peace in the iron industry. " No trades union has done so much," one observer wrote, " to introduce and render arbitration popular as the Amalgamated Association. Its former president John Jarrett rarely lost a strike which he was forced to enter." [103] On the whole, though he was not entirely sold on the English system, especially as it seemed to work in the iron industry of North England, Jarrett followed in the footsteps of his old mentor, John Kane, who was the prime mover in the establishment of boards in that area.[104] He managed generally to keep his men in conformity to the employers' pricing arrangements for nearly a decade.

Arbitration and conciliation, prior to the First World War, were not as important in America as in Britain; and even there their significance can be overrated. But the principles, as distinct from the practices, spread widely and focused attention on some of the alternatives for securing industrial peace. By the eighties every major industrial state, either through private or state agencies, had scrutinized English procedures, even though many of them later turned to consideration of the compulsory machinery operative in Australia and New Zealand.[105] Mundella's influence, nevertheless, was not restricted to puerile discussion. In Connecticut, for example, his views had a pronounced impact and, as the Secretary of the Connecticut State Board of Education admitted to the Nottingham Trades Union Congress in 1872:

The people of my state are very grateful to Mr. Mundella for spreading the truth of the grand principles of arbitration there. I have by tongue and pen often given circulation to the views expressed by Mr. Mundella and I am happy to think that by this means he has contributed greatly to the welfare of the workingmen of Connecticut.[106]

---

[103] Simonds, p. 652. U. S., Senate, *Report . . . upon the Relations between Labor and Capital,* 48th Cong., 1885, I, 1124, 1150; III, 573. *Final Report of the Industrial Commission,* 1902, XIX, 834-61. Barns, p. 237.

[104] Barns, pp. 235-36. McNeill, pp. 299-300.

[105] *Report of the Industrial Commission, Labor Organizations . . . Railway Labor,* 1901, XVII, 519-46. Caroline Lloyd, *Henry Demarest Lloyd* (2 vols.; New York: G. P. Putnam, 1912), Vol. II, pp. 113-16; also pp. 110-112. *Final Report of the Industrial Commission,* 1902, XIX, 858-62.

[106] Armytage, p. 111.

Likewise, in Ohio the Englishman left his mark. There Daniel J. Ryan, author of *Arbitration Between Capital and Labor*, and the member of the Ohio legislature who introduced a bill calling for the creation of a system of voluntary arbitration, acknowledged himself to be in Mundella's debt.[107] So it went almost everywhere that arbitration was discussed or examined. . The press, state and federal publications, also circulated the British plans. An early and excellent study of British and French arbitration and conciliation was prepared by Joseph D. Weeks, a man of great competence and a pioneer advocate of these programs in America. In the seventies, Weeks served for a time as a government labor expert, while in a private capacity he helped edit the influential *Iron Age*. The discontent in the mining and iron industries which threatened Pennsylvania's economic stability worried him greatly and he reasoned that " if arbitration has been successful in averting or mitigating industrial strife in these trades in England this fact should be a consideration of no small weight in favor of its trial here." [108] Under the auspices of Governor Hartranft of Pennsylvania Weeks conducted studies along this line, and he did a vigorous and effective job of circulating his findings among the workingmen and employers of the state. A believer in strong, incorporated unions, he wisely concluded that peace would come to industry only when labor had " a past to preserve and a future to care for," and since the " genius of people and institutions " was the same in America as in England he felt that voluntary arbitration would prove satisfactory to all parties.[109] Carroll Wright, one of the most competent students of labor in the last quarter of the century, and first U. S. Commissioner of Labor, moved in the same direction as Weeks. He too published a paper on British arbitration

---

[107] *The Nation*, Sept. 3, 1885. Barns, pp. 242-43.

[108] *IMJ*, Aug. 10, 1879. Joseph D. Weeks, *Rules for the Formation and Government of a Board of Arbitration and Conciliation of the Coal Mines of Western Pennsylvania* (Pittsburgh: By the Author, 1879); also see, *Report on the Practical Operation of Arbitration and Conciliation in England* (Harrisburg: 1879); *Industrial Arbitration in England and France* (Pittsburgh: 1879). Pa., Bureau of Industrial Statistics, *9th Annual Report* (1880-81), IX, 373.

[109] *Report of the Industrial Commission, Labor Organizations . . . Railway Labor*, 1901, XVII, 693-94. Barns, p. 239.

that elicited widespread attention and was reprinted by more than half a dozen state bureaus of labor.[110] British ideas were broadcast so widely by men of stature that it cannot be seriously doubted that they penetrated the thinking of labor leaders and employers all over the land.

These accomplishments of state and federal experts and their publications were augmented by private organizations and individuals. Among the stoutest proponents of British procedures were Nicholas Paine Gilman, Henry R. Seager, Henry Demarest Lloyd, and Arthur C. Pigou, each of whose analyses added to the general understanding of methods used to achieve industrial peace abroad.[111] One of the several organizations that spoke out for British ideas was the New York Society for Political Education which, by placing a broad construction on the term political, advertised the Mundella and Kettle plans. Of even greater interest, however, were the activities of a small band of New York positivists who were in touch with and influenced by Frederic Harrison, E. S. Beesly, and Thomas Hughes. They also championed British arbitration. It is not possible to determine their precise influence but they were directly affiliated with the local labor movement and several of the band were personal friends of Samuel Gompers. Among them, for instance, were Richard Foster, whom Gompers called "one of the finest men in the early labor movement," Hugh McGregor, J. J. Hill, Dick Holbert, Joseph Vanderheyden, and Edward King. Harrison sent King, who prided himself on his intimate knowledge of British labor, one of the best treatises on Mundella's ideas, *Industrial Conciliation*, written by the positivist barrister Henry Crompton. On both sides of the Atlantic, of course, the positivists had a wide audience of intellectuals and were generally recognized as friends of labor, hence it is not surprising to note that Gompers was immediately attracted by Crompton's work. Perhaps his refusal to consider

---

[110] See, U. S., Department of Labor, *Index to All Reports of State Bureaus* (Washington: U. S. Government Printing Office, 1902).

[111] Lloyd, *Henry Demarest Lloyd*, II, 113-16. Gilman, *Methods of Industrial Peace*; A. C. Pigou, *Principles and Methods of Industrial Peace* (New York: Macmillan, 1905); H. R. Seager, "The Legal Status of Trade Unions in the United Kingdom with Conclusions Applicable to the United States," *Political Science Quarterly*, XXII (Dec., 1907), 611-29.

compulsory arbitration was strengthened by his reading of British experience. But this is speculation; we need to know more about the positivists and their bearing on certain developments in American labor.[112]

Arbitration and conciliation did not stop the rising incidence of strikes and unrest. They did center attention on ways to secure peace, however, and convinced many persons that benefits could come with strong unions. Above all they encouraged the intelligent public, labor leaders, and industrialists to think out the problems raised by industrial warfare. Laws such as the Wallace Act in Pennsylvania, one of the first acts providing for voluntary arbitration in the United States (1883), and subsequent acts passed in Massachusetts, New York, and twelve other states before the close of the century, owed much to events abroad and to the discussion they had catalyzed in America. That portions of them remained dead letters should not obscure their educative function, nor their role in the long process of trial and error as Americans evolved collective bargaining techniques. Americans, of course, devised plans of their own; the Lynn Board in Massachusetts and the famed Straighton and Storm Board in New York were extremely intelligent approaches to specific problems of labor unrest. Yet the prestige of British industry and labor favored the circulation of the Mundella and Kettle plans. As British labor entered what Americans generously dubbed an " era of arbitration," its ideas served as a yardstick by which Americans could measure their own advance.[113]

### III. THE AMALGAMATEDS

The most typical of Britain's moderate trade unions had a pronounced influence in America. These were the " new model " or amalgamated unions which included the organizations of engineers, carpenters and joiners, and some of the iron

[112] Gompers, I, 272; also pp. 103-104 and p. 49n. U. S., Senate, *Report . . . upon the Relations between Labor and Capital*, 48th Cong., 1885, I, 557-65, 687-713. *Report of the Industrial Commission, Labor Organizations . . . Railway Labor*, 1901, XVII, 695.
[113] Barns, p. 234. Mass., Bureau of the Statistics of Labor, *1st Biennial Report* (1877), Chapter I.

and mine workers. The first of such unions was the Amalgamated Society of Engineers established in 1851 by the Scottish engineer, William Allen. Out of this union and others imitating it grew a whole new generation of tireless, methodical, respectable labor leaders. Gone was the flamboyant, ill-organized, colorful, anti-capitalist menagerie of the eighteen thirties and forties. The new union attitudes were tailored to suit Victorian society. Unions encouraged their members to "get knowledge . . . [and] intelligence instead of alcohol," and one enthusiast, converted to the new thought, announced that he had "left off buying beer and [had begun] buying books to improve my mind." [114] If everyone's sacrifices were not so heroic, this nevertheless was the spirit of the "new models." The collapse of the Grand National and the subsequent failures of the Chartists apparently knocked the scales from the eyes of skilled workmen and confronted them with realities. Capitalism was obviously not to be taken by storm, and sieges were too costly for serious consideration. From capital labor sought no capitulation in the revolutionary sense, but only concessions. And at mid-century concession was feasible. Capitalists were prosperous and secure; Britain was the workshop of the world, and they were the country's masters. In their established positions they could at last afford to divvy portions of their wealth and power. Therefore survival, to the new union leadership, meant conformity to the tenets of the bourgeoisie, to respectability, thrift, practicality, moderation, and sound businesslike trade unionism.

Convinced beneficence would take them farther than belligerence, the new unions, despite having launched their careers with sharp fights, bent to the currents of their age; they yielded to the wisdom of their not impossible situation. Centralization, association, and affiliation were their watchwords, when they could agree upon any, and in time the directing force behind them centered in the hands of the "clique" or Junta, a "cabinet of the Trade Union Movement," [115] located in London.

The amalgamated unions drew their strength from several sources. Their leadership, for one thing, welcomed assistance

---

[114] Cole and Postgate, p. 331.     [115] Webb, p. 233.

from intellectuals not themselves in or of the workingclass. They also relied upon the recruitment of skilled workers who were able to pay the high dues that assured the unions' financial stability. Moreover, they derived power from their eschewal of wildcat strikes. When they fought—and it was not often—they tried to select their own ground and concentrate their resources, which a centralized financial system made easy, and usually this was sufficient either to gain victory for them or at least prevent the struggle from becoming one-sided.

Lacking the color and dash of their forerunners, the amalgamateds had the usual difficulty of keeping their ranks at full strength, yet they did survive and endure—no small feat. They hardly offered workingmen the chance to enter the Promised Land but they did touch a substantial, if vulgar, sentiment that has since become a great twentieth century theme, the love of security. This they achieved through creation of benefit programs covering sickness, accidents, unemployment, and death payments to members or their survivors. Much of their success stemmed from their functions as provident societies that eradicated some of the more fearsome uncertainties from their members' lives at a minimal cost in strife.

Benefit unions and the Trades Union Congress dominated the British labor scene for over thirty-five years, and they proved a great example to American labor. They were copied or closely studied by trade unionists in several different crafts, and their structure and policies were often translated into action by Americans. Especially was the imprint of the " new models " discernible among the anthracite miners, textile operatives, carpenters and joiners, iron workers, cigarmakers, tobacco workers, granite cutters, stone cutters, and engineers.

Almost from the start, for example, American mine unionism adopted certain new model principles. Restrictions of output, insistence on compulsory maintenance of the standard wage, proposals for benefit programs, refusal to work with non-union labor, requests for high dues, conciliation, arbitration, joint agreements, collective bargaining—the latter a term Americans borrowed from the British—and the outright duplication of British union constitutions, all, in whole or in part, found their way across the sea. Nor did miners monopolize the use of British ideas. The constitutions and overall policies of both the Granite Cutters' National Union and the Soft Stone Cutters' Union were faithful reproductions of their British counterparts.[116] Likewise, when Adolph Strasser, a personage of great influence among the cigarmakers, was asked by Senate investigators where the cigarmakers derived their ideas of union structure, he replied, in part, "We have borrowed from the political government under which we live, but most particularly from the English trade unions. Our relations with the English unions during the early years were very close. We have borrowed from them our present financial system and the system of popular initiative and referendum."[117] William McClelland, leader of the American branch of the Amalgamated Society of Engineers confirmed this, informing Senators in 1881 that his union had an "equalization fund which has been adopted by various organizations and found to be of immense benefit. Mr. Gompers . . . informs me that he took the idea from our society and engrafted it onto the organization of cigarmakers."[118] Still further, the secretary of the Tobacco Workers' International declared before the Industrial Commission of 1901 that "our financial system is similar to the Cigarmakers' and another one. It was adopted or copied from an English organization called the Amalgamated . . . Engineers."[119] In those unions with a substantial British immigrant membership, like the iron molders and the Sons of Vulcan, there were demands for the institution of benefit programs comparable to those known to workingmen in the old country. When it is recalled that the structure and policies of both these unions were impregnated with British influences this is no surprise. Even William Sylvis, perhaps

[116] Ware, p. 168. *Granite Cutters' International Union of the United States and British Provinces of America, Constitution and By-laws* (Rockland: 1877); *Stone Cutters' Association of North America, Constitution* (1892) both in the Trade Union Collection (The Johns Hopkins University Library).

[117] Jacob Hollander and George Barnett, *Studies in American Trade Unionism* (New York: Holt, 1907), pp. 45-46.

[118] U. S., Senate, *Report . . . upon the Relations between Labor and Capital,* 48th Cong., 1885, I, 673-75.

[119] *Report of the Industrial Commission, Capital and Labor in Manufactures and General Business,* 1901, VII, 399-405.

the first of the great native labor leaders of the war and post-war period, copied many ideas used in the Iron Molders' International from Britain's labor movement,[120] just as did leaders of the other organizations mentioned above.

American eclecticism went even further. The largest constituent union of the American Federation of Labor in its early days, Peter McGuire's Brotherhood of Carpenters and Joiners, was directly inspired by and in large measure modeled after the Amalgamated Society of Carpenters and Joiners. Statements in the union's official journal, in fact, leave little doubt that this English organization was the Brotherhood's prototype and ideal.[121] The structure of the Federation of Trades and Labor Unions, forerunner of the American Federation of Labor, was likewise British-inspired. The proceedings of its initial convention in September 1881 indicate clearly that the British Trades Union Congress was to be the model.[122] Hopes were also expressed a year later that " our basis of representation and revenue [will] be assimilated to that of the Trades Union Congress of Great Britain," and that " frequent correspondence " and the mutual exchange of documents between the two groups might take place.[123] Efforts were made within the Federation to form a body " after the manner of the Parliamentary Committee of the Trades Unions of England," so that it might " urge and advance legislation in Washington." [124] It is difficult to tell which unions or delegates labored hardest to imitate the British; whether it was the cigarmakers, or the typographers, or Jarrett, Gompers, or McGuire, there is no question of their model. It was fitting therefore that the temporary president of the F.T.L.U., John Jarrett, should be a Welshman, and that two Englishmen, Robert Howard and William H. Foster, should nominate a third Englishman, Samuel Gompers, for the presidency of the Federation.[125]

[120] Grossman, pp. 88, 148.
[121] *The Carpenter*, Feb. 24, 1891. Simonds, p. 655. Ware, p. 166.
[122] *Report, 1st Annual Session of the Federation of Trades and Labor Unions of the U. S. and Canada, Pittsburgh, Sept. 15-19, 1881*, p. 7.
[123] *Ibid.*, (1882), p. 10.
[124] *Ibid.*, (1881), p. 7.
[125] *Ibid.*, (1881), p. 8; also *ibid.*, (1883), p. 15. *CMOJ*, Nov. 15, 1882; Feb., 1883; Nov., 1883; Aug., 1884.

After the formation of the A.F.L. little changed in these respects; in addition to the British and Irish organizers in its ranks, of whom we have already spoken, British-born intellectuals also helped orient the new union towards England. William Trant, an official pamphleteer of the A.F.L., for instance, had launched his own career by writing a prize-winning essay for the British Trades Union Congress, and with slight changes the same essay became one of the chief statements of the A.F.L.'s objectives.[126] No wonder those men who grew tired of conservative business unionism blamed its influence on the British-styled American unions.

There were, of course, direct transplantations of new models in the United States, and these were influential in their own right. Under the leadership of William McClelland, an Englishman, the Amalgamated Society of Engineers founded about a dozen locals in the United States during and immediately after the Civil War.[127] Their main purpose was to provide services and benefits for immigrants who wanted to retain their old union associations. Membership was never very great and probably averaged 1800 to 2000 members in the period from 1862 to 1914; 4200 members was perhaps a maximum number.[128] Yet because it was the first of the new model unions, the A.S.E. was widely known and highly respected in American labor circles; as late as 1897 some labor officials regarded it as the " best trade union in the world." [129] Planting of the A.S.E. was shortly followed by the appearance of the Amalgamated Society of Carpenters and Joiners. The first locals were set up in February 1868 and before long it boasted of fourteen branches with a membership that ranged variously from 1800 to 8000 men, depending on the conditions of the trade.[130] Both of these

[126] *Trade Unions, Their Objects, Origins, Influences, and Efficacy* (Washington: American Federation of Labor, 1890) in a collection of A. F. of L. writings by Trant in the Trade Union Collection (The Johns Hopkins University Library).

[127] U. S., Senate, *Report . . . upon the Relations between Labor and Capital*, 48th Cong., 1885, I, 673-85. *The Workingman's Advocate*, Aug. 17, 1867; June 10, 1871. *CMOJ*, July 10, 1875; July, 1878; Sept., 1887. *Report of the Industrial Commission, Labor Organizations . . . Railway Labor*, 1901, XVII, 222-27.

[128] *Ibid.*, XVII, 222. Mitchell, p. 86.

[129] *CSJ*, Sept. 1, 1897.

[130] U. S., Treasury Department, Bureau of Statistics, *Special Report on Labor*

small British unions created problems of "dual unionism," subtracting, or so it was thought, from the membership of the International Association of Machinists, and the Brotherhood of Carpenters and Joiners; occasionally they came under fire as "foreign organizations."[131] Nevertheless, they were highly publicized in the labor press and many of their features provoked discussion and imitation.

The benefit programs of the amalgamateds exerted a particular attraction and insofar as nineteenth century American unions developed provident features at all they were inspired by or copied from similar features in British unions.[132] Laborers on both sides of the Atlantic, faced with mounting uncertainties in an increasingly impersonal world, cultivated a powerful craving for security, hence the lustre of the benefit programs. Ordinarily the annual reports of the engineers and the carpenters and joiners were reproduced in whole or in part by American labor papers and trade journals. Comments were almost uniformly laudatory.[133] " Before us lies the 12th Annual Report of the Amalgamated Society of Carpenters and Joiners," read *The Workingman's Advocate*. ". . . It is replete with instruction and valuable information from which the skilled mechanics of America should take a lesson. A cursory glance at the statistics furnished convinces us that the strength of these . . . organizations lies more in their morale and discipline than in the number of their members." The British unionist, added the writer, wielded " immense influence" through this organization, preferred the " live trunk to dead branches," " a good substantial foundation to an imposing superstructure built on sand," and the " beneficial feature forms . . . a con-

*in Europe and America* (Washington: U. S. Government Printing Office, 1875), p. 201. McNeill, p. 375.

[131] *The Workingman's Advocate,* June 10, 1871.

[132] *Bulletin of the Bureau of Labor,* XII (1906), 699.

[133] *CMOJ,* Aug. 10, 1878; Mar. 10, 1880; Nov., 1883; July, 1885; Aug., 1887; Sept., 1887. *IMJ,* Aug., 1873; Apr., 1875; July, 1876; Mar., 1877. *Fincher's,* Dec. 12, 1863; July 16, 1874. *The Workingman's Advocate,* May 5, 1866; Jan. 1, 1870; Mar. 30, 1871; Sept. 28, 1872; May 24, 1873; Sept. 20, 1873. *Report of the Industrial Commission, Labor Organizations . . . Railway Labor,* 1901, XVII, 38-39. *Final Report of the Industrial Commission,* 1902, XIX, 828-30.

spicuous position." [134] Other editors dwelt upon the obvious lessons to be gleaned from observation of these British unions. Figures published by the amalgamateds, asserted one liberal paper in 1883, revealed British provident societies that " were as great a benefit to the state as they were to workmen." [135] One editor, who was opposed to British unions opening American branches, nevertheless described the amalgamateds as being " formed on the true principle that every trade union should be formed on, as they take the apprentice, learn him his trade, protect him all his life by assisting him when sick or out of employment, giving him at all times a living rate of wages, then they bury him " and still continue care for the widow and orphan.[136] Prior to the coming of the American New Deal in the nineteen thirties, this was as close to a modicum of security as workingmen could get— and alert men realized it. As a member of the Chicago branch of the A.S.E. put it: " I would sooner cut off my right arm than lose my membership because I know that in difficulties I am provided for." [137]

Fewer unions in America than in Britain adopted benefit programs, and few of the programs adopted were as sweeping as those functioning abroad. Benefits required cash reserves, and American unions, thanks to the myopia of their members, were generally poorer than Britain's amalgamateds. Nevertheless, by the turn of the century most American leaders favored extensive benefits administered by the national treasuries of the individual unions on the British plan. Forty of one hundred important unions by that time had provisions for funeral or death benefits; about a dozen national unions featured payments for sickness, and scores of locals drawing on their own funds (contrary to centralized disbursement in Britain) conducted similar payments. The great railroad brotherhoods pressed benefits farther than most other unions by including payments for insurance, disability, family sickness or death, fire, accident and tool insurance. Wherever such programs appeared, whether in large or

---

[134] *The Workingman's Advocate,* Sept. 28, 1872; also July 4, 1868.
[135] *The Nation,* Oct. 4, 1883.
[136] *The Workingman's Advocate,* May 16, 1868; May 31, 1873.
[137] *Ibid.,* Jan. 1, 1870.

small unions, they were operated largely, as an early student noted, " in the English manner " and were " based upon English models." [138] Where such programs did not exist, unionists who were aware of English efforts in this direction were apt to agree with the labor editor who commented that " it is much to be regretted that all unions are not formed on this basis." [139]

It is less important that thousands of organized workingmen in America gained security through imitation of the British than that the new models conveyed to American labor leadership, and a sizable part of the articulate public as well, the conception of unionism as a broadly social and economic phenomenon. Men were encouraged to think of unions as bringing with them not just higher wages, shorter hours, and the instruments of survival, but dignity, respect, a feeling of belonging, a new center of loyalty, security, and a measure of industrial democracy within the framework of a capitalist society. And because British labor experience extended beyond the confines of trade unionism, Americans were able to discover anew that industrial democracy and industrial harmony had many branches, that if arbitration, the constitutional and provident features of the amalgamateds mapped out one course, distributive and productive co-operation and industrial partnership marked out still others.

[138] *Bulletin of the Bureau of Labor,* XII (1906), 699. *Final Report of the Industrial Commission,* 1902, XIX, 828-30. *Report of the Industrial Commission, Labor Organizations . . . Railway Labor,* 1901, XVII, 38-42. Mitchell, pp. 106-10.9

[139] *The Workingman's Advocate,* May 16, 1868. *CMOJ,* Aug. 10, 1878; Mar. 10, 1880; Nov., 1883; July, 1885; Aug., 1887; Sept., 1887. *IMJ,* Aug., 1873; Apr., 1875; July, 1876; Mar. 10, 1877.

# Part Five

## SELF-HELP: THE PLANTING OF AN IDEA

---

### I. The Panacea and the Propagandists

On October 12, 1858, three days before the close of the Lincoln-Douglas debates, Horace Greeley's New York *Tribune* surveyed the social and economic horizons in America. The nation, according to the *Tribune*, was rapidly filling up; the gulf between producers and consumers was widening and substantial portions of the national wealth were accruing solely to the few. These problems, pregnant with significance, had to be mastered. What was to be done? As a fresh approach the *Tribune* suggested that " next to a pure national religion " the most promising solution lay in " co-operative combinations like those at Rochdale." [1] Unwittingly the *Tribune*'s proposal that economic and social embarrassments be resolved by the adoption of an English form of distributive co-operation signaled the end of one phase of American co-operation and forecast with accuracy the main direction in which co-operators would move in the war and post-war years.

Co-operation came as naturally to a people with frontier experience as did individualism and it was not a new thing on the American scene. In the thirties and forties, side by side with the early trade unions, harness and saddle makers, printers, molders, tailors, shoemakers, weavers, and farmers scattered throughout the East established both productive and distributive co-operatives. If we include the Utopian and sectarian communal experiments, co-operative enterprises must surely have been numbered in the hundreds in the mid-forties.[2]

---

[1] *Fincher's*, Nov. 28, 1863.  George Jacob Holyoake, *Among the Americans and A Stranger in America* (Chicago: Belford, Clarke & Co., 1881), p. 67.

[2] There is, of course, an extensive literature on this subject.  Commons, *Documentary History*, X, 195-96.  Edward Bemis, et al., *History of Co-operation in the United States* (Baltimore: The Johns Hopkins University Press, 1888).  Egbert and Persons, I, 44, 61-63, 207-208, 230-31, 265.

They were first responses to industrial change, the arrival of machinery, the unpleasantness of new shapes and noises, and the fluctuations of what we now call the business cycle. Aesthetic and emotional revolt had much to do with the creation of many co-ops, but many also grew out of practical situations. "Standing idle is not the true cure for our grievances," declared a Cincinnati iron molder in 1849; "why not employ ourselves?" [3] Thus at about the time the weavers of Rochdale resuscitated English co-operation, Americans, owing only a little inspiration to the British, and most of that to Robert Owen, were fashioning co-operatives very largely out of indigenous materials.

Time changed this. After the Democratic Party split at Charleston, after President Buchanan yielded office to Lincoln and the sectional armies locked in combat, established co-operatives, like so many raw recruits, went down in the general melee. The enthusiasm of the Owenites underwent eclipse; the élan of Brook Farm, the promise of scores of protective associations and other enterprises atrophied. Only a few distributive stores, like the ones at Natick, Worcester, and New Bedford, Massachusetts lingered on as heirs of the endeavors begun so hopefully in the thirties and forties and ended so dismally on the shoals of panic and impending war. [4]

Yet the autumn of 1862—the blight of war notwithstanding —found a few workers turning to co-operation, undeterred by previous failures. And well they might, for the quickening tempo of industrialism did not erase, but rather aggravated, the injustices that forced men into co-operation. Many who were imbued with craft traditions, with the notion that labor was mantled with dignity and rights of its own, [5] viewed the rise of the new order with distinct misgivings. Moreover, in mines, foundries, textile mills, and at the workbench Americans often labored longer, tended more machines, and were expected to produce more than Europeans. [6] The good times of the

[3] Commons, *Documentary History*, VIII, 310.
[4] E. C. Rozwenc, *Co-operation Comes to America* (Iowa: 1941). Richard Ely, *The Labor Movement in America* (New York: Thomas Y. Crowell, 1886).
[5] James D. Burns. *Three Years Among the Working Classes of the United States* (London: Smith, Elder & Co., 1865), p. 19.
[6] U. S., Senate, *Report . . . upon the Relations between Labor and Capital*,

fifties had left them relatively unprepared for the ups and downs of the sixties.[7] Thus labor, ostensibly supporting a conflict designed to emancipate the slave, to preserve free labor, and inaugurate a new era of liberty, talked of its own emancipation—a matter of greater concern than the freeing of the Negro. Behind the lines workers began fighting against low wages, loss of status, exploitative capital, inflated prices, and the specter of degraded lives not only with trade unions but also with English programs of co-operation.

Because workers painted their situation all too starkly, the inspiring intelligence about the successes of British co-operatives stood out in brilliant relief and their ideas and methods were soon eagerly assimilated. The spirit in which they were introduced was captured by Samuel Leavitt, one of the co-operators who claimed to have introduced the Rochdale idea to Americans:

> In common with many others I hailed the fact [the success of the Rochdale experiment] with delight and printed a pamphlet about the matter, scattering it over the country. . . . Robert Owen had come and gone and his followers had failed to accomplish any permanent success. . . . Fourier, St. Simon, Cabot [sic] and others had raised an uproar in France and America but the wrecks of their experiments were to be seen on both sides. . . . Hope came from Rochdale.[8]

No event was of greater importance for the spread of British co-operation than the appearance of *Fincher's Trades' Review* in Philadelphia on June 3, 1863. A national labor paper of high quality, *Fincher's* was a landmark in the evolution of an American labor press second to none, but equally as important for present purposes, it brought co-operative ideas into the mechanic's daily reading matter, presented them to him intelligently, and pressed them home with the editor's praise. Indeed, Jonathan Fincher, secretary of the important Machinists' and Blacksmiths' Union, and an intimate of the country's chief labor

48th Cong., 1885, I, 63-636; II, 436-38; III, 492-501. *IMJ*, Aug., 1873; Feb. 28, 1874; July 10, 1875; Mar. 10, 1876; Oct., 1876; Feb., 1877; July 10, 1878. *CMOJ*, July, 1885; Sept., 1887. *Fincher's*, June 11, 1864; July 25; Sept. 30, 1865; June 6, 1866. *The National Trades' Review*, Mar. 21, 1866.

[7] E. D. Fite, *Social and Industrial Conditions in the North During the Civil War* (New York: Macmillan & Co., 1910), for general background.

[8] *The Workingman's Advocate*, June 5, 1875.

figures, was well prepared not only to edit the paper that bore his name, but also to disseminate British co-operative schemes. Like so many Northern workingmen, Fincher was conscious of the sacrifices endured by English operatives in order to facilitate the destruction of the Confederacy. Grateful for the sympathies of British laborers and trade unionists he recognized the bonds of affinity that stretched across the Atlantic.[9] Fully confident, therefore, that Anglo-American workingmen faced a common enemy and common problems, that close understanding between them was essential, he sailed for England on the "George Griswold," a wartime relief ship sponsored by Northerners who wanted to aid their British friends.

Seeking to cement Anglo-American relations Fincher mingled with the patrons and the chieftains of English labor. Speaking engagements, for instance, found him on the same platform with Bright, Cobden, and John Stuart Mill. His tour likewise carried him among the competent, bourgeois-looking group of "new-model unionists" that included George Potter, John Wilson, George Howells, Lloyd Jones, and Charles Vincent.[10] He talked at length with Henry Pitman, editor of England's principal organ of co-operation, the Manchester *Co-operator*, and a person eminently qualified to illuminate the subject of self-help.[11] Fincher's limited stay, spent largely among the operatives of Manchester and Lancashire, did not give him the opportunity to "learn all [he] desired to know of Co-operation in England," but he saw and heard enough to cultivate a deep and enduring interest in it. Back once more in Philadelphia a few weeks later he commended it warmly to working people, asking, "When shall we be able to describe such scenes [of co-operation] as these in America?" and implying that it was up to his readers to answer, "Very soon."

Using the *Trades' Review* as a vehicle for English co-operative ideas, Fincher did more than any other labor editor to circulate them through the labor world. During its three years of publication, his paper carried more than 110 leading articles,

---

[9] *Fincher's*, Oct. 17, 1863.

[10] *Ibid.*, Mar. 11, 18, 1865. Fincher also met the American agitator Washington Wilkes.

[11] *Fincher's*, Mar. 18, Apr. 29, 1865.

sometimes half and occasionally full page affairs, about British co-ops and their methods. Twice the complete rules of the Rochdale Equitable Pioneers appeared in full; similar treatment was accorded articles of association of several Rochdale subsidiaries, the Halifax Society, and dozens of less well known institutions.[12] Many articles written by or about leading co-operators were featured so frequently that names like Thomas Hughes, Lloyd Jones, J. M. Ludlow, and especially George Jacob Holyoake, England's foremost and most authoritative spokesman of the co-operative movement, became by-words in American labor literature. When, in addition, the progress reports on English societies, evaluations of their moral and ethical aims, reports of their legal status, comments on their methods of organization, dividends, growth, merits and demerits are noted, the breadth of Fincher's coverage of co-operation becomes apparent.[13] Reaching over 11,000 subscribers in nearly every state and territory in the United States, and in England and the Continent as well, Fincher's paper proved of inestimable value to the disciples of British co-operation,[14] so much so that years after publication had ceased, Thomas Phillips, himself one the country's leading co-operators, summed up the editor's work as follows:

[He] put the question of true co-operation [Rochdale] before the American workingmen and was instrumental in building up . . . co-operative sentiment unequalled by any agency previously employed in this country. Co-operative societies [sprang] up in all directions and had they taken the advice given them by the *Review* they might today be the masters of the country and owners of its wealth.[15]

Important as he was, however, Fincher did not toil unassisted. Four of his personal friends, William Sylvis, John Samuel, Jr., Richard Trevellick, and Thomas Phillips, supplemented his educational campaigns. Each of these men was a

[12] *Ibid.*, Sept. 19, Oct. 17, 1863; Nov. 26, Dec. 10, 1864; Aug. 5, Sept. 23, Dec. 30, 1865, for instance.
[13] *Ibid.*, Oct. 31, Nov. 28, 1863; Apr. 2, Nov. 4, 19, 1864; Jan. 14, 21, Dec. 16, 30, 1865; also Jan. 30, Aug. 13, Nov. 4, Dec. 3, 1864; Feb. 11, 1865; Jan. 6, 1866.
[14] For a breakdown of circulation see, *Fincher's*, Dec. 9, 1865.
[15] Thomas Phillips to Uriah S. Stephens, Oct. 12, 1879, Phillips Papers.

leader of real merit; each believed in self-help, and except for Sylvis, each was British-born, trained in the labor movement of the mother country and in close touch with developments there. All of them, except Trevellick, were long active in the Philadelphia area, where *Fincher's* was published, but their reputation among working people was national.

The determined, professorial-looking Sylvis, whose reputation outshone his colleagues', established his first contact with Samuel Ashworth of the Rochdale Society in August 1863. Having questioned the Englishman about the efficacy of co-operation, Sylvis shortly received a number of documents from England in reply.[16] Thereafter, although he never mastered the details of the Rochdale Plan, he remained " an advocate of co-operation with few peers and no superiors "; moreover he identified himself with several co-operative ventures in Philadelphia and in those sections of the nation where as a unionist he could influence iron molders.[17] Through the rest of his life he remained vitally interested in the Rochdale idea and he took both pride and pleasure, his biographer tells us, in reciting the statistics of growth of the English society.[18]

Also an enthusiastic co-operator, John Samuel, Jr. served the cause for nearly forty years. His deep knowledge of British co-operative methods made him an exceedingly valuable man to preachers of the panacea such as Fincher, and it is hardly surprising that Samuel turned up on the staff of the *Trades' Review* during the war years.[19] Certainty is not possible, but it seems very likely that much of the information about British co-operation that found its way into the columns of the paper came from Samuel. He had a great deal to do with orienting American co-operative energies toward British programs, and as we shall see in detail later, he ranked as one of the country's chief practical co-operators by the mid-seventies.

[16] *Fincher's*, Aug. 22, 1863.
[17] Spanding to Phillips, date obscured, Phillips Papers. *The Workingman's Advocate*, Aug. 21, 1869.
[18] Grossman, pp. 195-96; also pp. 189-218. *Fincher's*, Oct. 3, 1863. Like so many others, Sylvis believed himself to be a pioneer in introducing the Rochdale Plan to the United States.
[19] *Fincher's*, Sept. 19; Oct. 3, 1863; Mar. 4, 1864.

Like Sylvis and Samuel, Trevellick regarded England as the birthplace of self-help and quite early in his career, as an adjunct to his many agitational activities, he started championing the creation of Rochdale-model stores in the United States. Widely travelled, in touch with labor's notables, he used his ample opportunities to spread the word. He frequently addressed co-operative meetings and rendered the cause such great service that he received a special tribute from co-operators themselves during the eighties.[20]

Similar interests, sympathies, training, and personal friendships, in brief, developed in the staff of the *Trades' Review* and among the leaders associated with Fincher a fertile source of co-operative information and a powerful instrument for its dissemination. In addition, the exertions of Sylvis, Samuel, Trevellick, and Fincher were paralleled, if not surpassed, by the practical co-operative enterprises and the propaganda of their colleague, Thomas Phillips.

Hardly significant enough for a full-scale biography,[21] a prominent personality only in the context of a small, though very important movement, Phillips provides a welcome case study of a man whose career encompassed labor activity on both sides of the Atlantic. From his life come clues about why and how that tenacious breed known as co-operators developed. His perspectives were those of a skilled worker in a rapidly changing craft, a pioneer advocate of distributive co-operation, an active organizer in four great labor organizations, and the first president of the International Boot and Shoe Workers' Union. Furthermore, his activities are a rough index to the ideas, the methods, and personalities of scores of British-born or British-inspired co-operators who were largely responsible for a revival of co-operation in America after 1862. If American trade unionists profited from the influx of immigrants and the disperson of British ideas, American co-operators, who can today count their earnings in the hundreds of millions, owe even more to the impulses generated by immigrants and ideas from across the sea.

---

[20] *Ibid.*, Aug. 19, 1865. *Chicago Post*, Dec. 21, 1865.
[21] For greater detail see my, "Thomas Phillips, A Yorkshire Shoemaker in Philadelphia," *Pennsylvania Magazine of History and Biography*, LXXIX, (April, 1955), 167-196.

Background and training fitted Phillips eminently well for his role in American labor. Son of a farmer, he was born on March 22, 1833 in Whitson, near Rotherham, a Yorkshire town famed for its iron forgers. In 1833, British labor had just begun its portentous advance; that year Robert Owen mobilized a conglomeration of tradesmen, co-operators, and malcontents into the most sizable and the most formidable labor organization in Yorkshire, the Grand National Consolidated Trades Union, " a giant Tree the top whereof shall reach to Heaven and afford a shelter to succeeding generations."[22] In Phillips' world one heard again and again the echoes of Owen's name, and the shadow of the Grand National proved a long one.

Like many agitators, Phillips' formal education was meager, yet it supplied him with many of his more substantial characteristics. Christened in the Anglican Church, given additional religious and secular training in Methodist, Episcopal, and day schools, he learned the canons of the faith as a boy; consequently, like so many labor leaders he reflected prevailing Christian mores, cast his thoughts in what he believed to be a Christian mold, and framed his objectives in Christian terms. Throughout his life he displayed an intense evangelical fervor: that of the labor revivalist.

When he was thirteen his schooling ended and, despite parental objections to bondage of any kind, he was bound out to his brother-in-law as an apprentice shoemaker. He practiced the shoemaking craft the rest of his life. At the time of his apprenticeship, the several types of craftsmen who labored at the bench could and did take pride in an ancient and proud profession. Crispins, as shoemakers were called for their patron saint, were distinguished by their spicy tongues, their wit, and intelligence. However, this craft, and it did not differ from others in this respect, had already begun to undergo fundamental changes as its scores of operations were rationalized, sub-divided, and taken over by machinery. The passage of kings, queens, and politicians, in fact, did not affect these men as vitally as did the appearance of the beating-out machine,

---

[22] Cole and Postgate, p. 240.

the power sole-molder, the foot-die machine, the power toller, and the McKay stitcher.[23] To a considerable degree these new conditions accounted for Phillips' partisanship in the labor movements of England and America.

As was the custom he labored from twelve to fifteen hours a day at his bench, and, as was equally common, his apprenticeship proved the period of his indoctrination in labor agitation. " My boss," he wrote realistically of his brother-in-law, " was an active Chartist and an ex-Methodist local preacher and with him I attended Chartist and other meetings and became interested in all the reforms of the day." [24] How much Chartist ideology he imbibed is uncertain. The movement late in the forties, of course, had already lost some of its potential. But within its purview he could have ruminated among a variety of ideas, from trade unionism to co-operation and the Christian Socialism of Maurice, Kingsley, and Ludlow.

In 1849 Phillips and his master withdrew their union cards from the Rotherham shoemakers' union and, tramping into industrial Lancashire, set up shop in the textile center of Bolton La Moore. There Phillips claimed the distinction of being the only union apprentice in town; moreover, his master was secretary of the union. There, too, he formally linked himself with the Chartist Association, " Ernest Jones, the great Chartist leader [making] out my membership card with his own hands in the Temperance Hall in Bolton." [25] One cannot doubt that for a time Phillips was swept up in the exciting spirit of the movement; but the spirit shortly waned. Although Jones was capable of arousing great enthusiasm, it is clear that neither he nor the Association was able to relieve the young shoemaker of discontent.

Bolton also lost its appeal and despite the fact that the " hungry forties " were over and a flood tide of prosperity had surged back into the cities and towns, Phillips decided that industrial England offered him insufficient opportunities. It is probable that the waning influence of Chartism hastened his

[23] Albert S. Bolles, *Industrial History of the United States* (Norwich, Conn.: Henry Bill Publishing Co., 1879), pp. 444-56. McNeill, pp. 192-94.
[24] "Autobiography," Phillips Papers.
[25] *Ibid.*

decision to quit his country for he was, after all, a self-styled
"English Radical," a reformer, an admirer of Cobbett and
Paine.[26] Thus when social disinfectants failed to cleanse the
land, when politics failed to serve as the mechanics' servant,
it was, in his judgment, time to leave.

Working overtime, earning a sufficient sum to purchase his
freedom from his master, he went to live with an Irish family,
one of the thousands in Lancashire, and prepared to emigrate
to the United States. He sold his few books, visited his family
for the last time, and sailed from Liverpool on August 4, 1852.
Several weeks before Pierce's election as President, Phillips
disembarked in New York with eight shillings in his pocket.
An acquaintance from Bolton, then in the United States,
secured him a job in a Brooklyn shoe shop owned by a Welshman, but since this job and a subsequent one in New York
City proved unsatisfactory, he moved on to Philadelphia.[27]

In the early fifties the City of Brotherly Love was already
a city of "remarkable manufactures," boasting more than
six thousand industrial establishments, including facilities for
making iron, brass, chemicals, cotton clothing, locomotives, car
wheels, carriages, and, of course, boots and shoes. Phillips
had every reason to consider his trade a highly respectable one
in Philadelphia. There, as in nearly every major city, boot and
shoe establishments outnumbered many industries both as to
shops and operatives.[28] There, too, shoemakers had a distinctive tradition of craft organization and labor agitation dating
back to the formation of the nation's first cordwainers' union
in 1792.

A skilled man, never unemployed for long, the young immigrant moved with great frequency from shop to shop. Whether
these shifts reflected seasonal conditions in the trade or the
normally high mobility of labor in his adopted land is difficult
to say. In one case, however, he confessed that his discharge
followed involvement in a strike, and, while his personal role
in that affair seems to have been slight, his labor activity,

---

[26] "Autobiography," Phillips Papers.

[27] *Ibid.*

[28] J. Leander Bishop, *A History of American Manufacturers from 1608 to
1860* (2 vols.; Philadelphia: Young & Co., 1864), Vol. II, pp. 530-75.

according to his own admission, steadily increased. After 1855, the year in which he took out his first citizenship papers, Phillips devoted a great deal of time to organizing shoemakers, cultivating in the meantime an ardent interest in the eight hour question, slavery, and general labor matters.[29] The forces from which he had fled had apparently overtaken him in the United States; like many immigrants he had changed his location more easily than he had changed the nature of his problems.

Although it is true that Phillips began his career as a trade unionist and that no hard, fast line ever separated him from unionism, he was nonetheless primarily a co-operator. Through most of his active life self-help was the focus of his energies. Moreover, his earliest and most enduring notoriety came from his advocacy of the Rochdale Plan of distributive co-operation. Strangely enough, while he had once lived within thirty miles of the town of Rochdale, he showed no discernible interest in co-operation as a young Chartist, rather he turned to it only after he was well established in Philadelphia. It was not a difficult transition, for British ideas as well as immigrants were freely flowing into the American labor world. Furthermore, he received his inspiration directly from the writings of George Jacob Holyoake, high priest of the English movement. In 1858 Holyoake kindled excitement among English workers by his publication of the first portion of his history of co-operation in Rochdale. Reprinted in substance by Greeley's *Tribune* hard on the panic of 1857-1858, news of self-help fired the imagination of many Americans seeking a palliative for economic distress; one of them was Phillips.[30]

Basically, Holyoake's writings on co-operation, which enjoyed wide currency on both sides of the Atlantic for forty years, dealt with the moral and intellectual values, as well as with the substantial economic gains of the Rochdale Pioneers and their disciples. His pen transformed the story of self-help into a drama; he told the tale of thousands of degraded mill

---

[29] "Autobiography," Phillips Papers.
[30] Several of Holyoake's pamphlets are in the Albert Hutzler Collection (The Johns Hopkins University). Also see, Goss, for bibliographical references to Holyoake's work and the *Dictionary of National Biography, 2nd Supplement* (1901-11), pp. 291-93. *New York Tribune,* Oct. 12, 1858.

operatives, of their elevation from perpetual indebtedness to positions, if not of affluence, at least of decency and competence. Self-help, the expression itself being marvelously Victorian, illustrated the effectiveness of united working men and women, how when joined in Christian brotherhood they could achieve relative freedom from their employers and the evils of the industrial system. The basic plan for accomplishing this was rather simple. Once a nucleus of co-operators subscribed enough capital through the purchase of shares, a distributive store (the term " store " having been borrowed from America), more familiarly a grocery or general store, was opened. Thereafter, cash operations were started and everyone, members and non-members alike, shared in a quarterly distribution of the profits according to the amount of capital invested and the amount of purchases made. Upon this simple foundation rested a hierarchy of co-operatives ranging from wholesale stores to manufacturing establishments, all operating on essentially the same " dividend " principle.[31]

Inspired by Holyoake, Phillips had no difficulty justifying co-operation as an essential element for the elevation of work-ingmen. In his judgment, the society about him was both unjust and corrupt, antagonistic to what he called " the natural genius of American institutions," to economic and social democracy. Examples of the accumulation of great wealth by the few in Europe and America preyed upon his mind. He foresaw fearfully the emergence of a landed aristocracy in America more formidable than England's, and this fear was accentuated by the rapidity with which western lands were being gobbled up by both British and American capitalists.[32] Worse yet, middlemen, whose economic value Phillips never understood, were milking the worker of his hard won gains, and political parties, allegedly a source of strength for enfranchised labor, failed to prevent or to alleviate this situation.[33]

Aware of injustices, desirous of forging a new social order,

---

[31] There are numerous authoritative explanations of the Rochdale Plan. See, for instance, George J. Holyoake, *The Co-operative Movement To-day* (London: Methuen & Co., 1891), pp. 35-39; H. C. Filley, *Co-operation in Agriculture* (New York: John Wiley and Sons, 1929), pp. 18-21.

[32] " Lecture on Co-operation," Ms, Phillips Papers. *Fincher's*, Jan. 23, 1864.

[33] *Fincher's*, Dec. 24, 1864.

Phillips was unwilling and unprepared to battle capital. A moderate Victorian, innocent of violating the conventions of his age, this handsome full-bearded man was essentially a liberationist, not a revolutionary. Time and again he emphasized that he was not opposed to particular capitalists, but only to an inequitable capitalist system. How he could be against one and not the other troubled him little; but then, too, not being a logical man he never solved the riddle of how to get co-operation and trade unionism to stretch out side by side.

Although he was later to lead a large trade union, his faith in co-operation prevented him early in his career from fully appreciating the efficacy of unionism and its major weapon, the strike. In his opinion, as long as men clung to unions they were sure only of making too few gains to justify their efforts. Because of their costliness to all concerned, strikes were especially deplorable, and Phillips once declared that if all the time and money lavished on them had been pooled for co-operative endeavor, the millennium would long since have arrived. Furthermore, strikes failed to fathom the depth of social injustice, which stemmed from the " prevailing mode of dividing the profits of productive industry." [34] Consequently, he urged mechanics " to emancipate themselves from slavery in a wrongly constructed society," [35] to substitute co-operation for strikes, and to confront capital with capital. Co-operation to this Yorkshireman meant a long-term, peaceful revolution. It provided an alternative to conflicts for which Phillips and other workingmen were neither economically nor psychologically prepared.

Satisfied that the United States offered a fertile field for co-operative revolution, sure that political parties, trade unions, and joint stock ventures could not effect it alone, he presented the Rochdale Plan as the most promising method of saving humanity and of providing a secure base on which other forms of co-operation could be built. This system, proven and practical, could " be realized by the people arranging the powers of production, distribution, education, and government, for

---

[34] " Lecture on Co-operation," Ms, Phillips Papers.
[35] *Fincher's*, April 30, 1864.

here the people possess the power and the time is not far distant when they will learn to use it." [36]

If anyone doubted the potentialities of co-operation, he had only to study the progress of the Rochdalers and observe the activities of English reformers:

Let the objector [wrote Phillips] read the history of the Rochdale Society . . . in England, and we think he will come to the conclusion that co-operative associations among workingmen are practicable.[37] The men who have stood by the people and suffered persecution—the radicals—the men that have the capacity to see the root of the evil and to apply the effectual remedy, these men see that the co-operative movement is producing more practical good than any other mode of reform.[38]

Therefore, in order to extricate Americans from " the galling tyranny of capital," to banish middlemen and monopolies, Phillips, always assuming that problems in the United States were similar to those in England, declared:

Let us on this side of the Atlantic profit by their [the English radicals'] foresight which their necessities and active battling against all forms of oppression have developed. Let us unite with them in an organized effort to apply the reform axe to the root and strike down the common enemies of both.[39]

This accomplished, he then caught visions of the millennium:

We claim that by co-operation . . . workingmen can, in time, raise sufficient capital to build workshops, factories or buy farms or to erect the most costly machinery and secure the benefits of every labor saving invention and turn them into a blessing . . . instead of as now to a large extent a curse from the fact that a few are able to monopolize these and reap the benefits which under a co-operative system would be divided among the many.[40]

It would be easy to misinterpret Phillips' objectives and to assume that he simply wanted to convert workers into capitalists. Such an assumption has too often been applied without discrimination to labor leadership. The Rochdale Plan, insofar as he was concerned, and this was true of other co-operators as well, implied the moral renovation of society. There burned

---

[36] *Fincher's*, Apr. 30, 1864.
[37] *Ibid.*, July 4, 1864.
[38] *Ibid.*, Apr. 30, 1864.
[39] *Ibid.*
[40] *Ibid.*, July 4, 1864.

within him the same fierce moral conviction, the same awareness of his Christian duty that sent British and American clergymen into the slums and dark streets of industrial cities, that
motivated Gladstone, for example, to found a private Magda-
lenian society, and drove scores of able men in both countries
into the ranks of the Christian Socialists. Co-operators and
co-operative ideas brought into the United States often arrived
replete with evangelical emotionalism and a zeal which defined
the connection between the secular reformism of Holyoake
and the religious fervor of his disciples.

To Phillips who was striving for a " Co-operative Republic,"
self-help was the movement of the future that would re-orient
industrial affairs in accord with what to him were equitable
principles. Co-operation was the "bright star to which all
enlightened humanity looked," "the friend of all mankind,"
"the reform containing the seeds of all other reforms."

. . . By equitable distribution of wealth the foundation would be laid
which would bring forth this fruit [the moral regeneration of society]
and the first efforts of the co-operator is designed to bring this about.
The co-operative arrangements are by their nature calculated to supply
the world with the most perfect system of economics that the most
advanced political and social reformers have ever been able to con-
ceive of.[41]

That such a steady fellow as Phillips believed this large utopian
order to be possible is an indication of how deeply rooted the
nineteenth century faith in progress was.

Excited, hopeful, entertaining not a scintilla of doubt as to
the ultimate triumph of co-operation, Phillips kept discussion
of the subject on a high plane, divorcing it from petty monetary
concerns, suffusing it with idealism. Emphasizing education,
scorning demagoguery, he sought to attract men of intellect,
good moral fiber, and sound judgment into the fold. There
was no place in his scheme of things for fanatics, hotheaded
youths, or revolutionary rabble.[42] Occasionally he upbraided
capitalism, to be sure, but on the whole as a co-operator he
conducted his operations with an almost gentlemanly balance.

[41] Untitled Ms by Phillips on Co-operation, dated 1876, Phillips Papers.
Phillips to John Butterfield, Oct. 10, 1874, Phillips Papers.
[42] *Fincher's*, July 1, 1865.

And it was perfectly feasible for him to do so. Unlike trade unions, co-operatives were not viewed with hostility by many of the more powerful employers. They saw in them no latent threat to the prevailing order; on the contrary, they frequently felt that business ventures by workingmen would have a healthy, sobering effect by teaching mechanics how hard the fortunes of business life really were. Some employers, in fact, were so convinced of the usefulness of self-help that they actively encouraged co-operative enterprises.[43] Small wonder Phillips could afford balance and optimism.

An idealist, and a naïve one at that, Thomas Phillips was also a man of practical sagacity. The new order would not come overnight. From his observations of English experience, he realized that the initial phases of co-operation must of necessity be humble, that the battle for survival would be prolonged. Counseling co-operators in patience, stressing the virtues of gradualness, he informed them that they had to " drill themselves " before competing with capital.[44] His first practical objective was the establishment of distributive stores " in every neighborhood in town and country throughout the land." [45] Since he based his entire program on precedents set by the Rochdalers, he arranged for shareholders in the store to receive interest on their capital and dividends based on the amount of their purchases. Non-shareholders, in the latest Rochdale fashion, were permitted to let their dividends accrue until they were credited with enough money to buy shares. Whenever possible, retail stores were to be buttressed by central wholesale stores, already experimented with in England. Here retailers could buy their stocks in anticipation of a dividend such as they returned to their own custom. Then, once both retail and wholesale stores functioned effectively, the co-operators could do as the Pioneers had done, namely, launch

---

[43] *The Merchants' Magazine and Commercial Review*, LVIII (1868), 249; also Vol. LXIII, 121. U. S., Senate, *Report . . . upon the Relations between Labor and Capital*, 48th Cong., 1885, II, 1104-1105. *Miners' Journal,* Aug. 13, 1875. Barns, pp. 75-112.

[44] *Fincher's*, Jan. 23, 1864; July 1, 1865. " Lecture on Co-operation," Ms, Phillips Papers.

[45] *Fincher's*, July 1, 1865.

co-operative workshops and manufacturing enterprises along the same lines.

Taking cues from the Pioneers, Phillips and a small band of Englishmen turned from preaching about co-operation to the practice of it. On December 16, 1862, they formed the Union Co-operative Association No. 1 of Philadelphia (UCA). With a capital collection of only $133.70, these twenty-two men, led by the Yorkshire shoemaker, started their revolution in a grocery store.[46] Their motto was " Co-operation, a means of harmonizing conflicting interests and securing exact justice to every child of Earth." [47] The entire venture was an imitation of the original Rochdale organization and the spirits of its members were high. As one of the exuberant members put it:

One of the brightest spots on earth to my vision is the little dingy, one-story co-operative shop, 917 Federal Street, Philadelphia. Its very reticence throughout the day and all but three nights of the week is pleasing to me because it speaks of economy. . . . The fact that the members are mostly of English birth argues that they have a fair amount of stability among them. Additional proof of this is found in the fact that they spent over a year studying this system and perfecting their constitution before they launched into buying or selling. . . . They adhere to the rigid [good] old Rochdale style.[48]

Then, paying tribute to English influence in the UCA, the writer proudly cited the fact that " the first shilling pamphlet " the members received came from George Holyoake.

For years it was believed that the UCA was the first Rochdale store in the United States. Such was the claim of the first competent historian of American co-operation, Edward Bemis. Bemis, to whom all later students are indebted, gave too much credence to Phillips' own statement about his organization.[49] The UCA was not the first such store and Phillips, at one time, was aware of it. During a heated newspaper debate with the

---

[46] See the *Constitution and By-Laws of the Union Co-operative Association No. 1 of Philadelphia*, and *Constitution and By-Laws of the Philadelphia Co-operative and General Manufacturing Company Associated*, Phillips Papers. *Fincher's*, Aug. 13, 1864.

[47] UCA letterheads; also Ms of an undated, untitled article by Phillips in Phillips Papers; *Fincher's*, July 4, 1863.

[48] *Ibid.*, Dec. 3, 1864. The writer who signed himself " Quaestor " was not Phillips.

[49] Bemis, pp. 141-42. Commons, *History of Labour*, II, 39-41.

leader of the Lawrence [Massachusetts] Co-operative Association, who also claimed to have founded the first Rochdale
store in America, Phillips declared: "We do not claim to
be the first organization in this country . . . on the Rochdale
Plan for we know that such an organization was formed in
Philadelphia in 1860 and one in Cincinnati in 1861." [50]

Precisely where the first English-model co-op was formed,
in other words, is a mystery and pending the discovery of new
materials it will remain so. There were many claimants, some
individuals and some organizations, that boasted of having
first planted Rochdale ideas in the United States. Of the
co-op which Phillips mentioned in Philadelphia in 1860 nothing
seems to be known, and there were actually two stores in
Cincinnati started in the late fifties. Confusing matters further,
an English friend of Phillips', Samuel Leavitt, who gained a
reputation of his own in the labor movement, insisted that he
had disseminated Rochdale principles in this country as early
as 1850,[51] and cited as proof the fact that Holyoake later
honored him with a special visit. Such a plethora of conflicting
assertions can only lead to the conclusion that word of the
" flannel-weavers' panacea," as the Rochdale Plan was sometimes called, reached workingmen in America before the
Civil War and had greater circulation among them than we
have previously supposed. The main point is clear, however;
Phillips' co-operative was the first to attract widespread attention and to leave adequate records behind it. The Philadelphia
shoemaker broadcast word of English-model co-operation as
none of his predecessors seems to have done, serving both as
a proficient propagandist and an ebullient, practical pioneer.

The founders of the UCA made haste slowly. They dedicated the fifteen months following the creation of their
organization to further studies of English co-operative methods.
They likewise corresponded extensively with the secretary of
the Rochdale Society, receiving important documents and
suggestions from him. Meantime, they hoarded their capital.

---

[50] "Autobiography," Phillips Papers. *Fincher's*, Apr. 25; July 1; Aug. 5, 12,
1865.
[51] *Journal of United Labor*, Jan., 1883, for Leavitt's remarks. *The Workingman's Advocate*, Jan. 15, 1876. *New York Tribune*, Oct. 12, 1858.

When their store opened for business in March 1864, they were, thanks to these precautions, well equipped in view of their resources. "We are few and poor," wrote Phillips of the members of the UCA, "but we know of no such word as fail." [52]

For two and a half years the store fared well. Morale among the co-operators was high. Not trusting to chance, they continually schooled themselves in English techniques. Speakers like John Sheddon, the Pennsylvanian who later led the Sovereigns of Industry, and John Samuel, Jr., himself a stockholder in the UCA, lectured on such topics as "Co-operation in England and America" and gave the group the benefit of their experience and reading. [53] In December 1864, the members formed a separate organization, the Self-Help Aid Association, designed to raise funds for the expansion of the UCA. [54] Samuel Leavitt induced several merchants to lend money to the co-operators, though he confessed later that this proved a mistake. By 1866 there were four stores in Philadelphia and prospects, especially after Phillips declared a six per cent dividend in April, were very good. [55]

"But," said Phillips, "trade and membership did not keep pace with expansion," which incidentally he had opposed as rash. "Profits ceased, Branch One closed, being in a neighborhood which cared not for co-operation. The summer soldiers and sunshine co-operators began to withdraw their stock and throw a wet blanket over the concern." In November it was all over. "It was a great disappointment. Our hearts were set on success but it was our fate to fail." [56]

Although the UCA was unsuccessful, Phillips' leadership and propaganda, coupled with the writings of his associates on *Fincher's Trades' Review*, elicited widespread attention. By May 1865, he was designated as that paper's chief authority on co-operation, and it was his job to answer subscribers' queries

[52] *Fincher's*, July 4, 1863; also Aug. 13, 1864; Apr. 25, 1865.
[53] Reasons for high morale can be found in the Balance Sheets, 10th Quarterly Report of UCA, Phillips Papers; also *Fincher's*, Apr. 1, 1865. A scrap of paper lists Samuel's $10 share, in *ibid.* Also see "Notebook," *ibid.*
[54] *Fincher's*, Apr. 15, 1865.
[55] *Fincher's*, Apr. 21, 1866; *The Workingman's Advocate*, June 5, 1875.
[56] The withdrawal slips are in the Phillips Papers; also see Bemis, p. 142.

about self-help. After the Trades' Review itself failed, the shoemaker maintained his position as an oracle for its successors, *The National Trades' Review* and *Welcome Workman*.[57] There is ample evidence that in this capacity he reached many working people. One of Fincher's Massachusetts subscribers, for example, credited "Worker" (Phillips' pen name) with the most lucid explanation of self-help that he had ever seen, and he wondered why, after such an illuminating commentary, workers remained so blind to their own interests.[58] Readers apprised of the operations of the UCA requested a great deal of information about co-operation. Hiram Lord, an English co-operator touring the United States, visited the UCA and was impressed by it.[59] Similarly, in Philadelphia the Kensington Mutual Co-operative Association, directly inspired by Phillips, modelled itself after the UCA.[60]

Enthusiastic workers also wrote Phillips personally for guidance. Having interested thirty men in a co-operative venture, a member of the Government Printing Office sought advice, instruction, and documents from him, and they were promptly forwarded.[61] From the bituminous coal district of Pennsylvania's Allegheny County, where co-operation was to enjoy some success among the relatively prosperous miners, Andrew Carney told Phillips: "We are about to start a co-operative store in this neighborhood and are at present without anything in the shape of a book or papers containing any information on the subject. I proposed writing to you as chief manager of the Co-operative stores in Philadelphia . . . to see if you'll send copies of your constitution and by-laws." Shortly afterwards Carney thanked Phillips for his assistance.[62]

There were other letters in the same vein indicating for us how far the ripples of Phillips' influence carried. The master mechanic of the Pittsburgh, Fort Wayne and Chicago Railroad's

[57] "Autobiography," Phillips Papers; *Fincher's*, May 6, 1865; Apr. 14, Aug. 16, 1866.
[58] *Ibid.*, Oct. 17, 1863.
[59] *The National Trades' Review*, Jan. 20, 1866; also *Fincher's*, May 6, Dec. 23, 1865.
[60] *The National Trades' Review*, Jan. 20, 1866.
[61] W. B. Berger to Thomas Phillips, Mar. 21, 1866, Phillips Papers.
[62] Andrew Carney to Thomas Phillips, Apr. 9, June 17, 1866, *ibid.*

Fort Wayne shop informed Phillips that the four hundred men in his charge were anxiously awaiting instructions from him, adding in a postscript, " Co-operation is all that's talked of among our shop men." [63] Occasionally more than one request came in from the same town. From one group in Mineral Ridge, Pennsylvania, came a letter asking Phillips to sell co-operators there copies of his constitution so that they might increase their membership and effectiveness; and from another group in the same town came word that it had adopted "nearly all" Phillips' Rochdale ideas.[64]

Blending propaganda with practical co-operative work, Phillips and his associates, especially those on the staff of the *Trades' Review*, were largely responsible for inspiring and counseling at least forty-five co-ops scattered through ten states in the period from October, 1863 to July, 1866. In all likelihood this is a conservative estimate. John Samuel, who was in touch with the situation, reported over sixty co-operatives were formed in the same general period.[65] That these organizations were similar to Phillips', that they were small, poorly capitalized, and composed mainly of the more fortunate or skilled workers would appear highly probable.

Certainly the intelligence purveyed by Fincher's staff struck home; their documents and ideas cropped up at co-operative meetings in numerous, if often obscure places. One soldier-reader commented, for instance, that a reprint Fincher had run from the Manchester *Co-operator* " ought to be read and pondered by every workingman that has to earn his living by the sweat of his brow." [66] From the fertile acres of York County, Pennsylvania, " Brutus " lauded the Rochdalers for originating co-operation and for helping it spread to America. Out of Litchfield, Illinois, in much the same vein, a former English co-operator announced that, " I was one of the first that commenced co-operation in Royston, my native village

---

[63] J. H. Harrison to Thomas Phillips, May 6, 1866, *ibid.*

[64] Charles Bowman to Thomas Phillips, June 28, 1866, *ibid.*

[65] Based mainly on letters in the Phillips Papers; " Co-operation," Ms, Samuel Papers; R. Heber Newton, " Co-operative Distribution," *North American Review*, CXXXVII (Jan.-July, 1883), 328.

[66] *Fincher's*, Feb. 13, 1864; also see, Nov. 5, 1864; Aug. 12, 1865. Special English contributors like Malcolm McLeod and " D. C." helped the staff also.

in Lancashire," and encouraged the editor and his staff to continue to sow their co-operative ideas in the American West.[67] These letters were fairly representative of the many that poured into Philadelphia and gave every indication that word of the English panacea was spreading afield. Moreover, so many of these correspondents were anxious to communicate with each other that Fincher accommodated them by opening a directory of co-operatives in his newspaper.

In this search for information it was Rochdale that caught everyone's eye and Rochdale's success that everyone sought to duplicate. Converts to the idea were everywhere. Tom Sellers of the Lawrence Mutual Benefit Society appealed to all potential co-operators to use the Rochdale idea, and he proudly reported that his own English-model store had become an object of great interest. Deputations of workers, as well as requests for advice and counsel, deluged his headquarters in Massachusetts. From Maine, Connecticut, New York, New Jersey, Pennsylvania, Ohio, Indiana, Illinois, Michigan, Kentucky, and Missouri hopefuls came to inspect his organization,[68] and what was true of Sellers' experiment and Phillips' was to a lesser extent very probably true of other co-ops.

There was certainly plenty of endorsement for the Plan. One prominent co-operator from Cincinnati and an old friend of Trevellick's, W. H. Gudgeon, praised it unreservedly, while an Englishman "lately landed," trained in the co-operative movement at home, took note of the excitement over the Rochdale Plan and volunteered to answer any queries addressed to him.[69] Another writer under a nom de plume cited the role of co-operation in "revolutionizing England," and insisted upon its acceptance in the United States. Joyously expounding its multiple blessings, a Quincy, Illinois co-operator reminded his readers that the movement in England had the sanction of the foremost minds of the century—Mill, Gladstone, Tennyson, Cobden, Bright, and Derby.[70] The English director of a large Ohio co-op, J. H. Gledhill, amplified these remarks and went

[67] *Ibid.*, Nov. 19, 1864; Mar. 18, 1865.
[68] *Fincher's*, Apr. 22, 1865.
[69] *Ibid.*, June 17, Aug. 19, 1865.
[70] *Ibid.*, Nov. 11, 1865; also Sept. 16, 1865.

on to show the value of self-help in solving the conflict between capital and labor. Finally, there were workingmen who rejoiced that the Plan was leaving economists and intellectuals, both of whom were fair game for American workers, baffled by its success.[71] On the whole, Phillips and his colleagues induced an interest in Rochdale among thousands of workers, and each new addition to their cause tended to become a new missionary so that word of the new cure-all, given the means of communication of the day, was widely scattered.

General economic conditions, of course, had already prepared many for conversion. Post-war deflation, demobilization, depression, and industrial unrest, all enhanced the appeal of self-help—and of other panaceas as well. But co-operation seemed to many a particularly happy solution to their troubles because it laid out a peaceful course and satisfied the workingman's conservative instincts. We have previously mentioned that it drew surprisingly little opposition from capital, except from local storekeepers who found themselves threatened with new competition on the block. Some of the larger business interests, however, felt self-help was simply another hobby to divert the masses. At any rate, employers could spare it an indulgent and benevolent smile, feeling that co-operation did nothing to interdict the free operation of natural economic laws or to overtax the fixed total supply of investment capital.[72]

Along this line there is no doubt that Phillips, and men of goodwill like him, spared few pains to point out that co-operation was not incompatible with the most venerable economic concepts of capitalism, and they insinuated that in practice, if not in theory, co-operators would fit themselves into the existing order of things. Of English co-operation Horace Greeley, a leading importer of ideas, announced:

---

[71] *Fincher's*, Nov. 19, 1864; Aug. 16, 1865.

[72] *The Workingman's Advocate*, July 21, 1866. U. S., Senate, *Report . . . upon the Relations between Labor and Capital*, 48th Cong., 1885, II, 1104-1105. Barns, pp. 75-113. J. T. Scharf and T. Westcott, *The History of Philadelphia* (3 vols.; Philadelphia, L. H. Everts & Co., 1884), Vol. III, pp. 2289-2290. US Mss 4A, *Sovereigns of Industry, Pioneer Council No. 1, Minute Books of the Executive Council* (Wisconsin State Historical Society, University of Wisconsin, Madison, Wisconsin). Cited hereafter as US Mss 4A, *Sovereigns of Industry*.

Their [the Rochdalers'] respectability is undoubted. Bishops and priests regard their orthodoxy as unimpeachable. Members of Parliament and mayors see nothing disorganizing or Jacobinic in their rules and practices and not an old woman of either sex in Rochdale . . . loses sleep any longer for fear of a Socialist raid from this quarter. . . . Co-operation is fully recognized in Rochdale as the most conservative, moral and beneficent idea . . . which it really is.[73]

Likewise only a year after the war, strife- and strike-weary iron molders heard from their leader William Sylvis that:

Co-operation [in England] has the approval of nearly all classes of society . . . [it] has enabled the workingman to provide against the necessities of strikes . . . or should he strike, he falls back upon the nest egg deposited in the co-operative store. Workingmen of America, if co-operation has accomplished such grand results abroad what might it not do here? Let capitalists see we are strong and there will be no necessity for strikes and conflict.[74]

Relatively detached observers, the Comte de Paris, for instance, writing for American audiences, lauded amicable relations between capital and labor springing from co-operative programs such as those at Rochdale, and others like them throughout England.[75] The findings of the Royal Commission also helped condition Americans to co-operation just as it had to trade unionism. Testimony of co-operative leaders before this body brought co-ops into the limelight, making them public affairs, revealing from several perspectives their aims and methods, and above all illuminating their gentility.

Respectably packaged, with no tariff barriers to hurdle, co-operation spread fanwise through the ranks of labor, though its progression, lacking the advantages of co-ordinated direction, was by fits and starts. Nowhere did there seem to be any hesitancy in placing an English label on these ideas. Indeed, during a period of alleged antipathy towards Britain, when the parochialism of the native mechanic was supposedly a dominant trait, labor leaders proudly displayed imported co-operative schemes and, like tweed suits, they took on a new

[73] *New York Tribune*, Oct. 12, 1858.
[74] *The Workingman's Advocate*, July 21, 1866.
[75] Le Comte de Paris, "On English Trades Unions," *Old and New*, I (1870), 565.

prestige because of their Britishness. As the iron molders put it:

To the laboring masses of the Old World goes the credit of first making manifest the advantages of co-operation . . . years of labor went into efforts to help themselves . . . but not until the clarion notes of ' self-help ' rang out from Rochdale did a gleam of sunshine light up their pathway. . . . It has been but a few years since an offshoot of the parent stem has been transplanted in this country and already there is glorious promise of abundant fruit.[76]

There were many individuals and agencies of one kind or another complementing the work of Fincher, his staff, and Phillips. Virtually every major labor newspaper and trade union journal (in these idealistic days before labor was entranced by visions of "bread and butter") featured articles, reprints, documents, discussions, reports, and even dialogues related to the myriad aspects of co-operative developments in Britain. The latest co-operative news from the Manchester *Co-operator*, the London *Workingman*, the *Beehive*, or *Reynolds'* was sure to appear in one form or another soon afterwards in American labor papers, in fact, in many papers outside of labor circles. From urban centers like Boston, Philadelphia, Washington, Detroit, and Chicago, and from smaller cities or towns like Worcester, Massachusetts; Sheffield, Connecticut; Tamaqua and Pottsville, Pennsylvania—for post-war co-operation was mainly a wage earners' show—explanations of self-help spread among workers and the ever-hopefuls of the lower middle class.

In 1866, for example, while the UCA still enjoyed favorable prospects, a special Massachusetts legislative commission endorsed the Rochdale Plan as an instrumentality capable of effecting both the moral and material elevation of the working class. More specifically, the commission pointed to the Plan as " one to which it is important the attention of our own working people should be called." [77] Reiterating what were substantially the recommendations of the commission, E. L. Godkin, himself a transplanted English liberal and the editor of *The Nation*, described glowingly to Americans the miracle

---

[76] *The Workingman's Advocate*, July 1, 1866.
[77] See *The Nation*, Mar. 22, 1866.

of the flannel weavers' panacea.[78] With a sizable volume of writings from or about George Holyoake, Thomas Hughes, George Potter, Lloyd Jones, and professors like Thornton, Fawcett, and Jevons, not to mention reports of the English Co-operative Congresses, with photographs of the original Rochdale Pioneers being hawked by *The Workingman's Advocate*,[79] it is clear that the Massachusetts commission and Godkin were simply swelling a growing chorus.

Naturally wherever there were appreciable numbers of Britons co-operative ideas flowered readily. Through the anthracite and bituminous fields, from eastern Pennsylvania on westward to the coal districts of Illinois and Missouri, immigrants who had known co-operation at home turned to it again. Noting the strength of co-operation among the immigrant miners of northern Illinois, the Chicago *Times* suggested it would be a good thing if English co-operation were given encouragement in that region.[80] The miners of La Salle County were especially active and there miners' unions early became involved in co-operative endeavor, largely as the result of leadership from men who had " known its practical workings " in England.[81] This sort of thing was duplicated in many other places.

Surcharged with moral energy and Christian fervor, the movement naturally solicited the attention of churchmen. Indeed, it raised a large following among clergymen, and co-operative ideas were soon echoed from many a pulpit. Since the better elements among co-operators as well as among the clergy were combating materialism and were under pressure from a social system in which Christian values were undergoing swift modification, friendship between them often came easily. Some divines, of course, brought their faith in co-operation with them to America. Reverend Robert Collyer, for many years a prominent lecturer to labor audiences throughout the

[78] *Ibid.*

[79] *The Workingman's Advocate*, June 2, 1866; also June 30, Sept. 8, 1866; July 17, 24, Sept. 18, 25, 1869; Mar. 7, 14, 1871; May 10, 17, 1873.

[80] See Nov. 21, 1863. Also the Chicago *Tribune*, Aug. 10, 12, 1867; and Mar. 27, 30, Apr. 13, 1867. *Belleville Democrat*, Dec. 3, 1868; Joliet *Republican*, June 15, 1867; *Illinois State Journal*, June 5, 1867.

[81] Chicago *Tribune*, Mar. 30, Aug. 10, 1867.

United States, remembering his personal trials as a worker years before in England, lent his voice and his pen to the cause.[82] Equally as significant as propagandists were Reverend R. H. Newton, Reverend Dr. Rylance, Reverend George Lorrimer, and Reverend E. Everett Hale.[83] By and large, the ministry brought additional sincerity, intelligence, and dignity to an already admirable movement; more important, they commanded a large audience and their social position argued well for the respectability of the cause.

Potentially the most promising vehicles for the spread of co-operation were the great trade and labor organizations. To workers galled by union defeats, hard times were a raw fact—not, as in the case of Reverend Collyer, half-recalled memory—and amid the disturbed atmosphere of transition years, before labor had set its sights on any single headland, panaceas were eagerly assimilated into trade union programs. Self-help was therefore a part of unionism until well into the eighties. Sensible of the political appeal of co-operative programs among the rank and file, labor leaders often engineered their inclusion in union platforms, some working strenuously for their advancement, others paying them mere lip service.

Consequently, as workers' associations blossomed in profusion during and immediately after the war, self-help became a matter of repeated discussion in unions. In October 1864 the Louisville Convention, largely under Trevellick's direction, formed the Industrial Assembly of North America and in the process adopted a co-operative plank to underpin its general program. Certainly Trevellick and W. H. Gudgeon, both of whom were advocates of the Rochdale Plan, must have tried to steer the Assembly towards the English method. Similarly, during the creation of the National Labor Union, which some have alleged was English-modelled itself,[84] co-operative ideas reared up among the welter of proposals for bettering labor's lot. Anxious to clear away the "debris of feudalism" and

---

[82] *The Workingman's Advocate*, May 26, 1866. Holyoake, *Co-operative Movement To-day*, p. 84.

[83] *Ibid.*, p. 84.

[84] *American Federation of Labor Encyclopedia Reference Book* (Washington: American Federation of Labor, 1919), p. 39. *Fincher's*, July 23, 1864.

usher in a new era of the hammer and anvil, the N.L.U. supported co-operation throughout its existence.[85] Unfortunately, while the years from 1866 to 1872 were marked by great interest in self-help, and despite the fact that many who were sympathetic to British co-operation—Sylvis, Trevellick, Hinchcliffe, Whaley, Cameron, and Siney—helped control the organization, the practical results of these repeated resolves were negligible. However, the N.L.U. did garner much information on the subject and helped educate labor leaders in co-operative ideas.

There is no question that the organization sought its inspiration abroad. Trevellick was specially selected in 1867 to study co-operation, among other things, in England. President Whaley likewise indicated the place held by Rochdale in his mind when he asserted that relief from capitalism lay in the kind of self-help "most successfully applied in England." [86] Many times the union's official organ hammered this theme home and its editor, Andrew Cameron, consistently made out a strong case for co-operation. In fact, Cameron functioned as the heir to Fincher insofar as he channeled co-operative information throught the columns of *The Workingman's Advocate*. Co- operative coal mining, the latest report of the London Co-operative Congress, Professor Thornton's co-operative program for abolishing strikes, Lujo Brentano's account of successful co-operation at Dumferline, profit-sharing plans, and co-operative workshops all fell within the ambit of his paper. His own views were well summarized in an address delivered before the National Labor Congress in 1867. According to Cameron, the experiment begun in Toad Lane had exceeded the wildest dreams of its founders, diffusion of its principles throughout the western world being ample proof of its efficacy. Tracing the struggle of the twenty-eight flannel weavers, he played upon a note familiar to workingmen everywhere and there can be little doubt that laborers, like children, listened eagerly to this morality tale in which middlemen and

[85] Commons, *Documentary History*, IX, 120-22. *Fincher's*, Aug. 13; Oct. 15, 1864.
[86] *Proceedings of the 2nd Annual Session of the National Labor Union*, Sept. 21, 1868: also see *The Workingman's Advocate*, Oct. 10, 1868.

monopolists were pottered and virtue triumphed. Cameron limned Rochdale as one of England's principal towns, flourishing and " prolific of the grandest results to workingmen." Simply to pronounce its various experiments a success was, in his estimate, but a feeble expression of their importance, and he became so enthusiastic that he asked Americans to adopt the plan at once. As for himself he never banked the fires of his ardor, but picked up all possible co-operative ideas on his visit to Basle in 1869 and, upon his return to Chicago, turned his office into a meeting place for co-operators as well as unionists.[87] He was, to say the least, a most representative spokesman for many leaders and men of the N.L.U.

Other trade unionists and labor reformers carried the message of self-help to their struggling brethren. On August 17, 1867 Colonel Richard Hinton, then Washington correspondent of the Boston *Weekly Voice,* sailed for Glasgow on a projected three month tour of Scottish and English co-operatives, intending to lay his conclusions about them before the American public.[88] Hinton was an Englishman, born into a trades union family, well versed in labor matters before he emigrated to the United States. " My father," he once wrote, " was president of a trades union when I was a lad. . . . I have heard him tell that at that period there was not a night that he initiated any member into the union that he was not in danger under the combination laws of Great Britain of transportation, of being made a convict." [89] This background kept him close to labor and in later years carried him into the socialist camp, though he continued his journalistic career. Returning from his trip in the spring of 1868 Hinton, too, sang the praises of Rochdale. Its shareholders, he reported, mechanics and laborers mostly, owned twenty-six stores, several rail lines, a large cotton mill, a flour mill, and a million and a half dollar store. Amazed by what he had seen, his exuberance spilling over, he exclaimed: " Workingmen of America, this is but a simple statement of

[87] See *ibid.,* Sept. 8, 1866; Nov. 2, 1867; June 20, Apr. 25, Nov. 7, Feb. 15, 1868; June 5, 1869; Sept. 25, Mar. 11, Apr. 8, 1871. Commons, *Documentary History,* IX, 141 and 148-150.

[88] *Boston Weekly Voice,* Aug. 17, 1867.

[89] U. S., Senate, *Report . . . upon the Relations between Labor and Capital,* 48th Cong., 1885, II, 405, 433, 437.

facts, but oh! what a conviction it must carry with it. The most powerful argument . . . is not as convincing as the practical effectiveness of co-operation as an alleviator of the miseries and privations that beset the toiler at every turn." [90]

Sufficiently intellectual to reach beyond the din of factory life, Hinton's writing circulated among a large and respectable middle class audience. Reprints of his articles, or parts of them, appeared in trade organs and labor newspapers, to be sure, but his writings on unionism and co-operation, based on his experiences abroad in 1867-8 and 1873, also appeared in *Galaxy, Atlantic Monthly, Old and New*, and the *North American Review*.[91]

Taking their cues from leaders such as Cameron, Fincher, and Phillips, and from writers like Hinton, trade unions often adopted the co-operative feature. Among those attempting this were Sylvis's iron molders, who operated a dozen widely scattered co-ops and made going concerns of them, at least for a while.[92] Carpenters in New York State, caulkers, machinists and blacksmiths in New York City, hatters in Yonkers and Newark, among others, engaged in co-operative enterprise.[93] Hugh McLaughlin's Sons of Vulcan under his personal direction organized a co-op among the families of employees in the Chicago Rolling Mills, while among the organized anthracite miners of Pennsylvania distributive stores, very likely offshoots of unions, enjoyed a heyday during and just after the Civil War.

Rochdale and other British-model stores not only influenced the organization of new co-ops among trade unionists, but also caused extensive revamping of some of the older co-operatives. One of these, for example, the Danvers Co-operative Union Society, in the famed Massachusetts shoe manufacturing center,

---

[90] *The Workingman's Advocate*, May 23, 1868.

[91] Thorndyke Rice, proprietor of the *North American Review* tried to found a trade union publication in England which he called *The Pioneer*. Holyoake described it as " the largest and best written trade paper that has appeared in England." See, Holyoake, *Co-operative Movement To-day*, p. 159.

[92] " Lecture on Co-operation," Ms, Samuel Papers, Box 13. *The Workingman's Advocate*, Nov. 6, 1869. Grossman, pp. 197-216.

[93] *Fincher's*, May 6, 1865. *Boston Daily Evening Voice*, Dec. 21, 1864; Oct. 20; Nov. 24, 27; Dec. 9, 1865; Jan. 24, 26, 31, 1866. Grossman, p. 205.

made the shift in 1869 and profited from it almost at once.[94] Similarly, in Fall River, so tightly packed with British and Irish immigrants that it smacked of a scene out of Lancashire, the town's main co-operative, the Fall River Workingmen's Co-operative Association, switched to the Rochdale Plan and thereby increased its capital and its membership. When Holy-oake visited the Bay State a decade later, this particular store covered an entire block, leading him to pronounce it as imposing as the better ones in England.[95] Needless to say, the conversion of these old establishments argued powerfully for the Rochdale idea.

Although intellectuals, at least native intellectuals, played a less significant part in the American labor movement itself than English intellectuals did in their own movement, there still were individuals whose abilities were thrown to the side of the co-operators. Horace Greeley was one; there is no need to review his service to the co-operative cause here. E. L. Godkin was another. Shortly after Hinton arrived back home late in the sixties from his English tour, Godkin joined vigorously in the cry for adopting English co-operative ideas. Dealing largely with materials drawn from the writings of J. M. Ludlow of the London Co-operative Board, Lloyd Jones, the Christian Socialist and sometime contributor to the American labor press, George Holyoake, and publications like *The Co-operator,* the *Friendly Societies Journal*, and sundry other British writings, he marshalled a formidable argument for self-help. Dismayed because he felt co-operation could hardly be said to exist in the United States, he stressed the ease with which Rochdalers had entered upon their work, moving from distributive stores to wholesale outlets, and on to more complex workshops and mills. Admitting Americans might have less need of such organizations than Europeans, he nevertheless regarded them as eminently desirable as a palliative for the problems of capital and labor. Like all others who favored co-operation Godkin was careful to highlight the immanent conservatism of the movement and he attempted to exonerate it from charges

[94] Bemis, p. 53.
[95] Newton, *North American Review*, CXXXVII, 329-30. Holyoake, *Among the Americans*, pp. 140-41.

fired by the Social Science Association that it intended striking a blow at laissez-faire or that it sought to infringe "in the smallest degree on any well settled economical law."[96]

Despite a revival of interest in co-operation during the sixties it is difficult to tell how extensively it was practiced or to determine just how many people were reached by British agitators and ideas. The number of co-operative associations formed, while helpful, does not of itself supply the answers. Many workers undoubtedly hoarded their capital but never set their plans in motion; some undoubtedly felt trade unionism would have to fizzle out before co-operatives could be propitiously launched[97]; others were content to preach and educate rather than act. How many men were set to thinking will always remain a riddle.

Moreover, men who had been co-operators in the old country did not always turn to it when they landed in America, nor did British ideas always produce positive reactions. Tom Jones, for instance, English-born founder of the National Iron and Steel Heaters' Union, had operated a co-op in Glasgow. Once in America he continued asserting that workers could gain their proper place in society only through self-help, yet there is no indication that he tried to implement his professions.[98] John Britton, a member of the famed carriage-making firm of Brewster and Company of New York, knew a great deal about English co-operation but decided it unworkable. A former laborer who had risen through the ranks of his organization, Britton, and a committee of workingmen in the Brewster firm, studied many plans of self-help throughout 1868-1869. They even struck up a correspondence with John Stuart Mill, John Bright, Thomas Hughes, J. M. Ludlow and other "advanced men" on the matter but in the last analysis gave up English ideas for a scheme of their own.[99] Ultimately it failed.

[96] E. L. Godkin, "Co-operation," *North American Review*, CV (July-Dec., 1868), 150-75.

[97] U. S., Senate, *Report . . . upon the Relations between Labor and Capital*, 48th Cong., 1885, I, 237, 457.

[98] *The Workingman's Advocate*, Feb. 14, 1874.

[99] U. S., Senate, *Report . . . upon the Relations between Labor and Capital*, 48th Cong., 1885, II, 1104-1105.

## II. CO-OPERATION AND THE CRISPINS

Among wage earners the popularity of co-operation continued growing from 1866 through the mid-seventies. Advocates of self-help busied themselves with propaganda, and trade and labor organizations insisted on mixing, or trying to mix, unionism and co-operative principles, this being feasible in a day when labor's objectives were neither so clear nor so simple as they would one day be. Indeed the very complexity of the co-operative movements in the United States, their unco-ordinated and highly individualistic activities, make them difficult to understand or to follow. Therefore, despite the danger of overemphasizing any one man's importance, we have traced the spread of the movement, insofar as this is possible, through the career of Thomas Phillips, a figure who was as representative and as important as any we know.

Like many co-operators, Phillips was not long discouraged by the failure of his initial enterprises; he merely shifted the points of his attack, writing numerous articles for Fincher's *Welcome Workman*[100] and generally chipping away at the barriers that lay between co-operators and their Elysian fields.

For a time he devoted himself to the task of changing the laws of association. Since there was practically no statutory allowance made for co-operation in the period prior to the Civil War, the laws that began appearing after the war suffered from all the defects of newness and experiment. Enacted without any apparent malice towards workingmen, they nevertheless posed a formidable barrier to associative activity by men of few means. Generally, at least in those few states with such laws, the statutes required accumulations of capital well beyond the capacities of working people; sometimes, too, they crippled those who raised requisite sums with additional fees and taxes due the state before co-operation was permitted.[101] Just such a law had been passed in Pennsylvania in April 1868. Co-

---

[100] "Autobiography." Phillips Papers.

[101] New Jersey, Bureau of Statistics of Labor and Industry, *12th Annual Report* (1890); U. S., Bureau of Labor, *Special Report* (1896), pp. 118-1177. Edwin G. Nourse, *The Legal Status of Agricultural Co-operation* (New York: Macmillan, 1927), p. 42.

operators were expected to amass $20,000 in capital, upon which they paid a tax; furthermore, they were expected to use the services of a notary, to pay special registration fees, and to pay for recording the charter of association.[102] This did not trouble business people for whom the law was really designed but it made things infinitely more difficult for the self-helpers.

Because Phillips was familiar with British laws of association he felt the Pennsylvania statute was a reactionary one. The irony of the situation did not escape him. If the creation of co-operatives was positively facilitated in a monarchy, why was the same thing not true—even more so—in a Republic?[103] Britain by its early laws of association, especially 15 Victoria 31 (1852), simply required that no fewer than seven persons agree to associate, and no serious exactions relative to subscriptions of capital, taxes, fees, or other charges were made. Charters were rather freely granted to men and women almost without cost, theoretically allowing even the poorest groups in England to form a co-op. Although Phillips denounced the Pennsylvania law and others like it as oppressive and obsolete, it remained on the books until a new statute more in line with his views was passed in 1887. By that time enough people were interested in the provisions of such laws to sweep them aside in Pennsylvania and elsewhere.[104]

Meantime Phillips was immersing himself more deeply than ever in the labor movement. In 1869, while working at Tillot's in Philadelphia, he learned through a circular of the formation of the Knights of St. Crispin, a powerful shoemaker's organization actually founded two years earlier by Newell Daniels in Milwaukee. By 1870 the order's 50,000 members easily made it one of the largest labor organizations in the United States. Phillips joined. Shortly afterwards he took up a new job at Shirley's and among the hands in this factory he organized the Philadelphia Lodge of the Crispins. Devoting himself to the enlargement of the lodge he often worked far into the

[102] "Notebook," Phillips Papers. Pa., Bureau of Industrial Statistics, 1st Annual Report (1872), pp. 393-94, 415-27.

[103] "Notebook," Phillips Papers.

[104] *The Union*, Sept. 9, 1881, Samuel Papers, Box 5. *Journal of United Labor*, Sept., 1882. "Notebook," Phillips Papers.

night, occasionally enlisting as many as a hundred and twenty-five men an evening. When the lodge could count 1100 stalwarts he was pressed by some of the men to form a separate branch, and to encourage him in this action they offered him the position of Sir Knight—which he readily accepted when the new lodge opened. Immediately afterwards, he carried a union election by a two-thirds vote, winning the rank of Grand Sir Knight and the additional title of "Crispin Orator" for his articulate campaigning.[105]

The Crispins, whose organization was impressive outwardly, drew their strength from among shoemakers all over the country who were disturbed by the technological changes sweeping over their craft in the late sixties. In particular, opposition centered about the introduction of the McKay pegging machine into shoe factories and about the practice of allowing numerous apprentices into the craft.[106] But it was none of these things that attracted Phillips; he saw in the new order another vehicle for his co-operative panacea—and he was not remiss in his missionary work. When a rash of strikes erupted in the industry, mainly in efforts to limit the number of "green hands," he was commissioned by the national order to write articles explaining its programs and principles in the Boston labor newspaper, *American Workman*. Availing himself of his opportunity, he argued that the Crispins should set up productive co-operatives, thus obviating the necessity of strikes by becoming their own bosses. Similarly in 1871 he had still another chance to drive home his ideas when, along with four other Philadelphians, he attended the Crispins' convention in Boston, where he exerted appreciable influence on the organization's Committee on Co-operation. Since the Crispins were shortly operating between thirty and forty co-operatives there seems little doubt that Phillips contributed materially to their formation.[107]

In Philadelphia, meanwhile, the main lodge, started with

[105] "Autobiography," Phillips Papers.
[106] Best studies of the Crispins are by D. D. Lescohier, "The Knights of St. Crispin, 1867-1874," University of Wisconsin *Bulletin*, No. 355; also Commons, *History of Labour*, II, 76-79.
[107] "Autobiography," and "Address to the Crispins," Ms. in Phillips Papers.

inadequate financial support, proved unable to maintain a co-operative workshop that Phillips had organized to serve unemployed Crispins, and it began to fail. As it did, the members divided into factions and fought one another, one group of partisans trying to restrict membership and to capture control of the co-operative shop. Such a move was fairly typical of older men who had developed a fetish for seclusion. More tolerant workers like Phillips were bound to oppose them since their objectives lay beyond the narrow confines of craft.

Leading the opposition, seeking to open the co-op to all Crispins, Phillips temporarily routed the " reactionaries " and plunged into the job of co-operative manufacturing along the latest Rochdale lines. Profits from the venture, the Knights of St. Crispin Shoe Manufacturing Association No. 1 of Philadelphia, were divided between " interest on capital, labor, and custom." [108] Chartered by the Commonwealth in August 1871, the new co-op was so shaky that its leader was forced to make stiff demands on the membership's cash resources. Nevertheless, initial obstacles were overcome and the Crispin Association fared well for a few years; like the UCA it also attracted attention. Unfortunately, the " reactionary " Crispins were able to rally their forces and, according to Phillips, brought such pressure to bear on their comrades that they prevented the mass of shoemakers from joining the organization. After four years of strife, its resources sapped, its programs sabotaged, its membership lists atrophied, the co-op collapsed.[109] Labor, as was so often true, had nourished the seeds of its own failure, for at no time had the enterprise been seriously attacked by employers.

Characteristically, Phillips remained undaunted and even as the co-op fought for existence, he recognized the urgent need for more training among his followers. Consequently, in 1871 he started still another venture, this time composed of what he called " choice spirits." Meetings of prospective recruits were held over the course of a two year period and over 20,000

---

[108] "Autobiography," Phillips Papers. *The Workingman's Advocate*, Apr. 13, 1872.

[109] Before it did it was signed over to the charge of Phillips. The legal instrument is in the Phillips Papers; also see "Autobiography," in *ibid*.

circulars, some of which drew the attention of the Manchester *Co-operator*, were issued to explain the purposes of the proposed organization. But it was too fragile a bark to launch upon the confused waters of co-operation and the attempt was finally written off.[110] Again, however, Phillips retained his perspective. He had witnessed many failures in co-operation, it is true, yet he had also seen considerable progress. A central figure in a city of great importance to workingmen, he had helped transmit British co-operative ideas throughout the labor world. Idealist, reformist elements among workers remained strong, building with that strength new vehicles for the movement—the Grange, the Sovereigns of Industry, the Central Labor Union of New York, the Knights of Labor, and the Sociological Society of America. British-model co-ops germinated in the coal fields of the Tuscarawas and the Alleghenies, in scores of obscure towns from the outskirts of Philadelphia to the prairies, and along the rail lines leading west into the heart of the Mississippi Valley. New, capable leaders armed with the legacies passed to them by British or British-inspired leaders, like Phillips and his associates, by trade unionists and journalists, came to the fore, while veterans like John Samuel, John Orvis, Phillips, and others kept pace with them, carrying their standard into the next decades.

Phillips was certainly justified in concluding that " good seed was sown." [111]

[110] *Ibid.*
[111] "Autobiography," Phillips Papers

# PART SIX

SELF-HELP: THE SPREAD OF AN IDEA

---

### I. Transition. Ideas and Men

Through much of the seventies co-operators labored in an exacting environment. The failure of Jay Cooke's banking house in 1873 symbolized but one aspect of a business cycle that hurled unionists and co-operators, along with their fellow citizens, into a severe, secondary post-war depression. Thousands of businesses failed. Men on the soil were cut loose from their moorings as commodity prices fell. Labor organizations that had weathered the crisis of 1867-1868 fell victim to the long recessional period that followed the panic and tens of thousands of workingmen faced disaster. There were lockouts and layoffs; there was unemployment and industrial strife.

Yet despite these handicaps, perhaps because of them, co-operators continued making gains. Drawing more extensively than ever upon British experience, they still tried to offer workingmen pacific and secure lives, for a time at least, within the framework of capitalism. The movements of the seventies, however, were marked by several new tendencies. For the first time self-help was adopted by the largest labor organization in the United States: evidence that it had become an integral part of the labor uprising. Even more significant was the fact that co-operation seemed to be spreading more rapidly from wage earners to farmers. This represented a transition that would ultimately make the countryside the stronghold of co-operation. It was also one in which workers proved to be the middlemen, thanks to the longevity of an old belief that farmers were part and parcel of the general labor movement. Significantly, too, the co-operative movement more than ever before was tending westward, penetrating the dissident areas of the Middle Border.

This was the general background against which we shall view the career of John Samuel, Jr., who, like Phillips, provides us with a tracer that shows the linkage of east and west, farmer and laborer during the critical years of the seventies and eighties.

John Samuel was one of the leaders produced by the crisis of the seventies. Photographed near the close of his life, his ruddy face framed in a mass of white hair and beard, a book clasped in one arm like Moses gripping the Tablets, he appears to have emerged from the Old Testament and indeed, some regarded him as an " Old Testament prophet," [1] others as an oracle and a patriarch. A man who could speak authoritatively on co-operation, his activities and influence surpassed Tom Phillips'. Like Phillips, however, his work lay mainly in the dissemination of British ideas.

Samuel fitted substantially into the pattern woven by the lives of the other agitators we have considered. He was born in Wales on February 3, 1817, the son of a druggist-ware glassblower who had taken an interest in associative enterprise well before the Rochdale Pioneers began their work. An obscure Englishman living in the United States recalled years later that the elder Samuel prided himself on having been born only a few weeks after the drafting of the American Constitution, which probably stamps him as a radical. This same Englishman also remembered that Samuel delivered a speech in Swansea in 1828 on " The Advantages and Uses of Societies of Mutual Improvement," [2] a sure indication that labor problems vexed and interested him. In 1831, or perhaps the year after, Samuel and family emigrated to Philadelphia in hopes of bettering their circumstances, and it was there that John Samuel, Jr., still an apprentice-boy of fourteen, finished his training.

The young Samuel, like Phillips, first acquired his local reputation as an organizer in his own craft. Craft-mindedness marked him, just as it did many immigrants, throughout his life. Philadelphia's glassblowers, most of whom came from

---

[1] Commons, *Documentary History*, IX, 281 for the photograph. Also E. D. Waldorf to John Samuel, Apr. 28, 1886, Samuel Papers.

[2] *Fincher's*, July 18, 1863, and Sept. 9, 1863; Mar. 5, 1864.

the British Isles, had already organized to a limited extent
before Samuel came on the scene. To encourage further
unionization, a convention of craft members met in 1852; in
attendance were representatives from Philadelphia and surrounding towns such as Temperanceville and Glassboro, New
Jersey. Fired with enthusiasm, the delegates left the convention determined to extend their activities, but in attempting
to do so they ran afoul of stiff opposition. In New Jersey, for
instance, courts were empowered to jail recalcitrant workers
who refused to continue working for the wages set in contracts
with their employers, and while this action was understandable
from the perspective of the employers, it—along with the use
of the lockout and blacklist—had the effect of putting the
quietus on the unionization campaign.

Hope was not abandoned however, and in 1855 Samuel
was dispatched to these same areas. He met with success;
even Glassboro, one of the more difficult targets in his itinerary,
fell into line. Why this occurred is not clear but it was
assuredly not solely the result of Samuel's personality—although it redounded to his credit. Triumphant in New Jersey,
he teamed up with two other agitators and worked in Mill-
ville, Williamstown, Waterford, and other glassblowing centers
near Philadelphia, and here again the results were heartening.[3]

Promising organizers like Samuel found that advancement
was swift. Philadelphia's glassblowers elected him President
of the Glass Bottle Blowers' Association in 1856 and in the
following year he secured his power by rallying several
hundred of his unorganized fellow craftsmen to the union's
cause. This and other additions to the Association's strength,
especially in the interior of the nation, resulted in the calling
of a national convention which established the Grand Union
of Glassblowers of the United States.[4]

Moreover, he had other opportunities to display his mettle.
When the national convention reassembled in 1858 the panic
of the preceding year had already caused serious rifts in the
organization. Several vital delegations refused to appear, and

[3] Simonds, pp. 629-30.
[4] "Sketch History of the G.B.B.A.," notebook, Samuel Papers, Box 5.
Simonds, pp. 630-32.

the members who did travel to Philadelphia were divided into two factions, one advocating reliance on the strike as the major bargaining weapon, the other arguing for a more pacific approach to labor problems. On the floor of the convention there erupted a heated debate which threatened to bring the meeting to an explosive end. At this critical juncture Samuel, through a series of adroit maneuvers which included the singing of a song he had prepared for the occasion, saved the day, mended matters, and kept the convention in session for another two weeks. As a vote of thanks to him, the delegates elected him their secretary and thereafter, through the remainder of his life, he retained positions of power or special status in the craft.[5]

Like thousands of other workingmen Samuel turned to co-operation during the Civil War. His service as an associate of Fincher indicates, as do his writings, that he had steeped himself in the subject of self-help. With Philadelphia as a kind of center of the co-operative movement, it was only natural that he should make the acquaintance of Tom Phillips and help him by participating in the activities of the UCA. There is little danger in assuming that they materially influenced one another. It is true that Samuel never ceased his active trade union work; in 1864, for instance, he was largely responsible for the meeting of organized tradesmen out of which grew the Philadelphia Trades Assembly and he served as vice-president of the order.[6] Nevertheless, his major interests were clearly those of a co-operator and directly or indirectly over the next forty years his name was associated with almost every major co-operative movement in the United States embodying British ideas.

## II. PORTRAIT OF A PROPHET

Samuel was one of the best informed practical co-operators active in America. In his unrelenting efforts to comprehend fully the cause to which he was dedicated, he conducted

---

[5] Simonds, p. 631.

[6] See, note dated Oct. 8, ?, announcing Samuel's lecture before members of the UCA in Phillips Papers; *Fincher's*, Oct. 3, Nov. 21, Feb. 23, 1863; May 21, Aug. 20, 1864.

research into self-help that was detailed, factual and, at least in terms of his instincts, scholarly. His knowledge of the panacea was much more substantial than Phillips'; professional students of the co-operative movement such as Edward Bemis, Albert Warner, and Daniel Randall regarded him as an authority on the subject, while George McNeill, Carroll Wright, and Richard Ely had the highest respect for his learning. Alive to his own importance as an expert on self-help, Samuel collected large amounts of information, in hopes of ultimately establishing a research library on co-operation. Replete with thousands of clippings, articles, annotated notes, scrapbooks and letters the collection is still the largest and most valuable aggregation of nineteenth century co-operative materials in the United States.[7]

For information Samuel relied almost exclusively upon printed British sources. He subscribed for many years in fact to Britain's chief co-operative papers, being especially fond of the Manchester *Co-operative News,* which he thought one of the most powerful agencies working to educate Americans in the principles of self-help.[8] Though his income from his trade or from his services to unions and co-operatives cannot have been great, his expenditures on newspapers, books, and tracts continued year after year and even when allowance is made for the re-sale of many papers and pamphlets that he purchased in quantity, his outlays must have taxed his resources.[9]

Samuel also depended heavily in many ways on his personal contacts among the co-operators of Great Britain. For several decades he sustained correspondence with prominent figures in the British movement, and he was on very friendly terms with

[7] See, A. Warner to J. Samuel, May 7, 1886; Samuel to D. Randall, Dec. 7, 1885; Dec. 28, 1885; G. McNeill to J. Samuel, Aug. 11, 1886; C. Wright to Samuel, July 8, 1892; J. Samuel to E. V. Neale, Aug. 24, 1891, Samuel Papers.

[8] J. Samuel to The Board of Managers of the Co-operative News Society, Mar. 30, 1882, Samuel Papers.

[9] Memo sheets of subscriptions and payments are scattered throughout the Samuel Papers but see, for instance, a memo dated Sept. 23, 1880 about just one batch of pamphlets appraised at $15 with a duty of $2.45. One year he spent at least $40 on papers and wrote off to Britain in perturbation if they were late.

British co-operative organizations and their officers. He struck up a particularly close acquaintanceship with E. V. Neale, Secretary of the Manchester Co-operative Board, in 1881 and their letters crossed the Atlantic frequently over the next twenty years. Furthermore, he cultivated similar relations with G. J. Smith, Hodgson Pratt, D. J. Sadler, and other co-operative leaders, and while he did not meet or correspond with George Jacob Holyoake until late in that man's career, he was familiar with all of his writings on self-help as early as the sixties. Finally in 1882, his link with the British was formalized by his election into the Guild of Co-operators, an organization charged "with the special promotion of Co-operative ideas," the intention of which was "to produce propagandists." There can be no doubt that Samuel amply filled the bill or that he facilitated bringing to the American scene a wide variety of opinions and intelligence from ranking British co-operators.[10]

Even before 1882, however, he commanded a wide circle of informants which included trade unionists, like George Howells, as well as co-operators. And these, even at long distance, enabled him to guide Americans into the intricacies of co-operation, to inform men interested in British progress who was best qualified to answer their questions, what books, articles, newspapers, and pamphlets would best serve their purposes. Moreover, since Samuel was intimate with co-operative developments and co-operative leaders in the United States, he was in a position to funnel the information gleaned from the British into the proper channels in America.[11] Dubious as he was of middlemen, he functioned as one himself.

Rather interestingly, Samuel's geographic location contributed to the increase of his influence. Though probably more from coincidence than not, he was always favorably situated

[10] J. Samuel to ? Steffer, Feb. 6, 1882; J. C. Gray to Samuel, Nov. 4, 1884; Mar. 12, 1886, June 18, 1890; Samuel to G. Smith, Dec. 9, 1880; Feb. 7, 1881; Apr. 13, 1881; D. Sadler to Samuel, July 4, 1881, Samuel Papers; Holyoake, *Co-operative Movement To-day*, pp. 47-48.

[11] See, Samuel to ? Hugot (date obscured), 1885; A. Fayram to Samuel, May 26, 1881; May 12, 1886; Samuel to E. J. Harris, Feb. 20, 1886; J. Samuel to Mr. Davis, Dec. ?, 1882; Samuel to D. Randall, Dec. 28, 1885; also see Samuel-Keuchter letters; Samuel-Fayram letters; Samuel-Nelson letters; Samuel-Osborn letters; Samuel-Fales letters, in Samuel Papers.

to function most effectively as a purveyor of information. At the beginning of the co-operative revival, as we have seen, he lived in Philadelphia, one of the centers of the co-operative movement, and a stronghold of unionism as well. As the co-operative impulse spread westward and buttressed the seedling organizations there, he again found himself in the heart of the movement, for in 1869 he took up residence in St. Louis, after the founding of a new glassblowing establishment. There he made his home until his death in 1907.

An articulate man, Samuel undoubtedly reached thousands of people through his writings. Despite the lack of a formal education, he proved a prolific, if not an accomplished writer. Like many labor leaders he turned to the production of propaganda early, in his case during the sixties with Fincher. Thereafter his ties with the labor press were close and he gained prominence in workingmen's and farmers' newspapers as "an advanced thinker on live questions." [12] In 1870, for example, at the request of the editor of the St. Louis *Times,* he contributed a series of articles on British and American co-operation; in 1874 he made similar contributions to the St. Louis *Republican.* As leader of the St. Louis Trades Assembly, he also directed the operations of the *Union,* its official journal, converting it into a co-operative vehicle whenever the opportunity beckoned. Throughout the seventies and eighties his opinions, and the opinions of others about him, were featured in various papers. Some of them, like the *Rural World,* were published by his friends—in this case by George Longmans, a native of Southampton; some were small, local papers printed in Iowa, Missouri, Kansas, and Illinois, papers such as the Casey *Weekly Times, The Daily Democrat, The Labor Compendium,* the Eureka *Union,* and the Carroll *Sentinel.* Others were of more general, often national, importance and included the *Sovereigns' Bulletin, The Journal of United Labor,* and, of course, *Fincher's Trades' Review.* After the founding of the Sociological Society of America early in the nineties, he became one of the editors of its official publications. Moreover by that time he com-

---

[12] "Co-operation in the United States," booklet, Samuel Papers, Box 4. *Casey Weekly Times,* Sept. 2, 1874, in Samuel Papers, Box 4.

manded wide coverage in the labor-farmer press and his reputation as an authority on co-operation was generally recognized.[13]

Pamphlets and lectures also helped Samuel circulate co-operative ideas that he had absorbed from the British. Though he never sustained the production of a book, he taught himself the disciplines of pamphleteering, and while his early efforts to summarize the historical origins of self-help were unsatisfactory and sometimes misleading, his skill increased with time. By the seventies he was regularly producing competent articles and analyses of co-operation and when W. D. P. Bliss commenced work on his *Encyclopedia of Social Reform*, Samuel was asked to make the contribution dealing with his beloved panacea, though for some reason he did not do so. Newspaper writing certainly helped him greatly and by the eighties he had hit his stride. One of his manuals, "How to Organize Co-operative Societies," emerged as a standard book of instruction on the subject in 1886, and his "Tract for the Times," and "A Chart of Rochdale's Progress," found large audiences in that turbulent era.[14] Equipped with the powerful lungs of a glassblower, he was likewise a formidable orator. Speech-making was an integral part of his routine and his papers indicate that his services were in constant demand, for his formal talks numbered in the hundreds. The contents of his lectures were uniformly brief, straightforward explanations of co-operation, coupled with sufficient idealism, for that he never lacked, to whet the listeners' appetites.[15]

Samuel's personal characteristics deserve mention too, for he was more than just another labor politician. His associates and acquaintances, and they were numerous, unanimously regarded him as a splendid man. Qualities of leadership

---

[13] *Times* (St. Louis), clippings from Feb. and Mar. 1870; Aug. 17, 1874 in Samuel Papers, Box 4. "The Union," annotated booklet; "Co-operation in the United States," Samuel Papers, Box 4. Clippings and notes on the Grange. Box 7. "The New Commonwealth, Co-operation, Journal of United Labor," collected in a notebook, Box 4. See too, Fales-Samuel Correspondence, Samuel Papers, Box 3.

[14] See, Samuel to W. D. P. Bliss, (date obscured), Samuel Papers; also the Ms of an article Samuel wrote for the *Encyclopedia* in Box 3, *ibid.*; The "Chart" was so popular Samuel ran out of copies. A copy is in Box 3, *ibid.* Mss copies of several lectures are also in Box 3, *ibid.* Bemis, pp. 396, 401.

[15] See Mss of lectures, Samuel Papers, Box 3.

placed him in a more fortunate position than his fellow workers but he preferred always to remain active in his trade. He kept intimately in touch with the little man in the labor movement and earned the reputation of being a thorough-going democrat. To these people, indeed to anyone who asked for it, he gave advice, time, and energy unstintingly. Many co-operators must have agreed with the middle westerner who called the Welshman " the greatest friend Co-operation has." [16] George McNeill, one of the more illustrious labor figures of his day, regarded Samuel as one of the greatest veteran co-operators and looked up to him with filial respect. Nor was McNeill his sole admirer. C. H. Simmerman, a laborer who had risen from the ranks to become chief of the New Jersey Bureau of Labor and Industry, always remembered Samuel as an "old time co-worker" in behalf of labor and he relied upon him from time to time for information on co-operative matters. To younger men like George Keuchter, the Welshman was "Uncle John," and to famed figures like George Jacob Holyoake, "the old War Horse." Men may not make movements but it is by their men that movements are often judged and few could deny that Samuel and others like him were ornaments to their cause.[17]

## III. Sources of the Faith

John Samuel's fundamental concepts of the theory and practice of co-operation were British, as we have earlier suggested, and because we shall use him as a tracer this point needs further illumination. Subsisting most of his active life on a flow of information that came westward from England, he carefully gauged the advance of self-help there and fed upon its intellectual roots. In the ordinary affairs of co-operation he proved capable, but very few of his ideas were in the slightest degree original. He studiously examined a great many varieties of co-operation, yet in the last analysis he faithfully adhered to the tested and successful principles of

[16] "Co-operator" to Samuel, Aug. 29, 1886, *ibid.*
[17] See, G. McNeill to Samuel, Aug. 11, 1886; C. H. Simmerman to Samuel, May 11, 1894; Samuel to C. H. Simmerman, Feb. 12, 1894; G. Keuchter to Samuel, Mar. 12, 1892; George Holyoake to Samuel, Feb. 1900, Samuel Papers.

his English mentors. Admiration for the work of his friends overseas is monotonously manifest in all that remains of his writings on self-help. As a propagandist he was superb; as a cipher he merits both the praise and the blame that inevitably go with that role. Certainly his enchantment was complete. The fearsome conundrums facing American labor, many of them more complex than those confronting British labor, failed to disenchant him entirely. His lifetime of vigorous activity, in fact, would have been as congenial to Lancashire and the Midlands as it was to Philadelphia and the Mississippi Valley.

Even Samuel's personal heroes were British. Robert Owen was one of his great favorites and he looked up to his memory not only as a co-operator but also as the guiding spirit of the short-hour movement, the leader of the Grand National and, in short, as the founder of the British labor movement. This was no less true of British political economists. Eager to create a basis of "economic literature" on which he could build a more impressive and useful reputation, he cultivated general acquaintanceship with the writings of John Stuart Mill, Arnold Toynbee, and, in the nineties, Alfred Marshall. The co-operators, of course, intrigued him and it is probably no exaggeration to claim that his readings in the works by these men was omnivorous. Books and articles by Holyoake, Lloyd Jones, Edward V. Neale, Thomas Hughes, and a host of others were his steady fare and a constant source of inspiration. He even tried to create a visual impression of British co-operation by collecting scores of pictures of co-operative stores and shops scattered throughout England. The entire co-operative movement, in fact, became an intensely personal kind of religion to him.[18]

From among the many forms of co-operation, Samuel selected the Rochdale Plan as the most perfect system. Into the promulgation of this program he sank the bulk of his energies. Despite fairly catholic tastes in some matters, he

[18] For instance see, Samuel to E. V. Neale, Nov. 26, 1889; also a Note from Holyoake, Feb. 1900; a lecture by Toynbee, "Industry and Co-operation," Box 4; and clippings and pictures of co-operation and co-op stores in Samuel Papers, Box 4.

was doctrinaire on the subject of Rochdale. Like Phillips and so many other men who fastened on the Rochdale idea, he clung to it absolutely and never seems to have felt that it could have been greatly improved upon. Once, for instance, a member of the Knights of Labor Co-operative Board, complaining of the slow growth of co-operation in the new order, suggested that alternative schemes might be preferable to the British plan. Samuel replied cryptically, " If you have read the Preamble of the Rochdale Pioneers and think you can improve upon it, let me know . . . I have carefully studied that Plan for the last twenty years and confess my inability to add to it or take away anything superfluous in it." [19] When, again, a dissenting faction within the Knights sought a fresh approach to self-help Samuel, in much the same vein as above, wrote them: " Some . . . members are racking their brains in devising some novel plan that will compare with the Rochdale for delivering the wage worker from poverty." [20]

While Samuel did develop an almost fanatical respect for Rochdale, it is only fair to point out that he did feel ample latitude was afforded him by his American work. He was impressed by the fact that the Rochdalers themselves had experimented freely in working out their system, so much so that by the eighties Rochdale really represented a complex of co-operative operations. Consequently, he championed both productive and distributive co-ops, although he believed distributive co-operation to be of preëminent importance. Distributive stores, in fact, as he told one co-operator in 1885, " represent the most advanced phase of practical co-operation," [21] and when one of his correspondents in Ohio doubted the efficacy of distributive stores, as opposed to productive co-ops, the veteran replied that if distributive stores were hard to operate, then productive co-ops must be impossible. [22]

During the early eighties, just prior to his assumption of

---

[19] Samuel to Peter McGaughey, dated only " 1886," Samuel Papers.

[20] Samuel to J. Osborn, Apr. 16, 1886, *ibid.*

[21] Note simply identified as being to a co-operator, dated June 2, 1885, Box 1, *ibid.*

[22] Samuel to W. H. Smith, Aug. 3, 1885; Samuel to J. Osborn, Apr. 18, 1886; Samuel Papers. " How to Organize A Co-operative Society," Samuel Papers, Box 4. *Journal of United Labor,* Dec. 10, 1884.

the leading role on the Knights of Labor Co-operative Board, he became vitally interested in "integral co-operation," an idea that really represented a logical extension of the Rochdale scheme. Under the integral system, distributive and productive co-operation became the foundations of a self-sufficient community; member co-operators were supposed to produce as well as to consume their own goods. As Samuel came to know it, the plan was brought forth in the United States by Henry Sharpe. An Englishman, Sharpe directed the Knights of Labor Co-operative Board in 1884[23]; the fact that he was a foreigner and was nevertheless given such a job is ample indication of the esteem in which British co-operation was held. A cautious person, Samuel was at first uncertain of the soundness of the plan, and curiously enough, so too was Sharpe. The upshot of this timidity was that Sharpe first wrote to Samuel for advice and then, still in doubt, wrote directly to Edward V. Neale, the Manchester co-operative leader and barrister. After respectful consideration of the plan, Neale supported it wholeheartedly, and suggested that it seemed to him the logical outcome of all co-operative endeavor.[24] Implementation of the new plan got under way almost at once. One integral colony was started at Eglinton in southwestern Missouri, and another was begun in Kansas. Unfortunately we know little of the details about either colony. Clearly neither was a howling success for Sharpe left the United States in 1890, travelling to the wilds of Brazil in hopes of founding a socialist community there.[25]

Nevertheless, the romantic and eccentric Englishman impressed many American co-operators. Richard Hinton, the labor journalist who was then well on the way to becoming a socialist, Frank K. Foster, one of the "intellectuals" in the A.F.L. and the editor of a co-operative newspaper, and John McClelland, leader of the Knights of Labor Executive Board,

[23] Bemis, pp. 398-99. Powderly, p. 635.
[24] H. Sharpe to Samuel, June 19, 1884; Samuel to H. Sharpe, July 2, 1884; H. Sharpe to E. V. Neale, July 5, 1884, Samuel Papers.
[25] *Globe-Democrat* (St. Louis), Oct. 14, 1899. *Co-operative News*, Jan. 8, 1881.

in company with Samuel all subscribed to the plan.[26] And Samuel, in particular, continued to champion it after taking over Sharpe's position as the leader of the Knights' Co-operative Board. In giving support to the integral plan, and certainly Samuel must have been aware of it, he was backing pure communitarian socialism and placing himself in the ranks of the most ambitious co-operators in the United States.

Taking Samuel's ideas as a whole, and that would include the integral plan, there emerged a coherent, though by no means a fixed, pattern. For the layman he summarized his views in shibboleths, mainly imported from Holyoake or other Englishmen—" fixed rates of interest on capital," " profits in the store to the consumer," " profits in the workshop to the producer." [27] But these were the oversimplifications of the propagandist. Spelled out his views were somewhat more complex. First, he called for the establishment of distributive stores, then, as conditions permitted, wholesale and retail agencies. Beyond this, whenever feasible, co-operators were encouraged to undertake the production or manufacture of their own products. Adapting his ideas to one of America's main resources, he even envisaged co-operators purchasing land for use by all the members of a particular co-operative society. Ultimately he hoped Americans would follow Britons in co-operative land purchase schemes, and in arrangements for securing workingmen's homes. For the socially unfortunate he had in mind a set of emergency measures. Members of co-ops who were unemployed, locked out, blacklisted, or on strike, were to be put to work cultivating lands owned by their co-operatives. Once all of these steps had been taken and self-help was under way, then by invoking the integral formula, members were to start self-governing, self-sustaining communities. By such a road did Samuel expect that the " co-operative idea of production, distribution, education, and government " [28] would be reached. But, of course, these were

[26] H. Sharpe to Samuel, June 19, 1884, Samuel Papers. This letter lists those men interested in the plan.

[27] Ms of the article Samuel was preparing for the *Encyclopedia of Social Reform*, dated 1895, Samuel Papers, Box 3.

[28] " How to Organize A Co-operative Society," Ms, Samuel Papers, Box 4.

long range plans and Samuel was a patient man. His counsel to workingmen co-operators invariably was, "Begin small, go slow, have patience, confidence, and courage." [29]

Viewed in its entirety Samuel's overall plan was an alternative to capitalism; above all it was a peaceful alternative. It contemplated neither strikes nor violence and evidenced no malice toward capitalists. Rather it was aimed at gradually supplanting the existing order with a more idealistic one in which Samuel and his associates would discover themselves independent of capital and the whims of markets, working for themselves in the present and for mankind in the future. [30]

Two typical nineteenth century themes are embedded in his ideas and in his writings—Christianity and individualism. His objections to capitalism derived as surely from Christian belief as from any sense of oppression. Being both zealous and devout, he easily convinced himself and many others as well, that he was a prophet leading his people out of Egypt. The disciplines he tried to instill in the rank and file were the disciplines of Churchmen embarked on a crusade and one of his more effective instruments, which he constantly exhorted workingmen to make use of, was the Bible. To Samuel self-help in Christian terms meant:

> Let each man find his own in all men's good,
> And all men work in noble brotherhood. . . . [31]

Although the Welshman was certain of the righteousness of his cause, he never managed to reconcile his individualism with government. His mistrust of state interference in the affairs of citizens was hardly less great than that of the staunchest laissez-faire capitalists. Men and women co-ordinating their strength and energies to remodel the world, to rejuvenate it morally, he could understand. Yet he had no faith whatever in political institutions that might be created or directed by these same people. Ironically, Samuel, like the Rochdálers whom he idolized, denied he was a socialist but there can be little doubt that ultimately he would have gone

[29] Samuel to W. Dawson, July 2, 1885, Samuel Papers.

[30] *Ibid.*

[31] Even as an old man Samuel continually tested himself on knowledge of the Bible. The tests are in Samuel Papers, Box 3.

as far, if not farther, towards changing society as the socialists of Britain or America. Had he pushed his programs to their conclusion he must have come into the possession of government and once in this position he was philosophically committed to changing the economic system, equalizing competition, and taking over the tools of production for "the people." [32] Nevertheless, during his active career he declared that the true co-operator desired nothing from the state.[33] That co-operation could have flourished within the economy as a countervailing power—as it has in Sweden—or that it might be aided greatly by government does not seem to have occurred to him. In short, dedicated as he was to his panacea, he revealed that there were rather serious gaps in the fabric of his thought.

## IV. SELF-HELP AMONG THE GRANGERS

Samuel's background and thought are significant because they illuminate specifically the more typical qualities of scores of co-operators, British-born and British-inspired, who carried their ideas into the mainstream of the American labor movement and then spread their message among farmers. During the seventies and eighties hundreds of men very much like Samuel started a number of small experiments and busily preached their gospel of self-help. In their zeal they sang,

> We will go down
> We will go down
>      To the lowest of all
>      To the lowest of all
> And carry our love
> And carry our love
> And lavish it there
>      In the spirit of Truth
>      In the name of God. . . .
> We will go up
> We will go up
>      To the highest of all
>      To the highest of all. . . .[34]
>      Etc.

---

[32] Holyoake, *Co-operative Movement To-day*, Chap. 19.
[33] "Co-operation," Ms dated 1895, Samuel Papers, Box 3.
[34] The official song of the Sovereigns of Industry; see *The Sovereigns' Bulletin*, Oct. 1875.

And it was in this spirit that Samuel and other co-operators began to function as middlemen, passing co-operative methods and objectives on from wage earners to the men who ultimately would do most with co-operation in America, the farmers. Indeed, the co-operators looked hopefully to one organization in particular that appeared on the scene late in the sixties and which soon became the greatest co-operative vehicle of its day, the Patrons of Husbandry, more commonly called the Grange. Thrown up among the lonely and restless farmers, and the town and village shop-keepers who served them, the Grange, founded in 1867, was designed primarily to alleviate the monotony and isolation of farm life. Swelling its membership rapidly under the stress of hard times and the discriminations of the great railroad companies, the Grange began to assume formidable proportions during the early seventies. During the first half of 1873, for instance, as the panic came on, 10,000 local granges were reputedly organized; membership doubled in 1874 and at the meeting of the National Grange in 1875 it was reported that there were 24,290 granges in operation, with an enrollment of 763,000 men and women. Power of this magnitude—especially in troubled times—naturally resulted in social activities yielding to political agitation and, in a decade singularly devoid of any remarkable workingclass gains on the farm or in the urban centers, the order won a series of victories in several states against the railroads—and with victory, however limited, the Grangers nursed their ambitions.[35]

Almost from the inception of their national organization many important Grangers displayed interest in co-operation. One early and popular form of self-help developed when Grange clubs resolved themselves into purchasing agencies which contacted wholesalers who were willing to sell them merchandise in quantity and hence at a discount. Business transacted on this American plan, at best an impromptu affair,

---

[35] Standard on the Grange are Solon J. Buck, *The Granger Movement* (Cambridge, Mass.: Harvard University Press, 1913), and *The Agrarian Crusade* (New Haven: Yale University Press, 1920). Membership figures must always be accepted with caution. See, Newton, *North American Review,* CXXXVII, 330-31; Thomas C. Atkeson, *Semi-Centennial History of the Patrons of Husbandry* (New York: Orange, Judd Co., 1916), pp. 20-30, 350. Commons, *Documentary History,* I, 114.

was unprecedented. An Ohio agency, to cite but one example, ran its business up from a few thousands to a million dollars a year by catering to these farm organizations, in the process saving Grangers over a quarter of a million dollars.[36] Summing up the order's startling progress one authoritative source declared:

> Turning to this country, we see two million or more Patrons successfully imitating their British cousins in this respect . . . their records show twenty state purchasing agencies, three of which do an annual business of $200,000 and one of which does an annual business of $1,000,000. Patrons have five steamboat or packet lines, fifty societies for shipping goods, thirty-two grain elevators, twenty-two warehouses for storing goods. . . . The Patrons . . . saved $5,000,000 in 1872 and $20,000,000 in 1874.[37]

Soon the Patrons focused their attention on purer forms of self-help and they began to employ British ideas. At the meeting of the National Grange in 1875, the organization's leaders unveiled a well articulated program for establishing Rochdale stores.[38] Broadcast throughout thousands of local granges, the program was widely adopted and Rochdale stores flourished as never before in the United States. There are only scraps of information about them, unfortunately, and little remains in the record of their experiences. Admitting the impossibility of securing accurate estimates of their number, it is perhaps worth notice that one source in 1876 claimed that there were 160 Rochdale-model stores in operation, another that there were nearly 1000, and still a third that there were several hundred. Some of these stores, or at least the impulse that gave birth to them, endured. A decade later in 1886 a Grange official declared that there were "hundreds of co-operative stores on the Rochdale Plan . . . in successful operation all over the country"; and, in the same year, the manager of the Texas State Grange listed 103 Rochdale stores in his state alone. "Our growth," he announced, "has astonished all alike. We have not had a single failure where the true

[36] Newton, *North American Review*, CXXXVII, 330.
[37] *The True Economist*, Nov. 8, 1876.
[38] Commons. *Documentary History*, IX, 114. Atkeson, pp. 74-82. *The Workingman's Advocate*, Jan. 15, 1876.

Rochdale principles have been adhered to." [39]  A year later the Texans could report 132 English-model stores with a capital of $629,644 and an annual business of $1,612,000.[40]

The story of how British influences permeated the ranks of American farmers is likely to remain nebulous; nevertheless there are clues about the way in which they won acceptance among groups whose offspring several generations removed have made co-ops an intimate part of their economic and social life.

Samuel's role among the Patrons may tell us much; indeed, it appears very likely that his personal activities were important to the spread of the Rochdale idea.  Although he was a wage earner and a trade unionist, not a farmer, Samuel joined the Grange in 1869 when he settled in St. Louis, hoping to convert the organization to co-operation.  Concentrating on a task he knew well, agitation, he became a figure of some consequence in the Missouri State Grange by 1874 and won a somewhat wider reputation, as his letters indicate, among grangers elsewhere.  In fact, despite his leadership of the St. Louis Trades Assembly and his editorial responsibilities, he seems to have given a large share of his time to agricultural affairs.[41]

We know something of how he worked.  In 1873 while busily circulating his ideas, he met J. H. Osborn, chief agent of the Wisconsin State Grange at the Patrons' national convention in St. Louis.  Osborn, with whom Samuel corresponded periodically over the next fifteen years, was fully informed by the Welshman of the potentialities of British co-operation, and was converted to the cause.  Once familiar with the British plans, Osborn in turn passed word on to his friends in his native state.  Time and time again, however, he drew upon Samuel, the original source of his intelligence, and thanks also to Samuel, relied heavily upon the Manchester *Co-operative News* for the latest details of British and American develop-

---

[39] Newton, *North American Review*, CXXXVII, 336.  Circular by the American Co-operative Union, Samuel Papers, Box 2.

[40] *Journal of United Labor*, July 23, 1887.

[41] "Grange Papers," notebook, Samuel Papers, Box 2.

ments.[42] Through this process of stimulating and instructing others Samuel helped create a missionary brigade that preached up and down the Mid-west.

The upshot of this advertising was the adoption of the Rochdale Plan as a part of the Grange's national program, an event of great importance to the labor world in 1875. " It is a very interesting fact," echoed the old co-operator Samuel Leavitt, " that the National Grange has formally recommended English co-operative trade to subordinate granges," and others reiterated this sentiment. Still more interesting is the fact that Samuel had the audacity to suggest that he was mainly responsible for the Grange's action. Writing to another co-operator in 1886, he claimed that when the Patrons met in St. Louis in '75 he had presented " Brother D. W. Adams, Worthy Master of the National Grange," with a chart that he had prepared illustrating the progress of Rochdale co-operation, buttressed by the opinions of many eminent sympathizers. Adams was allegedly so impressed that the chart became, according to Samuel, " the groundwork of co-operation in the Grange." [43]

Probably made in all sincerity, Samuel's claims taken by themselves cannot adequately explain why the Grange turned to the Rochdale Plan. Other influences similar to his were, unknown to him, receiving far wider support among the leadership and the rank and file than he could have realized. During 1874, for example, national leaders of the Grange contacted representatives of the Rochdale Society and drew from them information and encouragement. In this connection, it is worth speculating about the part played by William Saunders. Historians have generally credited the founding of the Grange more to Oliver H. Kelley than to any other single individual, but during the early days of the Grange William Saunders was regarded as an equally significant figure. Saunders was a Scotsman and, like Kelley, he worked for the Bureau of Agriculture, rising to become Superintendent of Gardens

---

[42] Samuel to J. Osborn, Apr. 16, 1886; Osborn to L. Allen, Dec. 18, 1873; Osborn to Samuel, May 18, 1886, Samuel Papers.
[43] Samuel to E. J. Green. Sept. 23, 1886, Samuel Papers; *The Workingman's Advocate*, Mar. 11, 1875.

because of his wide horticultural experience in England. A man of considerable learning, a scholar and writer of capacity in this field, he was widely recognized as " the father of the Order of Patrons of Husbandry." [44] A Washington correspondent of the New York *Times* went so far as to describe him as " the man who dreamed and thought out and inaugurated the Order." [45] Moreover, he is known to have " spent two years— 1865-1867—in corresponding with the principal agriculturalists of this country and Great Britain," and there is little doubt that the Grange's basic organizational features and its constitution were primarily his handiwork. Since Saunders was still a power among the Patrons in 1874 and 1875 we should like to discover specifically what he had to do with the switch to the Rochdale Plan and what, if anything, he derived from British co-operators.

Speculation about Saunders aside, however, it is worth re-emphasizing that word of Rochdale had undoubtedly spread among farmers earlier, thanks to the work of men such as Trevellick, McClelland, Siney, and Phillips. How extensively we cannot know, but we are entitled to believe that the rapidity with which local granges turned to British co-operation and the popularity that it enjoyed are at least partially explained by the fact that thousands of farmers had heard of the great panacea.

We do know that one of the Grange's boldest and most imaginative co-operative experiments, begun in 1874-5, contributed mightily to the circulation of the idea of self-help, and it is to that story that we shall now briefly turn.

During 1874 there was ample evidence to indicate that among certain groups of farmers internationalism was growing stronger and was taking the form of a transatlantic co-operative alliance somewhat like the trade union alliances discussed earlier. In 1874, for instance, leaders of the American Co-

---

[44] Jonathan Periam, *The Groundswell: A History of the Farmers' Movement* (Cincinnati: E. Hannaford & Co., 1874), pp. 363-68. Atkeson, pp. 317-18. H. R. Chamberlain, *The Farmers' Alliance* (New York: Minerva Publishing Co., 1891) is an old account of parallel movements in later years.

[45] *The Workingman's Advocate*, Jan. 10, 1874. There is an unidentified clipping about Saunders in " Grange Booklet," Samuel Papers, Box 7.

operative Union of Louisville, Kentucky endorsed the Rochdale Plan as the best known system of co-operation and immediately afterwards joined with the Grange Co-operative Congress to hammer out an agreement with the British that would lead to closer association.[46] Almost simultaneously, Edward V. Neale, as a gesture of friendship, invited Wendell Phillips, the old anti-slavery crusader turned labor reformer, to attend the forthcoming British Co-operative Congress; and George Jacob Holyoake dedicated an edition of his history of the Rochdale Society to the great Massachusetts leader.[47] Meantime in New Orleans a relatively obscure figure, Thomas D. Worrall, a grain trader, delivered what proved to be a significant paper on " Free Trade and Direct Trade " to the assembled members of the New Orleans Grange.[48] Within the year these events fitted into a more coherent picture.

February 1875, in fact, saw the unveiling of " one of the most promising developments of the day," plans for a full union between the chief co-operative societies of England and the Patrons of Husbandry. The ostensible purpose of the plan was the mutual interchange of commodities and manufactured goods between Britons and Americans without the intervention of middlemen. High hopes were expressed on both sides of the sea that this prospective alliance would quickly " spread throughout the civilized world" and result in a universal brotherhood of working people.[49] Apparently much of the initiative behind the proposed alliance came from Thomas D. Worrall. We can only wish that we knew more of his motives. Certainly he might have expected his grain trade to benefit from the proposal, but Worrall was also an enemy of the so-called grain trust and the railroads, which in later years he attacked in a muckraking book. He was, in brief, a product of the dissidence welling up among the farming peoples of the Mississippi Valley. Moreover, the readiness with which the

[46] Circular by American Co-operative Union, Box 2, Samuel Papers.
[47] *The Workingman's Advocate*, Oct. 24, 1874. Holyoake and Phillips, of course, had corresponded with each other before the Civil War.
[48] Denis Flanagan to author, July 7, 1953. Mr. Flanagan is Librarian at the Co-operative Union, Ltd., in Manchester where materials on the Mississippi Valley Trading Company are preserved.
[49] *The Sovereigns' Bulletin*, Feb. 1875.

British responded—and responded favorably—was an indication that the times seemed ripe to many men for an international experiment.

That the proposed alliance was no mere sentimental dream on either side of the Atlantic is evident from the haste with which both the British and Americans rushed to implement it. Soon after the original announcement was made in the United States, a delegation of Englishmen, members of the powerful Central Co-operative Board of the United Kingdom, arrived in Boston. Stopping briefly in Worcester, Massachusetts, the mission proceeded to Washington, D. C. where it met with the Executive Committee of the National Grange. Worrall, meantime, crossed the ocean and carried his plan in person before leading English co-operators and the Manchester Chamber of Commerce. It is worth noting here that the magnitude of the operation contemplated by the Englishmen, Worrall, and the Grange was unprecedented among either farmers or co-operators. It was daring and imaginative. The co-operators of the British Isles were half a million strong, and the Grangers claimed a membership of nearly two and a half million, though it may be doubted that they could count on more than half that many people paying dues. Nevertheless, it is no wonder that both parties were alive to the potential significance of the alliance; each stood to profit enormously from association, and interestingly enough, each had confidence in the other. The Americans, in fact, were extremely optimistic. "The eminent ability of those on the English side," wrote one of them, "make it certain that as soon as the project begins it will succeed." [50]

The Washington meetings were fruitful. The British and the Grange officials agreed that a direct exchange of products was feasible and would accrue to the benefit of all concerned. The co-operative societies of Britain were to send to the United States such national specialities as cotton goods, silk, hosiery, woollens, jewelry, cutlery, machinery, iron, fancy boots and shoes, stationery, chinas, earthenwares, chemicals, and various

---

[50] *The Sovereigns' Bulletin*, Feb. and Aug., 1875. American Co-operative Union Circular, Samuel Papers, Box 2. Denis Flanagan to author, July 7, 1953. Filley, pp. 32, 36, 43, 53.

categories of tools. These, on equitable terms, were to be exchanged for staples produced in the Mississippi Valley, wheat, raw cotton, corn, pork, tallow, hides, cheeses, butter, timber, flour, and beef. Since everyone appeared satisfied, preparations were launched to get the alliance into actual operation as soon as possible.[51]

The instrument designed to effectuate the alliance, the Mississippi Valley Trading Company, was incorporated on April 15, 1875 under the provisions of the English Company Acts of 1862-1867. The home office of the organization was located in London, though an American section was established in Louisville, Kentucky on April 19, 1876. Original capitalization amounted to £100,000 but additional money was to be sought on both sides of the Atlantic and business was not to start until £25,000 had been subscribed in both America and Britain. From the beginning, however, it appeared that the bulk of the capital came from various English concerns, despite the fact that the American papers announced that the " last 1/4% are in fair demand." [52]

A provisional administrative council was organized in England, its personnel—twenty of the most distinguished co-operators in the British Isles—having been selected by the Seventh Co-operative Congress. E. V. Neale, Samuel's mentor and correspondent, became the organization's legal advisor, while the monies of the concern were handled by the banking department of the famed Co-operative Wholesale Society in Manchester. As arrangements were being made for the formation of a permanent board of directors composed of both Americans and Britons, Thomas D. Worrall was invested with the tasks of managing director, aided by the foremost leaders of the Grange: Dudley Adams, who introduced the Rochdale Plan formally to the members of the Grange, Judge John Jones, soon leader of the Patrons, and four others. At the first meeting of the American board in St. Louis in September 1875, Worrall

---

[51] *The Sovereigns' Bulletin*, Feb. 1875; *Prospectus of the Mississippi Valley Trading Company, Ltd.*; *Memorandum of Association of the Mississippi Valley Trading Company*.

[52] *Prospectus of the M.V.T.C.*; D. Flanagan to author, July 7, 1953; *American Manufacturer and Iron World*, Sept. 9, 1875.

was instructed to establish a central office in Louisville and to visit the main seaports from Norfolk to Galveston and the railways in the South and in the Mississippi Valley with an eye to determining how well they could serve the new company,[53] and the wheels were soon in motion.

That the Mississippi Valley Trading Company sought to banish middlemen and their profits was obvious. Worrall had gone to considerable lengths to spell this out during his English visit. Trade between Britain and America, as he explained it, was subject to a triple toll, " 1stly and 2ndly to the English and New York firms who purchase . . . articles produced by either country and consign them to their correspondents on the other side of the Atlantic, and 3rdly to the Railway Companies by which these articles are transported to and from New York and the Mississippi Valley." Savings of as much as " 8 shillings per quarter," he argued, would stem from direct trade in wheat from Minnesota via New Orleans to Liverpool, and the cost of goods generally could be reduced from 10 to 25 per cent.[54] But the attack on middlemen was only a beginning as far as Worrall and the Grangers were concerned.

Less obvious, but perhaps equally as important, was the long range objective of the new organization. " It is the object of the present Company to bring about . . . direct shipment . . . and reduce to a minimum that self-imposed toll on the commercial intercourse between Great Britain and the United States, which, if once abolished by the free action of the people in each country, *would not be long in drawing after it a thorough revision of the U. S. tariffs.*" And, the directors added, " the future of the government of the United States lies in the hands of the population of the Mississippi Valley, who already outnumber all other states; and that population, when it has become thoroughly alive to the benefits of direct intercourse with Great Britain, *will speedily sweep away all artificial impediments to its full development.*"[55] Suggestions for a more imposing flank attack on the vested interests and

---

[53] *American Manufacturer and Iron World,* Sept. 9, 1875; *Prospectus of the M.V.T.C.*

[54] *Ibid.*

[55] Italics are mine. See, *Prospectus of the M.V.T.C.*

tariff-protected industries of the industrial states would be hard to imagine. Clearly the neo-mercantilist policies of the East, soon to become the great political issues of the age, were rousing resentment among the farming folk of the Mid-west and it is difficult to think of any groups that might have proven more sympathetic as allies than British co-operators.

Work necessary for getting the organization going continued at a steady pace through the spring of 1876. Worrall and his associates employed the services of Oliver H. Stratton, a capable propagandist, and a number of Britons were sent out to the United States to help spread information on the Rochdale Plan. A model store, in fact, calculated to impress Americans was established in Louisville in November 1875.[56] Not long afterwards Worrall published a pamphlet explaining how the American branch of the M.V.T.C. would operate on the most progressive co-operative principles known, those of Rochdale, and he went still further, claiming that he had introduced the Rochdale Plan to American workingmen and farmers—a claim so patently inaccurate it calls for no comment here.[57] Under his guidance, however, steps were taken to create co-operative depots, steamship lines, and all the ancillary means required to open direct trade. Exuberant over having brought forth what promised to be a momentous alliance, he triumphantly announced: "Both the South and the West are adopting the Rochdale Plan of co-operation and all the Patrons will soon be in the true path." [58]

Worrall, nevertheless, was soon struck down in the full flower of his enthusiasm. For some reason, he lost the confidence of the Grangers. It may be that his criticisms of their preparations were too cutting, though we cannot really be sure. In any event his place in the organization was taken over by Dr. J. W. A. Wright.

[56] American Co-operative Union, Circular, Box 2, Samuel Papers; also Oliver H. Stratton to the Editor of the *Rural World*, June 12, 1876, *ibid. The Workingman's Advocate*, Mar. 11, 1875.

[57] American Co-operative Union, Circular, Box 2, Samuel Papers; Thomas Worrall, "Practical Co-operation: A Manual Showing How to Conduct Co-operative Stores on the Rochdale Plan," (Louisville, n. d. 1875-6?), Labadie Coll.

[58] *The Sovereigns' Bulletin*, Oct. 1875.

A Patron of Husbandry, Wright had a rather impressive background. A native of Mississippi, he was graduated from Princeton in 1857 and then had gone on to a distinguished career in the Confederate Army. After the war he taught school briefly, then moved to California where he acquired nearly 4000 acres and soon became a prosperous farmer. He served as the Master of the California State Grange, one of the first to turn to co-operation on a large scale, and he won national fame in the farmers' organization by drafting the Grange's Declaration of Principles.[59]

Wright appeared in Worrall's place to address the British Co-operative Congress of 1876 in Glasgow, and while the latter was not inclined to relinquish his post without a fight, his successor went abroad armed with mandates from Grange leaders and several American Senators. The Californian had no difficulty winning the acceptance of the British as the new managing director. In other ways, too, his trip was intimately connected with the alliance of 1875, for along with Judge John T. Jones of the National Grange, he was the co-founder of the Anglo-American Trading Company, an organization designed to fit snugly into the scheme of direct British-American trade. Consequently, during his visit in the United Kingdom, Wright held "frequent and earnest consultations" with Edward V. Neale and the chief co-operators of London, Manchester, and Glasgow. Moreover, his tour of British co-operatives was comprehensive and included inspection of facilities at Leeds, Rochdale, Manchester, Oldham, Newcastle-on-Tyne, Paisley, and Woolwich. Once back in the United States in the summer of 1876, he reported fully on his findings, filling twelve columns of space in one rural paper. Broadly speaking, his thesis was the similarity between the Patrons' ideas and those of the Rochdalers and, apropos of the alliance, he declared, "After eight years of co-operation on our side and thirty on theirs we now for the first time are ready to combine our efforts to wield together our strength."[60]

[59] Atkeson, pp. 345-346; D. Flanagan to author, July 7, 1953; *Report of the Co-operative Congress, April 17, 1876, Glasgow.*

[60] Denis Flanagan to author, July 7, 1953; Nov. 22, 1955. There is an unidentified clipping on Jones and the Anglo-American Trading Co. in Samuel

Yet for all the vision, zeal, good will, planning, and prepara-
tory work it appears unlikely that the Mississippi Valley
Trading Company ever did business, though it remained in
existence until 1878. At that time, as we learn from statements made before the Eleventh Co-operative Congress, one
of the constituent English organizations " which held nearly
half the shares issued, refused to run the risk of any further
demands upon it, on the ground that they were taken up with
the expectation that the proposal would be supported more
extensively than appeared to be the case." [61] Obviously too,
there was a growing feeling among the British that the Grange
did not represent the " common people " but rather the big
farmers. Certainly the leaders of the Grange, Wright among
them, could not be said to have been peasants; indications are
fairly good, in fact, that the Grange represented a substantial
group of what might loosely be called middle class farmers
and country shopkeepers.

Whatever the precise causes of its extinction—which involved the loss of five shillings per share—the Mississippi
Valley Trading Company, with its emphasis on an international
version of the Rochdale Plan, helped greatly to spread the
popularity of the British idea. In this respect it did not differ
from most experiments launched by American reformers and
dissidents in the late nineteenth century, for its fundamental
service was educational.

The international stirrings of the alliance were felt throughout the rank and file of the order. British co-operative methods
could scarcely have been adopted under more favorable auspices, and letters praising Rochdale quickly appeared in farm
newspapers and grange journals. State granges likewise picked
up the theme. The New Hampshire State Grange, for example,
declared at its session of December 1875 " that the members
of our Order should examine the system of co-operation known
as the Rochdale System and recommended by the National

Papers, Box 7. Also see, clipping from *The Farmer's Friend*, dated 1876, *ibid.*,
Box 7; clipping from the Manchester *Co-operative News*, July 27, 1876, *ibid.*,
Box 7. *The Sovereigns' Bulletin*, Sept., 1876.

[61] *Report of the Eleventh Annual Co-operative Congress, April 14, 1879,
Gloucester*, " International Co-operation."

Grange for our consideration." [62] Oregon's Patrons resolved that " the best interest of this order in this jurisdiction requires that [there be] as little delay as possible [in establishing] such organization as is recommended by [Judge] Jones and known as the Granger Co-operative Association of the Northwest. That through it we connect ourselves with the Rochdale Co-operative Societies of England, and that it be made the accredited business agency of this state grange." [63] Similarly, from South Carolina came a resolution embodying the statement that self-help was " the panacea for all our ills," and this was followed by another resolution backing the plans for international co-operation as well as for the adoption of the Rochdale Plan. [64] Generally speaking, Grange sentiments about Rochdale were aptly summarized by one unknown spokesman for the farmers. " Why," he asked, " did this rebellion begin? Who is to blame for it? What is to be the end of it all? These questions are not British alone. They are international. . . . It seems to be recognized that the co-operative store either on the Rochdale Plan (which seems to be the best) or the Civil Service Plan [also British] is destined to hold on here." [65]

The Rochdale Plan did hold on in the United States, thanks very largely to the Grange and its work in behalf of the British program. Despite criticism to the effect that co-operative schemes brought about the decline of the Grange, [66] charges that cannot be conclusively proved or disproved, the weight of evidence would seem to point in the opposite direc-

[62] US Mss 16A, *The Patrons of Husbandry, Excerpts from the Proceedings of State Granges, 1873-1880* (Wisconsin State Historical Society, University of Wisconsin, Madison, Wisconsin). Cited hereafter as US Mss 16A, *Patrons*. See, US Mss 16A, *Patrons, Proceedings of the New Hampshire State Grange*, II, 65-66; US Mss 16A, *Patrons, Proceedings of the California State Grange: Declaration of Purposes and Resolutions*, July 15-18, 1873.

[63] US Mss 16A, *Patrons, Proceedings of the Oregon State Grange*, III, 16, 22, 29, 41-42.

[64] US Mss 16A, *Patrons, Proceedings of the South Carolina State Grange*, *5th Annual Session*, Feb. 7, 1877.

[65] Quoted from an unidentified clipping dated Apr. 7, 1881, Samuel Papers, Box 7.

[66] Atkeson, pp. 80-81. See the article by J. Clyde Marquis in *Country Gentleman*, May 15, 1920. Filley, pp. 358-59. Ellis Cowling and Dr. Edwin Nourse have differing views on the matter of co-ops and the decline of the Grange.

tion. Actually it appears that the Grange served as "middle-man" in passing on the spirit and methods of self-help in America. That it brought Rochdale to the attention of more Americans than had ever before been aware of the idea, that Rochdale never disappeared thereafter from the American scene as an important co-operative technique, and that Rochdale principles became the basis for the first significant state laws relating to self-help are undeniable.[67] The British idea was so firmly embedded among many of the Midwestern farmers that when Alliancemen in the late eighties sought to launch co-operative programs of their own, they were faced with "bitter opposition." "The people," they declared, "had been for twenty years taught the Rochdale system of conducting stores" . . . and "were wedded to the . . . Plan."[68]

## V. SELF-HELP AMONG THE SOVEREIGNS OF INDUSTRY

Other organizations also took their inspiration from the Grange. Late in August, 1874, *The Workingman's Advocate* reported without fanfare that the Sovereigns of Industry, "a new organization, started this year."[69] Destined to be one of the more important co-operative vehicles of the seventies, it was a "secret" society replete with all the ritualistic trappings so beloved by nineteenth century workingmen. Secret or not, the organization threw open its ranks to virtually everyone and its constitution announced that its objectives were "a better system of economical exchanges" and the promotion, "on a basis of equity and liberty," of "mutual fellowship and co-operative action among the producers and consumers of wealth."[70] Hopes were expressed that the wage system would likewise give way to a co-operative society sworn to "Christ-like giving."[71] The immediate practical aim of the Sovereigns

---

[67] Nourse, Chap. 2.

[68] Chamberlain, pp. 1-24. N. A. Dunning, *Farmers' Alliance History and Agricultural Digest* (Washington: 1891), p. 364.

[69] Aug. 22-29, 1874.

[70] Newton, *North American Review*, CXXXVII, 331. Simonds, p. 651. E. M. Chamberlain, *The Sovereigns of Industry* (Boston: 1875), for the frothy exuberance generated by the movement.

[71] *The Sovereigns' Bulletin*, Jan., 1875.

was to establish a network of distributive co-ops, their long term plan to expand into the realm of productive co-operation.

The new order grew swiftly; forty days after recruiting began there were reported to be councils in eighteen states, and by the opening of the first annual meeting in December 1874, a hundred councils claiming a total membership of 10,000 were represented. Just one year later membership went over the 100,000 mark, and while the bulk of this strength was drawn from New England, it was not strictly limited to that region.[72]

How the Sovereigns came to champion the Rochdale Plan is a story no less complicated than the Grange's adoption of the idea. That the order, under the direction of its deeply religious leader, William Earle, was an offshoot of the Patrons of Husbandry has long been known to scholars, but the details of its formation—and they seem to be closely linked with its acceptance of British co-operative ideas—have remained obscure. We do not now have all the facts, yet valuable information has come to us from John Orvis. Orvis was a co-operator and labor reformer with a long background by the mid-seventies; his experience, in fact, went back to the famed Brook Farm experiment of the forties. His entire career is an excellent example of the continuity of personnel in American reform movements. Among the Sovereigns Orvis served as chief lecturer, a role which made him an important force in the movement. Consequently, his particular version of the creation of the organization warrants attention despite the fact that it was written thirteen years after the events he described.

Orvis begins by confirming our knowledge that the influence of the Grange was central to the establishment of the Sovereigns of Industry. In July 1873 he had just returned from a year's tour of England and the Continent, where he was engaged in " studying different forms of co-operation." [73] Back in the United States he everywhere found the newspapers

---

[72] Such figures were usually exaggerated. Newton, *North American Review,* CXXXVII, 331-32. Simonds, p. 651. Bemis, pp. 37-51.

[73] " The Origins of the Sovereigns of Industry," in *Journal of United Labor,* May 5, 1888.

retailing the amazing progress of the Patrons of Husbandry. Profoundly impressed by his own experiences in Britain, he wrote to Oliver Kelley, one of the founders and a principal leader of the Grange, asking that the organization be opened to all who desired a "union of all classes of industrialists," by which he obviously meant wage earners. Personally Kelley appreciated the suggestion but he did not feel that it was then either wise or possible to remodel the Grange. He argued that it might rather be easier to establish an entirely new order, broadly based as Orvis suggested, and if and when it showed signs of vigor to merge it with the Patrons.

Being interested in the proposal, Kelley then went out of his way to help Orvis's idea along. Orvis was told that his initial letter to Kelley had been forwarded to the Deputy of the Grange, William Earle, who was busily spreading word of the Grange in Massachusetts. Not long afterwards, Earle, having been asked by Kelley to expedite matters, cleared with his superiors and replied to Orvis, inviting him to attend a meeting composed of "a few gentlemen . . . in Springfield on January 12, 1874 to consider the subject of a new order and if found practicable to proceed to organize the same."[74] Thus was the Order of the Sovereigns of Industry born in part through the efforts of John Orvis, a man whose dedication to the principles of Rochdale left little doubt about his conception of the organization as a vehicle for co-operation.

Not all of the Sovereigns were prepared to accede to Orvis's plan to make the organization the sponsor of British-model co-ops, but for those who were dubious there were plenty of important leaders to allay their fears. Recounting the great achievements of self-help, David Armitage took up arms for co-operation "as I have known it in England," and pointing to the examples of Rochdale and Oldham, called upon his American friends to imitate them.[75] A well-known labor leader declared that he had "read with deep interest the lecture of G. J. H. [Holyoake]. . . . I ardently hope its publication in the [Sovereigns'] *Bulletin* may lead the co-operative stores

[74] *Journal of United Labor,* May 5, 1888.
[75] *The Sovereigns' Bulletin,* Jan., 1875.

founded by the Sovereigns to adopt . . . the Rochdale Plan."[76] Similarly, in the Mid-west the Thomas J. Morgans turned to the Sovereigns primarily because the order stirred memories of their own days as the members of a Rochdale store in Birmingham.[77] John Orvis himself told a gathering of members in 1874: "Trade unions are a burden on labor. This new organization promises not only to give justice in the abstract but it will increase the purchasing power of wages. It will put something in everyman's pocket whenever he buys his supplies. It is not an experiment, for in Great Britain the same principle has been tried under the name of co-operation . . . we will institute the same principles."[78] Others hammered away at the same theme; John James, speaking for his Braidwood miners praised the Sovereigns' acceptance of British ideas,[79] and Amasa Walker, one of the country's leading political economists, told the rank and file of the order that the Rochdale Plan had his "unqualified approbation."[80] Subsequent events leave no doubt that these comments had their desired effect.

Once the organization was fairly launched, Orvis' plans were supplemented by yet another program sponsored by H. J. Burton. British in origin, the "Burton Plan" became "an invaluable aid to the [Sovereigns'] council in organizing co-operative stores."[81] Burton himself was English and the method he championed was, as he explained it, "successfully in operation in England [in] over five hundred societies and is the one lately adopted by the National Grange."[82] In other words, it was a version of the ubiquitous Rochdale idea. Through the adoption of his program, Burton felt Americans could achieve "English stability," and while he and Orvis felt at first that their respective plans were incompatible, they soon

[76] *Ibid.*, Apr. 10, 1880.
[77] *The Provoker,* Nov. 18, 1909. Clipping with a biography of Mrs. Morgan, Samuel Papers, Folder 21.
[78] Orvis' remarks are in an unidentified clipping, dated Apr. 21, 1874, Phillips Papers.
[79] *The Workingman's Advocate,* May 13, 1875.
[80] *The Sovereigns' Bulletin,* Jan., 1875.
[81] *Ibid.*, Aug., 1875.
[82] *The Sovereigns' Bulletin,* Aug., 1875.

recognized that in fact they buttressed one another. As the strength of the Sovereigns grew by leaps and bounds both men began urging the internationalization of co-operative efforts and Orvis, obviously enchanted with the Mississippi Valley Trading Company, declared that "hand in hand with the Patrons of Husbandry and English co-operators, I believe nothing under heaven can stop our progress." [83]

Of course, dissemination of British ideas took place at several levels within the Sovereigns of Industry just as it had in the other labor organizations that we have examined. The influences of Orvis and Burton, for instance, were manifested at the higher levels, but at an equally important, though somewhat lower level, veteran co-operators, John Samuel and Thomas Phillips among them, were likewise at work.

When the Sovereigns were just beginning to recruit their strength, Phillips, as we have seen earlier, was engaged in co-operative work among the Knights of St. Crispin, while simultaneously conducting a co-operative venture of his own.[84] In March 1874, his affairs took a new turn, however, for his fellow workers, aware of his long advocacy of the Rochdale Plan, secured for him, without his prior knowledge, a special deputy's commission from William Earle. With the commission, naturally, came organizational powers, hence only a few months after the Springfield meeting at which the Sovereigns of Industry was born, Phillips was in harness for the new organization. Within a matter of months, he managed to create five councils in Philadelphia, one of which, he cheerfully reported to his superiors, was composed exclusively of females. Agitation, of course, soon roused the usual local opposition, one newspaper suggesting that he be hanged, another that he be deposited in the Delaware, but dire though such threats might have been, and they were doubtless exaggerated, they were the spice of his life for they strengthened his sense of mission and helped him dramatize his own situation.[85]

And, whatever the obstacles of the moment, the Sovereigns

---

[83] *Ibid.*, Oct., 1875.

[84] See, "Autobiography," Phillips Papers.

[85] The original commission is in the Phillips Papers; also see his "Autobiography."

flourished in Philadelphia. On June 29, 1874, Pioneer Council Number One of the Pennsylvania Sovereigns was formed. As a charter member, Phillips must have noted with satisfaction that meetings, from time to time, became a forum for the discussion of British co-operative plans. For his part, he lost no chance to extol the opportunities presented workingmen by Rochdale, and he delivered a series of lectures on British co-operation to the rank and file. Apparently it was mainly through his exertions that the Sovereigns were able to launch several small co-ops in Philadelphia.[86]

If Phillips was galled by the Sovereigns' leaders' assertions that they were the first to bring Rochdale before the American public, he never gave vent to his feelings; however, the organization's secrecy did draw unfavorable comment from him. Trade unions, he felt, might conceivably prosper "underground"; co-operatives could not; either they flourished in the light of day or they could not exist at all. Therefore, hoping to remedy the situation, he wrote to the Secretary of the organization, telling him that "if we are to have a Co-operative Republic" the order must work openly in full public view.[87]

Meantime, his associates in the Pioneer Council were pressing for co-operation of the same type as Phillips. John Sheddon, the Pennsylvanian who subsequently became president of the Sovereigns in 1878, read into the Council's minutes praise for British principles and left no doubt that the Rochdale Plan was the one that the order should uniformly adopt. This was more easily said than done, for members of the Council represented a curious mixture. Side by side with Phillips and Sheddon sat Albert Brisbane, the veteran Fourierist, famed for his work at Brook Farm and Red Bank. Brisbane probably joined the order because of his long friendship with John Orvis. However, he proved anything but a pillar of strength, defaulting on his dues and retaining his membership only because his

[86] US Mss 4A, *Sovereigns of Industry, Pennsylvania, Pioneer Council. Membership Lists, 1879*; also see, *Minute Books, Jan. 4, 1877-June 18, 1879*; and *Minutes of the Executive Council, ibid.* "Lectures to the Sovereigns of Industry," Phillips Papers.
[87] Phillips to John Butterfield, Oct. 19, 1874, Phillips Papers.

colleagues were impressed by his "great services to Mankind"—which as Phillips and his friends must have realized was a small price to pay for the use of the old man's prestige.[88] Returning to our story, the significant bond holding the members together was a belief in the efficacy of self-help and its ultimate power to ameliorate the troubles that came with industrialization.

The opinions favoring Rochdale that were uttered in the East were reiterated in the Mid-west. There John Samuel, never losing sight of any chance to present his panacea, joined the Sovereigns as readily as he had the Patrons, promptly setting out to use his organizer's commission in Missouri and Illinois. Throughout the next three years he kept in touch with Earle and his deputies and apparently he was doing well, for in January 1887, the leadership sent him a letter of congratulations on his fine work in the area assigned him. As usual where the British program of self-help was being broadcast, Samuel put great energy into his work. Writing for the *Sovereigns' Bulletin* in 1875, for example, he exuberantly declared, "There never has been a plan presented to the working classes of the country to surpass the Sovereigns of Industry and the Patrons of Husbandry," [89] and no one could doubt the reasons for his opinion. Moreover, in St. Louis he fostered the creation of several co-ops and served as the Chief Lecturer of St. Louis's first council of the Sovereigns of Industry. He was so anxious to see the co-operative idea spread that he was chagrined when the leadership failed to levy a general tax on all members in order to finance their co-operative program. For the "Old War Horse" no sacrifice, even taxes, was too great, and quite incorrectly he assumed that other workingmen were equally as dedicated.[90]

We cannot tell with accuracy the extent to which Rochdale ideas were put into operation in Philadelphia and St. Louis,

---

[88] *The Sovereigns' Bulletin*, May, 1877. US Mss 4A, *Sovereigns of Industry, Pioneer Council, Minute Books, Jan. 31, 1877.* Commons, *Documentary History,* VIII, 28.

[89] See Samuel's correspondence with William Earle and John Butterfield. Samuel Papers, Box 2. *The Sovereigns' Bulletin,* Nov., 1875.

[90] *Ibid.*, May, 1876; Jan., 1878. Clipping on Samuel's association with the St. Louis Co-operative Coal Co., Samuel Papers, Box 9.

but nationally it was the assimilation of the very program that Phillips and Samuel advocated that accounted for the brief, yet considerable, success of the Sovereigns. Prosperity of the order was unquestionably greatest where British plans were employed and the General Council, conscious of this, made every attempt to " sell " these programs. Only a few years after the inception of the order, Earle announced that " a very large portion " of the Sovereigns' trade " had been secured on the Rochdale Plan." [91] Ten of the organization's leading stores with an average annual trade of $34,000 were Rochdale-models, while of twenty-six other stores that answered a questionnaire circulated by John Samuel in New England, nineteen were conducted on the same plan.[92] In 1877 all the stores operated by the order did a total business of over $800,000 and Earle noted that there were scarcely any that did not conduct their operations by the same methods.[93] Thus, in conjunction with the Patrons of Husbandry, the Sovereigns brought these imported programs of self-help to tens of thousands of farmers and wage earners, training and educating them. What these stores must have meant to thousands of hard-pressed men and women during the lean years of the middle seventies, psychologically as well as economically, we cannot ever really know.

By 1879 the current of events was playing havoc once again with the calculations of the Sovereigns of Industry and cooperators in general. Disaster on European farms raised wheat prices for the farmers of the Middle Border, the Mississippi Valley, and New England. There followed an increase in the acreage under cultivation that in turn stimulated fresh demand for rail construction. This unprecedented expansion of railroad facilities into the Great Plains created new jobs and caused large new expenditures of money. When these phenomena were coupled with scores of similar industrial and agricultural revivals, prosperity returned to a somewhat sluggish economy. Confidence returned to workingmen and farmers alike, and a partial collapse of the national co-operative move-

[91] *The Sovereigns' Bulletin,* May, 1877. *The True Economist,* Nov., 1876.
[92] " Statistics of the Trade of the Sovereigns of Industry," Feb. 28, 1878, Samuel Papers, Box 1. Newton, *North American Review,* CXXXVII, 332.
[93] *Ibid.,* pp. 332-33.

ments ensued. The Grange, while by no means extinct, atrophied, at least until the following decade. In 1880, however, the Executive Council of the Sovereigns, after months of misfortune, met in solemn conclave and buried the organization.[94] Elsewhere the ties that linked local granges or councils to their parent bodies commenced dissolving.

The grand achievements of co-operation appeared to have been swept away, but the damage, while serious, was in many respects superficial. Local co-ops in many cases remained strong, in some instances actually increasing their strength. British ideas were well established and could not lightly be pushed aside. In the East and in the Mid-west they had deep roots. Throughout the farm belt, Granger distributive stores continued to function, and in urban areas such as Minneapolis, for example, some co-ops did a booming business. In Pittsburgh there was even one small band of Sovereigns who managed to hang on for another decade. In Kansas the famed Johnson stores stayed prosperous; in Cincinnati and in Boston, John Gledhill and Josiah Quincy kept their respective organizations intact, and along with them scores of other British-model stores quietly worked on. Meanwhile, as Samuel had suggested to his disciples, they kept operations small, went slowly, and had " patience, confidence, and courage in [their] work." [95]

---

[94] Newton, *North American Review*, CXXXVII, 333.

[95] See, for instance, the way the barrel-makers of Minneapolis turned to the Rochdale Plan and continued a thriving business; clipping from the *Journal of United Labor,* Sept. 10, 1896, Samuel Papers, Box 6. Samuel to N. O. Nelson, Apr. 14, 1896; Samuel to Dawson, July 2, 1885, *ibid. The Sovereigns' Bulletin,* May, 1876. In 1888 a group of Sovereigns wrote to the *Journal of United Labor* indignantly reminding the editor that their order still lived on.

# Part Seven

# TOWARD A CO-OPERATIVE COMMONWEALTH

---

## I. "The Co-operative Wave"

Neither the grand sweep of economic forces nor the consequent reverses dismayed inveterate co-operators. Since their planning and activities had never been co-ordinated under a master scheme, the full magnitude of disaster was not realized. Lacking a single nerve center, the destruction of which might have imperiled the entire movement, co-operation continued during the late seventies and the eighties to manifest itself in scores of organizations across the country. These small co-ops, largely unaware of each other's problems, struggled on, their leaders and members waiting hopefully for a regeneration of workingclass energies that would bring them nearer the co-operative commonwealth.

Extreme decentralization accounts, in all probability, for some of the disparity in the then current estimates of the extensiveness of co-operative progress. In August 1880, the Chicago *Tribune*, less than sanguine about the prospects of self-help, reported the failure of more than five hundred distributive stores over the preceding five years.[1] Ominous indeed, yet only a month after this assessment was made, another Chicagoan viewed matters in a more cheerful perspective. After listening to a lecture delivered in Hershey Hall by James K. Appleby, a well-known co-operator of Lancashire and Yorkshire, this confident observer declared that "the co-operative wave in America is rising!"[2]—and he could just as easily have added that it was driven by fresh breezes from across the sea.

Late in 1879 George Jacob Holyoake arrived in America. He hoped to accomplish several things: he wanted to make

[1] Clipping from the *Chicago Tribune*, Aug. 9, 1880, Samuel Papers, Box 9.
[2] "Co-operation in England and America," Ms, Samuel Papers, Box 6; also see a clipping dated Sept. 6, 1880, *ibid.*, Box 6.

arrangements that would facilitate and simplify the passage of immigrants from Britain to the United States; he planned an overall survey of American conditions; and he intended to conduct missionary work for the Guild of Co-operators. The visit was destined to last about four months. If any single individual was symbolic of the co-operative movement, insofar as American co-operators were concerned, Holyoake was the man. As George Washington was famed for having presided over the birth of American independence, so George Holyoake had known " co-operation when it was born . . . stood by its cradle . . . and defended it in its infancy when no one thought it would live." [3] If, as one source claimed, "everyone in America . . . [had] heard of the success of English societies for distributive co-operation," [4] there can be no doubt that Holyoake's writings and the chain of events they helped propel forward had much to do with it; if the " initiation and rise of co-operation [was] one of the most memorable circumstances in the long reign of Victoria," [5] it was largely because articulate men like him were the preachers and historians of the co-operative spirit.

The Englishman received a warm welcome, was taken under the hospitable wing of friends and admirers in New York, and was rapidly introduced into the company of his American disciples. Guided by Dr. Holleck, with whom he lived while in New York, he swiftly made the acquaintance of many prominent figures from the ranks of workingmen, academicians, reformers, and literary people.

Holleck also introduced the celebrated Englishman to E. E. Barnum, nephew of the sensational showman. As much an idealist as his uncle was a charlatan, Barnum was an experienced co-operator, having directed Henry Sharpe's integral Co-operative Colony Aid Association in Kansas, and he was apparently the one who persuaded Holyoake to deliver his first American address at Cooper Union Hall. Needless to say,

[3] There are dozens of clippings on the Holyoake visit in the Samuel Papers. For this quote see, Goss, pp. lxxiv-lxxv.
[4] Remark by C. L. Brace in *The Epoch*, reprinted in *Public Opinion*, III (1887), 13.
[5] *Ibid.*, p. 261.

this created great interest among the labor-reformers and liberal journalists. Whitelaw Reid, E. L. Godkin, Felix Adler, Peter Cooper, and a host of clergymen including R. Heber Newton, E. A. Washburne, E. H. Chapin, and Dr. Rylance attended, thereby giving Holyoake the best possible advertisement. Furthermore, the gathering was presided over by Reverend Robert Collyer, a British immigrant, a reformer, and a co-operator. Holyoake's maiden address was thoroughly unexciting but fortunately this was not all that his disciples were to see or hear of him.[6]

Anxious to win friends and influence people, Holyoake then went on tour. Leaving New York City, he travelled into New England on a rather special mission. "If I had a personal object in visiting America," he later wrote, "it was to meet Mr. Wendell Phillips."[7] Indeed Holyoake and Phillips, first as anti-slavery crusaders, then as champions of workingmen, had much in common. Of their long correspondence we have spoken earlier, and clearly both of them were eager for a first-hand talk. When their meeting came, it lacked nothing in drama. As if they consciously sought to heal old wounds and encourage the growth of Anglo-American understanding, they journeyed to Boston's King Street, approximate site of the Boston Massacre, and solemnly shook hands. Accompanying Holyoake was a younger man who added to the imagery of the occasion, the son of a man who was perhaps more popular among citizens of the North than any other Englishman, John Bright. Aware of the debt he felt the nation owed the elder Bright, Phillips, exercising his histrionic talents with dignity, stepped forward, met the man, and bared his head in memory of Bright's work in behalf of the Union.

In Boston Holyoake met another native son and co-operator, Josiah Quincy. Born in 1802, a graduate of Harvard, and a prominent leader in local legal and political circles, Quincy

---

[6] Holyoake, *Among the Americans,* pp. 40-42. Amos Fayram to Samuel, May 12, 1881. "Tract for the Times," Samuel Papers, Box 13. "Co-operation in England and America," Ms. Samuel Papers, Box 6. Holyoake, *Co-operative Movement To-day,* p. 84. Barns, pp. 152-56. *The Workingman's Advocate,* May 26, 1866.

[7] Holyoake, *Among the Americans,* p. 70.

was one of New England's foremost exponents of self-help. He had long been engaged in distributing British co-operative tracts, including Holyoake's works, and, only a few years before the Englishman's visit, he had founded a co-operative store in Boston on the Rochdale Plan. Holyoake was quick to praise him by suggesting that the good man's fame reached all the way to England. Flattered, Quincy arranged for Holyoake to deliver his first major talk on co-operation; it was so impressive that Holyoake won a number of new and influential admirers, among them General R. K. Oliver, former director of the State Bureau of Labor, and George William Curtis, *Harper's* editorial writer and an important reform figure.[8]

Successful in Boston, Holyoake then travelled industriously over other parts of the East. He spoke with co-operators in Florence, Holyoke, and Fall River, Massachusetts. In Washington, D. C., he spent "time which seemed far too short with the Sovereigns of Industry," and moving to Philadelphia he delivered another series of lectures arranged for him by two of his former countrymen, put in an appearance before a branch of the Sons of St. George, and visited the home of one of the Rochdale Pioneers who had emigrated to America. The newspapers, meanwhile, followed his progress closely, writing about him, and occasionally, as in the case of the Cincinnati *Commercial,* soliciting articles from him on self-help.

Turning aside from the East for a short time, Holyoake went to Chicago where the "well known Manchesterian, the Reverend Brooke Herford," invited him to deliver lectures in his church. Thomas Morgan's Chicago Trades and Labor Assembly, of course, also claimed his services. The trip back to the East was by way of Cornell University (then only a few years old) where before a body of friends and many students Holyoake preached on the "Moral Effects of Co-operation upon Industrial and Commercial Society." Shortly afterwards he brought his journey to an end.

Careful of the reputation of his beloved cause, Holyoake

---

[8] Holyoake, *Among the Americans,* p. 51. Clippings of Holyoake's remarks on Quincy (dated Oct. 9; May 15; Apr. 10, 1880, and still another "The Obituary of Josiah Quincy," Dec. 2, 1882) are in the Samuel Papers. Also see, *New York Tribune,* Aug. 28, 1880. Bemis, p. 93.

chose with deliberation the places he visited, and his itinerary, which included many side trips, was as interesting for its omissions as for actual stops. Though he was invited, he did not, apparently, go to the languishing Socialist community at New Harmony, Indiana, then under the direction of Charles White; neither did he inspect the Oneida Community in New York State. The sexual theories of this latter establishment were anathema to the English Radical, and he obviously feared laymen might misconstrue a journey there, thus injuring the reputation of respectability cultivated by co-operators. Whenever possible he made every effort to protect the decency of co-operators and to convince Americans generally that English self-help was in reality an obstacle to faddist experiments, communism, and socialism. There can be no doubt that he had, instinctively, accurately sized up the middle class American.

It is interesting also to note that Holyoake's impression of co-operation in the United States was distinctly favorable. Everywhere, he later reported to his fellow countrymen, Englishmen and English ideas were welcomed. " Since leaving America," he wrote, " I have received many reports of public meetings held in New York and elsewhere to introduce co-operation on the English Plan. There appears no prejudice against any scheme which is good, whatever country may originate it." [9] In his judgment, even more emphasis would have been given to British ideas if there had been fewer embittered British immigrants in the U. S. and Canada to speak against the proposals he made simply because of their Britishness. Nevertheless, he was well satisfied with developments and was convinced that he had helped win many friends for self-help in America.

Much of his success he attributed to the American press which had, he thought, faithfully recorded the latest British co-operative events. " By the ability and generous trouble of the interviewers . . . the facts concerning co-operation and its progress in England came to be for the first time generally diffused over the United States." For special praise he singled out the New York *Tribune*, and one of its correspondents

[9] Reliance for the details of Holyoake's trip has been placed on his *Among the Americans*, and the clippings in the Samuel Papers, Box 6.

G. W. Smalley, who had freely passed on word of the virtues of the Rochdale system. That such intelligence had its effect on Americans Holyoake did not doubt: " It is to [America's] interest . . . that freedom, civilization, and social life should be strengthened by the solidity of English thought." [10]

Despite his air of condescension while " among the Americans," Holyoake was genuinely excited about the co-operators whom he had met in New York. Even before his arrival, of course, he knew of the work of his fellow countryman, John Gledhill. During the sixties Gledhill had figured in several scattered co-operative ventures, and in 1874 he took charge of the American branch of the great English Co-operative Wholesale Society, which had offices and agencies strung out between New York and Cincinnati.[11] In addition, Holyoake met another exceedingly competent man, Allan R. Foote, whom he described as New York's " foremost co-operative advocate." Foote, who was later an editor of *Public Policy*, a Chicago publication, was a friend of John Samuel and relied from time to time on the old veteran for information and ideas.[12] But Foote, as Holyoake indicated, had a " genius for organization " and was capable enough to have a mind of his own. At the time of Holyoake's visit, Foote and the Reverend Dr. Rylance were trying to form a Co-operative Wholesale Society in New York modelled after its British counterpart, and Holyoake hopefully concluded that since Americans were entertaining ambitions as grandiose as this, self-help must soon carry all before it.[13]

Important as Holyoake was, he was only one bubble on the stream, for American co-operators were receiving still other stimuli from abroad. Indeed, the noted Englishman had been

---

[10] Holyoake, *Among the Americans*, p. 205.

[11] Holyoake, *Among the Americans*, p. 135. U. S., Senate, *Report . . . upon the Relations between Labor and Capital*, 48th Cong., 1885, II, 1368-1371. " Co-operation," booklet with clipping dated Oct. 2, 1880 dealing with Gledhill, Samuel Papers, Box 6.

[12] Allen Foote to Samuel, Mar. 13; Apr. 16, 1882; Osborn to Samuel, May ?, 1886, Samuel Papers. Clipping on Foote dated July 3, Sept., 1880 and a lecture by Foote dated Jan. 8, 1881, *ibid.*, Box 4. Holyoake, *Among the Americans*, p. 138. *Report of the Industrial Commission, Transportation*, 1901, IX, 103-23.

[13] Holyoake, *Among the Americans*, p. 67. Wisconsin, Bureau of the Census, Labor and Industrial Statistics, *2nd Biennial Report* (1885-86), pp. 155-56.

gone from America less than a year when in August, 1880, Thomas Hughes, M.P., "six feet tall [with] side whiskers and dressed in the latest style," landed in the United States. Readers will recall that he had previously come to America with A. J. Mundella in 1870, speaking in behalf of arbitration and co-operation. These ten years later Hughes was more widely known than ever, and was perhaps as popular in the United States as in England. The purpose of this second trip was the establishment of a co-operative colony in the Cumberland Plateau of Tennessee, and the adventure into which he was plunging already had a preface. In 1877 an initial co-operative project had been started in Tennessee by several Boston gentlemen, but having encountered a long run of bad luck they were ready to quit in 1880. At this point Hughes and a few philanthropic British and American investors purchased and then reorganized the venture. Hughes, the guiding spirit, hoped to recreate in his 700,00 acre plot the atmosphere of Tom Brown's schooldays for young Englishmen; hence the colony was named Rugby. Rich in promise, the colony suffered a checkered fate, for the press of business carried Hughes back to England and the community was left in the hands of a controversial Englishman named John Boyle. Bickering, misunderstanding, and inanition soon destroyed the potential of the community.[14]

But while the Rugby experiment aborted, Hughes' American journey was not really without its important consequences for co-operators. The very fact that he headed such a large project, though it bore no relation to Rochdale or its principles, inspired the rank and file of co-operators in the United States, and almost immediately the premium on Hughes' opinions soared. The Fall River *Advocate*, for instance, enthusiastically reported that the Englishman was preparing to lecture to Americans under the auspices of the Central Co-operative Board of England.[15] In Boston, during October, he shone as an oracle on

---

[14] W. H. G. Armytage and E. C. Mack, *Thomas Hughes* (London: E. Benn Ltd., 1953) for the most recent biography. M. B. Hamer, *Thomas Hughes and His American Rugby* (Chapel Hill: University of North Carolina Press, 1928). Also see, "New Light on the English Background of Thomas Hughes' Rugby Colony," *East Tennessee Historical Society*, XXI (Knoxville, 1949), 69-85. There are numerous clippings on the Hughes experiment in the Samuel Papers.

[15] Unidentified clipping, dated Oct. 9, 1880, Samuel Papers, Box 6.

co-operative affairs, generously dispensing intelligence and advice.[16] Newspapers which had been so remarkably receptive to Holyoake treated Hughes so handsomely that he announced publicly that the American press was superior to the English. Like Holyoake, in other words, he understood the vital role of the fourth estate in spreading word of self-help. In November, his arrival having been presaged by the fanfare of reporters, he visited New York City and received an official welcome. Shortly before returning to England, he gave the usual address at Cooper Union Hall, thanks to the arrangements of John Gledhill. Of Rugby, and the subsequent work of Hughes, what can accurately be said? How did it really affect American co-operation? No one knows the answers in detail. But his trip came at a critical time for American co-operation, and the New York *Iron Age*, a paper of good repute and of considerable influence, declared that the Englishman "gave powerful impetus to movements in favor of co-operation." [17] Less direct, but nonetheless convincing, evidence lay in the events that crystallized in the wake of both Holyoake and Thomas Hughes.

Inspired by the Englishman, New York co-operators set about correcting the deficiencies in their work. Feeling themselves badly in need of machinery to co-ordinate their activities, they launched exploratory talks looking toward the creation of a central co-operative agency. Meetings were held in the Astor House among such notables as Allan Foote, John Gledhill, Reverend Dr. Rylance, William Sage, and several others. Foote submitted for consideration a paper he had written outlining the course of action he believed should be followed. His proposal had previously been sent to England to be read by George Jacob Holyoake, Edward V. Neale, and Lloyd Jones, each of whom had given it his blessing.[18]

[16] "The Interesting Letters of Thomas Hughes in Boston," clippings from unidentified newspaper, dated Oct. 1880, Samuel Papers, Box 6.
[17] Clipping from *The Iron Age,* n. d., Samuel Papers, Box 6. Clipping dated, Nov. 6, 1880, *ibid.,* Box 6; also see, clipping dated Dec. 4, 1880 with various of Hughes' comments in Box 6.
[18] "Co-operation," booklet with clipping dated Oct. 2, 1880 entitled "A Central Board Established," Samuel Papers, Box 6. Wis., Bureau of the Census,

Heavily indebted to the English for their ideas, the New Yorkers established a Central Co-operative Board identical to the one in Manchester. Its purpose was to foster harmony between capital, labor, and consumers through joint efforts to found and publicize co-operative stores. In addition to its founders, the membership included such well-known figures as Professor Felix Adler, Reverend R. H. Newton, and G. W. Smalley. Under the aegis of such distinguished men, the Central Board had one very significant effect: it encouraged a trend toward centralization and co-ordination of co-operative activity, especially among the Knights of Labor and the Sociological Society of America.

Other events were also unfolding so as to give wider currency to British co-operative ideas, and they pointed sharply to the fact that the co-operative impulse in cities and in rural areas remained vigorous. Farmers' clubs had begun springing up throughout the West and South in the post-Civil War years, for instance, many of them urging the formation of " a general association similar to the Trades' Unions which, in England, . . .were obtaining great power." [19] In April, 1880 the first of the more impressive of these organizations was created by Milton George and called the Northwestern Alliance. Similar bodies took form throughout the South and Mid-west almost simultaneously and, under the skillful direction of Dr. C. W. Macune, many of them were, over the course of a decade or so, absorbed into a National Farmers' Alliance. Basically, though there were variations, the purpose of these organizations did not differ substantially from those of the Grange. Like the Grange, of course, they became the vessels that bore the farmers' discontent, and they naturally experimented with many of the panaceas of the day, not the least of which was co-operation. While Alliancemen worked out co-operative plans of their own (co-operative exchanges, marketing arrangements, and impromptu schemes reminiscent of the Grange's early co-ops), they also seized on British ideas

Labor and Industrial Statistics, *2nd Biennial Report* (1885-86), pp. 155-56. Holyoake, *Among the Americans*, pp. 137-38.

[19] Periam, p. 224. Edward Wiest, *Agricultural Organization in the United States* (Lexington, Ky.: University of Kentucky, 1923), pp. 435-74.

and used them to implement their programs. In fact, they devoted considerable time to educating farmers in the ways of the English. Prairie newspapers like the Kansas *Stock Indicator*, for example, featured a series of articles on the Rochdale Plan, strongly recommending it to the austere, Puritan dirt farmers of the Sunflower State. Nearby in Iowa, growing center of a corn and hog kingdom, Alliancemen promoted self-help to the extent of adopting the Rochdale system and advocating that their fellow farmers apply it wholesale to the solution of their problems. In the same state, the *Farmers' Tribune* announced in 1882 that Alliancemen were "making arrangements with Eastern capitalists and businessmen to buy and run [Rochdale-model] stores in all the large trading centers." [20] Negotiations were placed in the hands of Alonzo Wardall of the National Executive Committee, a man who later led the American Co-operative Union, and an agreement between the lions of the business world and the lambs of the prairies was satisfactorily concluded. How many of these stores were actually opened we cannot say. Certainly stores were started in the Mid-west; some also appear to have flourished in Virginia and other sections of the East and South, and there is little doubt that many co-operative warehouses, grain elevators, and marketing arrangements utilized certain features of the Rochdale system. [21]

Developments in a few cities and towns duplicated those in rural areas, though accurate estimates of their number again, unfortunately, are not now and probably never will be possible. Distributive stores were reported in New Jersey, Pennsylvania, and New York, in places like Dorchester, Troy, Springfield, and New York City. [22] How they received their English ideas is not clear, but the Central Labor Union of New York, to cite only one example, may provide some clues. The Central, which was a "union" very much interested in co-operation,

[20] Clipping dated 1882, Samuel Papers, Box 6. Newton, *North American Review*, CXXXVII, 336. Walker, *Princeton Review*, X, 202. Simonds, p. 640. Dunning, p. 303. C. Vann Woodward, *Origins of the New South* (Baton Rouge: Louisiana State University Press, 1951), pp. 186-204.

[21] Dunning, p. 302. Newton, *North American Review*, CXXXVII, 336. Clippings on the Alliance, Samuel Papers, Box 6. Woodward, pp. 196-97.

[22] Newton, *North American Review*, CXXXVII, 337.

was primarily the brain-child of Robert Blissert, an English immigrant. Because of his staunch pro-Irish sympathies, Blissert detested the British government but his contacts with workingclass leaders and their intellectual " allies " were well established. John Stuart Mill and Thomas Carlyle both corresponded with him on labor matters, as did many unionists and co-operators; [23] as a consequence, the organization became one more link in the transatlantic chain.

Generalizations can only be tenuous yet it does seem that the co-operators of the early eighties were increasingly conscious of their role in national movements of reform and protest, and increasingly aware of international movements beyond their immediate horizons. More and more they came to grips with the logic of their situation, which seemingly demanded closer association with other reform groups, rather than sporadic, individual efforts. Viewing their labors in perspective, therefore, co-operative leaders concluded that they too belonged in the same context as trade unions, experimental colonies, Greenbackers, Single Taxers, Populists, loan and assurance agencies, mutual associations, profit-sharers, and co-operative credit institutions. This conceptualization of their functions may account for some of the attraction which the Knights of Labor exerted upon them.

## II. TWO VETERANS AND THE KNIGHTS OF LABOR

George Jacob Holyoake returned to the United States during the autumn of 1882. Unencumbered by a wearisome agenda, he took directly to the hustings to preach co-operation. While the visiting Englishman was in the field the Reverend Mr. Robert Collyer, himself an immigrant, informed him that, " We have been altogether too comfortable to do much in co-operation but by and by we will show you the biggest thing out of this line." [24] In the co-operative line, as Holyoake would soon learn, the biggest thing was the co-operative program of the Knights of Labor. The history of the Knights will already

[23] U. S., Senate, *Report . . . upon the Relations between Labor and Capital,* 48th Cong., 1885, I, 840.
[24] Newton, *North American Review,* CXXXVII, 337.

be familiar to the reader: founded in 1869 as a secret society by Uriah Stephens who was much under the influence of London's J. George Eccarius,[25] leadership passed in 1879 from Stephens to Terence Powderly, under whose direction the order came into the open and rapidly grew.

Converted into a huge national organization, the Knights of Labor held out great promise to co-operators from the very start. Its membership was literally comprehensive, and the fourth plank of its statement of principles and objects pledged the order to the "establishment of co-operative institutions, productive and distributive." Moreover its leaders, Powderly foremost among them, constantly stated that they hoped ultimately to create a co-operative commonwealth. It is hardly surprising, therefore, that many of the country's chief co-operators were swept into the order, among them Tom Phillips and John Samuel. After a quarter century of service to nearly every major labor or labor reform organization, these two once again demonstrated the fundamental continuity of American reformism, at least in terms of its personnel.

Tom Phillips learned of the Knights of Labor when it was formed in 1869, but his immersion in many other activities kept him from taking an interest in it. Not long after this, however, one of the founders of the order, "that grand old Irishman James S. Wright,"[26] persuaded Phillips to take a second look at the organization and, at Wright's behest, having casually stopped in on a meeting one evening, Phillips became the first shoemaker to join the order. Despite this, he nevertheless remained unwilling to devote much time to assembly affairs, preferring a passive role. But local leaders were not content to watch him waste his talents; both James Wright and the principal leader of the Knights of Labor, Uriah S. Stephens, prevailed upon him once more, and he was finally encouraged to undertake organization of the Philadelphia shoemakers for them. Thereafter, he served enthusiastically. Because of his broad background, he inevitably became an official of Local Assembly 64, the first composed of shoemakers

---

[25] Of the relations between Eccarius and Stephens see clippings about them in Samuel Papers, Box 13.

[26] "Autobiography," Phillips Papers.

in Philadelphia. Within a short time, this local expanded into one of the largest constituent units in the Knights of Labor.[27]

Phillips also entered District One Assembly as a member of the Committee of Progress, a body whose chief function was the production of propaganda. His task, in his own words, was " to act before the public . . . and push the work of labor's emancipation." [28] Searching for outlets for its ideas, the committee, which very quickly came directly under Phillips' sway, discovered in William Swain, a member of the Philadelphia newspaper family and the proprietor of the *Public Record*, a faithful angel. Swain donated the use of a column in his daily, his only stipulation being that whatever went into the column must be the " truth," a caveat that posed no problem to the righteous workingman. Uriah Stephens, Grand Master Workman of the Knights, promptly selected Phillips himself to produce the necessary 1770 words a day at an annual salary of $1,000, a figure that must have seemed fabulously large to him. Over the next fourteen months, the Yorkshireman published more than four hundred articles for the order; as he put it:

I stand on record as the first man ever employed by the Order of the Knights of Labor to publicly champion its cause and explain its principles and objects. From the time those articles began to appear abuse of labor began to be less bitter, sentiment grew on the side of the worker and the way opened for a great growth of labor organizations which had it been conducted on the lines first laid down, would have resulted in vast benefits to labor.[29]

His assessment of his writings was oversanguine; nevertheless, there is every reason to agree that he rendered a marked service to the Knights of Labor.

Writing propaganda consumed much of his energy but he never ceased to think of the Knights primarily as a co-operative vehicle. Among the members of District One, for instance, he initiated efforts to create Rochdale stores. At least one

[27] Augusta E. Galster, *The Labor Movement in the Shoe Industry* (New York: Ronald Press, 1924), pp. 48-55.
[28] "Autobiography," Phillips Papers.
[29] *Ibid.*

hopeful project was actually started and experience once again made him the logical choice as head of the organization. As usual, however, a couple of years of promise yielded to stagnation and ultimate failure and in this case the waning co-op was turned over by Phillips to the English-born goldbeater, then Secretary of the Knights, Frederick Turner,[30] who in turn made a success of the business.

Indefatigable, Phillips continued the good fight until 1889 when he began to think that "the enemy [Powderly] in the guise of a friend came in directing [the Knights] . . . in the spirit of the Dark Ages and murdered the grandest concept of labor ever put into shape on this Continent." [31] After years of hopeful waiting, he finally concluded that the Knights had utterly abandoned co-operation, and his harsh words were those of a man who had given much of his life to the movement. Moreover, a personal political quarrel with Powderly and what he regarded as a " disgraceful surrender " by District One during a lockout in Philadelphia [32] made him so furious that he quit the order and turned to trade unionism. In 1889-1890, he and Henry Skeffington helped found the International Boot and Shoemakers' Union, and Phillips served as its first President. In a very real sense, his move to pure and simple unionism symbolized a broader shift that was taking place in the labor movement, a shift which by the turn of the century left little doubt of the wage earners'—though not the farmers'—disgust with co-operation. It is significant that of all the organizations he had served, only the Boot and Shoemakers' outlasted him, testifying to the struggle of labor to found its house upon a rock. But even unionism proved a hollow reed when the old exhilaration was gone, for Phillips was now up against the professionalism of the younger trade unionists, hard, practical men with whom he could not work,

---

[30] "Autobiography," Phillips Papers.

[31] *Ibid.*

[32] Phillips ran for the office of Mayor of Philadelphia and played a part in state politics as well and Powderly went out of his way to throw cold water on Phillips' ambitions in this direction. See my, " Thomas Phillips, a Yorkshire Shoemaker in Philadelphia," *Pa. Mag. Hist. and Biog.,* LXXIX (April, 1955), 190-196.

who took pleasure in driving him, aged and disgruntled as he was, into permanent retirement.[33]

Meanwhile, during the early eighties John Samuel was busy burnishing a reputation that would shortly make him the chief co-operator in the Knights of Labor. Working vigorously among the co-operators of the Mid-west, apprised also of events transpiring in the East, Samuel continued strengthening his ties with England. Indeed, it was essential that he draw the bonds even tighter for he was dispensing British co-operative information at an increased rate. Throughout the late seventies, into the eighties, his correspondence with English co-operators was heavy. Letters that he wrote G. J. Smith of the Manchester Co-operative Board were typical. He had long been ordering publications from Smith: the "Rochdale System of Bookkeeping," "Report of the Rochdale Society," details of the Manchester Co-operative Printing Society, and the latest papers from such organizations as the Workingman's Protective and Provident League in London. Samuel frankly told him that only with the aid of the British could Americans "get to sound co-operation." On the whole, his letters to the Englishman formed brief progress reports on American developments and while they sometimes reported advances, sometimes retreats, their general theme was much the same: "It is difficult to get workingmen to take up co-operation," just as it once had been at Rochdale, "but as Lord B [Brassey] declared, it will carry all before it." [34] As the result of his general confidence and his extensive contacts Samuel enjoyed the prospect of watching his personal stock rise.

In 1880 Smith placed him in direct contact with Hodgson Pratt. Pratt was then the House Secretary of the Guild of Co-operators, which we had occasion to mention much earlier in this study. The Guild was an organization that greatly interested Samuel, for as early as 1878 he had praised its work in southern England in the columns of his St. Louis paper, *The Union*. The Guild, he informed his readers, "meant a spirit of faith in high purpose, close union . . . an association

---

[33] *Ibid.*
[34] Samuel to G. J. Smith, Dec. 9, 1880; Feb. 7; Apr. 13, 1881, Samuel Papers.

of ideas and diffusion of co-operative ideas." [35]  By January 1881, as we saw above, Pratt was able to notify Samuel of his election to membership, thus linking him to one of the greatest propaganda agencies of the co-operative movement, making him, so far as we know, its sole agent in America. Shortly afterwards, his fellow guildsmen wrote that they were looking forward to sending him materials " so that he could teach co-operation especially in the southern counties [states]," [36] and knowing his temperament we can hardly doubt that Samuel wanted to serve the organization zealously. After all, he was now associated intimately with his heroes, George Jacob Holyoake, Edward V. Neale, Abraham Greenwood, and the Guild's President, Thomas Hughes.

The Guild's induction of Samuel was an indication, too, of how much the English themselves desired closer bonds with their co-operative brethren in America. Holyoake and Hughes had both done spadework for the Guild during their tours and they clearly expected great things from the movement in the United States. There were even inklings of their encouraging formal association between Americans and themselves. After furnishing Samuel with quantities of Guild literature, which were promptly distributed, the Englishmen learned from him that because he hoped " to connect the co-operative movement here with your efforts in the same way, I shall bring a few earnest and sincere men together." [37]  Was Samuel responding to some specific proposal from the British? Or was he with his sensitivity about the movement accurately anticipating them?

Whatever the case may have been, Samuel's correspondence with Edward V. Neale augured well for closer ties between Anglo-American co-operators, for both men were internationalists. Working, thinking, and writing they acted as though the co-operative impulses of their two countries were in reality one. Each realized that he had much to gain from the other.

[35] Clippings from *The Union*, May 7; June ?, 1878, Samuel Papers, Box 4. Mass., Bureau of the Statistics of Labor, *17th Annual Report* (1886), p. 114. Holyoake, *Co-operative Movement To-day*, pp. 47-48.

[36] Pratt to Samuel, July 4, 1881, Samuel Papers.

[37] Samuel to H. Pratt and English Co-operators, Apr. 13, 1881, Samuel Papers.

Samuel felt that the Englishman had rendered signal service to self-help in America, in part because Neale had " [waked] up the workingmen of St. Louis," [38] and in part because of the masses of information and advice he had sent across the Atlantic. On the other hand, Neale appears to have looked on Samuel as a Welsh missionary at work in virgin territory, and he consequently relied upon him for latest word of the potentialities, the conversions, baptisms, and backslidings in the industrial wilds of North America.[39]

As Samuel was drawing his ties with England ever tighter, he enlisted in the Knights of Labor. His reasons for this are manifest: he felt that the " fundamental principle of the Order was co-operation," and that the Rochdale Plan was the only one " adequate to [its] needs." [40] The record of his first activities in the order is vague, although we know Powderly commissioned him an organizer in July 1882. Even prior to that time, however, he was busy lecturing, and he produced a series of articles dealing with Rochdale, the British Co-operative Congresses, the Co-operative Wholesale Society, and various other labor matters, for the Knights' official organ, the *Journal of United Labor*.[41] Moreover by 1883 he was involved in co-operation as an agent of the Knights, assuaging the misfortunes of a group of Missouri coal miners by skillfully getting them started in the Missouri Co-operative Coal Company, and not long afterwards, he and Samuel Leavitt presided over the creation in Illinois of the Belleville Coal Operating Mining Company.[42] In brief, Samuel's mind was running in its customary grooves and his successes were preparing the way for his subsequent rapid rise to one of the top posts in the organization.

[38] Samuel to L. Steffer, Feb. 6, 1882, Samuel Papers.

[39] See, Samuel to L. Steffer, Feb. 6, 1882, Samuel Papers.

[40] Samuel to Peter McGaughey, May 7, 1886, *ibid*.

[41] T. Powderly to Samuel, June 21, 1881, July 21, 1882; The Knights of Labor to Samuel, Aug. 4, 1882, *ibid*. *Journal of United Labor*, July 31, 1880; Sept. 1882; Jan. 1883; Dec. 10, 1884.

[42] " Record of the Missouri Co-operative Coal Association," letters dated, Sept. 7, 10, 13, Oct. 18, 25, Nov. 8, 1883; " Minutes of the Belleville Coal Operating Mining Co.," Aug. 3, 1883, Samuel Papers. *Journal of United Labor*, Apr. 1883.

### III. Self-Help Among the Knights

Samuel's personal achievements paled late in 1883 before the onslaughts of another depression and, as the business cycle plumbed the depths, the popularity of self-help reached new heights. Probably at no previous time had the principles of co-operation found such marked appeal. We are told that some workingmen turned to it as they might have to religion; [43] others thought it a quick, easy antidote to disaster; and still others saw it as the only non-violent alternative to the lockout and blacklist. More ebullient than ever as a result of the new trend, Samuel wrote Edward Neale that, " There is much greater interest in co-operation shown here now than when Mr. Holyoake was here last," [44] and this interest mounted until the tumultuous days of 1886.

Because the Knights were committed to co-operation, and because they were developing into the largest of American labor organizations, the brunt of the new demands for programs of self-help fell squarely upon them. Powderly found himself overwhelmed by petitions for action, and in a spirit of considerable perturbation he requested his English organizer Albert Denny to favor him " with such labor literature as you may come across . . . particularly such as relates to co-operation." [45] To the thousands of new recruits who looked to him for leadership, the Grand Master Workman declared, " I have during the past year felt it my duty to study the trend of the English co-operative movement and if possible to learn the lessons it has for us." [46] Personally he soon came to believe English methods too timid, but as a practical matter he made no moves to stop the organization from adopting the principles of Rochdale. His expediency may have stemmed from his belief that " many of our members grow impatient and unrea-

---

[43] Commons, *History of Labour*, II, Chap. 9.

[44] Samuel to E. V. Neale, Oct. 10, 1884, Samuel Papers.

[45] Powderly to A. Denny, Nov. 18, 1884, Powderly Papers. Powderly, Chap. 11. Carman and David, p. 203. Newton, *North American Review*, CXXXVII, 326.

[46] KL, *Proceedings, 1885*, p. 22.

sonable because every avenue of the Order does not lead to
co-operation." [47]

To carry out a co-operative program, the Knights created
a General Co-operative Board in 1882, although it was not until
the subsequent year that it got into operation. By that time,
demands for self-help were so insistent, pressure was so great,
that the Board modified its original policy of trying to cen-
tralize co-operative efforts and tossed the actual implementation
of the program into the laps of the locals. Once local assemblies had formed co-ops, the Board was empowered to grant
them aid when necessary. Approval of all grants rested with
the Executive Council, but the Board was permitted to draw
upon general monies, carefully watched by the leadership,
and to funnel them into various enterprises. Resemblance
between the Knights' Co-operative Board and the Central
Co-operative Board in England was as close, of course, as
circumstances would allow, and the resemblance was inten-
tional.[48] Like its foreign prototype, the Board's task was to
advise and educate co-operators, and attempt co-ordination of
their policies. Several forms of co-operation were officially
sanctioned, including one scheme by a former Blanquist, but
the prevailing predispositions were toward the Rochdale Plan.
Robert Layton, General Secretary of the Knights, made this
clear in testimony given before a Senate committee in the early
eighties. " I understood," he stated, " that the intention was
to adopt as nearly as possible the system which has been
adopted at Rochdale in England, that is as nearly as it could
be made applicable in this country." In addition, he declared,
the East Liverpool Pottery Works, biggest of the Knights'
co-operative ventures, operated on this plan, and " nearly all
our stores are adopting that system, or will adopt it when they
get going." [49]

There was no doubt of the course the Knights would
pursue when, in 1883, John Samuel replaced Henry Sharpe

[47] Commons, *History of Labour,* II, Chap. 9. Powderly, Chap. 11.
[48] The Samuel-Neale Correspondence clearly indicated that the Knights and
Samuel were eager to imitate the British Central Co-operative Board.
[49] U. S., Senate, *Report . . . upon the Relations between Labor and Capital,*
48th Cong., 1885, I, 5-6.

as the principal member of the Co-operative Board. Over the next four years he was the most influential co-operator in the order; potentially he was one of the most important in the labor world. His promotion to the Board also coincided almost exactly with the rising wave of interest in self-help and he was destined to ride the crest of it until it broke in 1887. In terms of qualifications it would have been difficult to have chosen anyone much better fitted for the job and Samuel probably regarded it as the fruition of a long career.

Samuel planned to direct activities of the Knights' co-ops as closely as possible by creating a sort of federal system of enterprises based on a uniform system of co-operation. However, if he and his associates thought their job would be easy, they were certainly ill-advised.

The great obstacle was the pluralistic nature of the organization they served. The Knights of Labor was not a body composed only of dedicated co-operators; on the contrary, it was a heterogeneous coalition of workingmen, middle-class reformers, radicals, and socialists, as well as a host of other disparate elements. As an organization, its objectives were unclear. Powderly, to be sure, spoke of the ultimate creation of a co-operative commonwealth and many undoubtedly agreed with this as a long range objective just as they might have agreed on the desirability of getting to Heaven, yet there seemed a fundamental conflict between trade union and co-operative economics which led to a fundamental dichotomy in the Knights' activities. How indeed could unionists secure higher wages if productive co-ops by lowering wages to secure larger markets pulled union wages down in the process? As it happened, this problem remained academic for the most part, yet there was nothing academic about the struggle on the mundane level concerning who got what from the leadership. For his part Samuel might have been expected to allay some of this dissension, having been a lifelong unionist and a co-operator, but divisions within the order were too deep and too serious for one man to reconcile.

Meantime, Samuel capitalized on an unparalleled opportunity to spread the gospel of self-help. Between 1881 and 1883 we know that he was responsible for counseling or creating at least twenty-four co-operatives; from 1883 to 1888, however, he rendered these same services to at least one hundred and four organizations.[50] Requests for his aid poured in from all over the country. About half of the letters preserved were from correspondents living in the northern reaches of the Mississippi Valley and the greater Mid-west; about a quarter of them came from New England and the Central Atlantic States, while southern, southwestern, and far western states were points of origin for only about a tenth each. Urban areas furnished many of the requests in Samuel's mail, and cities such as Philadelphia, St. Louis, Baltimore, Chicago, New Orleans, Milwaukee, Cleveland, Minneapolis, Indianapolis, Brooklyn, and New York are certainly represented. But the overwhelming preponderance of letters was from small towns and villages. Nearly ninety per cent of the information and advice dispatched by Samuel from the Knights' Co-operative Board went to places like Wapahonutee, Ohio; Zincite, Pierce City, Marysville, and Bonne Terre, Missouri; Philipopolis, Rockland, and Whitehall, Maryland; Burlingame, Hope, and Fall River, Kansas; Normal, Mattorn, and New Boston, Illinois; Janesville, Neenah, and Racine, Wisconsin; Sparta, Cheyboygan, and Coldwater, Michigan; Bentonville, and Argenti, Arkansas. By the mid-eighties, obviously, co-operation was the panacea of the farmer rather than the wage earner; the transition of the idea from city to countryside was to all effects complete. Some co-operators were claiming by that time, in fact, that " stores on the Rochdale Plan are not adapted to large cities." [51] Though overstated there was nonetheless a hard core of truth to this proposition, for Rochdale ideas were by that period finding their widest expression in one of the most typical and fundamental of American political and social organisms—the small towns.

Samuel's methods for popularizing his program were simple and we have good information about them. Inquiries directed

---

[50] Estimates here and below based on letters to and from co-operators as well as from various notes scattered throughout the Samuel Papers. How many of the original letters sent or received are preserved we have no way of knowing.

[51] Newton, *North American Review,* CXXXVII, 337. *CMOJ,* Mar., 1883.

to him were answered with a few generalizations on the nature
of self-help, followed by the citations of documents, tracts,
or articles giving fuller details. A letter he sent to one co-
operator of Streator, Illinois was fairly typical of the lot:

I would recommend you to confine your consideration of the subject
exclusively to the Rochdale Plan and carry it out as closely as circumstances permit. The Rochdale Pioneers began in a very humble way
and worked out their system slowly and gradually, their knowledge of
business increasing with their experience.

And he added, "All necessary information for starting a co-
operative store will be found in the *Journal of United Labor*,
December 10, 1884," a reference to one of his articles on a
St. Louis Rochdale-model store.[52] Numerous inquiries were
answered by mailing out the latest British tracts, or co-operative constitutions accompanied by specific letters of instruction.
Tracts from abroad Samuel considered especially valuable as
an aid to understanding the spirit animating old world co-
operators and, as he wrote his friend Neale, he felt, "There
is a good opening now for the judicious distribution of co-
operative literature if the [Manchester] Co-operative Board
would be kind enough to make grants for that purpose. The
leaflets of the Co-operative Guild, quarterly reports of large
societies like Leeds, Oldham, Rochdale, and Bolton are most
instructive."[53] More instructive still is the fact that Samuel
was using British co-operative materials to further the programs of the Knights of Labor; but the British, far from
objecting, actually paid half the toll on the literature dispatched
to America.[54]

Often Samuel placed his correspondents in direct touch with
English co-operative authorities for he was fully alive to the
international aspects of the movement he loved. A Butte,
Montana co-operator, for instance, was told:

---

[52] Samuel to W. Dawson, July 2, 1885, Samuel Papers. Dozens of co-operators
referred to this same article about the Jewel Co-operative Knitting Company of
St. Louis. The Ms of the article dated June 2, 1885, is in the Samuel Papers.

[53] Samuel to E. V. Neale, Feb. 19, 1886; Samuel to the Co-operators of
Bonne Terre, Feb. 11, 1886, Samuel Papers.

[54] Samuel to E. V. Neale, Oct. 10, 1884; Nov. 9, 1888; Nov. 26, 1889;
Samuel to J. Smith, Dec. 9, 1880; Feb. 7, 1881, Samuel Papers.

I take pleasure in sending you two copies of the work recommended
by the Secretary of the Co-operative Board. This constitution is framed
from ' Model Rules of English Co-operation.' The instructions ' How
to Organize ' will I hope be found satisfactory and I would be pleased
to learn of your progress in the work. As your assembly adopted the
name ' Pioneer ' I send you an interesting tract on the origins of the
educational feature of the co-operative movement. . . . If you will
send $5 to E. V. Neale, Esq., Gen'l Secretary of the Central Co-opera-
tive Board . . . with a request to have sent you the *Co-operative News*
for one year, the publication of the Central Board and the Guild of
Co-operators you will be able to plant co-operation in your own and
surrounding territories.[55]

To serve other individuals or groups Samuel would write to
England or make inquiries of British co-operators for them.

It is an almost inescapable conclusion that the popularity
Samuel enjoyed in the eighties resulted in part from wide
acquaintance with British co-operative ideas among farming
peoples. Work done in preceding years had made Rochdale
a familiar term, consequently many correspondents, already
determined to use this method, simply asked Samuel to fill
them in on details. The director of a fledgling co-op in Gun-
derson, Montana, for instance, asked Samuel for further information on Rochdale so that he would not have to send all the
way to England for it; another in Canton, Illinois, having read
some of the Welshman's propaganda in the *Industrial News*
" upon the Leeds and Rochdale systems " wrote just for
" definite details." A Pierce City leader reported, " I have
been recommending a Co-operative Society . . . on the same
principles as the Old English Societies," and he requested
essential technical information. A group of Illinoisians who
wrote Samuel knew of " two or three plans for forming . . .
stores," but hastened to add that they best understood " the
Rochdale method and perhaps that not as thoroughly as we
ought." From Samuel's experience in the " great and grand
movement " they expected to learn much. District Assembly-
men in Nashville who were under pressure to form a co-op
finally decided on the Rochdale Plan but, aware of Samuel's
repute in this field, they asked him for specific advice. A
committee of Belleville men similarly told him that they

[55] Samuel to E. Harris, Feb. 20, 1886, Samuel Papers.

wanted to " start on a small scale like the Rochdale Pioneers," yet they required a thorough explanation of the system from him. Letters of this sort reflect something of the "grass roots" nature of co-operation, and appear to indicate British ideas were more firmly and widely planted than scholars have shown.[56]

The influence of Samuel and the Co-operative Board reached a peak in 1886, a year of calamitous drought, unemployment, social unrest, and the Haymarket Affair. The Knights by then had established no less than a hundred co-ops and may have had several hundred, though we may doubt if many were as large as the East Liverpool Pottery Works.[57] Samuel's contacts remained sound; Amos Fayram in Detroit, George Keuchter in Cincinnati, and John Osborn in Oshkosh among others continued to reflect his influence in their bailiwicks. From Montana to Massachusetts, from Wisconsin to Texas, English panaceas were put to work. Through the enterprise of Samuel and Peter McGaughey, imported ideas and literature flowed through the district assemblies so briskly that Frederick Turner, the Knights' Secretary-Treasurer, wrote Samuel that the supply of English co-operative constitutions was exhausted.[58]

Thanks to stimulus from abroad, however, the domestic supply of co-operative materials was growing. Richard Ely, an academician of the German variety then revolutionizing American universities, published a series on co-operation in 1886 which Samuel told him were the best studies this side of Manchester.[59] At the Johns Hopkins University, a small band of scholars launched a pioneering study of co-operation in America, reaching, among other conclusions, the same one Samuel had thirty years earlier, namely, that the Rochdale Plan was the most effective mode of self-help. Similarly, new state

[56] Samuel to Manchester Co-operative Board. Mar. 30, 1882; Local Assembly 2330 to Samuel, Mar. 2, 1885; I. Atwater to Samuel, Nov. 30, 1887; J. Rowland to Samuel, Oct. 10, 1885; W. Dawson to Samuel, June 23, 1885; T. Gibson to Samuel, Oct. 13, 1884; Local Assembly 447 to Samuel, Mar. 31, 1885, Samuel Papers.
[57] U. S., Senate, *Report . . . upon the Relations between Labor and Capital,* 48th Cong., 1885, I, 5-6.
[58] Turner to Samuel, Apr. 9, 1885, Samuel Papers.
[59] Samuel to Richard Ely, Feb. 18, 1886, Samuel Papers.

bureaus of labor and industrial statistics by 1886 had over a score of reports in circulation about co-operation, most of them dealing in detail with British methods and ideas. Henry Cross of the Massachusetts legislature, for example, secured the passage of a resolution in 1885 directing the Chief of the State's Bureau of Labor " to prepare and publish for distribution a pamphlet descriptive of the history, methods, and present condition of distributive co-operation in Great Britain." Carroll Wright's excellent treatise, the result of this resolution, appeared the next year and was widely recopied as a standard treatment of the subject.[60] State reports, most of which were lucid and authoritative, greatly encouraged an understanding of co-operation in labor and industrial circles. Interest became so considerable that even American consular officials in the United Kingdom praised British self-help and the remarkable benefits that flowed from it. As one consul suggested, " I submit that the facts embodied in this report should be closely studied by all who have at heart the best interests of American working men and women to the end that our wealth producers may be as favorably surrounded as English operatives are" with instruments to help them get the most for their toil.[61] While the effects of all this material, private, state, and consular reports, were snowballing, Samuel wrote to Neale, " You will be pleased to learn that co-operation on the Rochdale Plan is making progress in this part of the world!" Samuel's own Rochdale store in St. Louis, which he named in honor of one of the Pioneers, flourished.[62] To a friend, the Welshman announced that at last co-operation appeared to have taken firm root in America; affairs took on such a happy complexion that Samuel's colleague, Peter McGaughey, asserted that, " Cloudy heavens opened when the Knights of Labor took an interest in co-operation," and even well-balanced men were estimating that the " emancipation of labor" would take only another five years.[63]

[60] Mass., Bureau of the Statistics of Labor, *17th Annual Report* (1886), p. 51.

[61] U. S., House, *United States Consular Reports, Labor in Europe*, 48th Cong., 2d Sess., House Executive Doc., 54, Part I, pp. 748-51.

[62] Samuel to E. V. Neale, Feb. 19, 1886, Samuel Papers.

[63] McGaughey to Wheeler, May 24, 1886; Samuel to J. C. Gray, Nov. 4, 1884; Mar. 12; Sept. 24, 1886, Samuel Papers.

McGaughey and those like him were oversanguine; but Samuel, cheered as he was, had been a co-operator for too long to be so naïvely optimistic. Though his hopes were high he detected serious flaws in developments; impatience with results, a desire to start big and grow still larger swiftly, were to him signs of weakness. Defections from established British methods, flirtations with untried ideas, deeply disturbed him. And, during the strikes of 1886, he apparently became more conscious than ever of the immanent dilemma created by the opposing pulls of trade unionists and co-operators within the Knights of Labor. Writing to a Kansan, he lamented the fact that the " Order is not yet educated up to your idea of the necessity and importance of co-operation as the full and final remedy for the evils of an unpleasant industrial system." [64] Evidence came from the rank and file that he was essentially correct, that lack of initiative, greed, mismanagement, and delusions about the qualifications for and purposes of self-help were undermining fundamental advances.

Faced after 1886 with an upswing in the business cycle and a mounting record of defeats, the Knights began to fade slowly away. Here and there constituent assemblies survived the debacle; Powderly lived on as a walking relic in the labor world, eventually accepting the post of Commissioner-General of Immigration to end his days on a Federal salary; and the contributions which the order made were passed on. But as a power in American labor the Knights had all but vanished by the mid-nineties. Far from perfect though it was, association of unionists and co-operators was never thereafter so close. Never again was there a vehicle with quite the same potential for men like Samuel. New, tough-minded labor organizations, most notably the A.F.L., saw to it that co-operation was divorced from wage-conscious unionism and they made the decree final.

Decline of the Knights raised serious questions about the value of self-help and there is no doubt that many hitherto sympathetic people began to wonder if it adequately answered

---

[64] Samuel to E. Green, Sept. 23, 1886; Co-operators of Marion, Kansas to Samuel, Mar. 9, 1888, Samuel Papers.

the problems of the workingman. Many critics were fair enough to recognize that co-operative failures did not appear disproportionately large compared to bankruptcies in business, yet this concession was scant comfort to discouraged and impatient workers in the cause. After appraising co-operation unionists eschewed it, or at best treated it with circumspection. Gompers, having decided it was useless, denied Henry Demarest Lloyd's request that two Englishmen be permitted to speak on the subject before an A.F.L. convention. Joseph Medill, publisher of the Chicago *Tribune*, nearly as disillusioned as Gompers, declared that, "At one time co-operation was hopefully regarded as the solution of the capital-labor contentions. But after many trials in this country its advocates have become discouraged and it is fading out as a feasible remedy for the ills of labor." And by the turn of the century Emile Levasseur argued that those who held out hopes of co-operation to laboring men were willfully deluding them, a charge that was not true but quite understandable.[65]

One of the by-products of labor's disenchantment with self-help was the increased popularity of profit-sharing and industrial partnerships. While it is not within the purview of this study to trace them out in any detail, these ideas were likewise in many cases imported from Britain. Most of these plans originated among British humanitarians and capitalists but their transition to America was through the American labor press, thence to reformers and capitalists. By the eighties and nineties the experiences of the Crossley, Briggs, and Halifax firms as well as the Whitwood Colliery, were generally familiar to the leaders of organized labor in this country, and so were the writings of Mill, Fawcett, Thornton, and Jevons on the subject. More specifically, what had been attempted at the Leeds Woollen Company, the Oldham Iron Works, the Ouseburn Engineering Company, and the Paisley Manufacturing Society was also tried, in substance, in the United States by the Pacific Mills at Lawrence, the Millvale Glassworks in New Jersey, the Peacedale Manufacturing Company of Rhode

---

[65] Lloyd, *Henry Demarest Lloyd*, II, 86.  U. S., Senate, *Report . . . upon the Relations between Labor and Capital*, 48th Cong., 1885, II, 963. Levasseur, p. 470.

Island, and by the Cameron and Hazard Companies of New York. Similar ideas were elaborated in more than a dozen other plants scattered across the nation.[66]

One of the more successful practitioners of profit-sharing was N. O. Nelson, president of the St. Louis Manufacturing Company, and an old and devoted admirer of John Samuel. For years Samuel kept Nelson abreast of the latest British developments and there was real rapport between the two men. Like many small capitalists, Nelson was as anxious as his men to reach a working arrangement in the new industrial society, and his own words speak eloquently to those who think only of " robber barons " in the years of the Gilded Age:

It is not benevolence but justice that the man asks, who lives by the work of his own hands. Is his product measured by the wages he gets? Has he no equity except that of a contract made under the duress of necessity? Have we no dispute with the man who reaps a lordly income from the midnight stitching of sad-faced women? The dense fog of money making does not blind us to human obligations. We put the brand of Cain upon the man who imperiously declares that he is not his ' brother's keeper.' [67]

Less important when they began to circulate in America than distributive co-operation, these British-inspired ideas stimulated American capitalists and workingmen to think along still other lines as they tried to solve their complex difficulties. And, while profit-sharing and various partnership schemes did not flourish, they never quite died out; moreover, in the last twenty years they have come to life and now play a vigorous role in the extension of American industrial democracy.

Thus although Rochdale underwent eclipse late in the eighties, statements about its disappearance were both pre-

[66] *The Workingman's Advocate*, May 26, Sept. 8, 1866; Nov. 7, 1868; Sept. 18, 1869; Nov. 12-19, 1870; Mar. 11; Sept. 30, 1871. Jelley, pp. 259-60. Barns, pp. 200-30. McNeill, pp. 497-505. Simon Newcomb, " The Labor Question," *North American Review*, CXI (July-Oct., 1870), 140. Le Comte de Paris, *Old and New*, II, 557. Francis Peabody, " Industrial Co-operation in England," *Forum*, VIII (November, 1889), 274-85.

[67] See the Samuel-Nelson Correspondence in Samuel Papers. Holyoake, *Co-operative Movement To-day*, pp. 120-21. Barns, pp. 87-89. *Report of the Industrial Commission, Capital and Labor in Manufactures and General Business*, 1901, XIV, 368-62.

mature and erroneous. The idea was not so popular in the nineties as it had been in the previous twenty years but it was in no danger of dying out. Some of the veteran co-operators, it is true, died—Barnum, Quincy, Leavitt among them—and others like Tom Phillips retired to unionism, politics, and then entirely to private life; but the ideas they espoused retained most of their virility.

## IV. THE SEED SOWN

For Samuel, who had been punished as much as anyone by the deflation of the Knights of Labor, setbacks meant only brief interruptions to his work. Still in touch with his English comrades, he kept them aware of the condition of affairs in America. "I have not been idle," he wrote Edward Neale, " though it is still uphill work here as it was in England forty years ago. The seed sowing done through the generous donations of the Central Co-operative Board tracts . . . has not been in vain." [68] Propaganda continued apace; he wrote articles and letters for the *Journal of United Labor* while it lasted and for various small newspapers, meantime distributing English tracts to his American contacts.

Availing himself of the gains made in several states where associative laws had been modified to the advantage of co-operators, he participated in the movement for reform in Missouri. As a lobbyist he was more successful than Phillips had been years earlier. Having drafted a bill after years of study and much advice from men like Michigan's Joseph Labadie, he entrusted it to a friendly politician in the state assembly in 1890. Its object was to place co-ops in the same legal position as businesses conducted on the joint stock principle; this, in fact, he regarded as an " absolute necessity." " Under the present law of incorporation," he explained, " all profits derived from business, commercial, industrial, and financial, are allotted to capital in proportion to the amount of capital invested. Under the co-operative system capital receives a fixed rate of interest from the gross profits of the business, the remaining profits after meeting the necessary

---

[68] Samuel to E. V. Neale, Nov. 26, 1889, Samuel Papers.

expenses being divided among those who have created or produced the profits regardless of the amount of capital invested." [69] Unfortunately while Samuel had started the ball rolling, a law of the kind that he sought was not passed until 1915, though when it was passed it was of the Rochdale type.

Practical co-operation also continued. In a letter to Neale, thanking him for his "heroic efforts" on behalf of American co-operators, Samuel gave details of a Rochdale store which he and a few surviving Knights had founded. "Its first quarter's experience," he wrote, "brings forcibly to mind the words of the Rochdale Committee of Management in the 21st Annual Report 'The Weavers' Dream.' Should this weakling of ours survive and acquire the strength and robustness of its great example, it may prove to be a landmark in future co-operation in the Western World." [70] Five years later, as the co-op struggled on, his ardor waxed hot and his faith in his panacea remained unshaken.

Early in the nineties, Samuel joined with an organization in which he invested his last energies, the Sociological Society of America. Viewed broadly this order was one of many attempts to weld the co-operatives of the nation together into a single co-ordinated force. Basically it was an outgrowth of the unrest that produced a proliferation of reform, labor, populist, alliance, and socialist groups. In many respects it was a transitional affair standing between trade unionism and co-operation on the one hand, and the Populist Party on the other. Like many other groups it sought the ultimate abolition of the wage system and the substitution of profit-sharing or co-operative industry in its stead. Political action, propaganda, and distributive co-operation were the devices upon which it relied. Taking as their motto, "Co-operation, the law of the new civilization," leaders of the order announced in the language of the new economics that:

the measure of reward should be based upon the productiveness of labor instead of upon the 'law of supply and demand'; that competi-

---

[69] Samuel to Butler, Aug. 5, 1890; Samuel to Fales, Jan. 5, 1895; J. Labadie to Samuel, Mar. 21, 1880, Samuel Papers. Wis., Bureau of the Census, Labor and Industrial Statistics, *2nd Biennial Report* (1885-86), pp. 223-25.

[70] Samuel to E. V. Neale, Feb. 19, 1886; Aug. 24, 1891, Samuel Papers.

tion—while it has produced good in the past, despite the suffering it has occasioned—is now reversing its action and is working against the further progress of society; that the very nature of the principle of competition is to break down and destroy the weaker industries, and to concentrate wealth to such an extent as to disturb the entire industrial system.

Moreover, they declared:

Labor as it organizes and becomes united in various unions should recognize that those unions while necessary as a means of protection are incapable of changing the present condition of things and placing Labor and Capital in harmonious relations. What is needed is not so much an advance in wages as the concession of the right of labor to share in the profits—in other words to introduce a new industrial system where Capital is restricted to a fixed rate of interest and Labor over and above the market rate of wages is allowed to share in the profits of the business.[71]

Originally the Society was a feminine order; it was founded May 24, 1882 in New York City by a band of women attending a lecture course on co-operation, then being delivered by Mrs. Imogene Fales of Brooklyn. Exuberant and emancipated, Mrs. Fales was one of those women who vented her emotions in every reform movement open to her in the eighties and nineties. A humanitarian and an idealist, she proved an effective, if somewhat overemotional, leader. During the organization's first decade of existence she expanded it and opened its ranks to males as well as females—a sound start for a co-operative commonwealth. Furthermore she attracted the services of several prominent co-operators and, most significantly for us, she made the order a stronghold of British ideas.

Samuel, ever alert to co-operative developments, heard of the Society almost immediately. At its inception it began to reprint and distribute English co-operative materials, and J. H. Osborn, Samuel's Wisconsin friend, wrote the veteran telling him how he had secured a number of Holyoake's pamphlets from the Society for use in his work. Thereafter, as his scrap-books show, Samuel followed the progress of the organization, even going so far as to note in a marginal comment: " The

---

[71] Simonds, pp. 659-660. Clippings dated Dec. 23, 1882, Samuel Papers, Box 6. McNeill, p. 529. Bemis, p. 105.

Sociological Society might do for American societies what the Central Co-operative Board does for England." [72]

By 1890 Samuel was in touch with Mrs. Fales; he already knew of her selection as President of the National Board of Co-operators, and he had watched closely her efforts to teach self-help to Chicagoans.[73] Experienced, cautious, and steady, he seemed to have little in common with her, yet somehow by 1892 he had been encouraged to write several reports for her and to furnish members of the organization with his manual, " How to Organize a Co-operative Society." Mrs. Fales then asked for his assistance at the forthcoming International Co-operative Congress in Chicago and he joined the Society, becoming in a short time one of its mainstays. Over the next few years he contributed to and for a time edited the *New Commonwealth*, the order's journal, and in 1894 Mrs. Fales persuaded him to accept the General Secretaryship of the National Co-operative Union, one of the constituent parts of the Society entrusted with co-operative matters. Service in this post must have given him pause; he was an old man, periodically in ill-health, with a right arm so diseased as to make writing a painful luxury. Yet he has made clear why he took the job: " Nothing," he wrote Imogene Fales, " but the fear that the movement to which I have devoted the best years of my life may languish if placed in untried hands tempts me to assume the responsibilities of the position." [74]

Taking up the burdens of his post Samuel at least had the consolation of being in familiar surroundings intellectually, for despite the grandiose declaration of principles announced by the Society it actually dedicated itself almost exclusively to the promulgation of British co-operative methods. This was true very largely because of Mrs. Fales' personal predilections. For years she had studied the works of Holyoake, considering herself his faithful disciple. Zealous interest in self-help led her to England in 1887 to attend the Carlisle Co-operative Congress,

<hr/>

[72] Note by Samuel, Samuel Papers, Box 6. McNeill, p. 529. J. Osborn to Samuel, (?) 1882, Samuel Papers.

[73] " Clippings and Announcements," notebook, Samuel Papers, Box 2.

[74] " Co-operation," Ms, Samuel Papers, Box 4. Fales to Samuel, Jan. 11; Feb. 22; Aug. 5, 1892; Samuel to Fales, Jan. 28, 1892, Samuel Papers. Samuel's articles for the *New Commonwealth* are in Box 3.

where she conferred with the delegates and leaders there assembled, and met the principal speaker, George Jacob Holyoake himself. Returning to America she continued writing to such English co-operators as Esacustis Phipson, leader of one of the co-operative colonies near London, and to Holyoake, upon whom she made an enduring impression.[75]

Nothing excited Mrs. Fales more than the example of English successes in co-operation. " If we could only measure up to English progress "—" and if we could only stick together as they [at Rochdale] did fifty years ago "—were typical of her comments. " I am still very anxious," she wrote an American friend in 1894, " to see a . . . colony started by real, solid and true Rochdale co-operators," [76] and when she gathered her disciples in James Freeman Clarke's Boston Church to organize a central co-operative body in 1886, she devoted most of her time to eulogizing the achievements of the United Kingdom's Co-operative Board. When, in time, her own organization's board was functioning, she made it patently clear that it was " earnestly endeavoring to follow in the path outlined by its predecessors in the movement and [that] every step taken in England in pursuance of this work is studied with a view to its reproduction in the United States." [77] What Imogene Fales was saying publicly to her followers was repeated in the Sociological Society's publications, first the *Co-operative News*, and later the *New Commonwealth*, and both organs buttressed their opinions with ample material drawn from the British co-operative world.

Sensitive, emotional, intelligent, and visionary, Mrs. Fales has left us a number of insights into the personal difficulties of the co-operator. Being a woman she gave freer reign to her moods than men like Phillips and Samuel, who nevertheless must often have felt much as she did. Convinced that British co-operative methods would make it possible for her to come

[75] Fales to Samuel, May 19, 1893, Samuel Papers. Holyoake, *Co-operative Movement To-day*, pp. 50, 174. Also see, Fales to Samuel, Feb. 23, 1893, Samuel Papers.

[76] Fales to Samuel, July-August letters, 1894; Fales to Samuel, Jan. (?), 1894, Samuel Papers.

[77] Bemis, p. 105. " Booklet on Co-operation," unidentified clipping, Samuel Papers, Box 6.

to terms with the American industrial juggernaut, she quickly learned what veteran co-operators surely already knew—that tasks of social education require generations to produce their effect. In the process of learning this, however, she poured out her heart to John Samuel. Her letters ran the gamut from discussions of occult readings to will power to affirmative Christianity and over the whole range of British and American co-operative experiments as well.[78] But it was a long letter written in May 1893 that gives us the best picture of what co-operators probably felt beneath their often stoical resolve, a resolve especially noticeable in the cases of Samuel and Phillips:

I think there is nothing so desirable in life as rest. Each time I feel I cannot go on, that I cannot any longer bear the burden I am carrying . . . it seems altogether too heavy for my strength. The clouds are heavy and dark. I lose sight of the heavenly vision and feel that I am pursuing a hopeless task. When these periods come over me and it is not once or twice but many times they come, then I pace the floor and reason the whole thing out—and then I see that I cannot without being false to myself drop this work. It is when the outlook is particularly dark that I give way and am assaulted by these doubts and feelings. . . . At such times I feel almost like a double person or one with a double consciousness. There are my own feelings and questionings appealing to one side with almost superhuman force. There is the calm judicial power of reason that impartially goes over the ground and then says,' Peace be still.' It is not the mere fact of publishing a paper or teaching but the constant effort and determination underlying that work to do all that is possible toward wiping out this competitive system . . . and bringing in a co-operative system. That seems Utopian and yet it is the sole motive of my labors.[79]

Although Mrs. Fales' Sociological Society was never large—probably it never included more than a dozen other co-operative societies—it was important as a part of a larger process and it was influential. When viewed in context with other enterprises such as the Ruskin Co-operative Association, the Cooperative Commonwealth, plus scores of smaller organizations, and when considered side by side with the preachings of Edward Bemis, Nicholas Gilman, Jane Addams, Edward

---

[78] Fales-Samuel Correspondence, Mar. 1892 through May, 1893, Samuel Papers.
[79] I. Fales to Samuel, May 2, 1893, *ibid.*

Bellamy and Henry Demarest Lloyd, its place in American reformism becomes obvious. Moreover, acceptance of British co-operative ideas by Mrs. Fales' group represented a penetration of the middle-class reform movement. Initially, the reader will recall, immigrant workingmen had been largely responsible for carrying self-help to America and for spreading its message among their own kind; then, wage earners had passed these ideas on to farmers, from whom humanitarian, reformist, and Populist elements borrowed it in the eighties and nineties.[80]

After doing its share of bearing self-help to middle-class reformers, the Sociological Society struggled on manfully during the early nineties. After the failure of a proposed co-operative congress, similar to England's, in 1893, the leaders of the organization sought to vitalize their institution by importing a new organizer from England. James Rhodes, whom the Society chose, was a well qualified co-operator but his much sought-after talents were ill-adapted to the task of leading Americans, for too often he lost patience with them and instead of adopting a positive line for them to follow, berated them for their stupidity. His tours fizzled; he lost confidence in his mission, and turned in anger on those who had hoped for his success. While the Englishman debated with his American mentors, George Dewhirst, one of the secretaries of the Society, learned from England that Rhodes was "a scoundrel and wife beater" and his association with the organization quickly terminated. Although Rhodes remained in America, befriended a number of prominent reformers such as Henry Demarest Lloyd, and became the Secretary of the International Co-operative Alliance, he was of no further use to his sponsors, or to John Samuel upon whose aged shoulders there fell the task of keeping the Society going.[81]

Samuel kept in touch with England, wrote many reports on co-operation, helped edit the Society's publications, and served as its General Secretary. In mid-summer 1896 he

---

[80] T. Morgan to H. D. Lloyd, Dec. 29, 1898; Jan. 22, 1900. Lloyd Papers. Quint, pp. 280-85. Lloyd, *Henry Demarest Lloyd*, II, 68-93.

[81] Fales to Samuel, Oct. 21, 1893; Rhodes to Fales, Oct. 26, 1893; May 25, 1894; Fales to Samuel, June 2, 1894, Samuel Papers.

accepted the chairmanship of the St. Louis Committee participating in the Co-operative Congress, and he played a prominent part in what proved a fiasco, for its deliberations showed little more than the disorganization of the co-operative movement. With him in the meetings were old acquaintances like Edward Bemis, Alonzo Wardall, Norman Lermond, and Imogene Fales. After the Congress created the American Co-operative Union, the function of which was " to promote Co-operation on the Rochdale Plan," Joel Duse, one of its representatives, offered Samuel leadership of the Committee on Information and Federation because of his wide experience. But Samuel barely assumed office before the Union crashed about him.[82]

Thus the failures continued. Nevertheless, if co-operation was not sweeping the country it had arrived to stay and to flourish years later. There were occasional bright spots, of course. H. C. Goodrich, a Chicago manufacturer, wrote Samuel that he wanted to " quit commercial war and enter co-operative peace," and he asked the old Welshman to " throw out the lifeline," to " teach [him] co-operative science." [83]  Reports from California indicated that " co-operative ideas were in the air " in all parts of the state, and throughout the nation distributive stores prospered here and there. And in the world of the co-operator these conversions and demonstrations of the faith were as important as they were in religious movements. Besides the converts, too, English immigrants still poured into the United States, continuing self-help in the same spirit Samuel had evidenced through his long years of service. By 1913, in fact, James Ford pointed out in his study of the co-operative movement that " the English immigrant brought with him what has become the most familiar type of co-operative association to be found in New England. He saw reproduced in America the same needs that had created the consumers' associations to which he belonged . . . and he instinctively urged

[82] Note dated June 2, 1896, Samuel Papers, Box 3. Rhodes to Bemis, Aug. 8, 1896, Edward Bemis Papers (Wisconsin State Historical Society, University of Wisconsin, Madison, Wisconsin). See also, J. Duse to Samuel, Aug. 29, 1896, Samuel Papers.
[83] H. Goodrich to Samuel, Aug. 14, Aug. 25, 1894; Ferris to Samuel, Oct. 23, 1894, Samuel Papers. Quint, pp. 282-83.

co-operation. Thus throughout New England where English immigrants have congregated, consumers' stores have been started, always on the Rochdale model." [84] Ford's study was limited to New England, but much the same story was true of the Middle Border, and of many industrial centers from coast to coast.

Samuel was too old to ride the next co-operative wave, as were most of the veterans who implanted the ideas of self-help in the United States, and even the younger and more vigorous Mrs. Fales had given up the cause for service in the National Women's Progressive Political League. The veteran took things philosophically, however, retired, and began the research which he hoped would prove valuable to co-operators younger than himself. Old friends flattered him with assurances that he was as hale as ever, but he certainly knew that after forty years of toil the game was over. He had no reason to be sorry. The movement of which he was a part, and which he has helped the historian trace in greater detail than has ever before been possible, had permanently fixed the Rochdale Plan in America. Moreover, the principles he symbolized were an enduring, if modest, contribution to American liberalism.[85]

---

[84] James Ford, *Co-operation in New England* (New York, 1913), pp. 20-30.
[85] Fales to Samuel, May 19, 1896; Samuel to Nelson, July, 1907; Nelson to Samuel, July 11, 1907, Samuel Papers.

# Part Eight

# THE WANING OF BRITISH INFLUENCE

## I. New Patterns

When John Samuel died in 1907 British influences in American labor were already disappearing. For nearly fifty years, Anglo-American labor leaders had steered more or less parallel courses, had moved in essentially the same direction. Like two vessels at sea they had been close enough during this period to size up one another's crew, to shout the latest word across the void, and to swap passengers and mail—even though traffic was heavier in the direction of the Americans. In the end, however, despite talk of going into port together, the masters took different star sights and their courses diverged.

It would be untrue to say that Americans entirely lost interest in the British. Just as it is difficult to discover the beginnings of the phenomena we have been studying so, too, it is hard to pinpoint their ending. Certainly American leadership watched the allied forces of Liberalism and Labour march towards the capture of British government with rapt attention. When the Labour Party at the close of the First World War unveiled its reconstruction program, its visions of a new social order, American political actionists sprang forth from their long hibernation refreshed, and the old leadership, in industrial states such as New York and Illinois, was hard put to squelch the uprising.[1] Similarly, British victories or defeats in the courts were closely observed. In fact, because the British did not carry their doctrine of " conspiracy to injure " as far as the use of the injunction was carried by " wealth worshipping Federal Courts," many felt that if " we would learn some of our British brothers' methods in this line of business . . . we

[1] For the influences of the British Labour Party on Sidney Hillman and other American leaders see, William E. Walling, *American Labor and American Democracy* (New York: Harpers & Brothers, 1926), pp. 64, 104-107, 110. 125-26. Staley, pp. 361-62.

303

would find a shorter, surer way to put a stop to some of the present infamous injunction juggling." [2] And so it went with respect to other developments abroad. British efforts to win compensation from employers and a greater measure of security from government drew considerable notice in the United States and played a minor part in demands advanced by a few labor organizations, while the famed Boston Police Strike was triggered by the activities of policemen's unions in London and Liverpool in 1919. Quite naturally, too, the older immigrants, while they lived, remained alert to the trends taking shape across the sea and there can be no question about the significance of their own or their parents' British backgrounds in the case of labor personalities like William Green, William Haywood, Philip Murray, or John L. Lewis. [3]

The twentieth century, nonetheless, found American labor standing solidly on its own feet. For the most part, the outlook of organized workers and their leaders tended to become increasingly parochial and opportunistic rather than international and idealistic. The Age of the Professional had arrived and, in terms of material gains, this was unquestionably all to the good. Basic constructive processes begun during the Civil War seemed well advanced. After much experimentation and many informative failures, labor rejected dogmas, turned to an instinctive pragmatism, formed its own cadres of leaders, and built organizations designed primarily to safeguard the interests of skilled and semi-skilled workers. If the co-ordination of labor's scattered armies was faulty, as the steel strike of 1909 proved it to be, at least the armies were permanently in the field; if the American Federation and the independent unions faced years of crucial struggle, as they did, they were nevertheless two million strong by 1905 and were slowly growing more powerful and more skilful. Unions, it is true, had failed to overawe industrialists but they had clearly won the battle for survival. Moreover, labor had attracted allies.

---

[2] Webb, pp. 599-601. *U. S. Labor Journal* (Memphis), Dec. 2, 1901. T. J. Morgan-H. D. Lloyd Correspondence, 1898-1903, Lloyd Papers.

[3] Green succeeded Gompers as leader of the A. F. of L. Haywood led the I.W.W.; Murray led the United Steelworkers' Union, and John L. Lewis now leads the United Mine Workers' Union.

Organized reform groups increasingly meshed some of their efforts with labor's in movements seeking to ameliorate the more flagrant abuses of the economic system, and co-operators, though no longer an intimate part of the trade union world, were firmly planting and profitably developing ideas that have flourished in our own day as sound and respectable economic activities.

Once it had been shown how to marshall its native resources, American labor evidenced increasingly less desire to borrow extensively from the British. By the turn of the century, in fact, Americans were leaving their own stamp on British labor; a number of American socialists and social novelists—Daniel DeLeon, Jack London, Henry Demarest Lloyd—were being heard and read in the United Kingdom. Towering above them all in terms of influence was Henry George, whose resuscitation of the British socialist movement, ironically, set the labor movements of the two countries more pronouncedly than ever on divergent paths. For as British workingmen and women turned in ever larger numbers to socialism, the unions affiliated with the American Federation of Labor, and the independent brotherhoods, eschewed such a course, despite vociferous dissent, for safe and sane unionism.

Many things contributed to the decline of British influence and each factor is so blended with others that little could be gained by ranking them in any ascending order of importance. There can be no doubt, however, that a relative decline in British and Irish immigration in the first decades of this century was an element of vital significance. The so-called " new immigration" which, symbolically enough, reached a peak in the year of John Samuel's death, inundated the labor market with a heterogeneous array of Slavs and southern and eastern Europeans. Generally unfamiliar with industrial society, hence with trade unionism or co-operation, these people temporarily sapped the strength of labor organizations, drastically altered the labor environment, and especially in the lower echelons of union organization, gradually reshaped the character of labor leadership. Nowhere was the influx of these immigrants more dramatic than in the coal mining districts which had been the traditional preserve of the English, Irish, Scotch, Welsh, and Germans. When Terence Powderly, for example, went into the Pennsylvania anthracite fields to deliver a eulogy over the grave of his hero, John Siney, he spoke at some length before realizing that almost no one in his audience understood English. Times had changed, not only in the mining industry but in most of the heavy industries where " hunkies," " polacks," and " wops," some of whom were especially imported to labor docilely, took over tasks Britons and Irishmen had earlier performed. As suggested, British and Irish immigration bulked numerically large until 1920, yet relative to the new immigration it declined. Unsure of all the motivations behind the great transatlantic exodus, we cannot be sure why it tapered off even before the ultra-nationalistic immigration laws of the '20's. Perhaps it resulted from a spreading belief that trusts had gained the upper hand and converted America into a bastion of conservatism, that greater opportunities were offered by British industry. Or perhaps it was due to the power of Britain's twentieth century unionism, its extension to the unskilled, and its possession of its own political vehicle. In any event, changes in immigration apparently meant a change in influence.

Over the long run, too, deep differences between British and American labor, some of them national and environmental, manifested themselves. Unlike the British, Americans at the opening of the century saw little reason to alter a free enterprise economy, or their form of government. Although labor piled up a fearful record of aggressions, it was the modification of capitalism and the correction of its abuses workingmen sought, not fundamental revision of their cherished institutions or beliefs. Given the American environment this was quite natural. American labor lived within the framework of an enormously expansive economy that promised ever brighter horizons. Yet for the workingmen and the industries of Great Britain, the halcyon days of the mid-nineteenth century were passing. To be sure, the British economy was also expanding, but less rapidly than in the day when Britain had been the unchallenged workshop of the world. Britain felt each year with increasing keenness the biting competition of German and American industry. Basically, therefore, the problem for the British laborer was how to secure more bread from a loaf in which the yeast was working less expansively. Under these circumstances he placed great emphasis on the role of his union; he expected a great deal from it, politically as well as economically and socially, and he broadened the goals of his labor movement until they were sufficiently comprehensive to envisage the direction of national life.

Americans could discover few reasons for living as fully within the ambit of unionism as their brethren across the sea. Incorrigible optimism, seemingly unlimited opportunities, the fact that wealth and not lineage was the only approximation of a real class barrier, all led them to anticipate a more varied and interesting life, and encouraged them to place but a small premium on organized labor activity. As changed patterns of economic growth caused British unionism to widen its programs, a mushrooming economy in America persuaded all except a few left-wing unionists and socialists to give to labor's goals the strictest and narrowest definition.

There were other elements, of course, that diminished British influence. Americans toiled in a vast continental market larger than Western Europe, immune, or at least protected by prohibitively high tariffs, from foreign competition. This meant that in time American unionists tended to support policies of fierce economic nationalism which—though they did not always suspect it—injured workingmen everywhere. In many respects labor, identifying itself with the welfare of this or that industry, reflected some of the habits and economic thinking of its industrial leaders. Thus, for instance, John Jarrett, himself a Briton, leader of the iron, steel, and tin workers, backed the high tariff policies of Pennsylvania's iron and steel kings, despite the fact that he was fully familiar with all of the arguments for free trade. This brand of nationalist sentiment, which was but one facet of an even less tolerant kind of nationalism then rising in America and in other western nations, undermined the old international spirit and substituted in its stead "America first." By the twentieth century, in spite of a general widening of liberties in many areas, "un-Americanism" was a cardinal sin which labor could flirt with only by taking the heroic and disastrous course into the maw of its enemies. Unwilling to do this, labor conformed—as it did all over the western world—and became more markedly and avowedly nationalist. Perhaps there is consolation in the fact that Marxism and other varieties of socialism fared no better in their struggle to advance internationalism over nationalism.

Certainly, too, a diminution of Christian missionary zeal on both sides of the Atlantic inhibited transatlantic influences. British organizers who came to the United States, as well as British visitors, like Mundella, Holyoake, Hardie and Macdonald, were preachers of a cause. It was primarily as missionaries that they viewed themselves. Even the avowed secularists among them possessed an undeniable religiosity; they felt a responsibility to their God to liberate workingmen everywhere, believed they were under deep moral obligations to do so, and never admitted that their zeal should be contained within particular national boundaries. Embattled men, often pariahs, they derived their exaltation from the wellsprings of their own righteousness. Amazingly like nineteenth century empire builders in many respects, these organizers were sure of themselves and of the efficacy of their programs. They were imbued with the notion that it was their calling to bear the workingman's burden, and they shouldered their burden with an indefatigable dedication that accurately reflected much that was good in British character and British society at mid-century. When these Englishmen, and their comrades from other parts of the United Kingdom, struck hands with American labor leadership, which was among the most religious in the world, positive action resulted, and the gain to the workingman was enormous.

The transformation of affirmative Christianity in England and America, despite the subsequent liberating effects this had in some areas of social and political life, dealt the labor movement in the United States a subtle but devastating blow, depriving it not of economic power, to be sure, but of idealism and moral dignity. Neither the socialists in England, who ironically have done less than their religious predecessors to internationalize the labor movement, nor the economic opportunists of America's huge unions have made up the deficit. There is the danger now in the Age of the Relative that economic opportunism will become an end in itself. In this regard, of course, labor's problem was and still is the general one—namely, whether democracy would degrade the working-man by pandering only to his economic appetites, or whether it would help him build new institutions that would make him a more complete human being. Excellent arguments can be advanced in behalf of either contention, but the challenge does exist and is a fundamental one in Anglo-American life, for what were once called God and vision seem to have yielded somewhat to the cost of living index.

Sheer miscalculation also discouraged efforts to bring the two labor movements together in the twentieth century. It is worth noting that the friendship of British and American labor was, to a considerable degree, based upon misunderstanding. British influence in America was attributable in large part to the work of skilled propagandists who tended to exaggerate the cohesive-ness and the progress of labor abroad. There was nothing inherently or even consciously sinister in this fact; the propagandists were simply overzealous, uncritical, or too anxious to drive home their points by oversimplifying. No one would seriously contest their main theme, namely, that Britain had the most powerful and effective trade union movement in the world but the divisions within British labor were all too often ignored. Differences between men like George Potter and the London Junta, between socialists and other socialists, and socialists and non-socialists, between new unionists and conservative unionists, were scarcely ever mentioned. Samuel Gompers, George McNeill, and a few other accomplished American labor leaders were aware of these things, but men of their experience and perspicacity were relatively rare. Co-operators were afflicted with the same blind spot. John Samuel and Thomas Phillips hardly ever alluded to the cleavage be-tween federalists like E. V. Neale, and individualists like J. M. Ludlow in the English co-operative movement.

Reading nineteenth century materials published in America dealing with labor in Great Britain, the impression that all was sweetness and light, loyalty and unity, is almost over-whelming. It reminds one of the long distance stereotypes of the Soviet Union that intrigued many Britons and Americans twenty years ago. These impressions naturally led Americans to believe that British labor was less heterogeneous and much more formidable than it actually was. The urgent exhortations of the agitators, for example, that American labor lagged behind British labor were, to say the least, misleading. Without unions American labor generally was more fortunate politically, economically, and socially, than the bulk of British labor, and it hardly requires the wisdom of hindsight to discern that since large-scale industrialization came at least a generation later in the United States than it did in Great Britain, the American labor movement could not, without more careful allowances than were then made, be compared with the one across the sea.

Because of these and many other distortions, leaders in each country tended to overestimate the resources and the potentialities of the other's labor organizations. To some extent this helps explain the practical failure of the series of attempts at international alliance and closer working agreements. The propagandists undeniably rendered great services to American workers, yet we can lament their refusal to speak and write of problems rather than promises.

These, then, were some of the factors that made co-operation between the two movements less feasible after the first decade of the century than it had been during the previous forty years. To be sure, the President of the British Trades Union Congress declared in the mid-nineties that strong common ties bound the workingmen of the two nations, that they were " one in doctrine and in charity." [4] In the old spirit Ben Tillett wrote John Mitchell, leader of the United Mine Workers, during the great coal strike of 1902 that " we are watching with interest the fight you are making in behalf of the men who work in the great deeps of the earth," and suggested that strike assistance between the miners of the two countries " would do a great deal to bring together the English-speaking races." [5] Similarly, as late as 1905, Daniel J. Keefe of the Longshoremen felt the need of importing British agitators and lecturers to

[4] British Trades Union Congress. *Parliamentary Committee, Reports and Circulars,* 1895, p. 48.
[5] Tillett to John Mitchell, Apr. 7; July 28, 1902, John Mitchell Papers (Catholic University Library, Washington, D. C.). Cited hereafter as Mitchell Papers.

help him in organizational work—a need that was still felt in the nineteen thirties when mass organization got under way in the United States.[6] But these gestures simply indicated all of the old bonds were not broken; in the labor movement as a whole, they failed to prove that impressive new links were being forged.

In the long run there are factors that might override differences in perspectives held by British and American labor. If American consciousness of less abundant resources, international interdependence, and international responsibility remains strong, the two labor movements could move much closer together. Broader concepts of self-interest than the traditional brand of ultranationalism, a distrust of extremist methods or immoderate philosophies, a spirit of kinship, and a great deal of vision might work to create new and closer relationships than have prevailed over the last forty years. Yet there is nothing inevitable or at present even likely about the development of deeper understanding; certainly the real spirit underlying this once significant trend has long since atrophied.

## II. CONCLUSIONS: BRITISH MEN AND IDEAS

As the gulf between laborers on either side of the Atlantic widened, the chief characteristics of British and Irish men and ideas emerged in bold relief. Agitators, propagandists, and co-operators brought with them a knowledge of the spirit, strategy and tactics of an experienced and effective labor movement. In key American industries, crafts, and shops they won positions of leadership; in mines and factories throughout the country they organized new unions and new co-operatives, or revitalized and resuscitated old ones. Every major union or co-operative order from 1860 to the mid-nineties felt their impact and in each of them they pioneered numerous advances.

Stimulated by these men and their ideas, American working-men (though how many we cannot tell) and without question American labor leadership, borrowed extensively from them. The talents of immigrant organizers alone were invaluable to

---

[6] Daniel Keefe to Mitchell, Jan. 4, 1905, Mitchell Papers. Interview with Florence Thorne, former A. F. of L. Research Director, March, 1953.

a young labor movement stopping its way to light, yet even beyond this, British labor became a great example that provided working criteria by which Americans could more easily measure their progress and plot their courses. British experience, moreover, focused American attention on such important instruments as arbitration, conciliation, collective bargaining, centralized union structure and finance, benefit and welfare programs, profit-sharing, industrial partnerships, various cooperative schemes, a vast range of socio-economic legislation, legal precedents, and statistical information.

Furthermore, in stressing the negligible role of intellectuals in the American labor movement, historians have overstated the case. The American worker, it is true, did not rally around a Marx, an Engels, an Owen, or a Henry George; there was no single mind or dogma that he placed on a pedestal and in this sense he managed to retain a pluralistic outlook during the nineteenth century. Nevertheless, the rising American labor movement did not lack, nor did it fail to seek, intellectual guidance. That such direction came less from native talent than some might have wished is beside the point. Labor relied heavily upon European intellectuals, but more heavily still on British intellectuals—radicals, socialists, utopians, humanitarians, reformers, political economists, and academicians. It is impossible to ignore the frequency with which we encounter names such as Owen, Oastler, Sadler, Shaftesbury, Mill, Ricardo, Adam Smith, Cairnes, Jevons, Rogers, Kingsley, Ruskin, Hughes, Mundella, Holyoake, Beesly, and Harrison in labor materials. If we included a list of less prominent persons, most of whom would now be classified as "experts," the roster would be even more impressive.

Opposition to intellectuals is more a twentieth than it was a nineteenth century phenomenon. In the overwhelming number of cases studied here, labor leaders were under an inner compulsion to improve their minds and to seek out the ideas of the principal political economists and labor-reformers. They were under an external compulsion to win the respect of a society that was not prepared to accept them; hence whenever possible they adorned their arguments with the names and ideas of thinkers and experts whose positions seemingly were unchallenged. They were obliged by the nature of their circumstances to premise their demands on factual pleas as well as humanitarian ones, and they sought and found intellectual succour where other Americans often did—in Great Britain.

On the whole, these men, intellectually and otherwise, would not, in my judgment, compare unfavorably with the present generally mediocre leadership which C. Wright Mills has recently delineated. They were far less under the inhibitions of the elected official, far less narrowly professional, far less able to bury their inadequacies in the ranks of a salaried bureaucracy, far less sure of their future. They were also, though there are still important exceptions, more dedicated, more imaginative, and more idealistic—but alas! they were unquestionably far less effective—and the twentieth century worker appears to have made his choice. It may, of course, prove the wise one.

It is of critical importance to mark the period during which maximum British influence was exerted upon American labor. The preponderance of it came roughly between the late fifties and the middle of the nineties, a period in which there existed what C. R. Fay has described as "a blank in English socialism." [7] The failure of revolutionary uprisings on the Continent, coupled with the decline of Chartism, shattered the English worker's faith in revolutionary politics or radical action. At the same time, increasing national prosperity, a new feeling of security among capitalists who by mid-century had "arrived," and optimism in regard to the future, channeled the Englishman's energies into new model unionism and what may loosely be called a middle class approach to labor problems.

Almost inevitably, therefore, the most prominent feature of British influence was its moderation, its pacific reflexes in the face of opposition or obstacles. Among the immigrants from the United Kingdom there were extremists and occasionally they would gain prominence in a strike, yet they were mainly distinguished by their absence, by their rarity. Few and far between were the men who tried to drive Americans into direct action or revolution, despite the fact that many agitators were accused of plotting to do so. This remains true even in

[7] C. R. Fay, *Life and Labour in the Nineteenth Century* (Cambridge: The University Press, 1920), p. 245.

the face of the wide varieties of individual opinion these men entertained. Some like John Francis Bray, Richard Hinton, and Thomas Morgan were ardent socialists; others like Phillips regarded themselves as radicals; not a few professed to follow in the footsteps of the Chartists. Many of them thundered against the multiple demons that beset workingmen and raised a terrible din, yet their actual tactics and methods, as distinct from the sound and fury, were pragmatic, and often designed to get back to harmonious relationships with capital. Even employers commented at times on the conservatism of some of the trade unions these men founded or led, and spoke of their potentialities as barriers against radicalism and communism. Many of them appear to have been in substantial agreement with Amos Fayram, the Detroit co-operator, who declared in 1881 that " with successful co-operative production and distribution and well managed Trade Unions we shall not need Marx's Socialism." [8]

Immigrants from the United Kingdom brought into the labor movement attitudes with which Americans were already familiar. Essentially, they could be included under the term " common-sense." Though the men with whom we have been concerned in this study had generally high ideals and genuine convictions, they showed little hesitancy in modifying them to conform to American conditions. At the same time, however, they carried with them just enough class consciousness to make them magnificent organizers. This moderate, but nonetheless real, class and in-group feeling, which in the main American workers lacked, was almost indispensable to the growth of early unions. It steeled them and supplied them with fighting élan essential to their survival. Yet it was never the extreme, frustrated class spirit of the true, the alienated revolutionary. Britons and Americans alike tended to feel that they faced a " labor problem "—something to be solved, not to be disputed from behind barricades. Indeed, it appears very likely that the moderation characteristic of the early British leaders, while it did not prevent the American labor movement from becoming as tumultuous as any other in the western world, did help curtail

---

[8] A. Fayram to Samuel, Dec. 13, 1881, Samuel Papers.

violence. British-trained and British-born leaders were seldom addicted to active aggression.

Because moderating influences came just as the modern American labor movement was beginning to emerge, they decisively shaped the future course of its development. A few speculative questions, I think, make the point clearer. What might have happened, for instance, had Slavic or southern European immigration—the " new immigration "—preceded the great influx of British and Irish workers into the United States? What course might American labor have pursued if radical German immigrants who arrived in the late forties had come fifteen or twenty years later? What, indeed, would have been the effect upon American labor, if British labor had turned to " new unionism," organization of the unskilled, and socialism twenty years earlier than it did? Needless to say, there is no neat answer to any of these queries. Nevertheless there are a few things of which we can be reasonably sure. Immigration generally, as the researches of William Bernard indicate, was a positive, contributing force in American economic life. Furthermore within that overall picture, British workers with their skills, inventiveness, and experience made special contributions to American industry as workers. Finally, the British and Irish were a powerful force in the rise of American labor organizations and made special contributions to the creation of countervailing powers in the economy that could modify capitalism and hence keep it both social and vital.[9]

It is certainly fair to suggest very strongly that by following British leaders and adopting British ideas, Americans materially shortened the apprentice stages of their labor movement. A great part of Britain's wealth, for instance, and a sizable portion, though not a majority, of her population were in industry by the eighteen forties, yet in the main, effective, enduring, national unions were from twenty-five years to a generation or more away. A regular Trades Union Congress, in fact, did not convene until 1868. In the United States industrialization—usually considered to have begun on large scale just prior to and during the Civil War—was well under

[9] *American Immigration Policy.* ed. William S. Bernard (New York: Harper & Brothers, 1950), pp. 55-97. Berthoff, Chaps. 2-8.

way by 1880. Yet despite stiffer opposition and greater handicaps than Britons faced, enduring, effective, national unions, by and large, were organized in from five to fifteen years among skilled and some semi-skilled men, and the American Federation of Labor, which was an imitation of the British Trades Union Congress, came in just six years (1886). With all the hazards and pitfalls involved in such comparisons, it would appear that perhaps as much as a decade, in some cases even two decades, of painstaking, costly experimentation was spared American unionists. This hard won experience was among the most valuable of all British influences, and it is to the credit of American workers that they selected and borrowed from others' experiences in order to forge their own institutions. Had they refused to do this the history of labor would not be what it is—the history of the rapid rise of the anonymous man.

The finest legacy of British labor was its general contribution to American democracy. Britons demonstrated that by peaceful methods labor could go far toward achieving its goals, even alter the complexion of government without smashing existing institutions. The ideals that they helped transplant, revitalize, and buttress in America were premised on democratic habits of negotiation, compromise, political bargaining, economic pressure, and gradualness. Unquestionably many of their ideas proved useless and were necessarily discarded; many of the organizations they created or led proved notoriously unstable and fell by the wayside. Yet in the vital task of pointing up new problems, of putting old ones in sharper and fresher perspective, they conducted a magnificent campaign of social education, effectively presenting to thousands of Americans the meaning of social, economic, and industrial democracy. By an insistence upon elevating the lowly through trade unionism and co-operation, by demands for the brand of social and economic justice that was applicable to workers as well as to employers, British and Irish organizers aided the survival, and ultimately the expansion, of American democratic traditions at a moment in history when they were in some ways seriously weakened. Co-operators in particular, even though they may have somewhat delayed the rise of pure and simple unionism, kept alive the finest and most unselfish nineteenth century Christian standards. They synthesized Anglo-American love of individualism with social traditions of co-operative endeavor based on Christian brotherhood. They posed for all who turned wholeheartedly to profit-making, or economic opportunism, the problems materialism would almost inevitably bring to Western Civilization. They banded with other idealistic elements to keep alive in the small towns and among wage earners a healthy repugnance toward unbridled and socially uncreative capitalism, and joined with other liberal forces to mitigate the most anti-democratic phenomena in American life. A generation before the co-operative revival of the nineteen thirties, with its emphasis on the creation of a co-operative commonwealth and the revitalization of the Social Gospel, they planted the seeds of and pointed the way toward what has become a flourishing " middle way."

Thus during labor's formative years, inspired, dedicated, if rather sober, dogmatic, and commonplace men on both sides of the Atlantic linked British and American democracy in a century during which democracy was the " wave of the future." No doubt many Americans then, as now, believed that the forefront of their democracy was in their own West. That view, however, while substantially correct, requires modification. The drama of the frontiers was not the only one. Undeniably, as in the development of Colorado or the growth of Mormonism, British and Irish immigrants were a part of it, yet their role as a group was relatively small. Plain and forest were alien to many of them. Many of them never looked upon the ocean of land tilting up from the Mississippi River to the Rockies, nor did they know the bleak world of the plains, cattle trails, or sod huts. By and large, they were not pioneers who rushed into harsh new physical environments, cutting their ties with the past. On the contrary, along with hundreds of thousands of native American working people whom they influenced, their instruction in the implementation of industrial democracy came from the sooty factories, the darkened mine shafts, and the tidy co-operative shops in the drab mill and mining communities of Great Britain.

# NOTES ON SOURCES

## Bibliographical Aids to Labor Materials

An old but useful guide to union constitutions and official journals is Barnett, George E. (ed.) *A Trial Bibliography of American Trade-Union Publications.* Baltimore: The Johns Hopkins University Press, 1907. Helpful for the eighteen seventies and eighties is Black, J. W. " References on the History of Labor and Some Contemporary Labor Problems," *Oberlin College Library Bulletin,* No. 1 (May, 1893). The newest, best, and most comprehensive thing of its kind is Reynolds, L. G. and Killingsworth, C. C. *Trade Union Publications, The Official Journals, Convention Proceedings, Constitutions of International Unions and Federations, 1850-1941.* 3 vols. Baltimore: The Johns Hopkins University Press, 1944-1945. An invaluable guide to state labor reports is U. S. Department of Labor. *Index of All Reports of State Bureaus of Labor.* Washington: U. S. Government Printing Office, 1902.

## Personal Papers, Collections, and Correspondence

Heavy reliance has been placed on the following primary materials: the *John Francis Bray Collection,* in the University of Michigan General Library, which includes excellent notes on Bray compiled by the late Agnes Inglis plus scores of clippings and pamphlets; the *Arthur C. Cole Collection,* in the Illinois Historical Survey at the University of Illinois, containing many invaluable clippings on Illinois labor during the eighteen fifties and sixties; the *John Frey-William Appleton Correspondence,* in the personal files of Mr. Frey, Washington, D. C., representing a twenty year exchange of views by moderate labor leaders on either side of the Atlantic; the vast 300 volume *Samuel Gompers Collection,* in the American Federation of Labor Headquarters, Washington, D. C., filled with illuminating and invaluable correspondence, letters, directives, editorials, and notes pertaining to all aspects of labor's problems; the *Rutherford B. Hayes Papers,* in the Hayes Memorial Library, Fremont, Ohio, " Excerpts on the Railroad Strike of 1877," which includes selected scrapbooks, hundreds of newspaper clippings from scores of papers, and letters bearing not only on the rail strike but on a broad range of labor matters as well; the *Albert Hutzler Collection* at the Johns Hopkins University which yielded a few scarce writings on co-operation; the *Joseph Labadie Collection* in the University of Michigan General Library which proved rich in clippings and pamphlets; the *Labor Collection of Manuscripts: Bio-*

*graphies and Papers, A-Z, US Mss 12A* in the Wisconsin State Historical Society, University of Wisconsin, Madison, Wisconsin, which includes the *Trevellick Memoranda* and the *Edward Bemis Papers*, plus, for this study, the far more important, 500-piece *Thomas Phillips Papers* covering this co-operative pioneer's correspondence, record-minute books, co-operative constitutions, manuscripts on a variety of labor matters, and balance sheets and *John Samuel* (*Jr.*) Papers which amount to 15 packed boxes of invaluable materials on reform, labor, and co-operation on both sides of the Atlantic; the *Henry Demarest Lloyd-Thomas J. Morgan Correspondence, 1890-1903* from the *Henry Demarest Lloyd Papers* in the Wisconsin State Historical Society which was helpful for the light it threw on the Socialist fight within the A. F. of L., co-operation, and Morgan's own views and career; the *John Mitchell Papers* in the Catholic University, Washington, D. C.; the extensive *Thomas J. Morgan Papers* in the Illinois Historical Survey, University of Illinois, Urbana, Illinois, which include 64 folders and 19 bound volumes of material; the *Patrons of Husbandry, Excerpts from the Proceedings of State Granges, US Mss 16A* in the Wisconsin State Historical Society; the *Terence Powderly Papers* in the Catholic University Library, which contains important materials on the Knights of Labor and some of the proposals for a Transatlantic labor alliance; the *Sovereigns of Industry, US Mss 4A*, in the Wisconsin State Historical Society; the *Trade Union Collection* in the Johns Hopkins University Library.

I also profited, thanks to Mr. Denis Flanagan of the Co-operative Union, Ltd., Manchester, England, from use of the official papers and records of *The Mississippi Valley Trading Company*, and from interviews with Mr. Mark Starr, A.F. of L.-C.I.O. Educational Director (February, 1953), Miss Florence Thorne, former A.F. of L. Research Director (March, 1953), Miss Fannia Cohen (February, 1953), Dr. Solomon Barcus (February, 1953), Mr. James Francey, Director of Adult Vocational Education, Baltimore City (June, 1956), Dr. Richard Heindel (November, 1952).

*Government Documents: State and Federal*

Official publications, reports, hearings, and investigations are too numerous for full listing here but extensive use was made of: U. S. *Bulletin of the Bureau of Labor*, 1895-1903; U. S. *Bulletin of the United States Department of Labor*, 1903-1913; U. S. *Bulletin of the U. S. Bureau of Labor Statistics*, 1913-1916; U. S. *Annual Report of the Commissioner of Labor*, 1886-1910; U. S. Senate, *Reports of the Commission on Industrial Relations*, 64th Cong., 1st Sess., Senate Doc.

415, 11 vols. (1916) ; U. S. Senate, Committee on education and labor, *Report of the Committee of the Senate upon the Relations between Labor and Capital*, 48th Cong., 5 vols. (1885) ; U. S. Senate, *Report of the Immigration Commission, Immigrants in Industry*, 61st Cong., 2d Sess., Senate Doc. 633, vols. 6-25 (1910) ; U. S. Senate, *Report of the Immigration Commission, Immigrants in Industry, Statistical Review of Immigration, 1819-1910*, 61st Cong., 3rd Sess., Senate Doc. 756 (1910) ; U. S. House of Representatives, *Reports of Consuls in the Several Countries of Europe*, 46th Cong., 1st Sess. (May 17, 1879) ; U. S. House of Representatives, *United States Consular Reports, Labor in Europe*, 48th Cong., 2d Sess., House Executive Doc. 54, Parts I and II (1884-1885) ; U. S. House of Representatives, *Report of the Committee of the House of Representatives, Labor Troubles in the Anthracite Regions of Pennsylvania, 1887-1888*, 50th Cong., 2d Sess., H. R. 4127, Vol. IV (1889).

The reports of state bureaus of labor which began to appear after 1870 contain a wealth of valuable material, statistical and interpretative. The following reports were especially helpful: Colorado. Bureau of Labor Statistics, *4th Biennial Report*, 1893-1894. Denver: 1895; Connecticut. Bureau of Labor Statistics, *7th Annual Report*, 1891. Hartford: 1892; Illinois. Bureau of Labor Statistics, *1st Biennial Report*, 1881. Springfield: 1882; Maryland. Bureau of Industrial Statistics, *1st Biennial Report*, 1884-1885. Annapolis: 1886; Commonwealth of Massachusetts. Bureau of the Statistics of Labor, *1st to 31st Annual Report*, 1870-1899. Boston: 1871-1900; Missouri. Bureau of Labor Statistics and Inspection, *11th Annual Report*, 1889. Jefferson City: 1890; Nebraska. Bureau of Labor and Industrial Statistics, *1st Biennial Report*, 1887-1888. Lincoln: 1889; New Jersey. Bureau of the Statistics of Labor and Industry, *10th Annual Report*, 1887; *12th Annual Report*, 1889. Trenton: 1888, 1890; New York. Department of Labor, *3rd Annual Report*, 1885; *8th Annual Report*, 1890; *16th Annual Report*, 1898. Albany: 1886, 1891, 1899; Ohio. Bureau of the Statistics of Labor, *9th Annual Report*, 1885; *10th Annual Report*, 1887. Columbus: 1886, 1888; Commonwealth of Pennsylvania. Secretary of Internal Affairs, Bureau of Industrial Statistics, *9th Annual Report*, 1881; *10th Annual Report*, 1882; *12th Annual Report*, 1884; *15th Annual Report*, 1887; *16th Annual Report*, 1888. Harrisburg: 1882, 1883, 1885, 1888, 1889; Wisconsin. Bureau of Census, Labor and Industrial Statistics, *2nd Biennial Report*, 1885-1886. Madison: 1887.

*Newspapers*

Newspapers are an important source for students of labor history. Reluctantly but necessarily I have relied heavily on the following:

*American Manufacturer and Iron World,* Pittsburgh, 1873-1875
*American Workman,* Boston, 1868-1872
*Baltimore American,* 1885-1886
*Baltimore Sun,* 1870-1875, 1883-1887
*Chicago Times,* 1892
*Chicago Tribune,* scattered issues, 1893-1896
*Commercial and Financial Chronicle,* New York, 1868-1880
*Co-operative News,* Manchester, England, scattered issues, 1873, 1875-
    1876, 1880
*Daily Evening Voice,* Boston, 1865-1867
*Detroit Tribune,* 1864
*Fincher's Trades Review,* Philadelphia, 1863-1866
*Iron Age,* New York, 1863
*Journal of United Labor,* Marblehead, Pittsburgh, and Philadelphia,
    1881-1882, scattered issues 1884-1887, 1888, 1889
*Labor Leaf,* Detroit, 1886
*Labor Standard,* Paterson, scattered issues 1878-1890
*Miners' Journal,* Pottsville, 1855-1879 (Microfilm courtesy of the
    Pennsylvania Historical and Museum Commission, Harrisburg,
    Pa.)
*National Labor Tribune,* Pittsburgh, 1874-1875
*National Trades' Review,* Philadelphia (the successor to Fincher's),
    1866
*New York Tribune,* 1858, 1870, 1883
*Sovereigns of Industry Bulletin,* Worcester, Mass., Washington, D. C.,
    scattered issues, 1874-1878
*Workingman's Advocate,* Chicago, Philadelphia, 1866-1877

*Trade Union Publications*

The following were indispensable sources:

*Amalgamated Engineers' Monthly Journal.* Vols. V-VII, new series
    Vol. II. London: 1901-1906.
*American Federationist.* Vols. I-XIII. Indianapolis and Washington:
    1894-1906.
*Carpenter.* Vol. I-II. St. Louis: 1881-1882.
*Cigarmakers' Official Journal.* Vols. I-XXX. Suffield, New York,
    Buffalo, and Chicago: 1875-1906.

*Coast Seamen's Journal.* Vols. I-XIV. San Francisco: 1887-1901.

*Craftsman.* Vols. I-V. Washington: 1884-1888.

*Garment Workers' Journal.* I-V. New York: 1894-1906.

*Granite Cutters' Journal.* Vols. V-XXIX. Rockland, Boston, Westerly, Quincy, Philadelphia, Barre, Concord, Baltimore, Washington: 1879-1906.

*Iron Molders' International Journal.* Vols. II, IX, X, XII-XXXVI. Philadelphia, Cincinnati: 1866-1867, 1876-1900.

*Machinists' and Blacksmiths' International Journal.* Vols. VIII-IX. Cleveland: 1870-1872.

*Miners' Magazine.* Vols. I-VII. Denver: 1900-1906.

*Printers' Circular.* Vols. I-XXII. Philadelphia: 1866-1888.

*Provoker.* Chicago: 1909-1911. (Thomas J. Morgan's Socialist journal)

*Shoe Workers' Journal.* Vols. III-XVII. Boston: 1902-1917.

*Stone Cutters' Journal.* Vols. I, V, VII-XX. Washington: 1886, 1895-1906.

*Tailor.* Vols. I-X. New York, Bloomington: 1887-1900.

*Typographical Journal.* Vols. I-XV. Indianapolis: 1889-1900.

*Union Boot and Shoe Worker.* Vols. I-V. Boston: 1900-1905.

*United Mine Workers' Journal.* Vols. I-XXX. Columbus, Indianapolis. 1891-1920.

---

A listing of the tracts, pamphlets, biographies, published and unpublished monographs, and secondary sources, including periodicals from England as well as America, would prove too tedious. Naturally where I have borrowed directly from other studies or followed them closely I have cited them in the footnotes throughout the text.

# INDEX

Adams, Charles Francis, 51
Adams, Dudley W., 247, 251
Addams, Jane, 299
Adler, Felix, 268, 274
Allen, Robert, 168
Allen, William, 184
*Allen v. Flood*, 161
Amalgamated Association of Iron and Steel Workers, 144, 146, 179–80
Amalgamated Iron Workers of Great Britain: on alliance with American ironworkers, 58–59, 143
Amalgamated Society of Carpenters and Joiners, 167, 173, 187, 188, 189
Amalgamated Society of Engineers, 43–44, 56–57, 68–69, 168, 173, 184, 186, 188, 190
Amalgamated Trades and Labor Union of New York, 151
Amalgamated unions:' British, 49, 90, 143, 162, 183–91
American Boot and Shoe Workers' Union, 80
American Co-operative Union, 301
American Co-operative Union of Louisville, 248–49
American Federation of Labor: organization of maritime workers, 77, 78; fraternal ties with British, 81, 82; fight over Plank, 10, 113, 114–20; contact with B.T.U.C., 163; structure of, 187, 316; mentioned, 61, 69, 75, 83, 86, 107, 108, 138, 139, 144, 149, 152, 155, 158, 240, 291
American Miners' Association, 34, 93, 124, 125, 131–32, 137
American printers: address of to British, 54
American Typographical Union, 54
Anglo-American Trading Company, 254
Anglo-American union, 52, 52 n.
Anthracite miners: immigrant organizers among, 39, 126, 128, 129–36. *See also* British agitators and organizers.

Anti-truck bill, 140
Appleby, James, 266
Applegarth, Robert, 167
Appleton, William, 82
Arbitration: British plans of, 170–83; in English hosiery trade, 171; American reception of, 171–72; compulsory, 180; in Connecticut, 180–81; in Ohio, 181. *See also* Mundella, A. J.; Kettle, Rupert; Mundella-Kettle Plan.
Arthur, Peter, 86
Ashby-Macfayden, Irene, 152
Ashton, Thomas S., 21
Ashworth, Samuel, 197
Australia, 68, 74, 75, 79, 106, 180
Avondale disaster, 135
Ayrshire miners, 116

Barnum, E. E., 267
Barrel-makers of Minneapolis, 265 n.
Barry, Leonora, 151
Basle, 58
Bates, John, 32–33
Bayard, Thomas, 51
Beard, Charles and Mary, 45
*Beehive*, 216
Beesly, E. S., 167, 182
Belgian immigrants. *See* Immigrants.
Bell, John R., 69–70
Bellamy, Edward, 300
Belleville Coal Operating Mining Company, 282
Belleville tract, 32–33, 124
Bemis, Edward, 208, 233, 299, 301
Berger, Victor, 121
Bernard, William, 315
Blair Committee, 149
Bliss, W. P. B., 236
Blissert, Robert, 88, 149, 151, 276
Block Printers of Massachusetts, 30–31
Boston Eight Hour League, 44, 107
"Bound boy laws," 30
Bower, Robert, 150
Boyle, John, 272

Braidwood, Illinois, 137
Braidwood, James, 127
Brassey, Thomas, 167, 171
Brass Workers' Independent Union, 108
Bray, John Francis, 26, 50, 107, 156, 314
Brentano, Lujo, 219
Bright, John, 47, 50, 195, 213, 223
Brisbane, Albert, 262
British agitators and organizers in America: early influence of, 31, 34, 45; positions in American unions, 84–86; spirit of, 86; ages of, 87–88; moderation of, 89–90; character of, 90–91; Irish organizers, 92–94; relations of English, Welsh, Scotch with Irish, 92; religious beliefs, 92; as general labor reformers, 94–106; among miners, 123–41; among metalworkers, 142–47; among textile workers, 147–50; in other trades, 150–52; female organizers, 151–52; summary of influences, 303–17
British capital: in American railroads, 53
British economic thought: in American labor movement, 161
British immigrants. See Immigration.
British industrial conditions, 41
British labor: views of American labor on, 27–28; as model for Americans, 49–50, 153–191; legal advances of, 109; prestige of in America, 154–55; in advance of American labor, 155–56; American use of statistics of, 162–63; outlook of, 165–68; influence of in America, 170–317 passim. See also British agitators and organizers in America.
British Labour Party. See Independent Labour Party.
British Trades Union Congress, 48, 78, 80, 81, 113, 116, 117, 163, 168, 185, 187–316 passim
British Seamen's Union, 73
British short hour movement, 31
British workers: internationalism of, 26–27; zeal of, 27; views of America as economic frontier, 28; views on American Civil War, 48–50, 50–317 passim. See also British

labor; British agitators and organizers in America.
Britton, John, 223
Broadhurst, Henry, 76, 81, 163
Broderick, James, 93
Brook Farm, 193, 258, 262
Brooklyn Female Burnishers' Association, 151
Brotherhood of Carpenters and Joiners, 187, 189
Brothers, Thomas, 45, 45 n.
Brown, James R., 71
Bryan, William J., 77
Bryce, Lord, 51
Building trades: extent of unionization, 21
Bunker Hill, Colorado, 141
Burke, Martin, 93
Burns, John, 76, 81, 117, 119, 120
Burt, Thomas, 65, 76, 81, 104
Burton, John, 260–61
Burton, Plan, 260

Cabet, Etienne, 194
Cairnes, John E., 162
California State Grange, 254
Cameron, Andrew Carr: background, 106–107; in Illinois labor movement, 107; in N. L. U., 107; mentioned, 58, 89, 99, 105, 123, 128, 133, 161, 162, 178, 219, 220, 221
Campbell, Alexander, 106
Cannon, William, 150
Carlyle, Thomas, 88
Carpenters and joiners, 57, 185, 221
Central Co-operative Board of the United Kingdom, 250, 284
Central Labor Federation of New York, 114
Central Labor Union of Chicago, 113
Central Labor Union of New York, 151, 275–76
Chamberlain, Joseph, 51, 171
Chapin, E. H., 268
Chartists, 21, 27, 28, 31, 32, 33, 36, 44, 90, 106, 123, 125, 133, 184, 200, 202, 313, 314
Chicago Federation of Labor, 112
Chicago Trades and Labor Assembly, 269
Chicago Trades and Labor Council, 112

Chicago Trades Assembly, 99, 107
Cigarmakers: relations with British, 57, 60–61; mentioned, 62–186 *passim*
Cigarmakers' International Union, 60, 150
Civil Service Plan, 173, 256
Cluer, John C.; in New England short hour movement, 31–32, 43, 45
Coal Mines Act (1872), 160
Coal regions: U. S., 124
Coast Firemen's Union, 75
Coast Longshoremen's Union, 75
Coast Seamen's Union, 69, 75
Cobbett, William, 122, 201
Cobden, Richard, 47, 195, 213
Coeur d'Alene, 141
Collective bargaining, 185
Collyer, Reverend Robert, 217, 218, 268
Combination Acts of 1824–25, 165
Commons, John R., 22–23
Compositors, London, 80
Comte de Paris, 215
Conciliation, 180. *See* Arbitration.
Conseils des Prudhommes, 171
Conspiracy trials: British immigrants involved in, 38
Conway, Moncure Daniel, 156
Cook, Joseph, 159
Cooke, Jay, 229
Cooley, Justice T. M., 178
Cooper, Peter, 104
Co-operation, distributive, 60, 174. *See* Rochdale Co-operation.
Co-operative Colony Aid Association of Kansas, 267
Co-operative Congress (British): Seventh, 251, 254; Eleventh, 255; Carlisle, 297; mentioned, 217, 282
Co-operative Wholesale Society (English), 271, 282
Corn laws, 100
" Cotton famine," 47, 48
Cotton Spinners' Association of Fall River, 149
Coxe, Eckley B., 175–76
Coxe Family, 176 n.
Crispins, 199
Crompton, Henry, 182
Curtis, George William, 269

Daniels, Newell, 225
Danvers Co-operative Union Society, 221–22
Darwinism, Social, 15
Davis, John M., 93
Davitt, Michael: on Anglo-American labor alliance, 66–68
Debs, Eugene V., 112, 121
DeLeon, Daniel, 112, 305
Denny, Albert, 65, 163
Derbyshire and Nottinghamshire Miners' Union, 87, 140
Detroit Trades Assembly, 98, 99, 150
Devyr, Thomas Ainge, 36
Dilke, Charles, 51, 52
Dillon, James, 45 n.
Dissenters, 92
Dolan, Thomas, 150
Douglass, Charles, 42
" Dual unionism," 78, 189
Dues, union, 185
Duncan, James, 86, 150
Durham Miners' Union, 87, 88, 123, 140
Dyer, Josiah, 87, 150

Earle, William, 258, 259, 261, 263
Eccarius, J. George, 57, 277
Edwards, John O., 144, 145
Eight hour movement: in New England, 52
Elderkin, T. J., 70, 71
Elthringham, John, 141
Elwell, Judge William, 176
Ely, Richard, 179, 233, 289
Emigrant Aid Society, 58
Emigration funds: in British unions, 28
Employers' Liability Acts (1880, 1896), 161
English Company Acts of 1862–67, 251
English Factory Acts, 42–43, 112–13, 160
English Fraternal Democrats, 44
English Radicals, 201
English Social Democratic Federation, 119
Evans, Chris, 139
Evans, George Henry: career and life of, 36–37, 45

Fairley, William R., 88
Fales, Imogene, 296–301
Falkin, William, 171
Fall River, Massachusetts: British agitators in, 39, 147, 150, 164, 222
Fall River Spinners' Association, 149
Fall River Workingmen's Co-operative Association, 222
Farmers' Alliance, 100, 103, 257, 274, 275
Farquhar, John, 90
Fawcett, Henry, 162, 217
Fay, C. R., 313
Fayram, Amos, 289, 314
Federation of Trades and Labor Unions. *See* American Federation of Labor.
Female organizers. *See* British agitators and organizers in America.
Fenians, 66, 92
Fielden, John, 95
Fincher, Jonathan: on amalgamateds' statistics, 162–63; on British arbitration, 170; and *Trades' Review*, 194–95; mentioned, 99, 198, 211, 219, 221, 232
Foote, Allan R., 271, 273
Ford, James, 301
Foster, Frank K., 240
Foster, Richard, 182
Foster, William H., 151, 187
Fourier, Charles, 194
Fraternal relations: British and American unions, 80–83, 155
Frey, John, 82
Furuseth, Andrew, 74–75

General Federation of Trades and Labor Union of Great Britain, 82
"General strike," 32
George, Henry, 66, 69, 71, 312
George, Milton, 274
German: agitators in U. S., 89
German immigrants. *See* Immigration.
Gilman, Nicholas P., 182, 299
Glassblowers, 30
Glass Bottle Blowers' Association, 231
Gledhill, John H., 213, 265, 271, 273
Godkin, E. L., 168, 216, 222, 268
Golden, John, 150
Gompers, Samuel: contacts with British labor leaders and organizers, 75–79, 81; on British in American

labor, 85, 152, 156; on Trevellick, 95; on T. J. Morgan, 114; fight over Plank, 10, 115, 119; on British labor movement, 154; on eight hours in England, 158; on English factory acts, 165; on Mundella's speech, 154; on arbitration, 177; and Positivists, 182; mentioned, 82–292 *passim*
Gowen, Franklin, 132
Grand National Consolidated Trades Union, 31, 184, 199, 238
Grand Union of Glassblowers, 231
Grange, National: American schemes of co-operation in, 244–45; and Rochdale Plan, 245–57; mentioned, 228, 264. *See also* Mississippi Valley Trading Company; Rochdale Co-operation; Burton Plan
Grange Co-operative Congress, 249
Granger Co-operative Association of the Northwest, 256
Granite cutters, 150, 185
Granite Cutters' National Union, 186
Gray, John, 38
Greeley, Horace, 192, 202, 214–15, 222
Green, William, 304
Greenbackism. *See* Greenback Party.
Greenback Party, 100, 103, 107, 139
Greenwood, Abraham, 281
Griffiths, Richard, 90, 150, 177
Gudgeon, William H., 213, 218
Guild of Co-operators, 234, 267, 280–81
Guile, Daniel, 55, 167
Gunton, George, 107, 150

Hale, Reverend E. E., 218
Hall, Bolton, 71
Hardie, J. Keir: relations with Gompers, 76, 81; influence on T. J. Morgan and Plank, 10, 116–17; visit to U. S., 120–22 308
Harney, George Julian, 45
Harrison, Frederick, 167, 182
Hartranft, John F., 181
Hatters' Guild, 30
Hay, John, 51
Haymarket affair, 110
Haywood, William, 304
Heenan, John, 151

Heighton, William, 37–38, 45
Hewitt, Abram S., 173
Hill, J. J., 182
Hillquit, Morris, 110
Hinchcliffe, John: life and activities of, 124–26; mentioned, 90, 129, 137, 160, 219
Hinchcliffe, Richard, 107, 150
Hinton, Richard, 89, 154, 157, 220–21, 240, 314
Hockaday, Joseph, 90–91, 151
Hocking Valley, 32, 139
Hocking Valley Mine Union, 139
Holbert, Richard, 182
Holleck, Dr., 267
Holmes, David, 48, 81
Holyoake, George Jacob: writings on co-operation, 202–03; contacts with and influence on John Samuel, 234, 237, 238, 239, 241, 281; American tours, 266–76; mentioned, 49, 196, 206–298 passim
Homer, James, 40
Howard, Robert: on Ten Hours Bill, 43; life and activities of, 90, 148–49; on arbitration, 177; mentioned, 88, 156, 187
Howells, George, 170, 195, 234
Hughes, Thomas: and Royal Commission on Trade Unions, 167; trip to U. S. in 1870, 172–74; and Positivists, 182; trip to U. S. in 1880, 271–73; and Guild of Co-operators, 281; mentioned, 47, 171, 196, 217, 223, 238
Hunter, Robert, 110

Illinois Grand Eight Hour League, 107
Illinois Miners' Federation, 93
Illinois State Federation of Labor, 87, 113
Illinois State Labor Assembly, 107
Immigration: U. K. to U. S., 19–22, 28, 38–317 passim; European to U. S., 19; German, 22, 85, 315; Scandinavian, 22, 138; problems of, 23–24; Italian, 138; Belgian, 138; Slavs, 315
Independent Brotherhood of Locomotive Engineers, 86
Independent Labour Party, 68, 110, 113, 303

Industrial Assembly of North America, 98, 218
Industrial Congresses of 1845, 1847, 36, 45
Industrial democracy: and propertied middle class, 18; British, 22
Industrial production: American, 13–14
International Association of Machinists, 189
International Boot and Shoe Workers' Union, 198, 279
International Bureau of Correspondence, 121
Internationale: Lausanne meeting, 150
International Federation of Ship, Dock, and Riverside Workers, 71
International Seamen's Union: relations with British unions, 69–71, 79
International Ship Carpenters' and Caulkers' Union, 91, 98, 100
International Transport Workers' Federation, 79
International Typographers' Union, 90
International Workingmen's Association, 57
Irish organizers. See British agitators and organizers in America.
Irish Republican movement, 66
Iron Molders' International Union: relations with British unions, 55–56; and co-operation, 221; mentioned, 95, 99, 147, 154, 187
Irons, Martin, 87
Italian immigrants. See Immigration.

James, Benjamin, 140
James, John: background and activities, 136–37, 138; mentioned, 90, 91, 105, 160
Jarrett, John: background and activities, 143–45; on arbitration, 179–80; mentioned, 87, 89, 146, 187, 307
Johnson, Andrew, 101
Johnson Stores, 205
Jones, Ernest: on industrialism and New World, 25–26; on closer relations with America, 29; mentioned, 44, 200
Jones, Judge John, 251, 254

Jones, Lloyd, 49, 195, 196, 217, 238, 273
Jones, Thomas P., 145–46, 147, 223
Journeyman Tailors' National Union, 151
Jude, Martin, 123

Kane, John, 58–59, 60, 143, 180
Keefe, Daniel J., 310
Kelley, Oliver H., 247–48, 259
Kensington Mutual Co-operative Association, 211
Kettle Plan, 177. *See also* Arbitration.
Kettle, Rupert, 171, 179
Keuchter, George, 237, 289
Kidd, Thomas, 120
King, Edward, 88, 151, 182
Kingsley, Charles, 200
Knights of Labor: relations with British miners, 63–65; British co-operative schemes in, 276–94; mentioned, 65, 83, 86, 87, 90, 93, 100, 102, 107, 139, 140, 151–274 *passim*
Knights of Labor Co-operative Board: John Samuel and, 284, 285, 286–89; mentioned, 239, 240, 242
Knights of St. Crispin, 225, 261
Knights of St. Crispin Shoe Manufacturing Association No. 1 of Philadelphia, 227
Kossuth, Louis, 27

Labadie, Joseph, 294
Labor: adjustment to industrial change, 16–17; moderation of organized, 17; opposition to organized labor, 19; crowding of its markets by immigrants, 28; international character of its problems, 53–54; mentioned, 54–317 *passim*. *See also* British Agitators and Organizers in America; and names of specific unions
Labor force: size of, 16, 29
Labor Reform Party, 100
Labour Electoral Association, 69
LaFollette Seamen's Act, 74
Lancashire, 88, 123
Lawrence Massachusetts Co-operative Association, 209
Lawrence Mutual Benefit Society, 213
Layton, Robert, 284
Leavitt, Samuel, 194, 209, 247

Levasseur, Emile, 153
Lewis, John L., 304
Lincoln, Abraham: letter to British workers, 47, 48
Lloyd, Henry Demarest, 81, 111, 117, 121, 163, 182, 292, 300, 305
Lloyd, Thomas, 33, 124
London Co-operative Board, 222
London Co-operative Congress, 219
London, Jack, 305
London Junta, 143, 170, 184
*London Times*, 167
Longmans, George, 235
Longshoremen's Union, 72, 79
Lord, Hiram, 211
Lorrimer, George, 218
Lowell, Massachusetts: immigrants in, 31, 40
Ludlow, J. M., 49, 196, 200, 222, 223
Luther, Seth, 41–42
Lynn Massachusetts Board of Arbitration, 183

McClelland, John, 240, 248
McClelland, William, 186, 188
Macdonald, Alexander: relations with Knights of Labor, 63–65; visits and influence in U. S., 126–29, 133, 134, 136; mentioned, 161, 167, 308
MacFarlane, Robert, 34–36
McGaughey, Peter, 289, 290–91
McGregor, Hugh, 182
McGuire, Peter, 115, 187
Machinists' and Blacksmiths' Union, 56, 109, 110, 194
McHugh, Edward, 71–72, 75, 78
McKay, Edward, 140
McLaughlin, Daniel, 137–39, 140
McLaughlin, Hugh, 58–59, 60, 144, 145, 146, 179, 221
Macnamara, Maggie, 151
McNeill, George, 17, 233, 237, 309
Macune, C. W., 274
Maguires, Molly, 62, 132, 134, 134 n
Malthus, Thomas R., 162
Manchester Co-operative Board, 234
Manchester Co-operative Wholesale Society, 251
*Manchester Co-operator*, 195, 212, 246, 278
Mann, Tom, 67, 68–69, 75, 81, 118
Marshall, Alfred, 238

Martin, William, 146
Marx, Karl, 27, 312, 314
Massachusetts: early labor problems in, 32, 40, 42
Massachusetts Mechanics' Association, 40
Mauch Chunk miners' conference, 176
Maurice, F. D., 200
Mechanics' Mutual Protective Association, 34–35
Mechanics' Union of Trade Associations of Philadelphia, 37
Medill, Joseph, 292
Methodism, 92, 199
Michigan Employers' Association, 98–99
Michigan State Labor Convention, 100
Mill, John S., 88, 109, 162, 170, 195, 213, 223, 238, 276
Mills, C. Wright, 313
Miners' and Laborers' Benevolent Association, 132–33
Miners' Association (Martin Jude's), 123
Miners' National Association of Great Britain, 63, 88, 127, 133, 136
Miners' National Union, 133
Miners' Protective and Benevolent Association of the Northwest, 137
Mississippi Valley Trading Company: background of, 249–51; structure and purposes, 251–55; mentioned, 261
Missouri Co-operative Coal Company, 282
Missouri State Grange, 246
Mitchell, John, 22, 22 n., 310
Morgan, Mrs. Thomas J., 151–52
Morgan, Thomas J.: relations with Irish in labor, 93; background, 107–12; positions among socialists, 112; in Greenback Party, 113; in K. of L., 113; fight over Plank, 10, 113–20; and Debs, 121–22; readings in British economists, 162; use of British labor information, 163; and Rochdale Plan, 260, 269; mentioned, 89, 123, 314
Morris, James F., 93
Mullaney, Kate, 151
Mundella, A. J.: influences on arbitration in U. S., 171–81 182, 183; mentioned, 272, 308, 312
Mundella-Kettle Plans, 172, 177, 182, 183
Murray, Phillip, 93, 304

Nation, The, 168, 216
National Association of Iron and Steel Heaters, 146
National Association of Sailors and Firemen, 70
National Cotton Spinners' Association, 149
National Federation of Miners and Mine Laborers, 138, 139
National Iron and Steel Heaters' Union (British), 223
National Labor Congress, 219
National Labor Union, 57, 62, 83, 86, 90, 99, 107, 125, 218–20
National Miners' Association, 123
National Miners' Federation, 139
National Mule Spinners' Association, 149
National Reform Association, 36
National Seamen's Union, 73
National Union of Boot and Shoe Operatives, 80
National Union of Dock Laborers, 67, 68
National Union of Sailors and Firemen, 73, 79
Neale, Edward V., 234, 238, 240, 249, 251, 254, 273–94 passim
Nelson, N. O., 293
New Hampshire State Grange, 255
New Harmony, Indiana, 37, 38, 270
"New model" unions. See Amalgamated unions.
New Orleans Grange, 249
Newton, R. Heber, 177, 218, 268, 274
New York: foreigners in unions of, 40
New York Society for Political Education, 182
New York State: early craft unions in, 29
New York Sun, 80
New York Typographical Union No. 6, 80
New Zealand: eight hours in, 96, 106, 180

*North American Review,* 66
*Northern Star,* 31
Northumberland miners, 123
Northwestern Alliance, 274

Oastler, Richard, 41, 42, 125, 312
O'Connor, Feargus, 44
Odger, George, 167
Ohio Miners' Amalgamated Union, 139
O'Keefe, Daniel, 79
O'Keefe, John, 87, 107, 150
Olive, Daniel, 151
Oliver, General R. K., 269
Oneida Community, 270
Oregon State Grange, 256
Orvis, John, 228, 258–61
Osborn, John H., 246, 289, 296
Owen, Robert, 36, 37, 38, 44, 82, 193, 199, 238, 312
Owen, Robert Dale, 42, 45

Paine, Thomas, 45 n., 201
Parks, Xingo, 132
Patrons of Husbandry. *See* Grange, National.
Pearce, W. C., 140
Peel, Sir Robert, 159
Pennsylvania: child labor, 40; factory legislation, 44; anthracite region, 129; laws of association, 224
Philadelphia Trades Assembly, 232
Phillips, Thomas: background and career of, 198–216; in Knights of St. Crispin, 224–28; in Sovereigns of Industry, 261–64; in Knights of Labor, 277–80; mentioned, 87, 150, 196, 221, 232, 248
Phillips, Wendell, 50, 172, 249, 268
Pigou, A. C., 182
Pinkerton, Allan, 62
Pioneer Council No. 1 of the Pennsylvania Sovereigns, 262
" Plank 10," 114–20
Pollock, John, 93, 105, 129, 177
Populist Party, 100
Positivists: in New York, 182–83
Potter, George, 195, 217, 309
Powderly, Terence: attempts alliance with British, 62–65; mentioned, 56, 104, 117, 163, 177, 277–306 *passim*
Pratt, Hodgson, 234, 280
*Priestley v. Fowler,* 161

Prison labor, abolition of, 35
Profit-sharing, 292–93

Quincy, Josiah, 265, 268

Rae, John, 91, 139–40
Randall, Daniel, 233
Raphael, Michael, 151
Reese, Daniel, 146–47
Reid, Whitelaw, 268
Repealers of Ireland, 27
Restriction of output, 185
Revolution, industrial, 26
Rhode Island: early child labor investigation, 40; textile operatives in, 149
Rhodes, James, 300–301
Ricardo, David, 109
Rochdale Co-operation: revival of in America, 192–207; U. C. A., 208–11; in N. L. U., 217–20; spreads to Mid-west, 229–65; in various unions and co-operatives, 221–23; among K. of St. Crispin, 224–28; integral co-operation, 240–41; among Grangers, 243–57; among Sovereigns of Industry, 257–65; among K. of L., 276–92; in Sociological Society, 295–302
Rochdale Pioneers, 205, 206, 207, 208, 217, 230, 239
Rochdale Society, 197, 205, 209
Rogers, Thorold, 162
Roy, Andrew, 105, 134, 137, 141
Royal Commission on Trade Unions, 129, 166–67, 215
Rugby Colony, 272
Rutledge, Walter, 140
Ryan, Daniel J., 181
Rylance, Reverend Dr., 218, 268, 273

Sadler, Michael T., 41, 125, 312
Saffin, William, 56
Sage, William, 273
Samuel, John Jr.: background and early career, 210, 212, 230–43; in Grange, 246–48; in Sovereigns of Industry, 263–65; in K. of L., 280–94; in Sociological Society, 294–302; mentioned, 88, 150, 196, 198, 228, 251, 261, 271, 303, 304, 305
Sanial, Lucian, 114

Saunders, William: and Grange, 247–48

Scaife, William, 87, 140

Scandinavian immigrants. See Immigration.

Schilling, Robert, 94´n.

Scott, Melinda, 151

Scott, Thomas A., 132

Scottish Miners' Union, 138

Seager, Henry R., 182

Seamen and Waterside Workers of Great Britain, 76

"Second American Revolution," 45–46

Select Committee of the House of Lords (1890), 161

Self-Help. See Rochdale Co-operation.

Seligman, Edwin R. A., 178

Sellers, Thomas, 213

Shaftesbury, Lord, 41, 44, 159, 312

Sharpe, Henry, 240, 267, 284

Sheddon, John, 210, 262

Shenango Valley, 139

Shipton, George, 81

Short hour movement: in New England, 43; in Britain, 158. See also Eight hour movement; Ten hour movement; Travellick, Richard; Cluer, John C.

Siney, John: background and career, 129–36; on arbitration, 175, 176, 177, 179; mentioned, 89, 91, 92, 93, 101, 105, 137, 138, 219, 248, 306

Skeffington, Harry, 279

Skidmore, Thomas, 29

Slavic immigrants. See Immigration.

Smalley, G. W., 271, 274

Smith, Frank, 121, 122

Smith, G. J., 234, 280

Smith, Goldwin, 47, 51, 172

*Social Economist*, 107 n.

Socialism: American, 27, 81, 93; Social Democratic Party, 112; Socialistic Labor Party, 112, 120

Socialists: Ricardian, 37; Utopian, 42; Christian, 49, 200, 206, 222; British agitators in U. S., 106–23; Lassallean, 109

Sociological Society of America, 228, 235, 274, 295–300

Soft Stone Cutters' Union: constitution of, 186

Sons of Vulcan, 144, 145, 186, 221

South Carolina State Grange, 256

Sovereigns of Industry, 228, 258, 264. See also British agitators and organizers in America; Rochdale Co-operation.

Spargo, John, 110

Spence, Thomas, 36, 106

Spencer, Herbert, 109

Spiers, James, 128

Standard wage, 185

Stephens, Uriah S., 62, 277, 278

Stewart, Ira, 44, 52, 56, 162

St. Louis: miners meeting in, 34

St. Louis Trades Assembly, 235, 246

Straighton and Storm Board, 183

Strasser, Adolph, 60, 81, 186

Stratton, Oliver H., 253

Strikes: comparative statistics of, 166

St. Simon, 194

Sunderland Seamen's Union, 73

Sweatshops, English, 161

Swinton, John, 24, 158, 159, 169

Sylvis, William H.: relations with British molders, 55–56; and N.L.U., 57; association with Trevellick, 95, 99, 100; views on and contacts with Rochdalers, 196–97, 198, 219, 221; mentioned, 177, 186–87

Tansey, James, 150

Ten hour movement: Ten hour convention, 31; Ten Hour Law, 43. See also Short hour movement.

Texas State Grange, 245–46

Textile operatives, 147–50, 185

Thompson, Robert W., 102

Thompsonville weavers, 38

Thorne, Florence, 81

Thornton, William, 109, 162, 217

Tillett, Ben, 68, 76–77, 81, 310

Tobacco Workers' International Union, 186

Toynbee, Arnold, 238

Tracy, Tom, 80

Transatlantic alliance: early spirit of attempts at, 25–45; early British organizers and influence on, 25–45; Anglo-American attitudes and problems in regard to, 45–50; relations between typographers regarding, 54; relations between iron molders regarding, 55–60; relations between cigarmakers regarding, 60–61; relations between iron shipbuilders and boilermakers regarding, 61–62; N. L. U. and, 61–62; K. of L. and, 62–66; maritime and waterfront workers and, 66–79. *See also* Mississippi Valley Trading Company.

Trant, William, 188

Trevellick, Richard: background and character, 93–106; in short hour movements, 95–96, 101–02; on Rochdale Plan, 99; in N. L. U., 99–103; and National Labor Reform Party, 102; and Greenback Party, 103–04; in K. of L., 104; mentioned, 58, 91, 123, 133, 137, 150–248 *passim*

Turner, Fred, 279, 289

Turner, Frederick Jackson, 13

Tuscarawas Valley, 32, 126

Typographical Society of Boston, 26–27

Typographical Union, 106

Un-Americanism, 24, 39, 307

Union Co-operative Association No. 1 of Philadelphia (U. C. A), 208–11, 216, 227, 232

Unions, American: condition of in early 19th century, 29; relations with British unions, 30–191 *passim*. *See also* names of specific unions.

United Garment Workers Union, 161

United Labor Party of Illinois, 113

United Mine Workers of America, 24 n., 91, 138, 139, 140

United Society of Boilermakers and Iron-Shipbuilders, 61

United Steelworkers' Union, 147

Vanderheyden, Joseph, 182

Vincent, Charles, 195

Vulcans of Albion, 143

Walker, Amasa, 260

Walker, John, 60

Walker, John H., 86

Wallace Act, 183

Wardall, Alonzo, 275, 301

Warner, Albert, 233

Washburne, E. H., 268

Watchorn, Robert, 87, 91, 140

Weaver, Daniel, 33–34, 124

Weaver, James B., 104

Weeks, Joseph D., 181

Wells, David A., 172

Welsh, John F., 87

Western Miners' Association, 138

White, Henry, 161

Wilson, J. Havelock: life and background in England and America, 68–75; mentioned, 78, 79, 117

Wilson, John, 195

Wilson, Woodrow, 74

Wilkinson, Joseph, 151

Woodrow, Fred, 107

Workers' Industrial Society, 138

Workingmen's Benevolent Association of St. Clair (later of Schuylkill Co.), 131–32. *See also* Miners' and Laborers' Benevolent Association.

Workingmen's Party, 112

Workingmen's Union of New York, 88, 151

Worrall, Thomas D., 249, 250, 252

Wright, Carroll: on arbitration, 181–82; mentioned, 144, 233, 290

Wright, James S., 277

Wright, J. W. A., 253–54

Yorkshire, 42, 123

Youngstown Ohio miners convention, 133, 137, 138, 139